At the Beach

At the Beach

Jean-Didier Urbain

Translated by Catherine Porter

University of Minnesota Press

Minneapolis — London

The University of Minnesota Press gratefully acknowledges financial assistance provided by the French Ministry of Culture for the translation of this book.

Originally published as *Sur la plage,* copyright 1994, 1996, Editions Payot & Rivages.

Published by the University of Minnesota Press
111 Third Avenue South, Suite 290
Minneapolis, MN 55401-2520
http://www.upress.umn.edu

Library of Congress Cataloging-in-Publication Data

Urbain, Jean-Didier.
    [Sur la plage English]
    At the beach / Jean-Didier Urbain ; translated by Catherine Porter.
        p.   cm.
    Originally published: Sur la plage, 1996
    ISBN 0-8166-3450-5 (hardback : alk. paper) — ISBN 0-8166-3451-3 (pbk. : alk. paper)
    1. Bathing customs—History.   2. Outdoor recreations—History.   I. Title.
    GT2845 .U7213 2003
    796.5'3—dc21

                                                                                    2003005068

Printed in the United States of America on acid-free paper

The University of Minnesota is an equal-opportunity educator and employer.

12 11 10 09 08 07 06 05 04 03   10 9 8 7 6 5 4 3 2 1

To Georges Perec, for the method

To my Belgian family, for my northern archives

To the Pieds-Noirs and the Corsicans, for my southern archives

And to Louis-Vincent Thomas, departed en villégiature . . .

Contents

The Shipwreck of Phileas Fogg

The transposition . . . in other words, the substitution of a story centered on an individual, governed by human passions, for a scenario originally wholly composed of gestures and the immemorial customs of society.
—Georges Dumézil, *From Myth to Fiction*

Phileas Fogg is a famous traveler, a man in a hurry. The hero of *Around the World in Eighty Days* is in many respects the literary model for the contemporary tourist. Let us imagine for a moment that, worn out by all his adventures, he suddenly disobeys his author and escapes from the novel.

When he arrives in San Francisco, Fogg changes his mind. Giving up on his wager, he abandons the attempt to set a record that has brought him this far. Still accompanied by his faithful Passepartout, leaving his planet-circling orbit behind, he decides to detour to the south.

Phileas embarks as a super-cargo on a British merchant vessel, using a false name so he cannot be traced. Passepartout signs on as an ordinary seaman.

The ship heads down the coast of California and Mexico past Panama and Colombia, toward the equator. Along the way, Fogg mixes business with pleasure; he is on good terms with the captain. They drop anchor in quiet bays, bartering here and there, then start to drift peacefully along the coast of Peru and Chile. All is well on board until a violent hurricane comes up.

Caught in the storm, driven away from the coast by the wind and "a raging wave, Mountain-like," the ship soon founders on a sandbank, its cracked hull filled with water.[1]

A rowboat is immediately launched, but a treacherous wave overturns it at once. The crew is hurtled into the raging surf. Dragged down, then tossed forward toward an unknown land, a breathless Fogg, brutally separated from his companions, clings to a rock. One last wave finally carries him to shore, where he finds shelter from "the Fury of the Sea."[2]

Phileas, the sole survivor, thus finds himself alone on a deserted island in the middle of the ocean, far away—at least so he thinks—from everything, presumably somewhere off the coast from Valparaiso. Here is the globe-trotter, lost on some Pacific shore: his travels brought to a halt, he is forced to come to terms with the solitude of this wild land surrounded by open sea.

As if condemned to a perpetual vacation, he makes the best of it and proceeds to settle in. For more than thirty years, he works at improving his living arrangements. The metamorphosis of the character is complete. Phileas Fogg is no longer Fogg; he has become Robinson Crusoe.

And Passepartout? As it happens, Phileas's servant does not drown. Clinging to a scrap from the wreck, he drifts for hours until he is picked up by a native in a dugout and taken to a cannibal village on another island. The natives make an exception to their rule and do not eat him: seeing his robust physique as the sign of uncommon strength, they adopt him. With the sun's help, his skin darkens. Passepartout adapts to his new way of life by adopting the cannibals' customs, practices, and rituals, and he quickly becomes a savage among savages.

Perfectly assimilated, Fogg's former servant lives happily within this primitive community—so happily that in time, separated from his master, he forgets even his master's name and his face. One day the master comes across his old servant, however, and saves him from the appetites of a rival tribe. Profiting from the occasion, Fogg-Crusoe makes Passepartout his companion and slave.

Still, and even though he notes that the savage has "all the Sweetness and Softness of an *European* in his Countenance,"[3] after such a long absence Phileas Crusoe does not recognize this tanned naked being as the old Passepartout and decides, as we know, to call him Friday.

According to this hypothesis, Phileas Fogg (accompanied by his faithful Passepartout) escapes from his own novel only to flee into a different one. This is obviously no accident. The ambition of my traversing fiction is not literary but pedagogical.

Just as the Northwest Passage or the Panama Canal allows ships to cross from the Atlantic to the Pacific, the imaginary connection between Jules Verne's novel and Daniel Defoe's has only one purpose: to suggest a way of linking two universes that are, like the oceans, not only separate but also totally opposite in nature. Whereas Fogg is the mythical image of the mobility of leisure, Crusoe is ultimately the best-known inverse figure of that mobility.

My recourse to this fiction, which allows us to imagine some incidents indispensable to Phileas's move into Robinson's universe, makes the difference between the two travelers—except of course for accidents—appear all the more irreducible. A shipwreck, that is, a break in continuity, is required for a shift in perspective and for the production of metaphor. The two heroes may both be travelers, but they belong to different worlds.

Correlatively, the use of this narrative of transference is a subterfuge that also allows me to draw the reader's attention for the first time to the astonishing symmetry and complementarity of these two adventure stories and their heroes.

The following question then arises: If Phileas Fogg appears in travel literature as the fictional archetype of the tourist, how do we categorize Robinson Crusoe? Of what traveler, what vacationer in the contemporary leisure universe, is Crusoe the model in his turn?

The present book is nourished throughout by the parallelism between Phileas Fogg and Robinson Crusoe. Starting with the realm I have chosen to explore, I shall attempt to answer the question formulated above by supposing that Robinson Crusoe leaves his cave and the interior of his island one day and, along with Friday, discovers the pleasures of the beach.

The Other Traveling Fool; or,
The Interrupted Voyage

> Nobody can describe or measure or demonstrate . . . how long a period
> endures in the spaceless and timeless . . .
>
> —Stefan Zweig, "The Royal Game"

"I hate seaside resorts and summer people." This is the first sentence
of *Sorry Shores*. Or at least it could be, if such a work existed, if its
author had finally decided to write it in order to describe his vacation
sojourns and record his memories. Still, Paul Morand's *Bains de mer,
bains de rêves* (1960), which I shall cite often here, approximates what
might one day be the memoirs of a summer vacationer, written fit-
tingly by a tanned Stendhal, with or without bathing trunks, someone
who lingers near sun-kissed ocean pools. While the central figure of
an earlier book—my *L'idiot du voyage*—was the tourist, our new hero
is a summer resident.[1] *At the Beach* deals with residential summer vacationers, in particular those who are attracted to the shore.

What is a summer resident? This figure, somewhat underappreci-
ated in its specificity, is first of all a character who suffers from a pronounced lack of recognition—even in studies on leisure and vacations.
The summer resident's lack of clear identity is reflected in the absence
of a precise label. In French the word *villégiateur*, which first appeared
in 1761, designated a particular type of vacationer who retreated to the
countryside or "took the waters," that is, went to the seaside; no precise
English equivalent exists. And even in French, the term gradually faded

from usage in the twentieth century; it has been replaced by terms such as *estivant* (summer resident), *vacancier* (vacationer), or—more disquietingly—*touriste* (tourist).

The term *vacances* (vacation) has a generic meaning in French. For centuries it has referred to the interval of time during which an individual temporarily stops working—a period of time when students put their studies aside (a meaning attested as early as 1625), a period of rest for adults (1669), or a break afforded by law to salaried workers (1907).[2] The term *touriste*, in contrast, has a quite specific meaning. It became current in the early nineteenth century, designating an activity that fills vacation time in a special way. While all tourists are vacationers, the converse is not always true, notwithstanding the approach taken by the contemporary typology of leisure, which makes "tourism" a generic concept and "vacation" a specific notion.[3]

Tourism, a special way of spending vacation time generally described as traveling for pleasure, is often subject to approximate definitions. The *tourist* becomes a person with some leisure time to spare that he or she devotes to traveling.[4] But the question remains: what does it mean to travel?

At the seaside, the "tourist" (but this is also true of the vacationer who stays on a farm or in a mountain cabin) does not devote his leisure time to traveling. He does travel; he may head for some remote corner of the earth. But his goal is precisely to stop. The point of his traveling is to bring traveling to an end. Psychologically, this form of travel must not be conceived in terms of circulation or nomadic behavior, but in terms of migration and the provisional transfer of a sedentary state. This second sort of traveler is a *villégiateur*—a seasonal resident or residential vacationer.[5]

The aesthetics of the trip or the itinerary is not a crucial issue for the seasonal resident—in this case, a summer vacationer heading for the shore. On the road that takes her there, her goal is not to complete a "circuit" or a "tour," but to arrive. Her destination is not a temporary stopping-place, a famous site, or an open space to be explored. It is a refuge, experienced as definitive. The visitor's pleasure lies wholly, exclusively, in that place.

In the French context, one can evoke the epic Route Nationale 7, a highway that has brought countless vacationers to the Mediterranean (the road was immortalized in song by Charles Trenet in the 1950s). But the summer traversal of France is not touristic in nature. It is not exploratory, and it is not the object of the trip itself. It is a waiting period, or better yet a rite of passage—a test, carried out along a trajectory dotted with pitfalls (breakdowns, bottlenecks, heat waves) that take the form of tribute exacted by the gods of leisure before one can reach the shore.

If the summer resident moves through space, if he travels farther and farther, it is precisely so he will not have to move again, and—in the exact opposite of touristic behavior—so he can settle into another sedentary existence. The tourist can modulate his mobility: he can either wander about or follow a circular route. He has a choice between vagabondage, itinerance, or something in between (in the intermediate case, which we may call semi-itinerance, he introduces fleeting periods of temporary residence into his nomadism). In contrast, the summer resident stays put (apart from excursions, which introduce brief touristic moments into an otherwise sedentary life); he is immobilized. As soon as he is transplanted, he becomes sedentary all over again.

This is why the second sort of traveler is "the other traveling fool." Not the tourist's "other" or opposite number—who is the tourist himself (and not even the native, as one might expect)[6]—but rather the "other" of travel, embodying a singular paradox: he moves in order to stop moving. Thus if we can account for this apparent contradiction, if we can identify its causes, we shall be able to decipher the psychology and the universe of this strange traveler who dreams of immobility, who travels in order not to travel. In fact, this traveler is all the stranger in that he is close to us, familiar, even an intimate acquaintance. Most readers of this book will have inhabited this figure at some point.

Thus we have reached the threshold of an exploration that was anticipated in my earlier book.[7] My goal here is not only to rehabilitate a distinction that has, regrettably, been abandoned, but also to explore the mysterious immobility of vacation sojourns, about which many writers have concluded that there is nothing to be said (unless it is something negative, on the pretext that nothing happens on the beach), that nothing happens in that formless, empty theater filled with passive, puerile idiots madly working on their tans.

But it is true, as Edward T. Hall wrote more than thirty years ago, that "culture hides much more than it reveals, and strangely enough what it hides, it hides most effectively from its own participants." And the anthropologist added: "Years of study have convinced me that the real job is not to understand foreign cultures but to understand our own."[8]

The German sociologist H. M. Enzenberger, for his part, sees the tourist—defined from this point on as a vacationer who travels—as a sort of inhibited revolutionary who finds himself unable to change the world and changes his own world instead.[9] He sublimates his frustration by gaining access, in the mode of simulation (evasion or exile, temporary disorientation or "reacclimatization"), to utopian situations and representations that are normally repressed by social standards. This interpretation is pertinent in a number of ways, given that vacations are most often perceived as a period of metamorphosis during which each individual can acquire what he or she lacks and live according to his or her own preferences.

Still, some questions remain unanswered. What does it mean to change worlds? What kind of change is sought? How is the change to be achieved? By wandering about, or by transhumance? And what new world is to replace the old one? To what end? While we may now have some notion of the regions into which the touristic universe is divided, and a certain idea of what is symbolically at stake in it, what can we say about the summer resident's seaside universe—one whose gregariousness has often been said to reproduce the world from which its denizens come: its crowds, its density, its concomitant rhythms, stresses, and constraints? What kind of change is involved, if the little summer revolution is just a return to the starting point, differing only in that sand, sun, and sea have replaced asphalt, gray skies, and the city?

Rather than settle for an overview of the phenomenon that denies both singularities and differences, we need to take a more nuanced approach. The world is not an objective given, but always a psychological construction resulting from perceptions. Whereas one sort of traveler circulates, traverses, explores, steps over, the other transplants herself, resides, sojourns, settles in. The nomad sees things in one way, the sedentary individual in another. In short, the tourist and the summer resident may encounter one another in the same physical space, but they nevertheless belong to two different worlds. For the former, the space is a place to pass through; for the latter, it is a territory to inhabit. The tourist traverses the planet; the summer resident has renounced that goal. Preferring immobility to vagabondage, the latter has interrupted her travels. Thus the former traverses a place as an outsider, while the latter belongs there, if not as a native, at least as a resident.

If this encounter recalls the mythic meeting between Stanley and Livingstone at the heart of equatorial Africa, what is particularly striking is the radical difference in perception that separates the two travelers, for this difference gives rise to a division of consciousness that separates two worlds. It is easy to experience this difference in everyday life, to feel the reality and the intensity of the psychological break it brings about, melancholic or euphoric in tone depending on the circumstances. For example, on the eve of a departure, we need only walk one last time through the familiar spaces in which we spend the greater part of the year. We shall leave them behind the next day; we know that they are unchanged, and yet at this precise moment the world is no longer the same. We experience it differently. In the imminence of departure, we are already out of place, we no longer belong.

Finally, why do I focus on the beach rather than the country or the mountains, other long-standing destinations that antedate the seashore as sites of summer residency? Personal taste and experience are doubtless contributing factors, but it is also the case that the seaside world (in the sense in which I am using the term here) is still relatively unexplored, whereas among all the sites that draw summer residents it is not only the most important in terms of the absolute numbers of people who elect to stay there, but also the one that has attracted ever-increasing numbers over several decades; the growth curve continues upward with no sign of abating.

It is high time to correct the misinformation imparted summer after summer in bulletins announcing the renaissance of "green tourism." One cannot help but wonder what lies behind such announcements—pious wishes, media promotion, sheer intoxication?—since, in France at least, the number of people who spend summer vacations in the mountains or the country has been steadily decreasing for the last quarter of a century.

In 1965, 19.5 percent of French vacationers chose to vacation in the mountains; in 1990, 14.9 percent. Sojourns in the country declined from 34.5 percent in 1965 to 23.4 percent in 1990. During the same period, with the exception of the seaside, only cities (urban tourism) and touristic circuits drew increased numbers of visitors, rising respectively from 4.5 percent to 8.1 percent and 2.5 percent to 4.7 percent (with a high point, in 1985, of 7.8 percent). As for the seaside, the figures are edifying. Approximately 36 percent of French vacationers chose to spend their holidays at the shore in the early 1960s; the numbers surpassed 45 percent in 1970 and reached 45.9 percent in 1990—and in terms of numbers of days, the percentage was 50.4 percent, as opposed to 14 percent for the mountains and 25.1 percent for the countryside.

Summer holidays at the sea are a widespread social phenomenon, leading to a concentration of "more than 25 million visitors (French and foreign) during the tourist year in seaside communities [in France] representing less than 4 percent of the national territory and 10 percent of the total population." This is the contemporary result of a century-long process that was summarized by M. Cassou-Mounat: "At the beginning of the twentieth century, one French citizen in four hundred spent summer vacations at the sea; the proportion was one in forty in 1936 when paid vacations were made mandatory, and it is one in four today."[10]

We should note that in 1991 the number of visitors to the mountains rose to 16.1 percent, and the countryside attracted 26 percent, whereas seaside destinations dropped to 45.1 percent. Still, it is too early to read the sign of a lasting reversal in these figures, for one fact at least is incontestable: the seashore is a vacation destination that exercises a considerable force of attraction, at both the national and international levels. Although this force of attraction becomes weaker outside France's borders, the sea nevertheless remains in first place. Thus 37 percent of the French citizens who spent holidays abroad during the summer of 1990 went to the sea, as opposed to 21.3 percent who chose tourist itineraries; 16.6 percent visited cities (that is, about 38 percent of overall tourist activities, which are particularly encouraged by travel to foreign countries); 18.1 percent went to the country, and only 7 percent to the mountains. Vacationing in the countryside abroad has nevertheless gone up noticeably in recent years: it registered an increase of 3.4 percent between 1988 and 1990.

Then, too, beyond these quantitative data, a motive of a different order dictated the choice of residential seaside vacationing, an anthropological motive that can be summarized as follows: when subjected to analytical scrutiny, the beach seems to be one of the privileged places where society puts itself on display, with its rites and symbols, its festive customs and conventions, its desires and norms, its rules and their transgressions, its strategies for coexistence and codes for settling in, its organizational logic, and, finally, its panoply of emotions.

The beach is spectacular. It is a theater in which society unveils itself, lays itself bare (literally and metaphorically), bringing to light "the affective and feeling dimension of social relationships" in the framework of a scenography that "stylizes existence and brings out its essential characteristic."[11] The beach, with its rituals and games, offers purification: it presents a hyperreal image of collective life that differentiates it from everything else, including "green vacations," which are associated with going "back to the land," returning to one's sources. Unlike the countryside, the beach is not so much a place of return as a place of new beginnings. It is not a patch of ground, it is a tabula rasa, a blank slate, an abstraction, an empty and rootless land, a "castle in Spain."

THE SUMMER VACATIONER ON THE VERGE
OF A NERVOUS BREAKDOWN

> These bodies, lying side by side on beaches, that bring to mind rows of chickens roasting under ultraviolet light—do they at least hide happy hearts? Is their Eden-like purity for real?
>
> —Paul Morand, *Bains de mer, bains de rêves*

But let us give free rein to those who want to proffer the cynical discourse about beaches that is fashionable these days. In keeping with a sectarian or nostalgic critical tradition whose ritual function of distinguishing among groups of people no longer needs to be demonstrated, seaside vacationers are classified as tourists.[12] They have their detractors and their purists; both groups take this form of vacationing to task, although from different vantage points. The detractors, whose arguments I shall discuss at greater length later on (see chapter 5), often adopt an uncomprehending tone. They declare, for example: "I never go on holiday. That's why I moved into this field in the first place. I always hated holidays, even as a kid. Such a waste of time, sitting on the beach, making sandpies . . ."[13]

Expressing scorn for emptiness on the one hand and obsession with the overfull on the other, purists frequently launch into a dirge, in something like the following terms:

> The beach? What about the beach? What are you talking about? Our very own beaches, with their changing cabins and their potted palms, or tropical beaches, with the cocoa-palm, "that giraffe of vegetables, so graceful, so ungainly," as its natural fringe?[14] Normandy beaches?

English beaches or Belgian ones? Mediterranean or Sri Lankan? Knokke-sur-Mer or Bora Bora? The Leeward Islands' paradisical Moana Beach, or the Ouistreham's Italian Riva-Bella in Calvados?

In any case, whether the beach you have in mind is in Brittany or Tunisia, Polynesia or Languedoc, on the Wild Coast or the Emerald Coast or the Silver Coast, whether it is hemmed with fine sand or studded with polished stones, there is nothing left to say about it. Look around: it's a disaster. And while it may still be resisting its invaders, it'll soon be polluted on one side and completely cemented over on the other, covered with clumps of bodies. It's relentless. Beaches are submerged under tanned corpses; they look as if there's been a gigantic shipwreck. This is what today's beach has come to: it's a place for wreckage to wash up at the end of a trip. From a distance, you'd call it a huge bivouac, a vast field given over to repose, lined with soft prone bodies and gleaming flesh that floated ashore under a leaden sun like scrap from a hull run aground.

The spectacle is hardly a new one. F. Scott Fitzgerald put words in an American woman's mouth as she passed by the summer people lined up on the sand on the Côte d'Azur in the early 1930s: "What do these people get out of it? . . . They just stick around with each other in little cliques."[15] Today, labeled as sun worshipping, the "new bronze age," or the "modern gold rush," the spectacle perpetuates itself as an epidemic on sun-drenched coasts all over the world.

The purist worships beaches the way others worship mountains, but he is a disappointed worshiper. He goes on:

In Italy today, what's happened to the Riviera, and the Adriatic? What's become of Rimini, Pesaro, Pescara, with their endless family boarding-houses and the fearful bathers muttering ten feet away from the water? What's happening on the other shore? Before the war, from Pula to Dubrovnik, there were nudist camps all over. But on either shore, what are we to make of this self-contained universe, this "schizophrenic society" closed in on itself, "with hundreds of yards of white sandy beach as its only reality."[16] It's zen, you'll say, because it's naked? But clothes or no clothes, there are far too many people in that garden!

The Spanish coast reads like a restaurant menu: Costa Brava, Costa Dorada, Costa del Sol—the coast "à la carte." The Algarve in Portugal, like Madeira, has been corrupted in a hurry by the vacation industry and its promoters. And the charters leaving for Florida? The

Canary Islands? Morocco? Miami Beach! Tenerife! Agadir! It's too late! Cuba and its seaside ghettos, the Petite-Côte in Senegal, the Black Sea on the Romanian or Bulgarian shores, the Kerala: all ruined! Cape Skirring! Constanza! The Isle of Mahé! Acapulco! Rio de Janeiro! It's too late, everywhere!

When I look at certain beaches, I'm sometimes reminded of Gustave Doré's illustration of the Inferno. We see Dante with his guide in the middle of a host of bodies. The damned are lying naked at the edge of the abyss . . .

Forget Matala, too, in Crete. In the late 1960s, a few dozen hippies were living there in caves facing the sea; others were doing the same thing in the Balearic Islands.[17] And Kuta, in Bali? During the same period, backpackers were in the habit of spending their days on the beach, which was "famous for the splendor of its sunsets as well as for its hallucinogenic mushrooms."[18] Now where can they go? Veracruz? Phuket? Penang? They're all spoiled! In Thailand, in Malaysia: it's devastating!

This beach-worshiper, whose discourse is reconstituted here on the basis of remarks heard or read hundreds of times, wants to cling to the myth of Eden. His purism collides increasingly with international realities:

But what about islands—other islands?[19] Away from crowds, sheltered from fashions. . . . In the Mediterranean, don't we also have Mykonos, Santorini, Malta, Cyprus, Corsica, Sardinia, Djerba, the Kerkenna, the Dodecanesus? No, let's stop right there! Even little Simi, off Rhodes, is very popular. As Morand said a long time ago: "Now you have to go much farther, to the Azores or the Canaries; Capri has become Maidenhead or Margate, painted blue."[20] Let's talk about islands far away . . .

The Antilles, the Seychelles, the Comores, Réunion, Tahiti, the Marquesas? They too are "à la carte"! The Bahamas, Cozumel, Mauritius, the islands of Cape Verde, the Maldives, or Hawaii? No thanks. I've just come from there, and I've read David Lodge. Hawaii! Jack London wrote as early as 1907 that Hawaii is "a paradise for someone who already has some property. It is in no way a paradise for the unskilled worker, or for the person who shows up without any money from his native country."[21] In short, those islands have been hostile to immigrants and adventurers for a long time. Hippies and others were smart to choose the beaches of Ibiza or Bali, sixty years later!

The purist is sometimes more than disappointed: he is desperate; and then his conscience is troubled. He still dreams of inaccessible places of refuge, even as he foresees their universal disappearance.

> Let's talk about getting far away—really far! From now on, we'll have to go farther and farther. I'm suffocating here! "Happiness," Céline says, "awaits us far from here ... on the other side of the world ... on the seas. The Tragacanth Seas!"[22] Can you still show me forgotten shores, undiscovered calanques, long-hidden lagoons, a miraculous bay spared by the masses, or an unknown coast bordered by indestructible reefs that still shelters a hospitable and empty shore? No, of course not!

The purist is an incurable nostalgic, his head full of lost paradises. His quest is mixed with regret and disillusionment:

> You'll probably find me quite sectarian, but it seems to me already so definitively past, the happy time when a Maupassant could still be surprised by suddenly coming upon the gulf of Porto, with no parking lots, campgrounds, or restaurants; and the moment seems so far away, too—it's incredible to think about it today—when a writer-navigator, sighting Nuku-hiva, could still compare the Polynesian beach to Europe's. "The trees, from our distance," Stevenson wrote, "might have been hazel; the beach might have been in Europe; the mountains modelled in little from the Alps, and the forest which clustered on their ramparts a growth no more considerable than our Scottish heath." We are, respectively, in Corsica in the fall of 1880, and in the Marquesas in the summer of 1888. . . .[23]
>
> And the deserted beaches of Brittany? When Flaubert went there with his friend Maxime Ducamp in 1847, they were still the earth's edge, a true finistère, land's end. The natives were exotic "savages" and the beaches were deserts. A century later, Paul Morand found that "the unknown, forgotten beaches, the hidden coves" were still there.[24] What has become of them since? They are indeed hidden, but not from everyone! With the Pointe du Raz threatened and "cement-itis" rampant, what was once there is gone! One has to go elsewhere. And when I read something like this in today's newspaper: "Annexed, trampled by Northern Europeans, Majorca has nevertheless managed to keep its purest landscapes for itself," I no longer believe it.[25]

On this point, the purist rejoins those who belittle seaside vacations: he is horrified by their popularity. The collective nature of vacation life at the shore makes him bilious:

As for me, the beach isn't so much about being in the tropics as it is about peace and quiet, and being alone. I don't want anything to do with beaches where people crowd together noisily, people who "seem as indifferent to the way they look as a baby toddling about or making his first sand castles."[26]

Still, the purist's reasons are different from those of the shore's detractors. His horror originates not in disgust or boredom, but in the destruction of a model seascape. His universe of reference is in danger, threatened by the invasion of the masses. Whether Corsican or Melanesian, his beach is above all wild and picturesque. He seeks an earthly paradise, a spit of land looking as though it had only just emerged from the limbo of the ocean's depths:

I want an untouched shore: a natural beach, unscathed by real estate, with no visible manifestations of tourism, no anachronisms. It would offer itself up as a world just beginning; it would have so few visitors that at first glance, except for the natives, it would appear unoccupied, and it would be all ours. It could be a beach like this one: "It was on a clear, perfectly calm afternoon that I first set eyes upon the village of Oburaku. Through the open entrance to the west, the soft, warm rays of the setting sun were streaming over the mossy-green waters of the lagoon. They fell on the shore, and lit up the wall of mangroves, playing on its glittering leaves of hard green."[27] An ethnologist's recollection in the form of a gentle shipwreck.

But today we have to come to grips with modernity and install the dream within the interstices of an invasive seaside reality. What beach will be the purist's ideal—or what will he find at least acceptable—now?

The beach will always be found at the edge of a modest fishermen's village, both being fairly far away from a newly constructed hotel fortress, with—as the times require—golf, tennis, and especially a pool. The pool is important. Why? Because it keeps timid, prudently hygienic, and casual bathers away from the shore!

As for the village, it will offer vacationers in search of authenticity only a few rustic residences belonging to the locals. Of course, that is where we shall stay. Lake-dwellers' bungalows around the bay are planned. But with all due respect to the natives, who are awaiting them like manna from heaven, it will be two or three years before they are built. For the time being, there is still empty space.

On our beach, there will be a scattering of canoes. Their sails drying in the sun will provide us with shade. No parasols here. Mornings, I'll help the fisherman shove their boats off to sea. We'll spend our days swimming, playing games, reading, and talking among ourselves. We'll bask in the sun like lizards. We'll settle in not far from the village, on the other side of the bay, on the natural beach, in contrast to the summer people who have crowded in across the water, below the hotel, on its manicured sands.

At dusk, on a beach once again completely deserted, we'll wait for the fishermen to come back. In their multicolored catch we'll soon find the ingredients for our next meal: groupers, crayfish, or thread-fins. That very evening we'll barbecue them at home, in the village, by torchlight, in front of our hut.

Except that here a certain "foreign" proximity suddenly intrudes. It throws a final shadow over the tableau of this idyllic vacation:

But horrible music erupts in the night. It's coming from the hotel, punctuated with laughter and shouts. The same thing every evening. This is the end of the peace and quiet we came for. Next year we'll go someplace else!

The acceptable has thus become unacceptable. Here we have Robinson disturbed on his island by the shouts of the savages and the noise of their revelry.

THE SUMMER RESIDENT ON THE COUCH

Lilliputian reveries are the antithesis of the dreams of escape that shatter the soul.

Thus the meticulous imaginary wants to slip in everywhere; it invites us not only to *go back into our shells* but to slip into any shell at all to experience a real retreat, life all rolled up, life curled back on itself, all the values of repose.

—Gaston Bachelard, *La terre et les rêveries du repos*

"I ask only for the right to the friendship of the void, the quest for the desert, the nudity of the site, on forgotten beaches," Paul Morand declares.[28] This sentence in its own way echoes the most intimate thoughts of our summer resident. More than the expression of a narrow concern with distinction, it offers in addition the image of a "pure product": beaches conceived as natural, authentic, and sheltered from the world, in contrast to beaches that have been invaded, denatured, and sullied by hotels. The latter fate is the frequent destiny of beaches, however, and for the purist it entails a disfigurement resulting from a collective rape, a disastrous deflowering of seashores by the modern world.

Faced with mass access to seaside pleasures, the distraught residential vacationer cries, predictably: "We have to avoid popular beaches like the plague!" The sight of this teeming world, established on the always still-deserted shore of his dreams, fills him with horror. A single cause, the same effects: the purist does not want to go where others, too many of them, have already trod. He feels followed, harassed, like a Robinson threatened in his refuge by cannibals. The summer resident herself, a vacationer following the model of Robinson Crusoe, marginalized and isolated, seeks to play the role with respect to the herd-like crowds of summer visitors that the Traveler plays with respect to sheep-like tourists (see *L'idiot du voyage*).

Thus as soon as a certain threshold of summer visitors has been crossed and a certain comfort level achieved, our lover of deserted shores rebels and flee. Down with marinas and ports for pleasure craft! Down with crowds! Down with the Bay of Angels and the Cap d'Ail, where he spent his earliest vacations. Down with Calvi! Down with La Bocca and Saint-Brévin-les-Pins. And down with the luxurious cocoon-clubs of the Fijis and the Caribbean, which are only very high-priced artificial paradises![29]

Our dreamer, who longs for pure mornings, cannot bear the spectacle of the Pacific archipelago or the Gulf of Mexico covered with palaces and bungalows, any more than she can tolerate the appalling sight of the so-called Virgin Islands deflowered by amusement parks and waterslides. All these iconoclastic vacation sites, from Fort Mahon Beach to Sandy Beach Island, whether popular or elitist, are so many physical and moral attacks on our protagonist's model.

Rich or poor, it makes no difference: avoiding these places and finding other beaches is rule number one. Unless, of course, it comes to seem hopeless: tired of the struggle, the dreamer may shift his seaside hermitage to some nonbeach site:

> Beaches, where once the sea offered us the products of its age-old tumult, an astonishing gallery of objects which showed that nature always belonged to the avant-garde, are now trodden by hordes of

people and serve only for the arrangement and display of nondescript rubbish.

It follows that I like mountains more than the sea, and for years this fondness took the form of a jealous love. I hated those who shared my preference, since they threatened the solitude by which I set such store; and I was contemptuous of the others for whom mountains were largely synonymous with excessive fatigue and a closed horizon.[30]

Paul Morand occasionally offers advice that is quite similar in tone. Discovering the Belgian coast and "the invincible monotony" of its seaside resorts (Middelkerke, Westende, Nieuport, Blankenberghe), he invites the summer vacationer to "rediscover the charm of the real Belgium" by taking "a cruise in the inland canals"—in other words, by leaving the beach behind and converting his stay into touristic exploration.[31]

But our summer vacationer is a purist. Nothing will keep him away from the shore. He shuffles crab-like along the coastline, always facing the sea, moving from beach to beach, turning his back on the world. He will not give up the shore, and he will resist the call of the back country as long as he can. He will become neither a tourist nor a Robinson of the crests nor a Crusoe of the countryside. He is a beach-worshiper, disappointed but stubborn. He belongs to a marginal category of intransigent travelers. In the wake of Morand and other travelers, those who have sought out Matala, Ibiza, or Kuta, he wants to be to the beach what the "routard" is to the road: an "elegant bum."[32] What he wants above all is the sea and a deserted beach where he can play Robinson to his heart's content, where he can settle down in the company of not too many Fridays, safe from the Savages. In harmony with the Crusoean model that he seeks to impose on his stint on forgotten shores or remote islands, here is the model of the utopian summer resident, and the mythology behind his jealous love of beaches.

The myth of Robinson Crusoe is perfectly complementary to that of Phileas Fogg (see Preamble). Although the two novels develop opposing themes (one describes the experience of endless sedentarity, while the other exalts the experience of incessant mobility), a brief comparative analysis reveals the presence of remarkable analogies within these two contrary universes.

If Fogg has Passepartout as his traveling companion (one whose behavior is often described as that of a mere "tourist"), Robinson for his part has Friday as his companion in exile. Each thus has a twin, an alter ego, not his equal in quality but his crude likeness, his "fool." Passepartout is in Fogg's employ, and Friday has Robinson as his master; the former follow and imitate the latter. In parallel ways, each hero has to confront a context that is the territory of the Other. For Fogg, this is the wide world and its multiple dangers; for Robinson, it is his island and the savages. We thus find the same tripartite division in both novels: the hero, his alter ego, and the Other.

Transposed into the vacation universe, the tourist who sees herself as a Traveler will clearly be more inclined to grant herself the status of a Fogg than that of a mere ignorant follower like Passepartout. Correlatively, our residential summer vacationer is more inclined to see herself as Robinson than as Friday.

Advertisers know what they are doing: they often invoke the name "Robinson," but rarely "Friday." Where the latter might say, "Me, a tourist? Never!" the former is more likely to say, "Be a Robinson!" Thus, in a 1993 advertisement in a special issue of *Paris-Match-Voyages* we find the following: "In the Grandes Comores, the Galawa Beach Hotel Casino offers an enchanting locale" and it proposes "a vacation fit for Robinson at the edge of a blue lagoon" (106). Not far away (that is, in the same magazine), we learn that "the K-Club of Bermuda, only fifteen minutes by plane from Antigua," welcomes "four-star Robinsons" (114).

In the vacation universe, Friday is either a crude double of his master, a caricature of the Summer Resident, or else a household employee, a servant. Even if he does offer the seaside Robinson companionship and assistance, he remains a secondary figure, confined to one of two roles; he is either a subaltern or a grotesque reflection of the hero. For it is the master who brings the slave into existence and allows him to live. The master stands face to face with the servant, who functions as a reference point. Only under exceptional circumstances in which the tripartite arrangement comes undone can this dialectical relation be interrupted—as is the case in a novel in which vacationers taken hostage by a military revolution are left without supplies or services in a hotel-village on a tropical island: "The staff has been captured by the Revolution. No more cook. No more maître d'. No more chambermaids. The Robinsons are alone on their island, deprived of their Fridays."[33] It is as though Friday, once saved by Robinson, had been recaptured by the savages.[34]

Let us note the presence of an atypical Friday, however, in a novel by Michel Tournier, titled *Friday*. This Friday's servility misfires, since the servant disobeys the master and reverses their roles. But we find no equivalent of that situation in the contemporary seaside universe—an equivalent would presuppose the submission of the early residential seaside vacationer to the model of the popular resort and thus his renunciation of the aristocratic or marginal practice of the beach. The second phase of the celebrated master-slave dialectic does not take place: in the face of danger, today's aristocrat either opts for a protectionist strategy by erecting an inviolable economic border guaranteed by luxurious ghettos between himself and the mass resort, or else, like our model summer vacationer, he chooses a strategy of avoidance and flight by taking refuge in remote or unknown beach interstices. Both leave the enjoyment of the invaded beaches to the new masters of the site, people on paid holidays and other Fridays.

As for the definition of the Crusoe myth, what are its specific signs, the ones that determine its meaning and outline its scenography? In 1857, to designate a person who lived alone in nature, Flaubert used the word *robinson,* turning the proper name into a common noun. In 1870, to express the fact that someone lived in Robinson's fashion, the verb *robinsonner,* "to robinson," was introduced in French. Then in 1872 the noun *robinsonnade* was borrowed from German to designate any adventure narrative inspired by Defoe's work, and beyond that the act of "robinsoning." Karl Marx himself, dismissing the idea of revolution espoused by historical materialism, used the term *robinsonnade* pejoratively to characterize the revolutionary utopia in its most reductive sense: "the revolution on fifty square kilometers."[35] And in fact the ideal theater of operations for our summer vacationer is a limited space, a very small world indeed.

Nevertheless, this characterization of the Crusoe myth is not yet complete. Beyond a certain solitude (but Robinson is after all not entirely alone) and a sphere of action that is by definition limited (by virtue of the island's boundaries), the space most suitable for a robinsonnade requires other dimensions—including the virginity of the site, whether it is real, apparent, simulated, or even imagined. The essential element is that this place can be construed as unexplored by a person who stumbles upon it: thus it can be encountered in the mode of discovery, and even as a place to be possessed. Advertising does not hesitate to pluck this sensitive string, one always ready to vibrate in the case of the vacationer who longs to "do a Robinson." "The Comores: The Indian Ocean's unexplored islands," reads a 1993 ad for the Sun International hotel chain; in an ad for Rev-vacances the same year, a tour operator's slogan, "the memory of your dreams," attests to the extent to which advertising discourse, in France as elsewhere, seeks to trigger the reemergence of myths in consumer psychology—among them the vacation myth of "doing a Robinson."

This mythological and sentimental memory of the unexplored is quite obviously present in our residential summer vacationer. It even comes into play in his behavior as a primordial necessity; in its relation to the shore and to the contemplation of a past that is not far off but nevertheless antedates the beach, it links him to a specific type of curiosity-seeker from the first half of the nineteenth century, one who is not yet seeking out virgin beaches along the coast of Africa or in the Polynesian islands, but who "discovers" Trouville, Honfleur, Étretat, or Saint-Tropez. Our vacationer's behavior has much in common with that of his precursor, whom Dominique Rouillard depicts as a "pioneer-artist": he has "an explorer's approach; he wants to understand the place in depth and to respect its population, whose dwellings, meals, and customs he will share, and to respect the site, whose natural beauties he will bring back home."[36]

But history repeats itself. Soon, imitators arrive and become a crowd. They destroy the vacationers' dreams, ruin their encampment, and in one fell swoop drive the discoverers out and bring the promoters in.[37] What becomes of the Crusoe dream in the minds of these pioneers who have been dispossessed of their discovery? The dream becomes an impossible one. The site must be abandoned! One must go elsewhere!

The portrait of our vacationer then becomes more precise: its niche is experimental vacationing. It leads our summer resident to reject developed shores, with their elaborate security precautions, their well-marked limits, and their rules and regulations. Our vacationer, like the experimental tourist who invents itineraries and breaks new trails, wants to invent places and open up new shorelines; he does not want to sink into a highly structured resort context, whether luxurious or inexpensive. He rejects the initiatory summer vacation, which is that of consumers, not creators.[38]

Ultimately, in our vacationer's eyes, it is only at the price of flight and discovery that the Crusoe myth resists historical fatality and that the dream of utopian residency, the true robinsonnade, protected against modernity, remains in the realm of the possible.

These are the first three characteristic signs of the Crusoean scenography: a certain solitude, a self-contained space bordered by the sea, and a virgin or unexplored site in the background—all of these disconnected from historical reality, that is, from time. The Crusoean beach is a prehistoric beach. But other signs follow, signs that are no less essential in the development of the myth. After space and time, there is the actor himself, the Crusoean hero. What does he do in this space-time? How does he settle in? What relations does he establish with his environment? And, finally, how and why does he end up in this particular place?

First of all, like Robinson, our vacationer settles into the space for a long period of time, or at least pretends to be doing so: the Crusoean situation requires this simulacrum. Then, in keeping with his model, she organizes her world, investing it with habits and comforts. Robinson is in fact a consummate "tinker, crop grower, and livestock breeder";[39] stories reworking the Crusoe myth have so fully developed the hero's demiurgic dimension that they can almost be described as "how-to" manuals.

Early examples include Joachim Heinrich Campe's *New Robinson Crusoe* (1779) and some of Jules Verne's novels, such as *The Mysterious Island* (1874), *The Robinson Crusoe School* (1882), and *Two Years' Holiday* (1888). More recently, other robinsonnades retain the character's competence and sometimes even exalt it as a quasi-mechanical virtue,[40] an obsessional virtue as well, one which, for Michel Tournier in *Friday*, tips the hero into maniacal delusion, and for Paul Theroux, in *The Mosquito Coast*, into suicidal madness.

What has become, then, of this demiurgic quality in our experimental vacationer? It is not absent, but it has become metaphorical. Compared to the mythical model, our vacationer's behavior is not so much a weakened manifestation of the heroic figure as its "displaced" translation. This vacationer is a hedonist and a contemplative sort. He is above all an inventor and an observer; he is not a literal demiurge. And if, like Robinson Crusoe, he discovers a world, he transforms it on an entirely different level.

The universe organized by our pioneer-vacationer is more moral than material, more empathic than technological. In fact, it is first of all diplomatic and amicable. What today's Robinson "cobbles together" is a network of sociability, woven on the one hand among the Fridays with whom he shares the beach, the not too numerous alter egos who have fled the hotel as he has, and on the other hand the natives, the local savages, with whom he establishes relations of exchange.

A sign of the times, in the lineage of nineteenth-century discoverers of shorelines, twentieth-century ethnologists, and 1960s utopians, our vacationer thus plays at integration and participatory observation more than he does at transforming the world. If he is a demiurge, he is a gentle one. He is attentive to local life, which he admires and to which he adapts his own; he wants especially to avoid modifying its natural equilibrium. Hence his rejection of hotels, luxury ghettos, vacation-villages, and other clubs: in short, all the seaside vacation enclaves that separate visitors from natives, that alter sites, remain ignorant of local customs, and degrade the environment.

The description of the Crusoean scene ends with this sign: the modification of the relation between the residential summer vacationer and the savages. In the framework of the experimental robinsonnade, contact between the two groups is in principle no longer conflictual. Robinson is no longer on the defensive. He has replaced his gun with a straw mat. He has made peace with the savages. The "real" savages are henceforth, instead, the summer people, as soon as they are numerous enough to constitute a crowd.

Is a shipwreck still part of the scenario? Unless it is voluntary, it too has disappeared, like the cannibals. Even if seaside vacationing is Crusoean, it presupposes a historical pacification of the coast, an already dedramatized relation to the sea and its shores, as Alain Corbin has shown.[41] Today, our residential summer vacationer reaches the utopian site under very different conditions: not requiring a storm, they are less perilous, but no less symbolic.

"Touch down off Catalina's magical coasts! Dive into African waters and share the customs of these happy people!" This excerpt from a 1993 advertisement for Peter Stuyvesant Travel (Odyssey) reflects the tone adopted today in commercial efforts to seduce new Crusoean vacationers and attract them toward their elective destinations. They will descend from the heavens, touch down gently on the waves like pacific gods, and then, once on land, will turn the hostile savages into friends. They will not live apart in a fiercely territorial and segregationist manner; they will live with the savages, among them, like them, in the shadow of their dugouts, in virtual symbiosis with them, according to the principles of a fusional strategy and a vacation ethics that would have been quite incomprehensible to the original Robinson.

To lay the shipwreck image to rest, it seems useful to recall that the actual incident on which Defoe based the Robinson Crusoe story did not include this dramatic event. The incident in question was the adventure of the sailor Alexander Selkirk, who participated in the Dampier expedition in 1703. After a dispute with his captain, Selkirk was left ashore at his own request on the then-uninhabited island of Más a Tierra (now Juan Fernández), off the coast of Chili, where he lived from 1704 to 1709.[42] Thus the origin of the model for utopian residential vacationing is found not in an accidental shipwreck but in a social rupture: a dispute, a quarrel, a falling-out between two men, an authority figure and an insubordinate subaltern. Our residential vacationer fits right into this historical scenario, for his outlook is not that of a shipwreck victim but rather that of an individual breaking with his own society.

The process of defining the Crusoe myth has already allowed us to identify some of its variations, its adaptations, and its anamorphoses. Let me simply enumerate a few of them here without commentary: in addition to the erotic or delirious versions, we should recall those in which the solitary hero is (or becomes) double or collective—a couple, a family, a group of scientists, a colony of children, or a society.[43]

For from this point on, robinsonnades and their real or imaginary variants will constitute the framework of my study.[44] Starting from Lévi-Strauss's principle that "the mythical value of the myth is preserved even through the worst translation," that is, despite the transpositions, distortions, and other operations that may alter its signs and confuse its readers, the robinsonnade will be considered here, in historical terms, as a powerful image that underlies the hedonistic uses of the beach and continues to function today as a model of symbolic behavior, even for overpopulated seaside locations that are not in the least remote.[45]

An archetype of installation, it would be strange indeed if the influence of the Crusoean model should have suddenly evaporated from the universe of residential seaside vacationing, despite the fact that every year the shores of France alone welcome millions of vacationers and see these inveterate lovers of the interrupted voyage settle down on their sands. Dreams of solitude resist the presence of the crowd as myth resists reality, and we must not forget that a society may be Crusoean and a crowd may be lonely.[46]

Still, the Crusoe myth has the value of an Ariadne's thread, not that of a straitjacket. The seaside universe cannot be reduced to this reference, any more than the Crusoean scene, as a utopian situation, can be reduced to the geography of an island. A mountain site, in certain respects, can play the same role: the sea may be absent, but the altitude compensates. For after all, seen from above with their chains of peaks breaking through an ocean of clouds, mountains—fantasized for centuries as the "top of the world"—quite resemble archipelagos.[47]

We may also recall the "ice Robinson," Captain Hatteras, trapped with his companions in a desert of ice, confined to a ship. They are prisoners of a frozen sea much as if they had been stranded on an island. Moreover, Jules Verne himself was aware of the connection: while he appreciated the differences between Defoe's story and his own hyperborean robinsonnade (a group forced to spend the winter at the heart of a hostile exotic terrain), he still compared the polar isolation of these shipwreck victims of the cold to that of Robinsons "tossed up onto the islands of the Pacific Ocean."[48]

The mythological framework is not exclusionary, moreover. The Crusoe myth incorporates other themes, has offshoots and combinations that give it a hybrid meaning and take it in the direction of other myths with which it comes to terms or within which it takes up residence.

For example, in the cinematic realm, *The Blue Lagoon* again comes to mind, as a characteristic example of hybridization of the Crusoe myth by amputation. Here the Robinsons (the two children), following the death of their Friday (the sailor Paddy), see their own robinsonnade shift because of Paddy's disappearance to a different mythic universe, the biblical universe of Adam and Eve, with savages thrown in for good measure.

Similarly, the film *Hell in the Pacific*, in which an American soldier and a Japanese soldier confront each other on a deserted island, uses a Crusoean framework (but this time without savages) to stage the myth of enemy brothers that goes back to Cain and Abel. The Adamic variant of the Crusoe myth gives way here to the agonistic robinsonnade, whose theme, in the case in point, can be summarized as follows: two Robinsons on the same island are one too many, especially when the two do not constitute a couple and when neither is prepared to become the other's Friday.

And in the literary realm, we can also invoke the philosopher-Robinson we know as Gulliver. From storm to shipwreck, from Lilliput to Brobdingnag, from piracy to mutiny, from unknown shore to flying island, from Laputa to Glubbdubdrib, does he not repeat Crusoe's discovery of the Other many times over? Except that here, in these places that are not only foreign but strange, the solitary shipwreck victim confronts fantastic "savages" of variable height, nature, and form: dwarfs, giants, immortals, soothsayers, necromancers, and horses—the latter holding power over the descendants of a degenerate human species, the Yahoos, who are the Savages.[49]

What do we find, then, on our own beaches? No immortals, to be sure, and no horses on vacation either; perhaps a few soothsayers, tireless readers of horoscopes, dispensing approximate predictions to family and friends. But if we look beyond these summer prophets, an entire world will appear to us—at least as soon as we begin to play the role of ethnologist in order to observe residential summer vacationers and their ilk more closely.

RETURNING FROM AFRICA OR POLYNESIA

Distrust those cosmopolitans who go to great length in their books to discover duties they do not deign to fulfill around them. A philosopher loves the Tartars so as to be spared having to love his neighbors.

—Jean-Jacques Rousseau, *Émile* (1979)

It is time to bring this introduction to a close and put a finishing touch on the portrait of our provisional model vacationer, before sending him back to his island or his dreams.

A partisan of an experimental, interstitial, and pioneering style of vacationing that combines *farniente* with discovery and sedentariness with adventure, this marginal summer resident means to distinguish the innovative universe of her vacation, on several points that are indispensable to the achievement of her utopia, from the initiatory form of summer holiday, a banal stay at the seaside. Our traveler belongs to a world outside the ordinary, one that has no place for organized vacations, whether for the wealthy or for the masses. In this world, she rejects both four-star Robinsons and paid-vacation Fridays.

Here is the first line of demarcation established by our vacationer between himself and the rest of the seaside world. By combining the privilege of a rare or protected place with simplicity of manners, this social demarcation establishes his sojourn halfway between the sumptuousness of one group and the banality of the other.

Another line of demarcation is the psychological one that his purism inspires in our vacationer. He wants his world to be outside of time, like the Crusoean site, as if it were inscribed in nonduration: an endless moment, or an eternal beginning. From this standpoint, he is probably one of the most perfectly realized incarnations of the relation to leisure; as Joffre Dumazedier points out, "though a product of the historical process, leisure is being lived, in effect as if it were a value outside history."[50]

Hence our vacationer's pronounced tendency to deny others access to her beach: she rejects all those licensed Fridays, detesting them not only because they are so numerous but also because they are manifest and invasive products of history. As such, they are unacceptable in her world. They violate its intimacy and destroy its atemporal ecology by their very presence.

In his desire to break with the social reality he comes from, our demanding Robinson has a horror of Sameness extending to the too similar and too numerous Fridays who remind him of his own origins with intolerable insistence. Thus he becomes one of the Cosmopolites, preferring "the Tartars so as to be spared having to love his neighbors"—a characteristic nativist attitude that brings us to a third type of demarcation, which is cultural.

The cultural distinction between experimental and initiatory vacationers is a crucial one. A vacationer of the first category privileges the relation to otherness, to wildness, whether human or environmental: he'll take either natives or nature. The integrated robinsonnade of this Robinson is ethnographic and naturalistic. It tends to minimize or even eradicate the relation to sameness. As we shall see later on, this tendency is reversed in the framework of initiatory vacations, by the institution of a strong relation to sameness, and by the prior institution of a weak or even nonexistent relation to otherness (see chapter 1).

In fact, we may say that the relation to the Other is so powerful in the experimental vacationer that it generally leads him to see the real Savage as the Same, thus producing a total permutation. Confronting a crowd of his own kind, our vacationer evokes Dante's Inferno. Or, as Paul Morand puts it, "They are a swarm of creatures from one of

Hieronymus Bosch's cauldrons, as many of them as there are sand fleas, vinyl suitcases in hand."[51]

Finally, there is a fourth distinction, common to all vacationers from the experimental category, whether tourists or residential summer vacationers. This distinction takes the form of a dream or obsession that interposes itself between these vacationers and the rest: it entails a virtually compulsive identification with the heroic model, the great ancestor, of whom these vacationers, sometimes unconsciously, see themselves as heirs. This mythological demarcation arises from a self-representation and a definition of one's behavior with respect to a symbol, an idol, and thus a divinity generative of adoration and mimeticism: the Traveler.[52]

But it would seem that the goddess of Travel has given birth to two sons, Phileas and Robinson, with completely opposite natures. The one never holds still, while the other dreams only of interrupting his forward motion. The former, whether vagabond, nomad, or globetrotter, traverses space without respite. He is the Traveler's kinephilic heir; he sees himself as an explorer and a great world surveyor.[53] The latter, a hermit, sedentary or shipwrecked by choice, suspends his travels in Eden-like sites as soon as he has a chance. He is, in contrast, the Traveler's topophilic heir; he sees himself as a discoverer of earthly paradises, and in particular as an inventor of beaches.[54] The one thus keeps moving through the realm of impossibility, while the other makes his nest in impossible nooks and crannies.

The great epic traversal of the one thus contrasts with the Edenic installation of the other. Phileas escapes to see the vast world, while Robinson goes back into his shell and shuts himself off in a tiny little world in order to forget all the rest. And if both are indeed pioneer travelers, there is nevertheless something of the escapee in the one and of the recluse in the other. In the religion of Travel, there are two high priests with contrary mystiques.

These four demarcations that allow the experimental vacationer to constitute himself in his difference are accompanied by a fifth. This last is devoted to the defense of the others; we shall call it strategic. If it becomes impossible to maintain one of the first four, our vacationer, losing his soul, his space, or his privilege, will have a crisis, a spiritual or nervous breakdown. Whence the fits of despair, the recurring condemnations, and the desire to flee on the part of our vacationer, who suddenly evokes the Adragantes seas, the other side of the world, that is, the possibility of breaking—and this time for good—the bonds of society that still hold him back. Will he make the attempt? Will he succeed? He thinks about it; it is his dream; and at this moment there is something in him of a Robert J. Fletcher seeking his own "real S[outh] Sea Island," or an Alain Gerbault—not the Gerbault of the trip around the world, but the Gerbault who dreamed, at the end of his life, of making the Polynesian island of Porapora a Crusoean refuge of "unsurpassable beauty."[55]

Facing a problem of strategic demarcation that appears insoluble, our vacationer is caught here in a full-fledged depression. What does he see now? One by one, his hidden nooks and crannies fall into enemy hands. The Other fades away: the Savages disappear or yield, collaborating with the order of the new occupying force; the gigantic scale of construction destroys his "Lilliputian daydreams"; his suspended time is now metered out and his territory has been invaded. His neighbors, whom he thought were far away, have moved in to join him: there they are, intruders, their feet in the foam, wading just a yard away.

He already catches himself regretting the time when there were still only a dozen Fridays and their children on his beach, three English governesses chattering for hours on end and only a few striped umbrellas.[56] It is too late. His invention and his discovery are done for. The beach belongs to everyone. Here is the impression he preserves in his memoirs: "At present, I am contemplating with horror millions of examples of my own caricature."[57]

Although in quite different circumstances (after the tourist, the residential summer vacationer), we rediscover here, from Fogg to Crusoe, the same sad, melancholic figure: the "empty-handed traveler," the desperate descendant of the great ancestor, the heir caught in the trap of his own utopia, who experiences seaside modernity in the persona of the postrevolutionary aristocrat, that is, who experiences the democratization of beach vacations as a process of despoiling.[58]

Threatened, surrounded by the new Savages, our vacationer looks on as his utopia takes on water from all sides and his purism is submerged in the eddies of a crowd of cannibals. His role has become untenable; his strategic line of demarcation gives way, like the others; and if in his heart of hearts he remains in spiritual conformity with the model, concretely he is like a Robinson caught in a new storm and another shipwreck. "Only Ischia, protected by its prices and by the absence of roads on the Western coast, still remains sheltered from 'vacationers.'"[59]

He can, of course, flee toward other shores; this is indeed what he has always done up to now. But is flight still possible? I am thinking here of an incident that can serve as a parable. An Englishman, fed up with modern life, decided to go off with his family, far, far away, to find peace. He studied the possibilities in detail and finally came to a decision. He chose an island in the South Atlantic, where he intended to raise sheep. He left with his wife and children and settled there. A few months later, in April 1982, savages, "visitors" armed to the teeth, landed on his island. A war broke out—he had settled in the Falklands!

For want of interstices or means, for want of information or owing to an excess of information, factors that are destroying secret hideaways one after another, he can also abandon the beach. But the vacationer who interests us is too much in love with the shore to make such a decision.

And if he were to resist? If he were to defend himself and declare war in turn on the invaders? Let's stop dreaming! Could he even bring off a guerrilla action? At the very most, like everyone else, he will come up with some avoidance strategies, some delaying tactics to postpone the inevitable invasion of his island.

If Service, one of the shipwrecked children of Verne's *Two Years' Holiday,* and an assiduous reader of Defoe and Wyss, can declare, optimistically, at the news that evildoers have invaded the island: "These scoundrels are like Crusoe's savages. There's always a time when the savages arrive, just as the time comes when they're beaten off!"[60] our fellow can't do this. Seriously outnumbered by the enemy, Robinson succumbs and falls back into place. You don't get the better of the seaside crowd: it swallows you up. And while our vacationer is looking at the horizon between two umbrellas, dreaming about inaccessible islands, in the film *M. Hulot's Holiday* Monsieur Hulot arrives on the beach, marking once and for all the end of utopia. And here come the clients of the Bella Vista hotel, the Seagull campground, or the Blue Waters boardinghouse.

But our choice is made. From now on, we are going to stick by our fallen, dreamy Crusoe, submerged in the crowd, one of millions on the beach. Here, our paths diverge from those of the vacationer setting out for Africa or Polynesia. Let him go where he likes; we'll see no more of him. And if we remember him from time to time, he is now the Other, the "caricature," of our residential summer vacationer; the latter demands our full attention.

PART I

The Origin of Beach Manners

> Perhaps it is finally time to start our own anthropology: one that will
> speak about us, will seek in ourselves what we have pillaged from others
> for so long. No more exoticism; it is time to turn endotic.
>
> Time to question what seems so obviously to go without saying that
> we have forgotten how it began. Time to rediscover some of the aston-
> ishment that Jules Verne and his readers must have felt when they came
> across a machine that could reproduce and convey sounds.
>
> —Georges Perec, "Approches de quoi?"

We need to be astonished. This is where we have to start. We have to
be astonished by the beach. Be surprised by its existence. Stop thinking of it as self-evident and start questioning its reason for being.
This is a hard thing to do: we are so used to the beach, so much in
the habit of seeing it as ours, available to us, an immediate element
in our thinking about vacations. You say "summer, sun, holiday"? I
think "beach"! And we all talk about "the beach." Some particular
beach? No, just "the beach"!

At this point, everything still remains to be done. Or rather, everything remains to be done again. Unlike Paul Morand, who is inclined

27

to see only "rows of chickens roasting" on the sand, we need to resist the temptation that leads us to think, rather foolishly, that "about summers, the vacationer has nothing to say. He has only to let himself drift, let himself be." We need to remember what an anthropologist remarked some time ago: "If one is at all given to analysis, one is impressed with the extreme complexity of the various types of human behavior, and it may be assumed that the things that we take for granted in our ordinary, everyday life are as strange and as unexplainable as anything one might find."[1]

But this time we have to do it on our home ground rather than on someone else's, rather than on terrain where we are astonished from the start by the strangeness of the space and the customs. To make the beach comprehensible, we have to start by making it astonishing; and to do this, we have to break with the usual attitude, oblivious to origins, that trivializes our everyday experience of the beach: we "do not question it, it does not question us, it seems to pose no problems, we experience it without thinking about it, as if it conveyed no questions and no answers, as if it offered no information at all."[2] Yet what is strange is not necessarily the province of strangers, not necessarily foreign. Very often it is right there before our eyes, unnoticed, implicit or forgotten—like the Paris neighborhood that remained, for the ethnologist, "as unknown . . . as the Amazon."[3] Just like the beach . . .

To begin with, we need to remember, simply remember. There is no need to repeat the work of others—generalists or authors of remarkable monographs—and retrace the history of the beach as a site, depicting the emergence of "the coastal stage on which unconscious desires and obsolete emotions gradually took shape between 1750 and 1840" and where, "between the dunes and the water, we saw the primordial circle form once again, and watched the beach being invented."[4] For despite its present self-evidence, the beach too was indeed invented, along with the country and the mountains. And people first tasted the sea the way they taste their first alcoholic drink: they made faces, then rose above an initial reaction of profound disgust. "The ancient shore is also the recipient of the sea's excrements: the sea purges itself and spews up its monsters along the beach."[5]

Thus at the outset we have to bring to mind not just facts but also the various feelings that arise when we are confronted with the sea. Summoning up these feelings will restore a forgotten distance and make it clear that the beach, a site of pleasure, is a place without precedent: an antinatural innovation, despite all the words and dreams that cloak it today, after the fact, in the garb of authenticity and spontaneity. The enthusiasm of the crowds that now rush to beaches every summer is not the least bit timeless or spontaneous. It stems from ritual behavior lately acquired, not from some instinctive attraction. In the early 1860s the historian Jules Michelet wrote, "On a first visit to the coast the impression is not very favorable. There is aridity, there is wildness, and yet there is a certain monotony. The novel grandeur of the spectacle makes us feel, by contrast, how weak and small we are, and that thought thrills the heart."[6]

Apprehension inspired by shores and waves, anxiety aroused by the sea and its enigmatic immensity—these reactions are of course not at all new. Ancient literature presents the Mediterranean, and later the Atlantic Ocean, in the same disturbing light.[7] But Michelet took the ancients' diffuse fear a step further. Far from weakening, this fear seems to have become more intense with the passing centuries:

> In the middle ages there was a perfect horror of the Sea. They libelled the great Sea, they called that fertile mother "the kingdom of the prince of the powers of air"—the very name which was given to Satan. The nobility of the seventeenth century would by no means consent to have its palaces near the huts of the rude seamen. The frowning castle, with its ugly and formal garden, was almost always built as far as possible from the sea.[8]

The sea: demonized, repugnant, horrific. Here it is, the sea of yesteryear, the very same sea in which we swim today, the sea that we have had to tame, to domesticate, in the meantime going against the grain of our age-old repulsion.

As Jean Delumeau wrote, if there is any space in which the historian of mentalities is certain to encounter fear, it is the sea—the sea, inextricably associated with death, darkness, the abyss. The sea that swallows up ships and sailors; the sea that brought the black plague, the Norman and Saracen invasions, and later the Barbarian raids; the sea that has been haunted by angry gods, pirates, and monsters; the sea that has seen storms, shipwrecks, and looting; the sea that terrorized Renaissance pilgrims: the sea, a hostile element that is "bordered by inhuman shoals or unhealthy swamps" and that "unleashes a wind that makes cultivation impossible along its shores." The sea ultimately perceived as an evil power.[9]

The sea, a never-ending menace: how could we be expected to swim in it? How could anyone have even imagined such a thing, when simply sailing on it was already a big problem? Out of the question! "From ancient times to the nineteenth century, from Brittany to Russia, countless proverbs have advised us not to risk our lives by going to sea."[10] Countless civilizations, too, although situated near some shore, preferred forests, valleys, plains, or mountains to the sea—like those castles located far away, "as far as possible from the sea." The sea is accursed and the coast is avoided, so much so that, as Fernand Braudel tells us, studies devoted to borders almost never mention the sea. "Such is the prestige, or the superstition, attached to terra firma!"—and indeed, such is the collective fear that views the coastline less as a border than as a gaping wound continually threatening the integrity of earthbound society.[11]

During this vast period, the seashore, bearer of numberless evils, was perceived and experienced above all as the space of every danger: invasions and landings, but also monstrous, seductive, terrifying, or divine apparitions—Homeric creatures, sirens, krakens, and other leviathans. On the lips of the fathomless, the shore is first of all a place of superhuman challenges, and such it remains right up to the heart of the modern novel. Let us recall Victor Hugo's hero in *The Toilers of the Sea,* the fisherman Gilliatt, a humble Nemo of the seashore who, for love of Déruchette, struggles heroically against a monstrous octopus and in a suicidal gesture finally disappears under the rising waters.

And then the human—this time all-too-human—shore is not simply a space for sublime tragedies, it is also the theater of archaic dramas and ordinary miseries. Besides Virginia's watery death in Bernardin de Saint-Pierre's eighteenth-century novel, Balzac gives us Cambremer's murder between Le Croisic and Batz, where the protagonist drowned his own son to settle a debt, and we have a drowned fisherman's sordid funeral attended out of curiosity by Flaubert, who happened to be passing through Carnac. These early images of nineteenth-century coastlines attest to a harsh and cruel reality, and to the mixed feelings inspired by the watery universe at the edge of the world: a universe both savage and social, captivating and disturbing—and not just because a few ghostly smugglers and other looters of wrecked ships haunt its shores.[12]

In addition to storms and tides, the assault of the waves, and the nightmarish legends connected with oceanic mythologies, what the earliest coastal vacationers discovered with the amazed eyes of explorers was not only an inhospitable nature that set many ambushes in their path—the shifting sands of the Cabourg dunes, for example, or the Deauville swamps—but also very often a miserable human reality, so wretched that it sometimes became almost monstrous and fantastic, as the Hyperboreans or the Cynocephalics were for Herodotus. Here is what Flaubert discovered in Brittany in 1847: "As soon as you arrive somewhere, the beggars swarm all over you and cling to you with the obstinacy of hunger. You give them something, and they stay; you give them more, and their numbers increase. . . . Such an existence does not enhance the races; thus one encounters many cripples, amputees, blind men, hunchbacks, people covered with scabs or deformed by rickets."[13]

The coastal populations in fact resemble the space they inhabit between earth and water, a shifting, swampy space when it is not steep and ragged. In this linear space at the world's edge, half solid, half liquid, an absolute limit and a place of rupture, the indigenous peoples mirror their milieu: creatures of chaos, they live at the very confines of humanity, like the lepers of old. And if the sea spewed forth its monsters on ancient shores, in the first half of the nineteenth century earthbound society seems to have purged itself of its own monsters here.

Today's beaches, complete with umbrellas, tanned and undressed bodies, children's laughter, and swimmers, are still well out of sight. Their birth is quite inconceivable in the context of the superior wildness of a nineteenth-century beach, which was not even that of the inland countryside, the sheltered rural existence of the interior. Here, where the salty wind made farming impossible and shriveled human bodies along with the leaves on the trees, the explorer of the period was confronted with such extreme rusticity that he retained not the picture of an idyllic primitive society, but the hideous anamorphosis of a crippled and suffering social life—an image of purgatory, not paradise.[14]

Still, let us be careful not to generalize this view—an extreme one—in space and time. For one thing, our ethnological reading of the human environment cannot be replicated with the same intensity on all France's coasts. Furthermore, in Brittany itself this reading is attenuated in the second half of the nineteenth century, as we can tell from an observation made by a tourist in the late 1880s: "You were wrong, my dear; however wild it may appear, the place we are in is quite civilized. French is spoken here at least as much as Breton."[15]

Let us note, however, above and beyond the softening of this coastal vision, that while the tourist's observation corrects a prejudice, it offers evidence by the same token that the "dewilding" of seaside space had yet fully to penetrate popular thinking at the end of the nineteenth century, and, a fortiori, that the psychological, emotional, and ideological resistances to the development of seaside holidays had not been eradicated.

If, as Alain Corbin demonstrates, "the fear of the sea and a repugnance towards visiting its shores" are still by and large the prevailing sentiments in the seventeenth and eighteenth centuries, it seems clear that although they may not be explicit, these negative attitudes remained present in the collective sensibility right up to the early years of the twentieth century.[16] This being so, and given that my aim is not to go back over the historians' ground but to bring the story up to date, here is the first question to be addressed: in the late nineteenth and early twentieth centuries, what events struck the decisive, if not the final, blow to the generalized fear and repugnance in the face of the sea? Today's seaside holiday, which presupposes the defeat of those sentiments, is at the origin of beach manners.

Educated individuals in the eighteenth century were not unaware that for Cicero, Pliny the Younger, or Seneca, seashores "had once been places of meditation, rest, collective pleasure, and unbridled voluptuousness."[17] People began heading for the sea to take the waters around 1750. The Prince of Wales bathed in the sea at Brighton in 1787; Napoleon III did the same at Dieppe in 1812, at the age of four, well ahead of the Duchesse de Berry, who bathed there in 1824. The Hôtel du Grand Orient was built in 1822 to accommodate the increased number of bathers at Luc-sur-Mer in Normandy; the first establishment for sea bathing in Sète was opened in 1834. All these facts point in the same direction and constitute clear evidence of the growing attraction of the seashore. There are many others, some even more telling: Brighton, for example, "received 117,000 visitors [per year] as early as 1835, and in 1862 it had 132,000 in a single month! Between 1860 and 1870, spas sprang up in the wake of the railroad and its stations along the Côte d'Azur and the Italian Riviera."[18]

But these early signs, however noteworthy, still fail to account for the psychological and symbolic conditions of the increase in, and then the satisfaction of, the new desire to enjoy the seashore. They explain neither the aesthetic of the terrain, which gradually became an imperative within this perspective, nor the meaning of the correlative practices that came to be associated with the site over time. However, the new aesthetic and the new practices are the origin of today's seaside vacationing: leisure on the edge—aquatic, topophilic, large-scale leisure.

When all is said and done, what is a beach? What is a holiday beach? What characterizes its terrain? What makes it special? What is it like? What plastic and physical, visual and corporeal modalities presided over its invention and characterize its appearance, use, and function today? The holiday beach has acquired its identity at the price of fundamental transformations and adjustments that cannot be ignored. And what psychological space are we actually talking about? What space for leisure? And for what sort of leisure? What does one do in that space? And why?—in particular starting from the moment when bathing (from the Latin *balneum*) became its primordial, universal rite?

When Gustave Flaubert and Maxime Du Camp went off to Brittany, what did they do? They engaged in tourism, to be sure: a form of cultural and natural tourism in which they combined the strategies of ethnologists and naturalists with occasional pauses during which they did nothing but stroll along a beach and lie on the sand—"where the rising tide wiped out the arabesques we drew with our sticks, and where, stretched out under the sun, we slept like lizards."[19] But the sea itself played no special role in the approach of these vacationers. They were practicing coastal tourism: that is, they were essentially exploring the country by way of its coasts, "over strand and field." However, these travelers never incorporated a seaside sojourn properly speaking into their journey as an experience, theme, or leitmotiv.

Compared to these dry-shod tourists, traveling along the Breton shores as explorers, do we move inevitably from coastal tourism to sea-oriented tourism the first time a bather who prefers a swimming costume to a frock coat and boots takes up temporary residence at the seaside? This new figure goes swimming, to be sure, but he no longer travels. He does not explore the coastline: an enthusiast for marine holidays, he remains immobile on the shore, in a site of his own choosing.

"Seaside tourism," like "health tourism," is a misnomer:[20] both terms stem from a misuse of language unless they refer specifically (but they do not) to vacations conceived as tours on which the points of interest would be beaches, swimming pools, spas, or sanatoria! In fact, these forms of "tourism" are generally nothing of the sort. They are more closely related to resort vacationing; recent attempts to rebaptize them "tourisme de séjour" or "sedentary tourism" have produced oxymorons, since such expressions refer to the paradoxical notion of immobile mobility and only add to the reigning confusion about how to categorize holiday practices.

And then to speak of the beach as a destination too often means speaking of what is in the vicinity rather than of the beach itself, focusing on the periphery and not the center, whereas for an anthropologist of leisure the beach is a world in itself. By looking elsewhere, are we not forgetting "the banal, the everyday, the obvious, the common, the ordinary, the infra-ordinary, the background noise, the habitual," that is, the essential, thus losing sight of the diffuse signs and vestigial indices that give rise to and account for precisely this world?[21]

Gabriel Désert has it right: "The seaside universe is beyond question the hardest thing in the world to grasp. It is exceedingly heterogeneous, and its witnesses, chroniclers, and the press have unfortunately tended to speak, with very rare exceptions, only about the most flagrant and famous minority, the one that is intent on being seen, recognized, and quoted"—"as if life could reveal itself only through the spectacular," as Georges Perec would say.[22] Now the contemporary vacation beach also proceeds from modest facts and discrete events, a priori infinitesimal but decisive ones; if these are not taken into account, its cultural significance—beyond the particular value of this space in the universe of leisure—cannot possibly be grasped.

"Space is subjected to time, is the product of time, bears time's traces, incites gestures and behaviors. . . . It authorizes events but does not contain them. These are subjects that shape history."[23] And these subjects, which have shaped and continue to shape the seaside space of vacations, are often anonymous or overlooked.

The task that remains, then, requires us to uncover traces and decipher the decisive gestures of these subjects. Sometimes famous, but often nameless, they are actors, ideas, and elements of varying natures, individual or collective, indigenous or foreign, human or nonhuman: symbols, idols, or have-nots, *gens de peu*[24] appearing in one place, disappearing in another, perhaps transforming themselves; all of them together have allowed the seaside reality to become what it is today—the space and mirror of a nontouristic leisure vacation.

1. The Death of the Fisherman

*(or, How Robinson and Friday
captured the Savages and did away
with savagery, one step at a time)*

Fishermen. People used by summer residents as barometers; frequently
asked to predict the weather.

—Pierre Daninos, *Vacances à tous prix* (1958)

We have reached the period of the blank slate, the moment when the
first holiday-goers tamed the seashore. This inaugural operation of
"attuning space with desire," required by the emergence and for the
satisfaction of "a new pleasure," was an *aesthetic* operation;[1] from
this perspective, the first material and visual arrangements of the
seashore were psychological and social, not to say *ethnic,* well before
they were architectural and urbanist. The "desavaging" of beaches
came at a price.

Thus Robinson Crusoe appeared in the first half of the nineteenth
century in the guise of a painter, writer, or enlightened aristocrat. This
new Robinson was the discoverer and inventor of the beach, a pioneer; he was followed a few years later by Friday, who appeared for his
part in the guise of a bourgeois vacationer, promoter, or speculator.
Friday was the imitator-exploiter, the agent who made seaside leisure
available to the masses, in the form of an *initiatory summer residency.*
In an eternal beginning, after the Norman and Breton coasts, the
Mediterranean, and other shorelines had been overrun, we can trace
the corresponding flight of the disappointed and bereft experimental
vacationer, who headed bitterly toward other seas, other shores, other

islands (see Introduction). Starting in the period between 1860 and 1880, the experimental vacationer could no longer stand to see his retreat assailed by the growing swell of travelers.[2]

The fact remains that in the early part of the century, in 1831 when Alexandre Dumas went to Trouville for the first time (after the painter Charles Mozin, who had discovered—or rather invented—it in 1825), the writer had the feeling that he had landed in a place "almost as unknown as Robinson Crusoe's island."[3] There, indeed, were Savages, natives whose destiny, as we shall see, was closely linked with the invention of the contemporary beach.

Who were these Savages? Who were these creatures who, in a space that had "never [been] trampled, contemplated, or perverted by any man [from a city], or represented by any artist," still living apart from the world as if on a moon: a satellite territory of which Mozin, Dumas, Alphonse Karr, Alfred de Musset, Gustave Flaubert, and others were to be the first cosmonauts?[4] They were the "toilers of the sea," harvesters of seaweed, swamp-dwellers, peasants working with kelp, whom Flaubert and Maxime Du Camp spotted in a sandy desert between Pouvan and Audierne.[5] They were also, and especially, fishermen. In sum, a population that was not only maritime but *exotic,* at least in the eyes of its discoverers, who saw, experienced, and described it as such, in the form of pastoral scenes or ethnographic clichés.

Thus these Savages were captured first by paintings and narratives that drew attention to an undiscovered land and an unknown population; from then on, they were frozen in their setting, domesticated by images and manipulated by novelistic techniques as if they were background figures on a stage. This artistic and literary appropriation of the shore condemned the space and its people to stereotypes, locking them into a highly codified picturesque realm filled with "typical" landscapes and timeless characters that appear even today in guidebooks and advertising. This "retinal" persistence is clear evidence that what alighted on the banks in those early years was first of all a gaze, not a foot in the surf or a body in the waves. In that period, the shore was above all a spectacle: its receding tides, which unveiled the sea's depths, supplied a theatrical effect, its storms offered grandiose new developments, and a sailor's funeral was a pathetic episode brilliantly interpreted by local actors.

Moreover, Mozin did not go to Normandy to swim any more than Flaubert went to Brittany for that purpose. The object was to see, not to touch—so much so that, beginning in 1880, when the holiday move-ment was spreading toward the shore, the sites selected were those from which "*the view of the sea* [was] *more precious than their actual use:* hills forming an amphitheater around large bays (Nice, Cannes, Monaco, Taormina), easily isolated capes and peninsulas (Antibes, Villefranche, Giens, Santa Margherita, Sorrento and its island extensions, Capri and Ischia)."[6] This is how postcards came into being, along with a whole panoply of images establishing the aesthetic of the emerging seaside world. From landscape to portrait: sites went the way of people.

At nightfall on Mont-Saint-Michel, we find in Flaubert an early trace of a stereotype that is immutable even today, that of the old mariner smoking his pipe, leaning on a parapet facing the sea—an individual with whom one speaks, with whom one gets one's picture taken, whose burnished features one takes in, whose tattoos one inspects with sidelong glances, and whom one invariably questions about the next day's weather: Daninos's barometer-fisherman.[7] In the Netherlands, in the late seventeenth century and in the eighteenth, "travellers rushed to Scheveningen in order to watch the activity on the beach scene and mingle with the fishermen."[8]

But to see is to interpret. So how does one interpret these men of the shore? At the beginning of the nineteenth century, "Philarète Chasles, for his part, and he is only one example, notes the presence of twelfth-century Norsemen all along the English shore: 'One feels that one is going back five or six hundred years in European history' (he says)." And Flaubert's ethnology of the shore people is hardly more nuanced. Along the shore on the road to Pontorson, he compares the long ragged line of carts loaded with soil from the sea intended for use as fertilizer to "some emigration of barbarians who have become aroused and leave their plains."[9]

The fishermen's village, too, is a prisoner of immutable representa-tions and received ideas. Even today it is frequently used as an advertis-ing motif, featured as the exotic and appealing heart of a coastal site. Like its inhabitants, the "primitive" village, to be authentic, must always be small, simple, modest, or worse. In her travel narrative, Mme de Lalaing tells us that Royan was "a poor little unknown seaport" and that for centuries "Biarritz was nothing but a miserable hamlet." Similarly, in a 1957 guidebook, we are told that Saint-Mandrier is a "little fishing village at the foot of a picturesque bay" and that Saint-Raphaël, when Alphonse Karr arrived in 1880, was a "just a little fishing town."[10]

Small, poor, and miserable, these ports, hamlets, and villages were inhabited by Savages, as we know. What was happening at this point in our society? What ideological and cultural relation to the shore and the sea was being established? And what consequences ensued from the "primitivist" gaze cast on the coastal universe?

Borrowing the metaphors of the day, Dominique Rouillard speaks of the holiday-goers' shift toward the Normandy coast as a "conquest of the West," noting that during the nineteenth century "artistic explora-tion evolved into a colonization of lands; flight developed into a strictly oriented westward movement." This colonial expansion of leisure start-ed from the principle that the coastal fringe belonged to no one, "no more than the territory of the Americas belonged to the Indians"![11]

Thus, far from integrating this new reality and assimilating its ex-oticism as a regional cultural given through and through, the solitary Robinsons and later the numerous Fridays of the Normandy coastline and elsewhere accentuated, even exaggerated, the strangeness of the shore. The former, leaving the exoticization of the sites and the people as their heritage, made the coast into "Indian" country, virgin and available; the latter, grasping the colonial opportunity, functioning as promoters, speculators, or property-owning summer residents, then took over the shoreline in large numbers. Here is where Friday tri-umphs and Robinson flees to the shores of other seas.

This initial artistic and literary "savaging," rather than leading to the recognition of a coastal culture, instead encouraged its distancing and contributed to the future reduction of its existence and its identity.[12] In its way, the gaze that saw local populations as "savage" prepared the ground for submersion of the local culture by leisure: exploitation, loot-ing, expulsion, extinction—pace Joseph Morlent, who declared in 1860 that "in a departure from the usual pattern, the bathers did not drive out the fisherman, the way the Americans drove out the Redskins."[13]

Still, the bathers were not singlehandedly responsible for the death of the fishermen, and in Morlent's day the concrete signs announcing the doom of the Savages along the shore were not yet irrefutable. But in the pictorial and fictional representations of the seaside, that future was already being sketched in.

THE SEARCH FOR SAVAGES WITH PAINTBRUSH AND PEN

While guidebooks, studies, manuals, and other treatises on maritime leisure were proliferating, an unmistakable evolution in painting was coming to light. Alain Corbin notes that, in the early decades of the nineteenth century, painters seduced by the seaside populations were still going to northern European coasts to study and represent the life and activities of workers along the shore. As of 1845, in these regions, the theme "had become an anachronism. The leisure class, in its quest for ever new ways of being seen, became the subject to be represented; paintings ceased to provide a direct expression of their longing for the shore. The social scene and the pleasure it procured became the focus, to the great regret of solitary Romantics," artists, pioneers, and inventors of beaches, fans of experimental vacationing and disappointed Robinsons![14] Alphonse Karr fled to Saint-Raphaël.

In 1805, in the great tradition of maritime landscapes of the seventeenth and eighteenth centuries, J. M. W. Turner exhibited *The Shipwreck.* In 1833, in *Plage à marée basse,* with its sordid thatched huts bordering the strand, Isbey depicted the poverty of the people along the shore. Just as John Constable had done earlier in *Brighton Beach,* in the early 1860s in *Falaises à Étretat* Gustave Courbet showed yet another wild stretch of wave-battered coastline with a fragile fisherman's skiff coming dangerously close to the reefs in rough seas. But these landscapes of storm and misery expressing the natural and social harshness of the shore gradually began to give way to a different model, that of the beach invaded and colonized by vacationers, the shore pacified, tamed, and "civilized" by city folk, turned into a stage for a very different sort of agitation, leisure-based and worldly.

"In the day the host of yellow gloves and varnished boots crowds the shore," Michelet noted.[15] This sort of spectacle is captured, for example, by Eugène Boudin's *Baigneuses sur la plage de Trouville,* depicting female "bathers" who were not actually "bathing." In this painting a group of women are portrayed in long dresses, carrying umbrellas; some are seated (not on the ground but on chairs), the others stand, chatting among themselves as if in a drawing room. In the foreground, two children, on the ground but also fully dressed, are playing in the sand. With the genre of "seaside" painting, breaking with the dramatic tone of seascapes and pastorals, Boudin won praise from his colleague Théodule Ribot in 1868 for having dared to paint people in contemporary dress on the beach.

To be sure, in 1886, Pierre Loti published *Iceland Fisherman,* a tragic evocation of the Breton fishermen's lot, and in Pont-Aven, five years before his departure for Tahiti, Paul Gauguin painted *Les ramasseuses de varech bretonnes.* But the evacuation of the shore people and their labor into painting was already under way, while the tendency to evoke storms, shipwrecks, and other maritime perils was fading—even if Gustave Courbet did triumph in the Salon of 1870 with *La mer orageuse.* In the second half of the nineteenth century, this evolution and the choices to which it led tell us a good deal not only about the new psychological and cultural status of the sea but also about the future of the natives of the coastal regions—a figurative evolution and figurative choices that offer a definitive prophecy as to their contemporary material and social fate, that is, their disappearance.

In the late 1860s, Claude Monet's *Étretat* is the polar opposite of Courbet's. At the foot of the cliffs and the famous "needle," the sea is now calm; and in the place of a fragile fishing skiff we now have the peaceful spectacle of a regatta moving away from an inviting bank. In 1869, three years after the publication of Victor Hugo's *Toilers of the Sea,* Courbet painted *La mer:* beneath the work's still-dramatic tone the metaphor is clear. The painting conveys a cruel prognosis. It represents a becalmed sea that comes to die on a deserted shore where an abandoned dinghy lies—not a wreck but a vestige, in the form of a trace on the beach of a time long past, when the shores were still the territory of fishermen.

Monet, who met Boudin in Le Havre in 1858 and became his student, painted *Sur la plage* in 1873. In the foreground, there is a couple on the sand. Dressed in the clothing of the period, the woman, seated, is reading; the man, half reclining, is looking at the ocean. What does he see? Or rather, what is there to contemplate? Here, too, are an empty beach and a calm sea, a blue-green stretch on which some black spots, some ghostly veils, flutter in the distance: they belong to fishermen's boats.

For from now on, fishermen are virtually out of sight. They are either at sea or in port; they are no longer found on shore. The contemporary holiday beach is beginning to take shape. It will be a stage without natives, empty of its Savages. Of course this disappearance did not occur everywhere at the same time or to the same degree. The south held out longer against disintegration, against the separation between natives and vacationers. The fact remains that, although the French Riviera was discovered as a seasonal resort as early as 1760, the Mediterranean coast was invaded later by the bourgeois vacation crowd.[16] In Edvard Munch's *Promenade des Anglais* (Nice, 1891), we still see fishermen's dinghies near the benches from which holiday-goers can gaze at the sea. On July 14, 1936, also in Nice, on the Quai des États-Unis, Max Gallo's fictional characters Denise, Giovanna, and Vincente are seated "in the narrow shadow cast by a fisherman's dinghy" in order to have a comfortable picnic on the beach.[17] Such proximity between material evidence of the fishing world and leisure practices was still possible in the early 1960s on the Spanish Costa Brava as well. Today this is no longer the case.

But in the north, signs of such juxtapositions were already disappearing early in the twentieth century. To be persuaded of this, it suffices to consider Albert Marquet's *Affiche à Trouville* or *La plage de Fécamp,* both painted in 1906. There are no boats and no fishermen on these Normandy beaches; instead, there are people strolling about, striped canvas cabins, and sailors from the Navy on leave looking at the sea from the promenade. And if Monet was still painting fishermen's dinghies cast up on the beach in the late 1860s (*La plage de Sainte-Adresse,* near Le Havre), the same year Marquet did his Normandy paintings, Raoul Dufy brought back from Sainte-Adresse a beach scene swarming with vacationers, full of Fridays; here too we find a breakwater and a fluorescence of canvas cabins.

We learn from painting, then, that from the mid-nineteenth century on, seashore cohabitation between fishermen and visitors was becoming increasingly rare. The spectacle of these worlds in coexistence ultimately gave way to separate representations, and even to representations of the second group alone. To find the first group still depicted in paintings, we have to turn our backs on beaches and go into ports—and even there, fishermen are not very common. Far indeed from the overcrowded port scenes of a Claude Lorrain or a Joseph Vernet in the seventeenth and eighteenth centuries, or of a Turner later on, we find that Georges Seurat's *Les quais à Honfleur* (1886), Georges Braque's *Le port d'Anvers* (1906), André Derain's *Gravelines* (1934), and Dunoyer de Segonzac's *Saint-Tropez* from the same period are all oriented toward simplified forms and abstraction; people are absent.

This contemporary modern painting leads unmistakably to a symbolic desertification of seaports, beaches (except for vacation sites), and their surroundings. Pierre Bonnard's *La plage à marée basse* (1922) depicts an almost deserted beach: except for the familiar dinghy washed up in the center of the painting, we can only make out the vague silhouettes of fishermen with their rods on the right, and that of a shrimp

fisherman and perhaps a child's head on the left. As for the surroundings, let us recall Paul Cézanne's *L'estaque,* or landscapes by Paul Signac,
who discovered Saint-Tropez in 1892: *Antibes, nuage rose,* or *Pin parasol.*
From these luminous sites, devoid of human silhouettes, a whiff of
Crusoean paradise emanates.

Images of fishermen and other shore-dwellers, propitiatory victims
of this aesthetic conquest, persist, significantly, through the end of the
nineteenth century and into the twentieth, in the case of certain painters: for example, Puvis de Chavannes, who kept his distance from the
artistic movements of his day *(Le pauvre pêcheur),* Paul Sérusier, one
of Gauguin's disciples *(La vieille du Pouldu),* and also local painters
or genre painters, precisely the ones who have been forgotten or have
remained unknown.[18] In the framework of a mystical pictorial haven,
whether they belong to the symbolist tradition or to an "outmoded"
realism that still gives them a certain presence, these images will survive, but in isolation, like refugees leading a marginal existence, apart
from the major trends of the period, oriented toward impressionism,
daily life, formal simplification, and, finally, abstraction.[19]

What meaning can we attribute to this evolution? To the marginalization and eventual expulsion of the populace from the seashores
shown on painters' canvases? To the abandonment of the theme? To
the figurative purification which, although symbolic and a reflection
of its time, nevertheless resembles a sort of ethnocide?

After leaving a series of Robinsons wide-eyed with surprise, and
after preempting the entire gaze of these newcomers with their local
exoticism, the Savages of the seacoast succumbed, driven out of images
by painters and excluded from texts by writers. Like painters, writers
mythified and magnified these strange outsiders during the period
of initial discovery, exalting their savagery before gradually pushing
them out of the foreground and then offstage altogether. After Honoré
de Balzac, Gustave Flaubert, Victor Hugo, and Pierre Loti, there were
Guy de Maupassant, Thomas Mann, and F. Scott Fitzgerald.[20] From
the cliffs of Le Havre to the rocky coasts of the Estérel via the Venitian
lagoons, these later writers appropriated beaches for an entirely different purpose. For them the coastal world was merely a backdrop, a
setting. Rather than producing narratives that would evoke the harsh,
miserable, and courageous lives of the shore people—or even the mo-
notonous lives of the bourgeois summer people such as Félicité and the
Aubain family in Trouville—these authors transformed the seashore

into a quite "civilized" stage: in one case, into "a love-market where some [women] sold, and others gave themselves"; in another case, into a world of subtle lies, "delicate jokes and politenesses"; in all cases, into a theater of passions, abstracted from the savagery of its origins, a theater for characters in search of identity, love, or absolutes, a place for observation, ostentation, seduction, and rivalry, a place available to new actors offering the spectacle of feigned conviviality, complex social protocols, and mating rituals.[21]

Whether pictorial or novelistic, this worldly socialization of the beach, "cleansed," as it were, of its native population, is a sign that presupposes a fundamental historical inversion of psychological and cultural relations at the seaside. This space now serves not for use but for exchange, not for labor but for contemplation, not for work but for play, not for production but for consumption, finally, so that the child's sandcastle comes to replace the fisherman's boat, and the bather's umbrella replaces the seaweed harvester's rake. By the time this aesthetic conquest was complete, the coastal landscape had gone the way of the rural landscape. The shore had become a "natural" framework devoid of work and workers, according to a perspective "from which the facts of production had been banished," visually abolished—a framework valorized as such by landlocked, urban society, the so-called leisure class.[22]

From this standpoint, can we not read the end of Ernest Hemingway's *The Old Man and the Sea* as a dirge for a world that is disappearing, an edifying parable? The fisherman's place is now on the high seas or in port; and the novel's conclusion confirms in its own way that everything that bears witness to the Savage's existence must henceforth vanish from the shore and from the vacationer's sight. Indeed, as soon as he has returned to land, the old fisherman disappears. Exhausted, he falls asleep in his isolated hut, in a deep death-like sleep. As for his catch, the pitiful trace of a heroic labor soon to be dissolved in the sea, it floats, a vestige of an unknown glory, like a siren's skeleton, in the dying waves along the shore:

> That afternoon there was a party of tourists at the Terrace and looking down in the water among the empty beer cans and dead barracudas a woman saw a great long white spine with a huge tail at the end that lifted and swung with the tide while the east wind blew a heavy steady sea outside the entrance to the harbour.

"What's that?" she asked a waiter and pointed to the long backbone of the great fish that was now just garbage waiting to go out with the tide.

"Tiburon," the waiter said, "Eshark." He was meaning to explain what had happened.

"I didn't know sharks had such handsome, beautifully formed tails."

"I didn't either," her male companion said.

Up the road, in his shack, the old man was sleeping again. He was still sleeping on his face . . .[23]

In short, the novel's ending takes the form of an allegory, recounting in its own way what the seashore has become under the combined aegis of modernity and leisure: an object of contemplation. The siren is dead, the fisherman has vanished, natives and other dangers have been removed; symbolically purged of monsters and savages, the beach is ready to be consumed as a world dissociated from the natural and social realities of production. It is an empty stage, reserved from now on for other activities, other forms of play; it is now available for the exercise of a collective simulacrum of the re-enchantment of the world, a simulacrum generally known as a "seaside vacation."

LAND AND SEAS DIVIDED

But all this still involves only pictorial representations and novelistic interpretations. What happened in actual fact? After the symbolic domestication of the bank by the artistic and literary elite, the real appropriation of the beach by the Crusoe myth was not achieved by brush and canvas or pen and paper alone. Whether we speak as prophets or as witnesses, we cannot rid ourselves of a world, we cannot abolish human beings and their culture, simply by ceasing to speak of them. Where the "death of the fisherman" is concerned, we need to shift our focus from the aesthetic conquest of the shore to the material conquest that resulted from its refurbishing for vacationers.

Unlike the suppression of local populations in painting and in literature (although these art forms did announce, attest, and even depict the event), the shore people's actual disappearance was polymorphic and complex. Although it coincided with the development of seaside leisure, in historical and technological terms it cannot be imputed to bathers alone.

In fact, nineteenth-century "bathers" did not do much bathing, and there were not even very many of them (see chapter 2). Other motives or imperatives prevailed at the time, such as air, sun, or views—that is, fresh air therapy, heliotherapy, and the taste for the picturesque—transported from the country and the mountains to the sea. In addition, the development of baths in certain sites appears less as a cause than as an effect of the local residents' disappearance. Michelet himself, though highly critical of the "host of yellow gloves and varnished boots," could not help but note with bitterness that bathers did not always drive out fishermen but on the contrary could facilitate the emergence of a substitute activity when fishing was in a state of crisis. During the rainy summer of 1860, on the little quay of Étretat, Michelet pursued the following reflection: "That very small Quay of Boulders, small as it is, yet is too large. I saw there a number of vessels, abandoned, useless. For . . . the Fishery has become so unproductive! The fish have fled that shore. Étretat languishes, perishes, so near to languishing, and, but for its sea-bathing, perishing."[24] For the disappearance of local populations also has to do with the evolution of the trades associated with the sea: as measured by a certain modernity, these maritime activities were already shifting toward industrialization and restructuring.

From the beginning of the nineteenth century to our own day, despite quite variable delays in application (relative delays, varying from one coastal region to another: comparing Spain to Belgium, for example, we note a lag related to the modification of the flow of vacationers toward the sea and a pronounced contemporary increase in flow toward the Mediterranean), we can nevertheless observe tactical repetitions from north to south all along Europe's coastline and thus catalog the principal ways in which the shore people were driven out. Their disappearance took on a variety of aspects, from sheer expulsion to the always ambiguous folklorization of the coastal world.

Among the very earliest tactics adopted, we shall focus on a historical reality comparable to the one depicted in painting: dissociation between worlds. Technologically, this operation was carried out via the construction of a pier-promenade. As Corbin points out, "Beginning in the 1810s [at least in the north], . . . the construction or improvement of a pier-promenade became a necessity for any resort with even the slightest ambitions."[25]

Each resort undertook such construction in response to a demand that grew entirely out of the new pleasure afforded by looking at the sea from a vantage point only slightly removed from shore: gazing down on the depths from a position of close proximity to the surf. But the pier-promenade, perpendicular to the shoreline, did more than offer a potentially picturesque view. In most instances, pier-promenades also facilitated the move toward a demiurgic parting of the waters, leaving vacationers on one side and fishermen on the other.

In the nineteenth century, a number of illustrations and comments bore witness to the material installation of these partitions, evoking their effects on both land and water. An engraving from 1889, a view of Le Croisic from the sea, offers an example that epitomizes the situation. The promenade at Le Croisic, built in 1840, is more than half a mile long. Officially intended to protect the port from storms, it is not only a wall but also a screen unambiguously separating bathers from fishermen. This division of aquatic space is echoed on land: on the left there is the port and the fishing village, and on the right the residential city with a line of bathing huts along the shore. Following its "resort-ification," the city of Le Pornic is described in similar terms:

> [The city] is divided into two parts: the upper city and the lower city, known as Les Sablons. The latter is inhabited by seafarers and customs officials; the upper city, the larger of the two, has the church, the city hall, the hospital, the justice of the peace, the marketplace, and the sea baths. These two cities communicate via large stairways, in most places carved out of the rocky ledge.[26]

Such stratifications were the rule, as ancient sites of maritime production were converted into vacation sites. "At the beginning of the century," the narrator adds, "Le Pornic was almost unknown; people were aware that cod fisherman had used it in earlier times, and that is about all. This almost entirely forgotten city has won a certain renown since the fashion of sea-bathing took hold. It is a very popular destination today"—owing to the separation between land and water, which in the process disconnected what had been "about all" from social life and relegated it to residual status with respect to the whole: the fishermen's territory, the former heart of the city, is now on the margins.

Beginning in the nineteenth century, then, we witness what today's geographers would call zoning. This process leads to the appearance of a "functional tourist zone" that is disconnected from the "traditional town."[27] On the side toward the sea, corresponding to the "old city," one usually finds the old port and the classic promenade space it offers summer visitors, most often all the way to the lighthouse that stands like an exclamation point at the end of the pier—a frontier that is also called a jetty, a dike, a breakwater, or something else again, depending on local circumstances. And what do the summer people do, during their ritual promenade? They come out to look at the vanished local folk, with their boats, nets, and supplies!

In the eyes of these strollers, who have provisionally abandoned the beach, the port—the fishermen's space, separated from that of the bathers—is from now on a different world. Whether isolated, remote, or marginalized, this world on the other side of the wall, outside the leisure universe of summer residency, the reverse side of the décor, is an exotic one.[28] The exploratory ritual of strolling is depicted in the engraving of Le Croisic. On the pier-promenade, between the beach and the port, we see curiosity-seekers, men in city clothes and elegant women outfitted with umbrellas. They are looking at the bathers' port on one side and the fishermen's port on the other—an exercise in comparative contemplation induced by the physical separation between the worlds that promotes the former as a universal place of health and pleasure and turns the latter into a curiosity, a local attraction, a vestige-site—reservation lands on which "typical" identity can be confined, but also a space of refuge for the Savages themselves, as if they had been captured, protected, and removed from the world by this front behind which they simultaneously hide and put themselves on display. They now offer themselves as a spectacle to the vacationers, who observe them in their aquatic pit like "curious beasts." For this withdrawal of the fishermen back into the ports is in part a function of the progress of sea bathing. Thus in the 1850s in the Belgian town of Blankenberghe (where sea bathing had only begun in the previous decade), "the maritime population . . . does not [yet] hide in the harbour as at Ostend, but rather spreads itself out on the platform."[29]

The pier-promenade was thus the first of the tangible tactics leading to the disappearance of maritime sites and practices of production along with native populations and their signs. This disappearance wasinitially more social than physical—even though cuts through the coastline and territorial redistributions were most often accompanied by rules and regulations in the public or commercial interest (adjudication, rent, and so on) whose application tacitly led to the expulsion of the shore workers.

For example, at the beginning of the twentieth century in Normandy, legislation concerning sea bathing prohibited "bathing horses" and "driving cars along the shore."[30] Under these conditions, in locales henceforth reserved for bathers, such legislation amounted to decreeing that people were no longer free to harvest "sea hay" on Calvados beaches, just as people could no longer rake seaweed onto beaches in Brittany in the 1850s except in specified areas.[31] What appeared to be an abstract law reforming the natural or traditional use of the shore was in fact a policy restricting beach use; from decisions at the prefectoral level to municipal decrees, such policies have grown more and more complex right up to our own day.[32]

But let us return to this evocation of the tactical realities that have led me to use the terms *vestige* and *reservation*—in the American Indian sense, needless to say.[33] These terms prefigure a more advanced form of confinement and segregation of the natives, one that is no longer based on distancing and simple partitioning of the territory but rather on the surrounding of one population by the other. The ghettoization of the natives is a process in which, rather than simply marginalizing the local beach population, the outsiders relegate them to enclaves, thus bringing about a shift in their social status: rather than remaining refugees, the natives become a besieged minority.

Robinson and Friday are no longer content, now, to distance, separate, push back, or set aside the territory of the Savages; instead, they encircle it. It is no longer a matter of condensing distance with the help of a wall, but rather of condensing the fishermen's world itself, shaping it as a kernel rather than leaving it as a margin. In our own day, the Algarve offers a good example of the process. On this Portuguese coast, "the smallest fishermen's villages have found themselves, in the space of some fifteen years, at the center of gigantic tourist complexes." Thus the city of Albufeira (10,000 inhabitants in winter, 350,000 residents in summer) "is intact today, with its narrow shady streets and its beach, which is accessed through a tunnel carved out of rock, but which is surrounded on all sides by huge concrete masses."[34] For all that, if the territory of the Savages is, properly speaking, isolated (from the Italian *isola*, "island"), the Portuguese case of enclave-creation is far from an isolated instance. The phenomenon is international, identifiable in multiple sites, with many precedents on the coasts of England, Belgium, Spain, Italy, France, Greece, and elsewhere.

This second tactic, a demarcation between worlds that is no longer linear but nuclear and that keeps the natives' territory in a central position, appears a priori more humane. Unlike the strategy of rejection exemplified by the preceding tactic, this one actually seems to be valorizing, and even integrative, in that it raises the ethnographic legacy to the dignity of a protected vestige. From this standpoint, the creation of "reservations" for people, places, and traditions can thus be perceived as relatively positive, technologically and morally satisfying—at least at a certain level of perception. On the scale of "sight sacralization" established by Dean MacCannell, it corresponds to the third stage, that of enshrinement.[35]

There is a problem, however. By vocation, the coastal site is not so much a tourist destination as a site of summer residency, not so much a place to pass through as a place to settle down in, given not so much to circulation as to sedentarization. This vocation is realized most often today at the cost of unbridled construction, leading to the "seaside Manhattans" resembling Miami Beach that form walls along the Spanish coasts, or to the strings of villas ravaging the environment on the mountains of the Estérel. It is in the very nature of the residential seaside vacation industry to promote the fidelity of its clientele, to turn it more than any other into a population of returnees, and thus to encourage it to move "from temporary enjoyment to the definitive appropriation of a vacation home."[36] In the context of enshrinement that interests us here, as soon as the goal of sedentarizing vacationers is achieved, the prolonged cohabitation thus obtained between natives and summer residents has specific effects, including infiltration, coastal erosion, and real estate pressures. In short, they entail a progressive encroachment on the indigenous kernel by the vacationing periphery, a process that gradually imperils the integrity and finally the very existence of the historical enclave and its original population.

A number of different signs point in this direction; they all attest to the reality of the threat and announce yet again "the death of the fisherman." Where material encroachment is concerned, and in the guise of rehabilitation, they include the renovation and densification of the old quarters of the village, converted into "typical" residential housing—which, in terms of protecting the patrimony, entails nothing less than the social falsification of the site and the disintegration of its inhabitants' daily lives. But the same reality, seen from the outside, can be described quite differently—with humor, for instance, as in the case of a schoolteacher commenting on a photograph taken at La Turballe, a seaside destination and fishing port on Le Croisic bay where she spent her vacation in the summer of 1984:

> Now here you can stroll through a port that isn't completely artificial, because there was already something there before. The village was there. But they've changed it; and besides, in earlier years, there wasn't this bank. And now you see ultramodern buildings, very recent. They've succeeded in combining what's modern with what's attractive: something like fishing for mussels in street shoes![37]

"The village was there. But they've changed it . . ." What has been changed? And what "success" has been achieved in the framework of this modernized, not "completely artificial" site? The schoolteacher's unvarnished testimony sums up the situation. Before, "there was already something there." In fact, only the form of eradication has changed, confirming the future of the historical enclave as a shrinking kernel, a core constantly being fragmented and altered by the vacationers' adjustments to the "something" that was there before.

As for human encroachment, it takes place not only in villages and ports as they are invaded by new residents and property-owners (not to mention the additional problem of pleasure boating), but also on the beach itself.[38] The beach becomes the theater of a confrontation between bathers and fishermen from which the former emerge victorious (occasionally in the face of some resistance), and from which the latter withdraw and disappear. Thus in Tossa, Spain, in the 1960s, "driven away from the beach by the tourists,[39] fishermen worked in their own doorways on the steep streets of the upper city, preparing their baskets of fishing line."[40] But the same scene had already been played out many times in other places.

In 1881 the village of Étretat as portrayed by Maupassant was deserted in winter, its beach wholly restored to local fishermen after the cheerful clamor of Parisiennes was gone. As in Spain, the encroachment in Étretat was temporary. In Port-Vieux, on the other hand, which was "all that remain[ed] of the once-lively old port of Biarritz," the encroachment was definitive as early as 1889.[41] At the base of this natural gap, once the fishermen's territory, a bathing establishment was built that stayed open year round. A very similar situation prevails in Albufeira today: there is constant encroachment, since access to the beach takes bathers through the narrow streets of the old fishing village.

My aim here, however, is not to lament, but rather to try to see, in the context of an overall strategy whereby the seashore has been converted to leisure use, to what reinvention of the beach or to what invention of a universe this disappearance and shift of sovereignty belong. Thus I do not mean to incriminate summer residents or bathers in particular. To point an accusing finger—and that is certainly not my intention in this book—would change nothing. Such an attitude would be not only banal but also excessive with respect to a socioeconomic and cultural reality whose evolution cannot be imputed to vacationers and the propagation of seaside leisure alone. In any event, this form of leisure did not really become a mass phenomenon until after the Second World War.

The fact is that after being marginalized and confined to enclaves, the Savages were deported. Village fishermen totally disappeared, socially and physically, through expulsion. This third and final tactic used to dissociate the two worlds does not originate in the development of seaside vacations but in the industrialization of fishing at the beginning of the twentieth century, with a shift toward "large-scale" or "deep-sea" fishing. And the example of the Costa Brava sums up quite well what took place during that period on most of the Western European coasts:

> If converging circumstances played an essential role in the current eradication of all fishing activity in the little ports that have recently been promoted to the status of international centers of tourism, such as Tossa, Cadaqués, or Lloret, a technological evolution was what triggered the first movement toward concentration, between 1910 and 1925. Just as the appearance of machinery had condemned rural craftsmanship and imposed the concentration of industry in cities, the evolution of fishing technologies toward intensive forms, implying significant investments and the use of motorized vessels, imposed the concentration of fishing in the best-equipped ports.[42]

This concentration clearly did away with the dissemination of fishermen along the shoreline and put an end to their traditional omnipresence in many small coastal villages. Symbolic in painting, the fisherman's disappearance was a reality here, and the removal of the workforce from the coasts was a prophecy realized. The contemporary beach, more than ever emptied of its native populations, emerged triumphant from this technological and economic upheaval that deported seafaring men into city ports in massive numbers.

Stripped of its workers, the vacation beach presents itself as a world dissociated from natural and social realities, cleared of Savages and savagery. Whether this particular industrial revolution is attributed to converging circumstances or to coincidence, it has favored a dynamics of semiologic denuding of the "old-style" beach: signs of the tradition that until recently marked a given site with their presence and stamped it with a local identity have been eradicated.

Individuals, technologies, activities, and objects have all gradually disappeared, not through any fault of bathers but because, functionally and socially, they no longer have any reason to exist. The great circular nets for tuna fishing that were still in use at the end of the nineteenth century disappeared in Roses in 1921. Old fishermen no longer weave traps on the shore; today, molded plastic traps are produced industrially. Cotton and hemp nets, replaced by nylon ones, now hang on restaurant walls. And the boats hauled up on the beach are also disappearing for technological reasons. Trawlers weighing thirty-five tons or more began to appear along the coasts of Spain (and elsewhere) in the 1930s; their vertical keels "required a minimum of installation in port," and by the same token they favored "the disappearance, or at least the perceptible reduction, of big flat-bottomed boats with lateral keels that made it possible to hoist them up on the beach."[43]

Coincidence? Converging circumstances? Sociologists, on the alert for the collective forms of logic that determine social evolution, will not settle for this sort of argument. In fact, if it is true that the industrialization of fishing preceded the extension of seaside leisure to the masses, it is equally true that the development of intensive fishing, by liberating the seashore, unwittingly favored—as a substitute activity or even as symbolic reparation for the death of artisanal fishing—the development of a different industry: seaside vacationing.

THE MUTANT FISHERMEN

So the fisherman is dead. Having been shunted from apartheid to ghetto, and from ghetto to exodus, he has now disappeared, has been declared disappeared, not at sea, but on land: on the shore. Who is his successor? What has become of him, this artisanal hero, along with his descendants, in the aftermath of an epoch that has no more use for him?

What fate claims this escapee from the revolution whose sons have told him, in some places, that they are not going to follow in his footsteps, while elsewhere he has seen the very name of his village—as in Fréjus-sur-Mer—or even of his region modified to attract vacationers?[44]

For this coastal Mohican, engaged in a strategy of reconversion, destiny is often a road paved with ambiguities and compromises. Heir to a lost trade, shipwrecked victim of a defeated world of which he has become the picturesque star, he may have nothing left to do but make fun of the outsiders, the summer people, to whom he nevertheless owes his survival. For it is imperative to recognize the cruel paradox. A victim first of industrial fishing, then of bathers, the fisherman in question manages to survive thanks to those who have driven him away from the beaches: "since 1950–1955, tourism . . . has played an essential role for the seashore and our small ports."[45]

The artisan-fisherman finds a new manna in the development of seaside vacationing. Thus when he does not head for a major port to become a deep-sea worker, when he does not sign up for the merchant marine or the police force, when he does not give up his trade and his way of life, this survivor of the tradition may well still be fishing today. He can supply "high-quality species that bring in very high prices in the summer: red mullet, sole, turbot, hake, rock fish, bream, perch, conger eel, grouper, moray eel, dentice, cuttlefish, squid, crayfish."[46]

By responding to the visitors' demands rather than to those of his own community, the fisherman breaks with custom. He begins to play the luxury trade game: he deals with a speculative market that depends on the flow of vacationers, and thus he shifts to a different economic universe. But this reconversion, required by modernity, enables him to keep functioning as a fisherman. This is the role that seems to do the least damage to his identity, by maintaining a certain truthfulness. For on a more distant horizon the fisherman discovers a space of reconversions that are often perceived as degradations. "We only hold on as small-scale fishermen," one of them told Roger Vailland, "because there aren't any trawlers yet between Toulon and Nice. I know perfectly well that we're doomed. In five years, there'll be nothing but pleasure boats in Saint-Tropez. Still, the day I have go to work for the 'torpedos' it'll break my heart."[47]

The "torpedos" are military factories. We are in the early 1950s. And Louis, the speaker, age twenty-eight, an independent fisherman, son of an independent fisherman, is desperate. Like someone afflicted with an incurable disease, he knows the end is near and is already resigning himself. His heart broken, his soul in agony, he will go to the factory. A total metamorphosis. An absolute renunciation. For someone like Louis, in the end, the anticipated reconversion, taking the form of a shipwreck with no survivors, will be tantamount to death.

Nevertheless, while waiting for the deadly trawler, Louis is still fishing. A confirmed bachelor, he even derives certain transitory benefits from the vacationers:

> In the summer, lovely ladies on vacation allow him to take them out in his boat, and they are said to take off their bathing suits to swim in the open sea. Jealousy only makes the ladies of Saint-Tropez more tender than ever.
>
> "Louis always brings something back in his net," his foreman says. "When it isn't sardines, it's girls. When they're not provincials, they're Parisians—or Danish, or English."

That counts too, in the quest for happiness.[48] But when the quest becomes a profession, what becomes of happiness? When this form of "fishing" becomes a trade and a one-day adventure becomes a business, it is called prostitution.

In this connection, Morand points out that in Capri, around 1900 to 1910, "men were supported by fishing and not by the old American women who competed for them with lords; the fishermen often dealt cruelly with the latter, for they preferred the local girls to both groups."[49] From the Neapolitan gigolos of the 1960s to the fishermen-pimps of today, under cover of flirtation and Don Juanism, the "garçon de passe," or male prostitute, has emerged.[50] The strategy is scandalous, the reconversion notorious: thus it is not often discussed. Still, there is no doubt about its existence, here as elsewhere. In this familiar secular traffic, the Savage, having become Friday, sells himself to lovelorn Robinsons.

Nevertheless, from one shipwreck to another, between factory and palace, other forms of reconversion are available to the natives. They are less pathetic, less cruel, and sometimes even fortunate. They belong not so much to the order of shipwrecks as to that of drifting and compromise: it is not a question of rupture, but of a shift in function. The shipwreck will come later, when these substitute activities are abandoned, replaced by others, or imitated by new arrivals and industrialized in their turn.

The first of these substitute activities, that of guide, appeared on northern beaches in the eighteenth century and was developed throughout the nineteenth. Fishermen would offer their services to guide the summer resident/stroller in his visit along the shore. This function was often enriched by that of tale-teller: the guide would regale his clients with regional stories and legends.[51] This supplementary function of the native has by and large disappeared today; it has been replaced by boat rides along the shore.

Following close on the heels of this seaside attraction came a second activity, the souvenir business. Curiosity shops were already appearing by the end of the eighteenth century; for example, in 1795, in the Dutch city of Scheveningen, the coastal population had taken to selling "shells, stuffed fish, marine plants," and "scale models of ships, launches, and other objects related to seafaring."[52] This presupposes that fishermen have turned themselves into suppliers, craftsmen, or even artists (we can picture the old sailor using his big gnarled hands to build a boat inside a little bottle), into vendors of trinkets or second-hand goods. Let us note, however, that these "shells," "scale models," and other typical products are frequently replaced today by decontextualized objects: items that are not specific to the locale and indeed often originate elsewhere. Some come from Polynesia, others doubtless from Asia; at best they are manufactured by more or less local artists.

It is not our place to judge this transformation by seeing in it only a "frightful load of junk for tourists," as Louis Bertrand did in Egypt in 1910.[53] The reorientation of trade, especially along the seashore, toward anachronistic products, in which a market shifts successfully from the sales of indigenous curiosities to that of nontraditional or international souvenirs (tee-shirts imprinted with maritime themes or humorous legends, imported coral and jewelry, exotic Mexican or Balinese objects, and so on), signifies an evolution in mentalities. In addition to making the relation between contemporary vacationers and the seacoast more artificial, this shift attests to the summer residents' psychological detachment with respect to local realities. Coming in the wake of a two-hundred-year-old commercial strategy, it is a detachment characteristic of contemporary seaside existence.

For want of inns, hotels, or residences built for the purpose, fishermen also took in the pioneer summer visitors and other avant-garde bathers. Visitors were housed for a few days at modest cost; homeowners sometimes gave up their own bedrooms and the best seats by the hearth.[54] This occurred in Normandy in the early nineteenth century, and in the Mediterranean region at the end of the century and the beginning of the next, during the period of experimental summer residencies.

On the Gerona coast in Spain, the early manifestations of seaside summer vacationing were "so dispersed that they were integrated into daily life." For local residents, taking in lodgers was thus an economic recourse that transformed natives into hosts, landlords, and even primitive restauranteurs. Hotels, villas, campsites, and other industrial structures of reception would come later. And lodging in private homes has continued, though in a more professional form that preserves the hosts' privacy.[55] Even today, it offers the possibility of integrated stays that residential enclaves or isolated vacation villages cannot provide.

In the second half of the nineteenth century and at the beginning of the twentieth, with the development of bathing, the sailor-fisherman could also transform himself into a watchman, thus joining the emerging category of "the old sailor sitting in his rowboat or canoe, 'resting his elbows on the oars,' and surveying the swimming zone that has been officially marked by ropes." Better still (but on the explicit condition of perfect trustworthiness, politeness, devotion, and prudence), he could become a swimmer's guide. His new function gave the transformed sailor real prestige in vacationers' eyes; this guide of a hitherto-unknown sort was viewed from the outset as a hero always ready to sacrifice himself in order to save "tired swimmers in mortal danger."[56] Thus promoted to the rank of chevalier of the waves and tides, protecting fearful or inexperienced swimmers (and before the swimming instructor arrived to challenge his monopoly), this ancient mariner will appear again in the next chapter, vigilant and ready to instruct, transfigured into an aquatic educator and worldly lifesaver. Later on he will be rechristened "master bather," "master life-saver," or, on the Anglo-Saxon beaches of England, Australia, and North America, "lifeguard," a title symbolically more in conformity with the quasi-mythic status of the role.

In this array of more or less satisfactory reconversions that have led to the gradual disappearance of the Savage as such from the beach scene, another possibility has opened up to the native more recently: pleasure boating, the armada of leisure craft whose arrival Louis of Saint-Tropez dreaded, knowing that it signaled his own end. And Louis was right. The number of pleasure boats in France grew from 20,000 in the early 1950s to more than 550,000 in the early 1980s; it reached some 800,000 by 1992. Of the 372 pleasure ports that dot the French coast, more than 300 have been created since 1964. These artificial havens distort the coastal outline here and there like enormous blisters, but they harbor a massive job-creating flotilla.[57]

Remaining on shore thus requires a change of port (and not just a change of costume, like that of the bathers' guide). We have to shift to a different port in which sailors find new roles—in maintenance, construction, surveillance, or navigation. We shall see once-independent fishermen transformed into workers, janitors, or crew, as we stroll through the pleasure port on vacation, admiring the pampered luxury craft in their moorings. The former fisherman is there, in the shipyard or on the docks, polishing hulls or using fresh water to swab the bridges of great white yachts that belong to others.

"I Am Legend"

Thus we have moved from shipwreck to drifting, from total reconversion to partial mutation, from rupture to compromise, and from exile to metamorphosis. The mere evocation of this social reality does not exhaust its diversity, but it suffices for our purposes here. We have to acknowledge that the presence of the fisherman, and more generally of "the shore people," has been ineluctably blurred in the seaside world.[58]

The death of the fisherman has occurred as part of a series of disappearances at the end of which the vacation beach came into being as a mythic space, that is, as a natural and depopulated world that has lost the memory of its own fabrication, and thus of the historical events that allowed its advent.[59]

Under the pressure of a new aesthetics of leisure determined by a collective project for which authenticity and the defense of local societies are manifestly not the principal objective, the evanescent indigenous community is doomed to extinction. The Crusoean model is thus not betrayed here; on the contrary, it is taken to the extreme, borne out by the facts. In the archipelago of seaside vacations, there will soon be nothing left but islands devoid of savages. After all, if Robinson had had the power, would he not have proceeded to exterminate them all?

Moreover, let us consider all the resorts that have been created ex nihilo, such as Deauville in 1861, Le Touquet in 1903, La Baule in 1923, or Juan-les-Pins in 1925, all the seaside islands that have arisen out of nowhere, born of no autochthonous seed, coastal cities without historical centers: have these not shown in their own way, once their hour of glory was past, the optional character of the Savage in the seaside vacation universe? And have they not by the same token set an example and opened the way to the widespread realization of such an abstraction? "Faithful" reconstitutions of fishing villages without fishermen are being built for the use of summer residents today.

Unlike the forces that move vacationers to go to the country or to some particular mountain,[60] the contemporary seaside imagination, oriented as it is toward artificial or simulated sites, seems to be fundamentally lacking in genuine social and cultural roots. It does not originate in some dream of returning to a lost landscape or territory, guided by the search for an earlier form of sociability, whether rustic, traditional, or native.[61] Consequently, what is imagined is translated into reality either by the progressive evacuation of the indigenous social and historical traces marking the environment, or by the choice of a place that is specifically free of this sort of trace from the start—for example, an uninhabited stretch of coastline consisting of dunes and swamps.[62]

From this standpoint, the death of the fisherman is undoubtedly the most notable symptom of the symbolic strategy, the aesthetics of the void, that underlies the vacation conquest of the seacoast. A cruel truth, but a truth nonetheless. The fisherman-guide recounting local stories and legends to summer residents has disappeared, and with him the living memory of the site. What remains is relayed by the laconic statements of standard guidebooks that present seashores chiefly as panoramas, that is, as beautiful features of physical geography, independent of any local human realities.[63] These landscapes are treated as today's souvenir objects. Behind them, a world is vanishing.

So under these conditions, and with the exception of the residual population that is still nesting for the time being in the old port, in the narrow perimeter of the historic kernel, what can remain of the inhabitants, the natives, the past? What indigenous presence is left? What has happened to the emblematic figure of the fisherman? In this universe that has been cleansed, unencumbered of its original maritime rusticity, to what place, by what right, or in what form can that actor still claim to survive? Here begins the semiology of a death agony—the terminal phase of an investigation that will come to its end in a souvenir shop, in front of a postcard display.

Roger Vailland may declare that "small independent fishermen are the last adventurers of the sea," but today they are chiefly the adventurers of a lost trade.[64] Our era has invented its own new adventurers of the sea, who travel around the world in less than eighty days; new fishermen, too, who are very dissatisfied with their lot, by the way. As for the small local fishermen, they now belong to the past of a past that was already dominated by summer residency. This is the point at which, a bit late in these ambiguous patrimonial times, a voice arises to proclaim: "We have to save the small fisherman! We have to preserve his culture and keep his tradition for ourselves!" What does this mean?

Save

The preservation of the pastoral scene in the religious or symbolist works of painters such as Puvis de Chavannes, Gauguin, or Sérusier has done much more to save a theme, a genre, or a symbol than to rehabilitate a reality. The small fisherman as an everyday social subject, purely and simply human, is transported here through allegory into the purified universe of myths, dreams, or ideas. The image of him we retain is thus a figure of legend projected onto the poetic universe of the tale: the indeterminate once-upon-a-time of a world in suspension, an imaginary place, an atemporal space in which the individual survives but carries no weight—denied as a historical subject. Once upon a time there was a poor fisherman . . .

Preserve

For this task there are museums. In 1889, anticipating a museum fever from which our society has never recovered, Mme de Lalaing evokes the museum in Arcachon, which "contains a fine collection of shells and fish; nets and other tools for fishing and model boats are also on display. It is a pleasant place to pass an hour."[65] The time has come for ethnography as entertainment, or archaeology as spectacle. The patrimony of the shore people has reached the stages of protection and display. Except for one thing: putting a fisherman in the museum does not save the man, but only preserves signs attesting to his existence: tools, clothing, products, various scraps and shreds of culture, accumulated images and imprints of an identity, an inventory of material attributes that do a good job of evoking the individual, but that by the same token, through this language of traces or dross, turn him into a vestige—the theme of a collection. Educational and recreational, this archival record, like any other of its kind, thus also has the symbolic value of a reliquary. Bringing together empty shells, mummified fish, vestigial boats, and other fossil-objects of the fishing trade, the Arcachon museum does a good job of saying what it has to say. In the late nineteenth century, it announced, expressed, and finally summed up the inexorable disappearance of the shore people, even while trying to save them.

A museum is a pantheon of words, images, and things, a resonating chamber for vanished worlds: what its closed doors retain, even enriched as it is today with models, photos, and films, are always, in the inevitable paradox of the place, symbols of an absence. However praiseworthy the "archival taste" may be, and however great the technological progress in conservation, the museum remains the ultimate condensation of a presence, the capture of a phantom, the cemetery of its object, a maritime object in this instance: the tomb of the fisherman. "Lives that have washed up in an archive cannot be restored."[66]

Keep

If, after painting (which finally settles for abolishing history magically by sending the subject off to some heaven or other), the sepulchral museum does not succeed either in conjuring destiny or in resuscitating the past, in safeguarding its presence, it then has to adopt a different strategy: it has to move from exposure to display, from representation to living spectacle, from evocation to reconstitution, or, better still, from ethnography to choreography—in short, from simulacrum to simulation. Down with mannequins. Long live actors. Now we have animation, with the fisherman as featured attraction: after the signs of man, we now have the man as sign.

In his novel *Paradise News*, David Lodge evokes the choreographic afterlife of the Hawaiian fisherman, a character who has become the patented actor of a nightly Hukilau, a "traditional shoreline fish-gathering ceremony in which," according to the brochure, "guests lend a hand to pull in the huge net."[67] Drawn by the promise of participation, the Fridays come in by the busload to this theatrical reef separated from the swimming sites (more than a thousand people crowd into Sunset Cove); they come to discover the last Savages, who are no longer mere fishermen, artisans of the living seashore, but fishermen acting the part of fishermen and earning their living by the spectacle they create.

A sign of the times, you may say, spurred by the leisure industry and the accessibility of seaside vacations to the masses? The most astonishing fact is that the thing is not new: the premises of this folk-lorization of the fisherman, of his foregrounding on stage to entertain excursion groups or to create an authentic "ambiance" are older than one might suppose.

In Menton, in 1909, from the promenade (where a horde of summer residents were crowding in to look), Henri Bolland watched a net being pulled onto the shore in a ritual very similar to the "traditional shoreline fish-gathering ceremony" on the beach at Sunset Cove; even then, Bolland detected something like a shift toward spectacle, a programmed display of the fisherman, the artificiality of whose presence and attitudes Bolland suspected at the time. Commenting on the scene, he confided: "I cannot keep from thinking and believing that these Mentonese fishermen are simply stand-ins paid from the [city] budget to offer a daily distraction to the guests of the winter resort." Henri Bolland was not mistaken when, in the table of contents of his book, he called this part of his narrative "Comic-Opera Fishermen."[68]

What is still just a suspicion for this early-nineteenth-century traveler becomes a certainty later on. The idea of animated "local color" through a staging of the tradition is hardly abandoned; on the contrary, in some instances, it is even quite explicit, as in this recent study on the demand for seaside vacations: "The colors, smells, and sounds of cables clattering on masts, the spectacle of boats coming and going, the work of men dressed in blue (this is a fishing port), contribute a great deal to creating an atmosphere. Thus it is important to call attention to ports, to put them in the foreground."[69]

When do we get the real-fake fishermen? When do we have fishermen who are not what they seem, who are fishermen in appearance only and who (at prescribed hours) will leave the port and come back after a nonfishing trip, their boats full of a cargo of fish loaded ahead of time, so they can play out the great scene of coming into port with gulls flying and foghorns blaring in the background?

We should note that in the context of the study cited, three types of animation are identified: the "animated event" (festivals, beach contests, parades, concerts, fairs, festivals, and so on), "structural animation" (mini-golf, little trains on wheels, bicycle rentals, and so on), and "natural animation" (native attractions: the port, the village square, the promenade, the market, the bistros, and so on). The actor-fisherman will thus take his place in the framework of natural animation—which is said to be "the most difficult to create"! Drive away the natural and it will come back at a gallop—but in what form?

The frenzied quest for "natural" animation can go even further; it can include a staging based on the illusion of participation. Helping the fisherman draw up his net onto the beach is already not bad; but—going far beyond the simple disinterested complicity that could once be established between vacationer and fisherman, between a Roger Vailland and a Louis de Saint-Tropez, for example, during a friendly fishing party[70]—discovering the fisherman's trade on a trawler, for a fee, is better still. This is done at Sables-d'Olonne, on the trawler *Kifanlo,* which has been classified as a historical monument.

And why is this so? Why do people go out for four hours at a stretch on this floating monument? To act like sailors. To act as if they were sailors, deck hands, or even cabin boys. The excursion becomes a role-playing exercise in which the fisherman-sailor is the principal organizer, not only a professional but also a professor to whom the vacationer-students submit themselves. One participant declared, moreover, that he was there to "obey the orders of a real fisherman."[71] A strange animation, in fact, one in which the summer resident, after paying some twenty dollars for a session, is happy to play his part in an ephemeral simulacrum of apprenticeship and submission.

This totally artificial type of animation, from the port-as-theater to the phantom trawler, in the guise of active rehabilitation and protection of the patrimony, marks the definitive achievement of the complete exoticization of the traditional fisherman: the capture of the Savage. In all this there is something that resembles a therapeutic endeavor; it is not so much animation as reanimation. Far from bringing the patient back to life, reinserting him, the undertaking encloses him in a bubble, a space of simulation that resembles life but is not life, a space exempt from the "law of the present," from duration, from history, a space within which the old-style fisherman-sailor, the man-sign, retains some existence, to be sure, and even acquires some autonomy, but it is the existence and autonomy of a legendary character, a ghost, or living death, a "situation from a fantastic novel." As in painting, as in museums, these "remains of a lost past" on the margins of the maritime universe—the fisherman and his boat—"open up escape hatches toward another world"[72]—a separate world, no longer the world of today's shore and sea, from which they have disappeared.

This is not the place to introduce a polemic or to formulate criticisms concerning a reality that in the final analysis may well provide more satisfaction than irritation to the parties involved, the locals as well as the visitors—Robinsons, Fridays, and Savages included. In this chapter, I have sought to bring to light the existence on various levels (symbolic, material, economic, social) of the objective process of the fisherman's disappearance and to pursue the process to its ultimate ramifications. This disappearance underlies all the other transformations of the coastal landscape, and the process that accompanies it is nothing less than the very first, symptomatic phase of the aesthetic conquest of the shore by the vacation ideology. The contemporary seaside world as a specific universe (unassimilable to other territories destined for tourism or residential vacationing) stems from the multiple erosion of the presence, real or figurative, of Coastal Man, Homo littoralis.

It is thus not a matter of judging the strategies of representation or arrangement, of reconversion, exclusion, integration, or rehabilitation, whatever they may be; rather, it is a matter of maintaining a critical distance so as to appreciate their significance in the framework of a global cultural evolution. Whether they set the Savage aside, abandon him, or make use of him, all these strategies—even if they aim to do just the opposite—abolish the Savage as such. A world emerges here, headed toward the void and toward simulation, a world from which the authentic, the historical, and the natural are gradually withdrawn. When we read in a magazine article about Cannes that the port is the "city's lung" and see the accompanying photo of a fishing boat, no one is fooled.[73] Anyone who goes to Cannes will see what remains, there as elsewhere, of the fishing port! The real "lung" is the port for pleasure boats, the marina. "Cannes seeks to retain its identity," the article adds. So be it! But what identity? That is the question, of importance not just to one city but to a whole world, within which the fisherman has from now on the fragile status of an optional label. The future of the fisherman is uncertain, and his image is rarely used any longer in such places except to seduce a minority of vacationers who are still consumers of traditional cultural indices.

As promised, at the end of our investigation we find ourselves in front of a postcard stand. The display case sums up the situation all by itself. What do we discover here? The fisherman—or at least his image—had earlier found a final refuge, an ultimate space for survival, when he reached the industrial stage of "mechanical reproduction."[74] By virtue of the epistolary diffusion of his portrait, there was once a time when the fisherman experienced a commercial fame that attested to his social and cultural recognition in the vacation mentality. People went to Brittany and they thought about Breton fisherman; in Royan, they thought about the fishermen of the Charentes. Up to the period between the two world wars, they sent postcards illustrated with a black-and-white photograph of a person in the fisherman's stance, holding a net over his shoulder or weaving a basket, with the legend "Typical Fisherman" or "Old Fisherman." All the traditional seashore trades had their place, and some success, in the framework of these souvenir-images: fishermen, but also fishermen's wives making nets, salt marsh workers, seaweed harvesters, oystermen and -women, and so forth.

But what does the revolving display stand tell us today? Although the old fisherman is still there, in color, he is quite obviously becoming a rarity. The display reflects a demand, and it tells us that here too the Savage has lost ground. What has happened to him in the realm of painting also holds true in the universe of postcards. Landscapes and vacation scenes, panoramas and wide-angle views of seaside resorts, and the naked bodies of female sunbathers on the beach predominate everywhere, in terms of quantity; and whether one is in Corsica or in the Vendée, nothing resembles one topless sunbather lying inert on the sand so much as another topless sunbather. The abstraction, the robbing of the shore's history, even in this ultimate symbolic ramification, is over the top—or rather, running on empty.

The revolving postcard stand is the wheel turning. Like a lapsus, it delivers a brutal statistic. Let the small fisherman die; long live summer vacations! Brigitte Bardot used to sing of "shells and shellfish on a deserted beach": there are no more natives. Their presence dissipated, they will appear here and there, folkloric, virtual foreigners in their own lands—survivors, attractions, as in Richard Matheson's fantastic novel *I Am Legend,* which tells the story of the last man on earth finishing his life in a cage in the zoo, in a society of mutants who come to look at him. Another novel by the same author is called *The Shrinking Man.*[75] The fisherman is shrinking too. The man who once regaled visitors with local legends has become a legend in his turn.

2. The Birth of the Bather

*(or, How Robinson finally
decided to bathe in the sea,
how he wrote a swimming manual,
and what happened next)*

Bath, *n.* A kind of mystic ceremony substituted for religious worship, with what spiritual efficacy has not been determined.

—Ambrose Bierce, *The Devil's Dictionary* (1906)

At the beginning of the twentieth century, in *Les cents métiers de Bécassine,* Pinchon (whose real name was Annaïk Labournez) has his heroine get a job near Plurien, a few kilometers away from Sables-d'Or-les-Pins, southwest of Cape Fréhel. Plurien is the actual name of a perfectly real place in Brittany, in the Côtes-d'Armor region. The comic use of the town's name says a good deal about the seacoast as the grand opera of the void. No longer simply the "territory of emptiness" but an *emptied* territory—a space where there remains precisely *Plurien, plus rien,* "no longer anything": nothing to contemplate but the shore, the land meeting the immensity of the sea.

This is the way the contemplative Romantic summer vacationer still thought most often of the shore, looking down on the open sea from his terrace, or even from the end of the pier, with the spray whipping his face in a rare and—for the period—adventurous contact with the marine element. This onlooker was far removed from everything: from the local population, from the land, and from the sea, all of which he embraced with a panoramic and solitary gaze. He was a spectator looking at a stage that was being cleared of players: the eradication of the natives was nearly complete (see chapter 1). At this stage in the aesthetic consumption of the shore, Antoine Blondin's comment about winter resort sites applies perfectly to seaside resorts as well: "at first glance, the resort offers the most artificial circus that can be given free rein in a natural circus"; to meet the requirements of contemplation, it was always installed on "the edge of a grandiose universe."[1]

The fisherman's disappearance was closely linked to the development of beach pleasures, as we have seen; indeed, the slow demise of the former prepared the ground for the latter. This process did not lead directly to the invention of "the seaside" in the contemporary sense, however. Ablutions were rare, discreet, circumspect, and excessively monitored: Boudin's female "bathers" actually bathed very little, preferring to take walks and to converse in groups. The progressive elimination of the Savages set the stage, but with respect to seaside enjoyment for the masses the site still awaited its founding heroes. Robinson had yet to come out of his cave and leap into the water for sheer pleasure.

Before thousands of bodies flung themselves gleefully into the surf, the beach, the beautiful beach, was first of all a theater of emptiness inviting onlookers to gaze into the distance and breathe the remote salt air. It was a space without personal use, a space whose uses were instead spectacular and airborne—a visual and olfactory territory, for the most part, not yet a territoriality devoted to bathing and bathers, direct contact between flesh and water. The initial conquest of the shore on behalf of leisure entailed a circumspect advance: a phase of observation and artistic, aesthetic, ethnic, societal, and finally health-minded colonization, before the unanimous physical conquest, the vast somatic annexation of the shore, the popular and ludic phenomenon with which we are all familiar. Thus some bodies—those of work—disappeared, while others—those of pleasure—were yet to come.

At the shore, Yves Lacoste writes:

> [W]e do not get the "best view" by staying on the beach, but by taking some overlook as our observation point, finding a dominant element of the relief from which we can see the outline of the coast, the land in the background, the valley that traverses it, and, in the far distance, the heights that frame it. These "viewing points" are dream sites for the most fashionable hotels and the classic sites of the largest fortified constructions of the Atlantic Wall![2]

What the original summer vacationer contemplates, with the gaze of a conqueror and not that of a shore-dweller—and sometimes, as in Dieppe, with the help of a telescope that makes it possible to study the open sea and the beach[3]—is above all a theater of distant operations: ships on the horizon, perhaps a storm, natives scattered along on the shore, groups of people walking or a few "immodest" women bathing here and there. In short, a battlefield without troops, just far-flung, microscopic bit players—a foreground that may have been dotted with "clusters of agreeable folk," but those cautious, clothed creatures animated an empty terrain that was still quite unlike the umbrella-strewn fields of our own vacations, invaded as they have been by stripped-naked crowds.

Moreover, as Yves Lacoste adds, "for the tourist, who has a hard time imagining that he himself is being looked at, the landscape is empty of people, as it were (even when he sees towns and villages), or at most it is a spectacle, a tableau without much relation to the people who live there."[4] This holds true as well for the seaside vacationer, at least in the early days: this "vacationocrat"[5] was no longer a pioneer, not yet a bather, but already a voyeur-vacationer observing society's domestication of the shore. At this stage, the observer on the sidelines transferred into the universe of summer residency a touristic strategy inaugurated in cities: that of Icarus, who was motivated by a taste for panoramas.[6] Only later, when our spectator abandoned his observation point and became an actor in turn by mingling with the earliest bathers, the "balneocrats," did he become a bather himself; in the process, the beach was gradually transformed into a vast "living theater" in which the boundary between audience and actors was abolished. But this made the fall all the harder: it presupposed not only that a gaze was coming closer, as through a zoom lens, but also that a body was approaching, exposing itself to the waves and to other people.

BALNEOCRATS AND HEDONISTIC PIONEERS

The point needs to be stressed: fishermen had not yet disappeared from the shores when sea bathing began. At Scheveningen, as early as 1768, "people bathed in the sea."[7] But who were these bold bathers who in the early nineteenth century could sometimes be counted in the hundreds or more? Where did they come from? And how did they go about their bathing?

In this transitional period of a primitive "seasidization" of the coast, these bathers did not foreshadow—or did not dare clearly foreshadow—either in numbers or spirit the playful, pleasure-loving swimmers who offer their bodies to the saltwater today. As with the houses rented to bathers in Dieppe during the Restoration period (almost all of which turned their backs to the sea), we should note that, beyond the discourse on the picturesque and the search for a viewing point, "the admission that contact with sand, water, and rocks was a source of pleasure" considerably antedated the material arrangement of beaches as such, and thus their collective use.[8] At the seaside, enjoyment of the environment might be expressed, in extreme instances; but it had to be practiced on the margins, at a distance; the shore and the surf had to be either enjoyed in privacy and solitude or else shared in virtual secrecy. In reality, this enjoyment, like the body itself, was not to be laid bare, exposed to the light, put on display. The beach was a blank page that could not yet be filled in at will, for pleasure. In the popular mind, physical contact with the sea, tactile and coenesthetic, was perceived for the most part as serious or dangerous, and perhaps even immoral or suicidal.

Indeed, if we are to circumscribe the identity of the "balneocrats" and their historical importance, we must first grasp the symbolic significance of their gesture. This inaugural gesture, seemingly a simple one, actually broke down a psychological barrier and prefigured nothing less than the cultural rift favoring the passage from seaside vacationing, which remains on the edge, to residential seaside vacationing properly speaking, which goes beyond the edge of the sea, with vacationers venturing not just *onto* but *into* the water.

Seen from afar, the first sea baths thus constituted only one small step forward for any given individual, but they represented a great and definitive leap forward for the "mankind" of coastal leisure. By leading the vacationer to the other side of the foam, this leisure activity transported the summer resident into a different sensory universe, countering an age-old repulsion in which a phobic fear of water was mingled with a nightmarish terror of being swallowed up. In short, by interrupting the standoff between human beings and the sea, in which fear of direct contact with water had instituted the contemplative stance that we have come to recognize, the "balneocrats" were not only the initiators but the instigators of an aquatic osmosis that was still conceived as an almost unbearable confrontation in both physical and moral terms.

In order to measure the intensity of the feeling of repulsion inspired by water itself, let alone the sea, let us recall Madame de Sévigné's testimony in a 1676 letter to her daughter from Vichy, where she had gone to "take the waters": "I began the operation of the pump to-day; it is no bad rehearsal of purgatory." She went on to point out that the torture of showering was compounded by the humiliation of nudity.[9] The following year, back for another treatment, Mme de Sévigné managed things so that she took only two showers! And the situation was hardly better in the early eighteenth century. If we are to believe a doctor in Saint-Ursin, therapeutic baths (which healthy people avoided) prolonged the torture: "Gathering all his courage, the patient descended into his tub as into his final resting place." And although water regained favor with the reappearance of public baths as the century progressed, "slowly, unevenly, cascading down the social pyramid," as Philippe Perrot nicely puts it, there is nevertheless no doubt that the modern phobia about bathing remained stubbornly present, persisting—under numerous pretexts governed by phantasms and assorted prejudices—throughout the nineteenth century and even beyond.[10]

But what about the sea? The sea! That gigantic saltwater tub, with no borders but the shore, with its unfathomable depth and its agitated surface, the tomb of thousands of sailors and captains, could not help but terrify the vast majority at first. And anyone who bathed in it, unless he or she was ill, could only be strange or mad, unconscious or sublime, endowed at all events with unfailing temerity or robustness. As Michelet wrote in 1861: "To live on land is to repose; to live on sea is to combat, and to combat savingly—for those who can bear it." And the historian makes his own perceptions clear further on: "Whoever has seen a poor creature come out of the water after taking his first bath, whoever has seen him come out pale and shuddering, must perceive how dangerous such experiments are for certain constitutions."[11]

To be sure, as early as the late 1820s, the beach at Dieppe, with its separate baths for men and women, was sprinkled with tents or canvas cabins; and before that, the beach at Travemünde, on the Baltic, near Lubeck, was equipped with mobile cabins tied to the shore by ropes; these transported bathers and kept them dry until they reached the surf.[12] But we need to look at this picture more closely. In Dieppe bathers went into the water fully dressed, up to the waist or torso, complete with top hat! And in Travemünde a complicated apparatus allowed bathers to immerse themselves under movable tarpaulins without getting out of the box and thus without confronting the great marine void in an anguishing body-to-body contact. All this, of course, constitutes a sign; and here we need to nuance our account of the so-called vogue for sea bathing, at least in its early stages.

A fully dressed bather in one place, a fearful bather enclosed in a cabin attached to the shore in another: the protocol of the coastal conquest of the ocean denotes in the beginning the meticulous attention to detail of a cosmonaut, a need for protective clothing and technological prostheses that tells us a great deal about the modern persistence of the phobia and the refusal to detach oneself from land in ocean bathing. Robinson still preferred his island to the surf.

Moreover, as the services offered in nineteenth-century beach spas attest, many people preferred to partake of the "delights" of the sea indirectly, via showers, footbaths, or tub baths, preferably in warmed or heated seawater, well protected from waves, wind, and sun. These accommodations served to prepare bathers for going directly into the water, but they also served as alternatives to sea bathing; thus in certain places, such as Saint-Valéry-sur-Somme, there could be spas even in the absence of a shore: "One can bathe without beaches!"[13] Here vacationers did not go to the sea, the sea came to them! We are looking at what was for the time being a fashion rather than a widespread practice, an experimental procedure and not yet anything like a habit. While vacationers may have headed for the shore in large numbers during the nineteenth century, on the whole they did not immerse themselves, or even get their feet very wet.

To gauge the relative scope of this fashion, it suffices to consider for example the place occupied by sea bathing in the early 1860s in the voluminous guide to mineral waters published by Dr. Constantin James. Of this work's 610 pages, only 16 are devoted to sea bathing.[14] Vacationers of the period, as soon as they abandoned their tubs, public baths, hot springs, or similar accommodations, remained essentially soft-water bathers.[15] For the time being, they preferred rivers or lakes to the Atlantic or the Mediterranean. When Seurat painted *La Baignade* in 1883–84, when Cézanne painted his series of bathers between 1879 and 1905, when Renoir (who nevertheless spent his final days at Cagnes-sur-Mer) painted *Les Baigneuses* around 1918, even if the scene was barer, the setting always involved fresh water and green fields, not sand or stones. People preferred to bathe inland, in the country.

Sea bathing was clearly something entirely different, as far as the spirit of the bath was concerned; and it was precisely in this phobic—or at the very least reticent—context that the founders of sea bathing, the "balneocrats," emerged. So who were they? Here again, the historical and literary celebrities tend to mask the importance of the anonymous individuals who, sociologically speaking, were unquestionably the true precursors of contemporary pleasure bathing, hedonistic immersion, lacking any constraints and feeling no disgust.

The aristocrats come to mind first of all: the Prince of Wales, who bathed in the sea in Brighton in 1787 to treat his gout, on the advice of his doctors; Mme de Boigne, in exile in England, who bathed in the same spot in 1792; the future Napoleon III in Dieppe in 1812; Queen Hortense in 1813; or the Duchesse de Berry in 1824, an intrepid swimmer who is listed (incorrectly) in all the encyclopedias as the heroine who inaugurated sea bathing—the same duchess who, on August 3, 1824, was "exposed to the waves" by Doctor Mourgué, the inspector of the baths.[16] But not everyone ventured into the sea; those who did so did it cautiously, and only in the presence of science: medical specialists, general practitioners, and other supervisors.

As for literature, we think of course of Robinson, who swam very well, according to Paul Morand: he did, of course, but in a context of necessity that was anything but a summer vacation. Crusoe plunged into sea bathing only to escape a shipwreck, or, later, to go back to his ship's hull to retrieve some goods. He preferred land to water; for him bathing was a confrontation, not a pleasure, and the sea had a dramatic and dangerous aspect. We may think, too, of Bernardin de Saint-Pierre's novel *Paul and Virginia*, in which Paul is said to "swim like a fish" and to play in the waves; "he would [sometimes] advance on the reefs to meet the coming billows."[17] The qualifier "sometimes" is not unimportant: it indicates a circumspect game; and it may be somewhat excessive to say that with "Bernardin de Saint-Pierre the beach makes its entrance into the novel"—especially if the beaches are "the shores of earlier times humanized by bathers."[18] Virginia's beach is not human, but tragic: it is here that Paul succumbs to melancholy during Virginia's absence, and it is here that we discover Virginia's body after the shipwreck of the *Saint-Géran*. This beach is a place of unhappiness, of mourning and death. Paul and Virginia find happiness on land, near freshwater springs, in the shady forests of their island. We need to avoid retrospective illusions and the soothing effects of the aesthetic work of modernity on this narrative, which deals not with a beach but with a shore that the sea has overwhelmed with despair.

Thus for Robinson, Paul, and Virginia, the beach was essentially sinister—a place of danger and a blurred border beyond which lay the world's dark and hostile coast. Moreover, even without swimming, when Robinson ventures onto the sea in the small boat he has built in order to reconnoiter the shores of his island, does he not once again risk death from it? It is thus better to remain on land rather than to "feel the power of the waves or the touching coolness of the sands against [one's] body."[19] This is still the "touching coolness" of a mortal trembling, as Michelet says: it is terrifying, and the sand is Virginia's shroud.

As for the beaches of the balneocratic nobility, beaches as places for bathing, we should not idealize them either. If seaside spas became pleasure sites under the influence of aristocrats, the fact remains that the pleasure lay on land, not in the water: on promenades, on the sand and boardwalks of Trouville, on the stones of Dieppe, or in the casino in Deauville, and not in the surf. Immersion thus partook of mortification rather than pleasure, necessity rather than entertainment, resignation rather than desire. Among the bourgeois and worldly Fridays who followed them, the example of blue-blooded balneocrats most often became only a hygienic or therapeutic pretext for their sojourn, with few consequences in reality. In 1882 Ernest Ameline describes these second-generation "bathers" as follows:

> See them settled on the beach,
> In huge armchairs, on simple folding chairs,
> Showing off, gesticulating, yelling,
> Real peacocks displaying their feathers, between
>   two o'clock and six,
> And returning to their lodgings, once they have
>   produced their effect.
> I am addressing only those individuals here
> Who have never been bitten by the love of bathing,
> And, contemplating the sea with a look of bluster,
> Stubbornly remain on the boardwalk like cattle.[20]

Then where do we find the origins of contemporary bathing and its true founding heroes, those who took obvious pleasure in it? They are elsewhere, on shrub-covered beaches, like strange scattered tribes that are framed neither by latent tragedy nor by vigilant doctors, neither by allegory nor by science. They have only the bath and the happiness of taking one, without cosmetics or ceremony, far from those scenes where one "takes the waves" the way one takes the waters, under strict surveillance.

Various sources attest to the existence in France of "wild" bathers, spontaneous in their practices, from the Basque country to Normandy. Thus, as if clandestine groups were in question, "in 1817, the assessor of direct contributions points out that in summer the inhabitants of Bayeux gather in Port-en Bessin" for the pleasure of walking or bathing. Similarly, in 1839, "an officer, sent south to reconnoiter in the Channel region, reports that for the past ten years 'much use' has been made of sea bathing. He even specifies that the bathers are thought to be in the habit of meeting at Saint-Jean-le-Thomas, Carolles, Saint-Pair, and especially Granville. This last city is thought to be frequented by a thousand bathers each year."[21]

We should note the use of speculative wording ("are/is thought to be . . ."), both for the information itself and for the estimated number of bathers. The phrasing alone sums up the stupefaction of the era: the exotic perception of the free bather, who is "pointed out" as if at the conclusion of an explorer's "reconnoitering" expedition into unknown territory. We have a different balneocracy here, a local, bourgeois, or popular balneocracy, whether we are in Bayonne or Bayeux: a different tribe of pioneers, quite unaware of their pioneering status. What we have is not a court society, but rather a society that exists apart from the aristocratic networks and protocols of fashionable bathing, a society that is set apart, too, by its simplicity and naturalness. In 1847 in Saint-Malo Flaubert waxed enthusiastic when he discovered the spectacle of young boys swimming at the foot of the ramparts: "Oh! How beautiful the human body is," he wrote, "when it appears in its native free state, just as it was created on the first day of the world! Where can it be found, masked as it is now, and forever condemned to appear no more in the sunlight?"[22] We are certainly not in Dieppe here: there are no bathing inspectors, and no heavy costumes to dissimulate bodies and repress nudity.

Similarly, in Spain, near Gerona, Martínez Quintanilla noted in 1865 with seeming regret that itinerant merchants (whose number was estimated at 850) bathed along the coast; there were also "some persons who [bathed] *on the beach itself.*"[23] The first group were travelers, while the others, "more or less well-to-do," were from Barcelona. But both groups seemed to appear odd to the observer, who preferred the natural setting of the Pyrenees to the coast. In the same period, in Royan, according to Eugène Pelletan, a few quail hunters sometimes came to bathe on hot days simply to refresh themselves, and not to "take the waves."[24]

In short, sociologically speaking, here we have a whole population of "unofficial" bathers who, on the margins of the luxurious displays and aristocratic snobbery of the principal spas, open up a different path and institute a different relation to the sea: a hedonistic and even naturistic approach that is not yet weighed down by health-related arguments, therapeutic motives, or moral alibis. However, these bathers are too often the forgotten souls of coastal vacationing—perhaps because history is more likely to remember celebrities whose influence on the "vogue" for sea bathing was considerable, but especially because, like a breaker, the medicalization of the sea surged up to repress and remove from common usage the marginal balneophilia of these undisciplined predecessors. In addition to its objective benefits, balneotherapy or balneology—if we set aside its treatments and head for the shores—in fact (with the cooperation of the bathing industry) came to regulate the public's aquatic behaviors in a marine environment.[25] By the same token, it subjected seaside practices to the technological and moral dictatorship of a discourse that substituted the useful for the agreeable.

BALNEOPATHS, OR THE SEA OF ALL EVILS

In the course of the nineteenth century, the practices of bathing and beach sociability were organized definitively around illness. Bathing was no longer merely a marginal adventure or a display ceremony. It became a preventive or curative method and a discipline defined by a veritable code governing the human body: a common language with multiple prescriptions. The medicine of sea bathing, promulgating rules and theories, constitutes a historically decisive instance of the surveillance and ritualization of fashion. Its power of normalization, even as it repressed pleasure in the name of good health and subjected the "natural" bather to its expertise, came to channel and homogenize the beach population in a dogmatic way. Medicine codified everything: bodies, gestures, actions, clothing, conviviality, space, and time.

But it is from this medical perspective, justifying sea bathing at a time when the conquest of the shore for health purposes was being superimposed on its aesthetic conquest, that the extension of the practice to the masses began. A certain number of summer vacation-ers were expected to master their phobias in the name of science and health—and thus to pass from an initial repulsion to a salutary ac-ceptance of contact.

By offering the sea to "all those who feared the miasma and sought out the foam instead,"[26] and by enclosing the practice of bathing for more than a century in a rigid straitjacket of principles, not only physiological and therapeutic but moral ones (which dealt, beyond the general and specific effectiveness of sea baths, with the periodicity of baths and their dangers, the fragility of children, the sensuality of adolescents, and the sexuality of all groups), this medicalization, as an ideological obstacle to pleasure, paradoxically paved the way for later liberations. By establishing a norm, by setting thresholds of tolerance and strict taboos, this "scientific" moralization of sea bathing was in fact at the origin of the naturist transgressions and the other emanci-pations that have marked the history of beach bathing from the nine-teenth century to our own day.

What exactly happened? Of course, the medical and hygienic rela-tion to the sea, both to the coastal site and to saltwater, was not a new one. As Paul Morand writes,

> I should not like to crush the reader [nor should I] under medical docu-mentation, citing Galen, Asclepiades of Bythinia, Celsus or Anthyullus, who recommend salt water for epilepsy and paralysis, already using—unwittingly—iodine, chlorine, potassium, sulfur, sodium, and magne-sium. But let us recall that in *Plutus,* Aristophanes brings his hero to the temple of Aesculapes, where he is advised to use sea water to ward off blindness.[27]

We may also recall that Herodotus deemed the sea and the sun ap-propriate treatments for most illnesses, and that Hippocrates advised treating oozing wounds with seawater in baths or compresses. The sea cures: Euripides wrote in *Iphigenia in Tauris* that "the sea washes every human evil away."[28]

Although this relation to the sea was slowed, weakened, and even interrupted for several centuries in the Christian West in favor of other therapies or freshwater baths, medieval steambaths and rural or mountain hot springs, the practice of sea bathing that had been established and attested from antiquity on was reborn in the eighteenth century, if not earlier. In the sixteenth century, Ambroise Paré recommended baths that were astringent, resolvent, rehydrating, and so on; Henry III took baths in Dieppe to combat the "stones" to which he was prey; and in 1661 J.-B. Ferrand wrote one of the first theses on the treatment of rabies by sea bathing.[29] But the great medical return to the sea took place in the eighteenth century, with the publication in England of *A Dissertation on the Use of Sea Water in the Diseases of the Glands* by Dr. Richard Russell, who declared, "One must drink sea water, bathe in it, and eat all manner of marine life in which its virtue is concentrated."[30] From this period on, we find numerous editions and translations of works on the subject—works that are often forgotten or little-known today, like one published first in England and then in French translation in 1770, titled *The Uses of Sea Voyages in Medicine*, by Ebenezer Gilchrist, head doctor of the Faculté de Médecine at the University of Paris. The French subtitle spells out the contents: *Pour la cure de différentes Maladies, & notamment la Consomption, avec un appendix sur l'usage des Bains dans les Fièvres* (For the treatment of various maladies, and consumption in particular, with an appendix on the use of baths for fevers).

But a great deal has already been said on this subject, especially by the recent authors I have cited, as well as in the many nineteenth-century guidebooks and manuals for bathers. These works begin for the most part with a brief history of baths among the ancients and the moderns. Without going over the ground again in detail, I shall simply note, in the first place, that it was indeed difficult for seaside vacationing in its infancy to escape the domination of medicine, and, given the therapeutic universality of the sea, for vacationers to avoid feeling drawn to this panacea. Thus they gave in, sooner or later, willingly or reluctantly, to the constraints imposed by authoritative opinion on the application of the remedy.

In the second place, and this is of particular interest for our study, the codification of sea baths by nineteenth- and twentieth-century medicine turns out to be a complementary or auxiliary phase, and not the final one, in the overall process of taming the shore. In addition to its therapeutic virtues and in parallel with ethnic pacification (see chapter 1), it comes into play as a pacification of bodies: beyond the disappearance of the Savages, it is still necessary to free Robinson's flesh, and Friday's, from their savage elements—for flesh is still weak and always ready to succumb anew, upon contact with the water, by virtue of its own body or that of others, and lapse into an uncontrollable sexual frenzy or the misbehavior of a rediscovered animality. In short, the sea—*la mer*—of all evils has to be prevented from becoming the mother—*la mère*—of all vices.

The lessons of history have not been forgotten. From this perspective, Dr. James notes in his preamble: "In the earliest times, men and women took their baths separately, and decency prevailed; but soon, owing to the mixing of the sexes, the baths became places of debauchery comparable to the worst houses of ill repute."[31] With respect to the dissolving and troubling effects of hot baths on the senses and to the too-numerous "wild immersions" consummated in complete nakedness in home bathtubs, private baths that were sources of moral slackening, of physical languor, or, on the contrary, of various nervous reactions, all prejudicial to health and proper moral standards, medicine preferred cold seas to hot seas and short baths to long ones, following Dr. Russell's advice in this regard.[32] For while it retained the discipline of treatment and did not deny the sea's regenerative and restabilizing force, medicine was obliged to warn against its pernicious aspects—"sea baths often having the effect of producing headaches, agitation, and insomnia"[33]—and to restrain or even halt the surge of desire that such baths arouse: the pleasant sensations, the sensual reactions, and the "enervating" practices that free contact with the element might provoke.

Cold

Starting with the medical renaissance of sea bathing in the eighteenth century, doctors continued to advocate "the virtues of cold sea water." Dr. James said as much at the outset: this is why he preferred Le Havre, Tréport, or Étretat to Marseille or Sète, and even Arcachon as opposed to Biarritz. Michelet himself, who recognized that sea bathing was "of all forms of hydrotherapy, the harshest and most hazardous," did not call into question "the violent emotion of cold baths." At the very most, he advised the use of warm baths as a transition phase between the bather and the ultimate shock of contact with the sea. Cold appeared to be an immediate given of hygiene: a categorical imperative of healthy seaside activity. For it would eventually be necessary, as the science of bathing required, "to encounter the severe shock, the horripilation of the really tremendous shock of the cold water bath in the cold open air." The spirit of sea bathing changed very little up to the 1880s and 1890s: it belonged fundamentally to this authoritarian therapeutics. At the end of the nineteenth century, virtually no one but heart patients, kidney sufferers, diabetics, menstruating women, and the elderly (owing to the risk of congestion) managed to escape the brutal hygienism of cold baths.[34]

Today we cannot help but be shocked by the violence that was associated with sea bathing—a violence all the more startling in that it was so widely accepted, even by those who found it cruel. There is an element here that must originate in a deep cultural source transcending even medicine and health, a quest for mortification: pleasure inverted and imprisoned by a hygienist rationale having a great deal to do with penitence, abstinence, purification, and self-sacrifice. And a certain Christian dogmatism has indeed always recommended immersion in cold or even icy water in order "to gain control over the flesh" or make it pay for its weaknesses—hot baths have been viewed, on the contrary, as a quest for sensuality and even, according to St. Jerome, a threat to chastity.[35]

Duration

In the name of caution, progress, or efficiency, the duration of baths tended in the same direction. By its organization of the bath, its rhythm, and the gestures that accompanied it, the time allotted for bathing attests to the imperative of violence and the underlying prohibition of pleasure. "While the initial immersion in the sea is usually somewhat painful, the well-being that follows is so rapid, swimming so easy, the expenditure of muscle power so imperceptible, that the bather could easily let himself be carried away by the charms of such an exercise. Its duration must therefore be limited," Dr. James declared peremptorily.[36]

This was indeed the first act of violence, its first degree and the first of the restraints imposed on the potential upsurge of sensuality in the bathing experience. Medical opinion of the day was unanimous on this methodological point: the summer vacationer, after getting used to the sea air during the first two or three days of his stay, would thereafter take up bathing only gradually, first by brief immersions of one or two minutes, then increasing the duration until the bathing period lasted fifteen to twenty minutes at most. As for the number of baths per day, there might be one or two, not more. To go beyond this number would be imprudent, abusive, even transgressive. "Some people take as many as three or four baths a day without discomfort: this is far too many," writes Dr. James, "and impunity by no means justifies imprudence in this case. A single bath normally suffices; two seem to me to be the maximum that may be permitted in certain cases."[37] This sums it up: "natural" logic, which is above all moral logic, wanted science to maintain that people would be punished for abusing baths.

With baths thus limited in duration, their medical codification extended even to their gestural content. Whether one bathed alone or with assistance, one had to do violence to oneself here again, for the goal of the operation was to provoke a healthful shock: a reaction stimulating an abrupt flow of blood. Thus bathers were advised to immerse themselves all at once, as soon as they got into the water; the accompanying sense of suffocation and breathlessness would produce the sought-after "positive" effect. The imperative of self-mortification was always present. Combining suddenness with cold, bathing had to hurt for it to do any good. One did not "take" a bath, one "inflicted" it on oneself, or had it inflicted. "Sea baths are administered, depending on the circumstances, by immersion or by surprise; as breaker baths, by exposing the patient to the shock of an incoming wave, or as showers or rainwater baths," Dr. V. Raymond wrote in 1840—the desired consequence was always the infliction of a sudden chill on the bather's "exposed" body, an effect of surprise or shock to the patient.[38]

In this universe in which, from the prophylactic standpoint, every bather was ultimately presumed to be ill, a real or potential balneopath, this shock effect was viewed as a "rational use of bathing"—a use whose methodological violence may in some instances appear quite unbelievable today. For example, here is the treatment inflicted on a poor soul suffering from "persistent headaches": "The patient sits on the sand, and we throw several buckets of water over his head, one after another; the water flows over his entire body and produces a powerful chill. These various means act chiefly by virtue of their temperature, cold being in such cases the most powerful sedative known."[39] We can imagine without difficulty—indeed, we can see perfectly well—by way of this extreme therapy where the medicalization of bathing was headed in the long run.

In addition to the sign of a "technological" transfer of treatment to the seashore, we find here the sign of a repressive continuity that goes from putting insane patients under a cold shower to the bathing of patients with "nervous disorders" in cold seawater. Michelet's "generous and beneficent" sea, orthopedic and tonic, was all the more healthful to the extent that it was mortifying and sedative: it turned out not only to regulate menstruation, the circulation of the blood, and digestion but also to cure blindness, wounds, ulcers, scabies, rickets, coxalgia, rabies, rheumatism, bone problems, childhood diseases, problems of the lymph system, depression, delirium, swollen glands, hypochondria, trembling, asthma, constipation, consumption, and syphilis.[40] It could even moderate, if not reduce or eliminate, the functional activity of certain organs that were known factors in "nervous illnesses."

Effects

Medicalized seawater was purgative, regulatory, productive of scar tissue, and calming, on several grounds—including the obscure zones of impulses and desires, the point of pride in its power to calm bodies. In his 1846 *Guide médical et hygiénique du baigneur,* Dr. Jules Le Coeur recommends that the bather practice "extreme continence in the pleasures of love" during his stay. In 1859, in the *Petit guide pratique du baigneur,* the tone has hardly changed. The author declares that it is "essential to avoid excessive muscular exercise, excessive drinking and eating, excessive voluptuousness [including even] of the intelligence." Hygiene had no limits, and treatments by way of sea baths were dispensed on all horizons, even as an antidote to masturbation: a stay at the seaside was also recommended not only to rejuvenate the elderly and to invigorate children, but also to revitalize young people "prematurely exhausted by pernicious solitary habits."[41] The soothing liturgy of the surf is unquestionably preferred to the "brief prayer fervently uttered."[42]

In short, the colonization of the shore for bathing came about in the beginning in the framework of a virtually total conformity of beach practices with the precepts of the medical empire—sea baths, baths in seaweed or kelp, but also in sand, air, wind, sun, or light. Everything was referred to science: no gesture escaped it; and we are still very far removed from a vacation practice of bathing clearly dissociated, through the sheer pleasure of immersion, from its thalassotherapeutic virtues.[43] In fact, from inland hot springs, spas, and sanatoria to the shore, there was nothing new under the sun. Medicine ruled undivided and distributed according to its principles—with violence and moderation—the benefits of the four elements, air, fire, earth, and water. And this situation remained virtually unchanged not only up to the end of the nineteenth century—when the "breaker bath" was still deemed an excellent remedy—but through the beginning of the twentieth; the methodical "wisdom" of medicine thus took root over time in collective knowledge. The bathing beach was not to be easily liberated from the therapeutic straitjacket that invented it; it was held in thrall to a general theory of bathing based on fear of excess and the threat of pleasure.

To become convinced of this, it suffices to consult the article "Mer" in the 1929 *Larousse médical illustré*.[44] In it we discover the astonishing persistence of the old norms into the period between the two world wars. After the seasons for bathing are indicated (let us note in passing that on one point at least Dr. James's opinion is no longer respected: the Mediterranean is mentioned), we find the "rules to follow during bathing." The first deals with the bathing costume. It should be made if possible "of wool, large enough to allow water to reach the skin [and] not to inhibit the motions of swimming." Women "will cover their heads with a waterproof cap," though no health reason is given for this discrimination. As for the time and duration of bathing, it should take place between meals, "from 10 A.M. to noon, from 3 P.M. to 6 P.M." Let us note the following prescription in particular: "The bath should last two, then three, then five, and finally ten minutes, as a strengthener; longer if a calming effect is sought." No, there is really nothing new here. Similarly, under the heading "Arrival, sojourn, departure": after spending two or three days becoming acclimated "to the sea air before taking the first bath," when one is ready to go into the water one must "hasten to get wet all over and remain completely immersed, except for the head, during the entire duration of the bath." Violence, still; and mortification: "general dousings with buckets of sea water over the head are a good practice for people who do not know how to swim." Finally, under the heading "Precautions for children," beyond the fact that they "must be brought gradually to the beach—a half hour, an hour at first," the text indicates that "even infants may become so naughty at the seashore that they can no longer be taken there"!

Still, an instance of bathing described by F. Scott Fitzgerald at the beginning of the 1930s tells us that behaviors are beginning to change—

for here, neither the hour of the bath nor the entrance into the water conform to medical principles: "Before eight a man came down to the beach in a blue bathrobe and with much preliminary application to his person of the chilly water, and much grunting and loud breathing, floundered a minute in the sea. When he had gone, beach and bay were quiet for an hour."[45]

The bath is still brief; but this early-morning bather, solitary, free, and unsupervised, is autonomous; and, as opposed to the brutal immersion once so highly recommended, his relation to the water has been modified, oriented toward gentle contact.

BALNEOPHOBES: BATHS, METHODS, AND TRANSGRESSIONS

The bather's body "must get used to the coolness of the water." Get used to the sea. Indeed, we have to get used to it; and this doubtless sums up everything that lies behind today's summer beaches: the abandonment of violent treatments, "surprise baths," and, more generally, of the collisions, the prescribed shocks to which people had quite clearly not become accustomed. Giving up this tradition allowed for the imperceptible establishment of a more peaceful relation between sea and flesh, preparing the way for a more sensual exchange.

To understand the revolution presupposed by the birth of the contemporary bather, freed from therapeutic dogmas, we have to measure the extent of medical power over the practice of sea bathing in the nineteenth century. This power was total, omnipresent, omniscient, and unchallengeable, not to say dictatorial; and, like all absolute power, it was all the stronger for being based on fear, threats, even terror, credulity, and superstition. Almost everyone (the exception being the balneocrat of the unsupervised beaches mentioned above), before being a "balneopath," was a "balneophobe." A balneopath is never anything but a sick balneophobe. Sea phobia was the keystone of medical omnipotence; and generally speaking one bathed only if required and forced to do so, as if in penance for a fault, with the soul of a sinner.

During this period, then, bathing was at the opposite pole from pleasure. It was a purifying trial, and a redemption: "The sea is the great redeemer of all afflictions of the bones," the *Larousse médical* states as late as 1929. "Moreover," Dr. James specified in 1861, at the beginning of the brief section devoted to sea bathing, "many people go to sea baths less to bathe than to breathe the exceptionally pure and invigorating beach air." Up to the second half of the nineteenth century, people continued to spend more time looking at the sea than bathing in it. The phobia, unvanquished, was still there. The same year, Michelet expressed this anxiety by raising questions: "How, between this great and salutary, but somewhat rude, strength and our weakness, can there be any connection? What union can there be between elements so greatly disproportioned?" The solution to these difficult questions, he added, "required an art, an initiation."[46]

This art was first appropriated by medicine, which granted itself a monopoly on initiating bathers and defining the rules governing the practice of bathing. While it is true that the extension of sea bathing to the masses got its start by way of balneotherapy, in initiating patients to sea bathing medicine was still only standardizing a practice; it did not make it an everyday occurrence. For sea bathing to become an unremarkable activity, a loss of seriousness was required, a dedramatization that the therapeutic justification of bathing was not in a position to produce. It was still necessary that a nonpathological, familiar, ordinary, and even euphoric relation be established in order for the initial timid, fearful relation of repulsion to be abolished.

In many respects, the conquest of the beach for health purposes and the medical justification of bathing seem to have exploited the bather's sea phobia rather than helping to overcome it. In terms of acceptance, resignation, and necessity, the medicalization of bathing led to a rational adherence to a practice invested with anguish and anxiety. A passionate adherence would come later, one that would presuppose a ludic conquest apt to promote joyous unanimity. In other words, attraction had to be added to reason; play, gratuitousness, and pleasure had to be added to treatment. That is what was needed, on the margins of the therapeutic sanction: a certain emulation transcending everyone's instinctive balneophobia.

The key to solving the problem was to conquer the phobia through pleasure—and for this, bathers had to gain confidence, had to be reassured; they had to tame the waves rather than submit to them. Just as "it is impossible to understand the fashion for the sea-shore that became widespread at the end of the eighteenth century without taking into account this desire to be present at the point of contact between the elements,"[47] one cannot understand the balnearization of leisure that took shape toward the end of the nineteenth century without taking into account the new desire to play with the sea, to establish

a ludic relation to the marine environment, which had been envisaged medically up to that point only as a way of getting children used
to water.[48] The bath became a distraction, even a regression, and the
adult bather became a player—thus a "grown-up child." For such an
adult it was a matter not only of defying the waves (instead of tolerat-
ing their aggressions) but also of looking to them for pleasant physical
sensations, drawing enjoyment from them, becoming intoxicated and
even giddy, allowing oneself to feel freely and "naturally" the small
unfamiliar pleasures, emotions, and excitements provided by the experience of aquatic weightlessness. The following beach scene in Biarritz
at the end of the nineteenth century attests to the henceforth collective
nature of this shift toward hedonism in sea bathing:

> We sat on the bank in order to observe the exploits of the modest
> bathers of Port-Vieux. The tableau was truly picturesque and animat-
> ed. Husbands, holding their wives in their arms, taught them to swim;
> students and teachers laughed aloud at the awkward movements;
> coaches bathed the most cowardly of the lot; the strong swimmers
> went out to the rocks; the novices, who wanted to manage on their
> own, were very amusing to watch. Taking a pair of gourds tied to-
> gether by a strap, they threw them out in front, paddled out to them,
> then, on their backs or their chests, floundered on until they reached
> the rope, not without swallowing occasional mouthfuls of salt water
> and making frightful faces in response.[49]

The scene is thus "amusing"; less than thirty years after Michelet's
description, we have come very far from the dramatic spectacle of a
"poor creature" emerging "pale and shuddering" from the sea.[50] Now
people are laughing on beaches. But this joyful relaxation of behavioral standards, which transgresses against medical seriousness and
leaves therapeutic severity behind, does not come about without precautions and method.

As Francis Ponge puts it, "the sea, up to the edge of its limits, is
a simple thing that repeats itself wave after wave. But in nature not
even the simplest things reveal themselves without all kinds of fuss
and formality."[51] So people learn to swim; and we also note, in this
end-of-century beach scene, the reassuring presence of actors indispensable to the dedramatization of bathing, namely, coaches, swimming teachers—"intercessors," Antoine Blondin calls them, "between
individuals and the elements."[52]

Swimming Teachers

Often a former fisherman, at least in the early days (see chapter 1), also called a bathing guide, and later a master swimmer, this character was essential in the history of the beach. He was indeed an "intercessor," and on more than one account. A collaborator in the enterprise of maritime hydrotherapy, he was the precious intermediary between medicine and the balneopaths. Historically, however, he was also much more: not only a mediator between a medical prescription and the application of the treatment, but also a sort of intermediary between the balneophobes and the joy of bathing. He was both master and servant, protector and seducer, the incarnation of both the reality principle and the pleasure principle; a therapist on the one hand, a tempter on the other, "taking care of" phobic patients in the guise of a tacit initiator to the pleasures of the waves—pleasures that intoxicated some bathers to the point of delirium. This is why, as Gabriel Désert insists, the bathing guide was "the key figure in bathing": he was very popular, highly appreciated especially among female bathers. "The well-known image of the guide carrying a woman in his arms and taking her to bathe is not a myth."[53] Here, under the pretext of safety, in the arms of this intercessor, the privileged object of all amorous transferences reappears, the scarcely disguised place of passage between morality and pleasure: the prohibition of sensual pleasure and the sensual self-abandonment to the other—whether a man or a natural element, water—and vice versa.

A savior indeed! Yesterday's bathing guide at Biarritz or Étretat, today's swimming teacher, a member of the military police, a bronzed beach athlete, an Australian lifesaver, or an American lifeguard, this person is truly a savior who protects bathers from their phobias and frees them from their inhibitions. He is the crack through which pleasure has been reintroduced to the beach universe. Countless caricatures depict the classic operation of saving a beautiful woman in danger as a scene rife with erotic implications.

Swimming

And then people learned to swim. The skill that transformed bathers into swimmers was the great liberator of seaside vacationing. Once they could swim, bathers ceased to be lumbering oafs harnessed and moored to the shore, every motion timed, like the horses that used to pull their wheeled cabins. On their own, of their own accord and by their own power, they could break free of the shallows and of the strict rules of hydrotherapy that had kept them near the shore, limiting them in space and time. "Today," as a 1927 guidebook declares, "we no longer heed the time of the tide. The custom is to bathe between 5:00 and 6:00, depending on the hour of lunch, which is often late." Observations of this type are unquestionably signs that the severity of the earlier rules is giving way and that balneophobia is declining. Guidebooks written around the turn of the century begin to acknowledge, against medical advice, that bathing is possible the very day after one arrives at the beach.[54]

But progress was slow, and the balneophobes' emancipation was gradual in the extreme. It took more than a century for them to conquer their fear. And while Dr. Raymond asserted in 1840, at the beginning of his *Traité de natation*, that it was "almost as natural to swim as to walk," in the face of a phobia that is mastered very slowly people remained cautious for quite a long time. If the naturalist Quatrefages, passing through Biarritz at the end of the nineteenth century, was ecstatic at the sight of intrepid Basque or Spanish women swimming, "without the slightest concern in the world [seeking] a handful of gravel at a depth of ten feet," Paul Morand recalls that not far from there, at Hendaye, in 1913, swimmers were still "holding hands, seated in the water, so as not to be carried off by the waves; that was called a half-bath." And later still, in a 1931 guide to proper etiquette, we read that "most people practice swimming, in the summer especially, at the seashore," but a clarification follows: "Swimming is a relatively uncommon activity in France."[55]

One must thus be careful not to suppose that at the turn of the twentieth century sea phobia, the desire for supervision or "reassurance" on the bather's part, or the influence of medical discourse on behavior had finally been eliminated. Lingering attitudes and rules, even if they were implicit or distorted, were no less present in people's minds (all the more so in that they had been widely diffused), determining the choice of destination, feeding fears disguised as requirements, justifying standardized corporeal strategies, prolonging prohibitions, and, on the beach, sometimes leading to excessive respect for certain principles. "Ah, yes! The hydra of hydrocution! You swallow one gram too many, you jump in one minute too soon, and you'll go straight to the bottom!"[56] In the face of the sea, the phobia persisted, polymorphic, perhaps less powerful, less obvious, no doubt somewhat calmed, but still tormenting the summer resident's unconscious mind and attitudes, on various grounds—for swimming isn't all that natural, after all! As the incurable balneophobe will exclaim: "Do you see the locals, the people who live here? They aren't crazy—they never go swimming!"

What is the situation today? To be sure, we no longer live in an era when an imperious doctor-inspector supervised patients' baths while bathing guides instructed the cowardly and rescued the novices. The pedagogy of the sport has made inroads: in 1992, 64 percent of the French population knew how to swim and this mass training has reduced the obsession with the "danger of going under."[57] After the shore, the sea has been tamed in its turn. But what could be called the "leviathan syndrome" has not disappeared for all that. This syndrome is even, in many respects, the ultimate refuge of the primordial fear, a source of shudders, that is a component of the contemporary seaside imagination (see chapter 9).

To appreciate the continuing influence of medical discourse and the demand for safety, it suffices to look at the table of contents of summer issues of weekly magazines and other specialized popular publications. Some propose the ritual "hit parade," a list or ranking of beaches that are "clean and safe" (pollution has to be taken into account), while others, such as the August 1992 issue of *Top Santé*, in addition to first-aid tips and medical advice on the effects of the sun and sea bathing, offer investigative reporting and articles with revealing titles such as "Are Your Vacation Spots Well Supervised?" or "How to Help a Child Who Is Afraid of the Water." Thus we note the enduring nature of the themes that, having been popularized by "mass communications, amplify the myth even as they share knowledge"—though this knowledge may be imparted incidentally and with reluctance, in the guise of "mere facts."[58] And what is the myth in question? In this instance, the myth that surrounds supervised bathing and fear of the water is woven in counterpoint to the Crusoean reveries and other seaside robinsonnades (see chapter 4), expressing the primitive balneophobia of most human beings: the myth of the sea that redeems but also devours; the sea that purifies, heals, restores to wholeness, but also mortifies and delivers a cruel justice. A violent element, an eternal unknown, the sea is always ready to punish the swimmer's excesses and to swallow up imprudent souls.[59]

Beyond the permanence of these themes involving health and safety (and the persistence of fantasies of repulsion that their mediatization betrays), this observation nevertheless leads us to nuance the dialectic between rational and passionate relationships with the sea. This dialectic no longer takes the form it had in the nineteenth century, when it reflected a rivalry between the scientific and the hedonistic perspective in which the former came out well ahead. The hedonism of sea bathing is now an immediate and incontestable fact of life at the beach—to such an extent that balneotherapy, starting in the early twentieth century, has become no more than a specialization limited to specific sites: centers for thalassotherapy and other treatments based on sun and seawater.[60] Choosing concentration over extension, this branch of medicine, by becoming a professional specialty, has thus given up its omnipresence and by the same token has left the field free for pleasure-oriented practices.

Outside of these specialized enclaves, one may nevertheless wonder whether the contemporary popular and media-based medicalization of sea bathing (replacing the earlier scientific and dogmatic discourses) does not still perform the same regulating function. Although it takes a different form (which is no longer that of the earlier treatises, manuals, or guidebooks), adopts a different tone (instead of prescriptions and threats, we find advice and warnings), and operates in an entirely different context (the presence of vast numbers of vacationers at the seashore), contemporary medical discourse may still have a similar "slowing" effect on the balneophile. The balneophilic practice of bathing, which induces a more sensual and transgressive relation to the sea and its surroundings, has its critics. For beyond the "reasonable" uses of the beach, what is at issue today is in fact "the use of pleasures," their multiplication and the correlative emergence of untamed bodies, invaded and driven by passion.[61] The manifestation of these "free" or "uncontrollable" bodies (depending on who is describing them) is moreover now the privileged object of other media, which exalt their most spectacular aspects: nudist, athletic, and sexual. We shall come back to this point.

If it is true that among "the great temptations of medicine (and perhaps initially one of its reasons for existing) there is the temptation to exercise its authority on healthy bodies, on daily life, thus on codes of behavior,"[62] the fact remains that here, on the contemporary beach, a body escapes, or tries to escape, from this authority: the desiring body of the balneophile.

BALNEOPHILES: THE EMERGENCE OF PLEASURE

The fact that pleasure emerges does not mean that it finally begins to exist, but only that it begins to be manifested, that desires and their satisfactions now dare to express themselves, let themselves be seen and heard, allow themselves to be read on faces and bodies, manifested by expressions, gestures, behaviors, words, or screams. We have gotten used to this. On the beach, we often observe the attitudes of others, or, when we are not participating ourselves, we watch their games, deciphering the signs of pleasure that they communicate. In fact, the beach today is something like a dance floor: a space instituted by a juxtaposition of bodies, a space of contacts, sensations, excitement, and pleasure whose free expression is broadly authorized. Although codified and highly ritualized, the language of pleasure is relatively clear—although this has not always been the case.[63]

For the language of pleasure was unclear at first: not absent, but encoded, its signs emerging here and there, incidentally, sporadically, like lapses or affronts to the good manners of the times—brief traces of abandon or insolence. It suffices to read Michelet to realize to what extent everything was concerted to keep that language from reaching expression. Thus, regarding "the hard ceremony of the first cold baths," Michelet indicates that "at least, the odious gaze of a mob of people is to be avoided. Let them be taken in private and with no one present but a perfectly reliable person who, at need, will help the nervous patient, and rub her with hot cloths and revive her with warm drinks."[64] Beneath the prescription there is a proscription: that of the spectacle of physical sensation and its uncontrolled effects.

We must not deduce from this that pleasure is not already present, even in cold baths and the most violent exposures. Yesterday's bather, like today's, is a complex being and cannot be reduced, according to the periods, to any one profile, phobic, pathological, or hedonistic. Historically, what is in question is more the affective nature of the individual than successive generations of bathers reducible to a type that would be, first, the "balneocrat," then the "-path," then the "-phobe," then the "-phile." Not only are there elements of the -path and the -phobe in the -crat and of the -phobe in the -path (and vice versa), but as we shall see there are also elements of the -phile in the -phobe and thus of the -phile in the -path. In short, if there are philic balneocrats and phobic balneopaths, there is also something of the balneophile in the balneophobe, and vice versa.

A drawing from the 1870s that depicts breaker bathing in both rough and smooth water offers a perfect illustration of the emotional complexity of bathers, their sensual ambivalence, and, correlatively, the surreptitious emergence of pleasure. In a turbulent sea, in order to receive the wave on her backside, the woman adopts an equivocal bathing posture from the outset: she is kneeling at the water's edge, her head at the level of the bathing guide's waist; he is holding her by her wrists. And in a calm sea, when the missing wave is replaced by a violent projection of water administered by the guide on the same spot with the help of a bucket, there is longer any ambiguity in the drawing. It suffices to see the bather's face, like that of Bernini's St. Theresa in Rome, "to understand at once that her pleasure is orgasmic; there is no room for doubt"[65]—and her neighbor, observing her ecstasy, envies her as she waits her turn. The only difference is that in place of the angel with his arrow striking the saint with happiness, here we have the famous bathing guide Zephyr, named after the wind, intoxicating, to be sure, and his "magic" bucket that is the equivalent conveyor of erotic pleasure.[66] The woman bather here can be compared to the mystics, whose essential testimony consists in expressing by their faces, gestures, or postures that they are experiencing pleasure without being aware of it. At least they act as if this were the case. They are simply present, with their trembling flesh, their beaming faces, and their semi-clandestine ecstasy. There also emerges, unexpectedly, at the heart of the most rugged balneotherapy, the pleasure in the shock of the waves, "the coenesthetic joy of violence," or "the whip of the sea," or even "the ambivalent suffering of flagellation so characteristic of masochism."

We have discovered the revealing lapsus; there remain the "insolences"—other incidents that are symptomatic of emergence. These other signs do not stem from the *acte manqué*, from self-abandonment, but rather from provocations or attacks—on modesty, as one would expect. We cannot examine all instances, but even a few of them—indices that spurred discussions and polemics in their own time—suffice to show that the tension between reason and passion was rising, that toward the end of the century the language of pleasure was increasing its pressure on hygienic and moral standards, and multiplying transgressions.

On the beaches that were frequented in those days, a naked or nearly naked man suddenly appeared as a public outrage defying the order of dress along with the moral and medical order. From north to south, reproaches were addressed to those who did not respect the code of modesty. Thus in Spain in 1833, the vice-consul of France complained to the mayor of Roses of solitary "nudist" practices and demanded that "men who bathe without any shelter have the decency to choose another part of the beach instead of bathing and undressing right in front of the cabins," which had been built by other, more modest bathers.[67] "I pull'd off my Clothes, for the Weather was hot to Extremity, and took the Water."[68] Robinson is back, but he is met with stern disapproval. Here is another shipwreck, for sure, but the ship is that of morality!

From the coast of Gerona to the Normandy coast, the struggle was organized—already!—against those weak-willed souls for whom the use of bathing costumes did not seem indispensable, people who preferred to offer their bodies to the sea without veil or obstacle, just like "savages," in fact, new Savages, at least in the eyes of a bourgeoisie that was still having a hard time opening its windows and exposing its body to the sun and the water, at a time when woolen pants descending at least below the knee were strongly recommended to women bathers in Normandy. Because in the Granville region in 1896 some girls had been caught "naked as Eve, or disrobing in a creek," the mayor of Jullouville responded to the "attack" with a scathing decree: "People who appear naked out of the water will be pursued before the appropriate tribunals."[69] With the cry of "the nude body shall not pass," the fight had only begun.

Given the increase in nudist pleasure, in nudity or denuding (which are not the same thing), in other words given the emergence—though in still widely scattered places—of nudist balneophilia, we have now arrived at the threshold of a hundred years' war. This conflict brought the advocates of bathing "costumes" into opposition with those who advocated the disappearance of costumes. From discussion to conflict, from polemics to concessions, from provocations to condemnations, and from detours to subterfuges, during a quarrel traversed by scandals and compromises, shaken by reforms and counterreforms, by dressings and undressings, censorship and trickery, a proteiform and multicolored minimalism finally invaded our beaches after a long struggle.

There is no need to decide who won and who lost. The important thing is that, for the second time, a world was transformed. "Conquest of the west" and distant contemplation first, connection, contact, and immersion next. From the discovery of the fisherman to the summer balneocrat, then from the seaside summer vacationer to the residential vacationer-swimmer, the coastal region continues to be transformed. "Nudity, complete in nudist villages or partial on so-called textile beaches is [today] an unconsciously very motivating element." What does this mean? And why is it so? Saint Cyprien (after whom a beach is now named, in an irony of fate) recommended, it seems, "not to expose the nudity of the faithful to the curious, on beaches."[70] Except that now, at Saint-Cyprien-Plage, and elsewhere, the "faithful," like Robinson, have shed their clothes. Their bodies remain; and on these, a "textile" detail that hardly counts: the end of the story of wool pants that have gone from mutation to mutation and turned into "briefs" and a "string"—the history of a vestimentary sign that tells in its own way the metamorphosis of a universe, setting and characters included.

To be sure, from the eighteenth to the nineteenth century, "for the first time, a shift took place from therapeutic aims to hedonistic ones" at the seashore.[71] But this was at bottom only an initial movement, which was to stop, in a cautious advance of pleasure, precisely on the edge, right on the bank, supported by promenades, casinos, mobile cabins tied up on beaches, baths and bathing establishments. From the nineteenth century to the twentieth, this movement did not simply expand; it changed in nature. In the person of the liberated bather, disclosed first as a balneophile and then as a free swimmer, it was to move beyond these ultimate protections. A complex character, both -phile and -phobe at once, in which exciting contradictory feelings coexisted; not content to set up his tent on the bank, this bather, naked and driven, would cross the foam barrier, the frontier of the breaker.

The frontier of the breaker, and the frontier of sensibility as well.[72] For we can say that it is here, in the traversal of the punishing wave, that contemporary beach society was born, no longer a society of repentance or redemption but one of pleasure, cutting off with this gesture the moral and technological moorings inherited from two centuries that in many respects prefigured its invention quite inadequately—a strange society, actually, unlike any other, founded peculiarly on the ambiguous desire for the void and the vertigo of a leap into the unknown: a depopulated shore, without natives, an unveiled body on display, and a leap into the sea.[73]

3. The Era of Scandals

*(or, How Robinson lost his modesty,
got a tan, built a shack on the shore,
and what happened next)*

"Ma, what is that fellow?"

"Why, that's a ho-bo."

"Ma, I want to be a ho-bo someday."

"Shet your mouth, that's not for the like of the Hazards."

But he never forgot that day, and when he grew up, after a short spell
playing football at LSU, he did become a hobo.

—Jack Kerouac, *On the Road* (1957)

So what was the beach like by the second half of the nineteenth century?
Except for some "wild" balneocrats, isolated nudists, and a handful of
other dissident hedonists who could be spotted now and again (see
chapter 2), the beach was a proper sort of place. It had gradually been
invaded not only by warmly dressed bathers but also by meticulous
rules that set limits on well-mannered conviviality. As early as 1847, as
we have seen, Flaubert cast admiring glances at some young naked-as-
Adam bathers he encountered as they were attempting to swim near the
Saint-Malo coast (Saint-Malo was still a distant shore and for the time
being still safe from the puritanical decrees of the mayor of Jullouville
or any other). Already passing judgment on the era, he exclaimed, "Isn't
what is required today just the opposite of nakedness, simplicity, truth?
Fortune and success to those who know how to clothe and dress things!
The tailor is the king of the century, and the grapevine is its symbol;
laws, art, politics, bathing trunks everywhere!"[1] Flaubert's exclamation

captures the spirit of the times. Its triumphant emblems, bathing trunks and their countless cousins, could be found everywhere—these symbols were particularly prominent on the most fashionable coasts, donned so that people could get themselves into the water with decency.

> On the beach at Beuzeval,
> When the sea bubbles up in the morning,
> You'd think it was Carnival time!
> You see green, red, blue outfits,
> For custom dictates
> That bathers be covered up,
> Each in his own costume.[2]

However, despite the obvious fantasy elements, this "carnival" had nothing really carnival-like to offer. It neither presupposed nor gave rise to a real reversal of moral standards, practices, or habits. On the contrary, at the risk of caricature, the versifier was perpetuating city manners here, although in disguised form. This is why, taking a critical view similar to Flaubert's, the author of these lines made fun of the "custom" dictating "that bathers be covered up." We are squarely within the antinaturist ethic of bathing that is denoted by an aesthetics of the clothed and not the unclothed.

On the beach, during this period, in the name of decency and in perfect synchrony, bathers and the site were thus "covered" with taboos. Bathers, even if they were decked out in bright colors, swaddled themselves in costumes that masked their bodies, while the site was garbed in laws, rules, and decrees that had to do not only with its physical arrangement, its commercial exploitation, or the amenities for summer residents along the shore, but also with the way people presented themselves and conducted their personal relationships in public. These ordering principles were thus in scrupulous conformity with the principles of distinction that governed social life away from the beach; they "staged" life at the shore.[3]

Among the discriminations adopted, the spatial distribution of the sexes was the most noteworthy. From the 1830s on, in northern Europe, in the Baltic and Channel regions first of all, the bathing zone was generally divided into three sectors: one for men, one for women, and in between, one for couples and families. Moreover, this "classical division by sex" along the beach was often paralleled by a social sectorization that separated the upper and lower classes within each zone.[4]

But a great deal has already been said on this subject. I shall not return to it, preferring to move closer now to the period that interests us here: our own. Still, as this sexual and social administration of space brings us to the threshold of the twentieth century, let us note on the one hand that segregation on the beaches lasted throughout the entire nineteenth century, up to 1900 and even beyond, and on the other hand that this segregation was accompanied by no less discriminating dress codes. Place and costume continued to be linked: a man who bathed in the mixed zone, reserved for couples and families, had to be covered from neck to knee; but if he bathed in the zone reserved for men, he could use a simple pair of bathing trunks. As for women, no matter where they were, they had to be completely "covered up": trousers, shirt, skirt, or camisole.

Let us also note that this insistence on rules and regulations, which traces simultaneous topological and vestimentary boundaries between modesty and immodest display, was not an intrinsic aspect of sea bathing, but always superimposed on it. On the less popular beaches, separation between the sexes did not exist, and dress codes, not being established by formal obligations, were followed in a much more random fashion. Indeed, rules increased in proportion to the presence of the aristocracy, the popularity of the site, and its therapeutic reputation; at the same time, via the rational bias of concern for health and safety and in the name of hygiene and social tranquility, institutions appropriated the invention of the beach, took over its management, channeled the desire that inspired it, codified and normalized the expression of that desire, and ultimately repressed its excesses.

Thus a geopolitics of the beach and a geopolitics of the body developed along parallel lines, defining the thresholds of tolerance of the covered and the uncovered. They conjointly divided bathing space in the sea and also the bather's body into visible and invisible zones: there was a place for dressing and undressing (cabins and tents), a place to bathe, and a place to walk about (public promenades, piers, streets), a place where one had to be dressed at least in a dressing gown or else had to pay a fine.[5] And on the body there were even "places," public ones in a certain sense, on which the gaze could alight and circulate, others that were reputed to be secret, intimate, or obscene. Hence the necessity of a bathing suit that "covered up," a guarantee that the bodily territory of each individual was protected and that its forbidden "regions" would remain invisible.

The phobia of water was now supplemented—and later replaced— by the phobia of the Other, or more precisely the gaze of the other, the gaze that "undresses"; the norms of modesty were established to counter the power of this gaze. According to Alain Corbin, this puritanical attitude, the added phobia aroused by the fear of both social and sexual contact, was intensified between 1811 and 1850.[6] It is clear that the double fear was not only present but powerfully experienced by Michelet in 1861. He expresses it as follows:

> And, as though the impression of a first sea-bath were not sufficiently strong, it is aggravated for a nervous woman by the presence of the crowd of bathers. For her, it is a cruel exhibition to make before a critical crowd, before rivals, delighted to see her ugly, for once; before silly and heartless men, who, with telescope in hand, watch the sad hazards of the toilette of the poor humiliated woman.[7]

A desire for visual protection is expressed here, and thus a desire for the necessary art of body camouflage. For more than a century, this art was universally practiced on most beaches. Its maintenance (proof that it was becoming more and more difficult to practice) led the mayor of Deauville to publish a decree in August 1929 spelling out ways to mask one's body on and off the beach. But it was also this art (proof that it was still being practiced) that led Paul Morand to recall in 1960 that, in the first decade of the twentieth century, "[a] naked woman was for us a spectacle of unheard-of rarity, unimaginable for boys of today, and the waves on which we turned our backs were less precipitous in their convulsions than our senses, at the sight of a bare leg or shoulder."[8] The mayor of Deauville, in his decree, specified in this connection that it was "obligatory to wear a bathing suit with epaulettes in order to take sea baths."

Shoulders were taboo for the gaze. Chests and thighs too, of course. In the late 1920s, the "places" subject to litigation, places for which propriety required invisibility, quite clearly betrayed a moral environment that we need to keep in mind to measure the extent of the upheaval: the break or rupture that, in this context, was constituted by the scandalous appearance of nude or minimally dressed bathers—a carnival actor without the costume, now, for whom the best of disguises was to have to all intents and purposes no disguise at all.

THE SCANDAL OF THE VISIBLE BODY

Michelet in 1861, the French vice-consul in Spain in 1883, the mayor of Jullouville in 1896, the curé of Biarritz in 1917 (protesting against cleavage),[9] and many others as well manifested their concern over the development of sea bathing, from north to south. During this first century of seaside pleasure, many well-known individuals spoke out against the humiliating or casual display of nakedness that this modern practice produced along the beach. In the name of hygiene, morality, or aesthetics, all these people in turn became vehement spokespersons for a bourgeois mentality that had abhorred a vacuum, particularly in the context of dress. And yet, in the biblical tradition, the absence of clothing symbolizes the nakedness of Eden! But this is the point: the new nakedness was iconoclastic. It was the sign of an obvious imposture. By definition, nothing in fact authorized sinners to carry out such a return to their origins by taking off their clothes, unless it was by way of simulacrum, a taste for untruths, perfidious provocations! What is more, the symbol was ambivalent, for in the context of this tradition nakedness might also have a negative value and signify shame.[10]

At all events, a bathing costume worthy of the name had to be ample, even bouffant, not only to envelop and protect the body from bad weather, but especially to blur its contours and hide its flesh. Letting nothing be glimpsed, preventing anyone from guessing, it "softened" personal appearance. Because it did not "emphasize" the details of the body, it did not "betray" the intimate morphology of the bather. For example, the little skirt "like the one worn by vivandières," added above the trousers, had ultimately just one purpose: to hide the breadth of the hips.[11] The main point, finally, was to encode the body's form and flesh, its shape and substance, and protect it from prying eyes. Just as the obligatory dressing gown, prescribed by the hygienists for getting out of a bath, served not only to protect against cold but also to avoid the provocation of a body becoming readable again upon contact with the water, for the cloth clinging to the skin then perfidiously offered the excessively visible spectacle of naughty or obscene hollows and bumps, folds, and recesses to the eyes of all.

This regulated, encoded, and controlled context, very attentive to respect for the intimate unreadability of bodies, led fairly rapidly to the disappearance of spontaneous nudist practices (see chapter 2), and provided the backdrop for scandal. Defying the established dress code, subjects for controversy and debate arose over the right to disrobe and how much clothing one could remove in the vicinity of the beach. In the early 1930s one summer resident/poet accounted in the following terms for the atmosphere of an era that was still oscillating between rejecting nudity and succumbing to temptation:

> Getting briskly out of the water,
> The woman puts on her pajamas,
> Puts a large Panama hat on her head,
> And walks through the town
> In queenly fashion.
> People get their pictures taken
> For others who could not afford
> The trip to the place of delight.
> Some say that the police
> Should never have tolerated
> Such a scandal, should have prevented it.
> They ought to know that the Code
> Is powerless against fashion.
> Some censors, in their virtue,
> Have a profound horror of nudity.
> They say it is an arena
> For seals running loose.
> Others, more taken by beauty,
> Contemplate the human form
> In its charm and voluptuousness.[12]

Here we have a first glimpse of the terms in which the controversy was developing. On the one hand, the code was pitted against fashion; that is, the standards of modesty inherited from the nineteenth century incriminated the evolution of moral standards and the accompanying laxity of behavior. On the other hand, the presumed animality of the naked body—the seal metaphor is edifying in this regard—was contrasted with the charm and voluptuousness of the unveiled body. One group appealed to the police and to chastity, while the other invoked beauty and the pleasure it procured. To sum up the principal charges brought by the ancients against the moderns, we may say that the former reproached the latter for a disturbing desire to transgress and regress.

For, alongside its recognized therapeutic virtues, its medical goals, which were its sole justification in the end, the taste for sea bathing and swimming was broadly perceived and fantasized as an essentially regressive ludic practice apt to damage human dignity. Here again, science—the science of swimming, in this case—had to take hold of the body to purge it of its bestiality. Swimmers thus had to avoid "up-and-down gestures that make them look like monkeys," said one nineteenth-century guidebook. Even before the grotesque comparison with seals, uneducated swimmers were thus already threatened with ridicule through comparison with monkeys and through other degrading analogies. It is true that Alphonse Karr reversed the primate metaphor in 1841 in favor of the moderns by writing that old-style women bathers, with "their woolen costumes, their jackets, pants, and hats of waxed cloth," were the ones who brought to mind "a crowd of cantankerous monkeys gamboling on the beach."[13] Cantankerous or not, the image remained. And in 1844, in his *Traité de natation*, Dr. V. Raymond offered in all seriousness the following anthropological reflection on swimming, which can hardly leave us indifferent:

> There is one other way of swimming used only among a few savage peoples. This is an imitation of the movements of quadrupeds in the water: a great deal of force is used without much result; swimmers make hasty movements that impede their progress, and long familiarity with this sort of swimming is required to make the most of it. I have seen Negroes who went upstream against rapid currents this way. But it is always a tiring and ungainly way to swim.[14]

Monkey, Negro, or quadruped: it is easy to see here what phobic imaginary was attached to the perception of leisure bathing and swimming, and the corrective function that the methodical and sporting aestheticization of swimming was to have as a result. It would take human aquatic behavior out of the realm of savagery and domesticate it. By the same token, we can also see what prophetic premonition lies behind this sort of discourse, namely the premonition among the "ancients" that sea bathing, as soon as it has surpassed its initial status as remedy and treatment, is an open door to primitivism or savagery—from which it follows that the beach, left to its own devices, is potentially an ideal stage for imitating Savages. Long after the death of the scrupulous hygienists, and far beyond anything they could have imagined, what followed was to prove them right.

Here then, after the danger of submersion, we have the "peril" of regression, which haunted and kept on haunting the spirit of seaside moralists! As for the desire to transgress, what are its chief signs? Here, between large and small scandals, celebrated coups de théâtre

and discreet dissonances, we have to distinguish between two categories of signs.

On the one hand, there were the ostentatious signs, generally produced in a sophisticated milieu, that stemmed from eccentric behavior, deliberate transgression, or atypical excess. Despite their always
indicative value, these signs nevertheless remained isolated symptoms
and are thus not very representative of the collective evolution. To illustrate this sort of transgressive manifestation, premonitory but not
really significant in terms of the era, we can invoke the "beautiful and
bold" Trouhanova who, in 1913, swam at Deauville bare-breasted;[15] or
Gabrielle Chanel, who got a good deal of publicity by exposing herself
to the sun on the Riviera in 1927.

On the other hand, there were the less spectacular but recurring
signs that were symptomatic of a profound shift in attitudes. These
signs, which were repetitive, thus widespread, did not stem from a
provocative and contingent exhibitionism but from a troublesome
and diffuse gap. In the process of being generalized, they already had
the power of fashion and denoted much more decisively the reality of
a global evolution of moral standards and sensibilities. Socially, these
signs are problematic. They reveal a rupture and announce a transformation in behavior. This is why, if the unexpected signs of the first
sort produce stupefaction or surprise, those of the second (like those
of an epidemic) instead tend to provoke anxiety: it is not so much
their novelty as their propagation that creates a scandal, by massively
betraying the old dress code.

At the origin of contemporary beach manners, registers of the betrayal of the "classic" costume can be analyzed in semiological terms.
What are the aspects of clothing through which the scandalous variation was surreptitiously introduced—the one which, by restoring a
visible body with its form and its flesh, gradually called into question
fallen man's duty to practice modesty?[16] The transgression of the
accepted standard was carried out by challenges in four principal
registers, four "safety devices," as it were: the opaque garment, the
covering, the long, and the closed, which were contrasted respectively
with the transparent, the clinging (or body-shaping), the short, and
the open (or half-open).

Transparency is one vehicle for scandal, operating paradoxically
by way of an ambiguous hygienist prescription. White, a color that
reflects and protects against the sun's aggression, was in fact deemed

medically desirable by nineteenth-century health professionals. But there was a problem: the known disadvantage of white fabric is that it loses its opacity when it comes out of the water, and, as Paul Morand notes, the obscene gesture is no longer so much taking off one's clothes to change into a white bathing costume as getting wet in one. Certain hygienists, more committed moralists than they were therapists, did not hesitate to advise bathers to wear dark colors (other than black). Others, less strict or more diplomatic, splitting the difference between morality and health, recommended bathing costumes in two colors. Thus "blue with white stripes" was a dominant pattern on Normandy beaches in 1875. Here, then, is the source of the sea-bathing fashion of striped suits. This fashion originated not so much from a desire to imitate sailor suits as from a concession made by science to morality.[17] Still, even striped, even with highly contrasting stripes, as if raked by the lines that continued to hide it, the body was no longer behind an opaque screen here, but behind a "palisade" that let light through. This compromise palisade was simultaneously one of censorship and of interstices: bars and window through which, in the late nineteenth and early twentieth centuries, the body began to appear, half decoded.

The first betrayal of the "classic" costume, the stripe, was thus a balanced betrayal, an artifice that, along with the ambiguity of white, which was simultaneously healthy and immodest, stifled the scandal of transparency. In the framework of this aesthetics of dress, in which hygiene and modesty made their peace and as yet left little room for the visible body, the transgression was reasonable and reasoned—the gap was small with respect to the model—and the variation, even if it was mocked by some for its carnival aspect, was in fact a novelty that was rapidly accepted and assimilated. On the other hand, starting in the first decade of the twentieth century, the arrival of the clinging bathing suit or, rather, its return led to much more forceful reactions.[18]

Paul Morand attests to the effects of the new "costume" on the social environment between 1911 and 1913 by relating a personal experience: "I remember having brought back from England at the time a championship one-piece bathing suit in black silk, which caused the crowds in Hendaye to stare." There is no doubt about it: the transgression here was clearer and the break with the cover-up model obvious: the silhouetted body was entirely visible, faithfully modeling the bather's body and its volumes of flesh. From here on, as soon as this hydrodynamic suit changed wearers, as soon as female bathers took it up, scandals broke out. In the 1920s, when it was coming into fashion, the form-fitting suit was the object of all sorts of attacks: the father of two girls deemed it "indecent," while others asserted that a married woman who wore one was "courting danger" and her husband was a "fool."[19]

From critiques to polemics, from rejections to condemnations, the body shaped in its clinging suit was an exposed body, expressed in its difference and its attractions, the body restored to its sex after a century of being kept secret. It was a resexualized body, offered to the Other, as it were—not only to the other's gaze, but to the other's desire. At least this is how the new "costume" was interpreted; this is how it was fantasized and feared in the framework of a psychosis of rape, adultery, or (provoked) return to a lawless and amoral sexuality. Underneath the transgression, there was a phobia of disorder, unbridled freedom, a return to savagery, and regression.

The success of the clinging bathing suit was more gradual than that of the striped suit, however, although the two were easily combined. Here and there, resistances were expressed, attesting to a more recent assimilation. As late as 1931, Liselotte wrote in her guide:

> The most convenient costume for swimming is the form-fitting suit. But the latter, accused (rightly) of being unattractive and inappropriate, has been abandoned by good society. Young men and women today wear either the so-called Canadian costume composed of black or dark blue shorts and a blouse that leaves the arms free and tucks into the shorts, or else the one-piece "American" suit, in which a narrow skirt hangs from the waist just enough to cover the shorts.[20]

The narrow skirt in question, although shorter, in fact fulfilled the same function as the earlier "vivandière" skirt. The form-fitting suit existed, and people wore it, but they still felt a need to blur its contours, to recode in some way what it invited viewers to decode. The transgression took place, but under cover, as it were, and it was fully accomplished only later on. We have not yet seen the last of the epaulets, the little skirts, and other "dressed" blouses covering the form-fitting suit. These are maintained, even in two-piece suits, up until the 1960s, in the form of "pant-skirts," "false three-piece suits that are really two-piece suits," the "combination" (top and bottom meeting), or even the "overskirt," considered to be "infinitely practical for strolling along the beach, playing ball, or lolling about."[21]

Still, the empire of cover-up garments gradually shrank, increasing the visibility of form-fitting suits accordingly, as the third betrayal of the costume made inroads in the period between the wars: the tendency toward shortness (or its variants, narrowness and thinness), which gave rise to bared shoulders, arms, and legs. From south to north, the testimony is consistent. "Bathing suits gradually got shorter, brassieres were increasingly minimal, baring the shoulders." The top went up less high and the bottom went down less far. New transgressions, more scandals. In Yport, a bather shocked public opinion because she presented herself "as if entirely naked . . . poured into a red suit, her breasts thrusting outward, her waist curved, her buttocks ripe, thighs and arms bare." Onlookers were shocked not only by the vivid color and the form-fitting aspect that drew the eye to her figure, but also by the nudity of her limbs, which revealed not just the body's shape but the flesh itself. We may recall "Homeric struggles between partisans and opponents of shorts" in the 1930s; at the heart of this debate remained the problem of short versus long vacation clothing. Losing sleeves here, dropping leg coverings there, the territory of the clothed was melting like ice in the sun, announcing the end of the medical, hygienist, and moralist ice age for bodies and beaches alike.[22]

Finally, after becoming transparent, form-fitting, and short, the bathing suit opened up in another direction by means of low necklines, to the great dismay of the curé of Biarritz. In the late 1920s, during the Belle Époque, if not even earlier, half-openings in articles of clothing came onto the fashion scene. "The provocation thus lies in allowing glimpses of the chest rather than in displaying it; the bathing suit is a means." And then "brown shoulders are spoiled by the white line left by straps."[23] Thus straps fell, shoulder coverings disappeared, and the "costume" opened up like a cocoon from which the naked— or "as if naked"—body would soon emerge.

There is no doubt but that, subject to one transgression after another, betrayed several times over, the "classic" costume was the very symbol of a world that was collapsing, a world born of the original colonization of the shore by bathers. While one universe was disappearing, another was being born, one in which the unclothed body would be not only the scandalous emblem of a new ideological definition of the sea-bathing space but its primordial dimension. Along with the unclothed body, a new seaside "culture of leisure" was appearing, oriented toward mass nudity—despite the signs of resistance manifested in compromises on the clothing front such as stripes or pants-skirts. These were not signs of retreat or rejection but of transition—as "monokinis" would be somewhat later, between bikinis and bare breasts (see chapter 8).

"A variation in clothing is inevitably accompanied by a variation in the world and vice versa," Roland Barthes wrote.[24] In fact the multiple transgression involving costumes also signified those involving customs and the correlative introduction of new ones. As a result, these transgressions also led to the organization and establishment of a new culture, a new seaside world at the center of which, poised to conquer the sensual shores of the robinsonnade, we now find a visible body, that is, a body emptied, as if "cleansed," of the signs in the realm of dress that once tended to deny it as a site of pleasure—just as the beach had been denied.

To the image of the stripped-down coastal environment, the extreme harmonization of site and actor, to the "territory of the void," there now corresponds the body of a naked man or woman, a stripped-down site in turn, a terra incognita finally discovered and henceforth exhibited in "intimate" regions that were once swallowed up under waves of clothing.

SCANDALS OF REVERSAL

From clothed to unclothed, or more clearly still, from dressed to undressed: these are the first of the reversals at the origin of contemporary beach manners, the chosen space of a parallel sociability that was thus favorable to the free expression of provocations and assorted excesses.

To be sure, as Pastoureau says, "at the seashore, one is freed from certain constraints, dares to do what wouldn't be done in the city, transgresses certain customs, sometimes even mixes with the riffraff," in this way playing roles that are out of the ordinary.[25] In addition, as Gabriel Désert emphasizes, the beach was justified as a theater for transgression during the Belle Époque by the fact that this period "saw woman liberated from certain constraints and becoming more provocative."[26] These remarks, which pinpoint certain characteristic aspects of the sea-bathing revolution with considerable accuracy, still fall far short of explaining the logic of reversal of the behaviors that mark it—a logic that is not only symptomatic, but generally applicable, irreducible either to a rite of slumming or to the emancipation of the female population.

The entire leisure class (first the aristocracy, then the bourgeoisie) in fact began to play the game. In the next wave (with the extension of vacations resulting from the institution of paid holidays in 1936), all of French society began to head for the shores in large numbers. The "rabble" did not go to the beach to go slumming, nor (despite its persistent therapeutic prestige) did people head for the shore simply to breathe the fresh air, bathe, and exercise. Mountains, spas, lakes, and rivers would have been just as satisfactory for all these purposes. As in the time of the earliest fashionable summer residencies, these objectives are often just pretexts. There is more than meets the eye here: there is a deeper desire or dream that social mimeticism does not adequately explain.

Why did people abandon the guinguettes, little restaurants with music and dancing along the Marne, to go to the seashore? Might this be another way of raising questions about the contemporary rush toward the coast? Guinguettes were places where members of the bourgeoisie went slumming, went fishing, took off their clothes to swim, and where workers for their part flirted with members of the upper classes, taking on worldly airs and seducing the tipsy nobility. These sites provided escape hatches, as it were, between the social classes—and they were already on the water's edge. We must then look for the aspects, signs, and significant indices that bore witness at the beginning of the twentieth century to the emergence of this general inversion. Through the process of jettisoning clothing along the shore, the "betrayal of the costume," we have to decipher much more than a transgression. What is at stake is the reform of a social morality, a form of leisure conviviality that involves concepts as relative as decency, modesty, hygiene, sociability, pleasure, and physical beauty: self-image, one's relations to others and to the world. A hedonist morality took hold of practices that had initially been subjected to medical standards; a morality of pleasure placed happiness above even health and made way for the physical expression of passions. Point by point, this new morality came to contradict the ethical arguments and aesthetic alibis of the nineteenth century.

Concerning the right to nudity, or, more modestly, the right to be unclothed, it must be made clear that nothing was clear—not even for Flaubert, for example, despite his virulent denunciation of the bathing-trunks ideology. The (segregative) requirement of beauty—the aesthetic alibi—still had a strong upper hand over the social recognition of the cautious but real demand for the freedom to go naked. The same Flaubert who in 1847 admired the naked bodies of young bathers at Saint-Malo or who in 1836 in Trouville envied "the soft and peaceful wave" that slapped the thighs of Mme Schlesinger, wrote in 1854 of his disgust with beaches and collective undressings, even though these were in the very early stages: "I spent a full hour today watching women swim. What a sight! What a hideous sight!" Flaubert's reflection is related to Georges Vanel's reactionary denunciation in the 1920s condemning the freedom of dress that was "transforming our beaches into more or less artistic exhibits of the anatomy of both sexes." Artistic: this is the master argument, still used today![27] As for Flaubert, he remained a man of his time, quite representative of contemporaneous standards in this matter and still lacking in the iconoclastic tendency necessary for revolution.

The real reversal, which went beyond the ancients' phobia of regression and the moralists' horror of immodesty or ugliness, came later. It erupted, whatever the late lamented Vanel may have thought, at the beginning of the twentieth century, with naturism or nudism, a movement that originated in Germany.[28] Despite their marginality at the time, owing to the fact of their very possibility we must not underestimate the ideological importance of these movements, along with their effects on mentalities and behaviors—effects ensured in particular at the time by the vulgarizing discourses of a somewhat complacent or even ambiguous literature, and spectacular enterprises that had wide echoes in the contemporary media: "There was much talk last summer of the creation by Drs. André and Gaston Durville of a naturist center on an island in the Seine, Médan, near Triel. This island has been called the island of naked men, and the press has devoted many articles to the project."[29]

The naked man now had his island. All he lacked to become an immodest Robinson was the surrounding sea. In 1933, four years after the mayor of Dieppe made it obligatory to wear bathing epauletes, and while people were fighting for or against shorts, the first naturist village—following the acquisition of the domain of Heliopolis and the tolerance of the municipal council of Hyères—was created on the Île du Levant. From then on, facing the shore, circled by boats or observed from afar through a telescope by curious souls, as if they were discovering King Kong, uneasy and fascinated before the palisade that hid the primate from view, there was thus the island of the naked monkey, whose population was biding its time while waiting its turn to land on the coasts. It would have to be patient for nearly half a century.[30]

Still, we must not overlook the "obscure" roots of naturism, starting at the very beginning of the century with the Wandervögel, who were proselytizers for nude bathing in lakes and rivers (like other innovations in leisure activities, nude bathing thus had a nationalist inspiration).[31] Similarly, we may wonder about the ideological import of certain declarations, like this one by M. K. de Mongeot, one of the major supporters of nudism in France:

> In founding Vivre, we had not decided to lead a campaign in favor of nudity; it was only later, after the publication had been in existence for a year, that this means of regeneration struck us as indispensable to our work.... Free physical culture is working miracles in many countries by recreating strong races; why should it not dispense its power just as well among ourselves?[32]

Without question there is ambiguity here. The text deals with work and with race; it appeared during the between-the-wars period with whose outcome we are all too familiar. Considered from this angle, we may agree with Jacques Laurent that "the nudist movement was born like a religion, before the last war"—with its powerful priests and its zealous fundamentalists, as one would expect, practitioners of a demanding cult: that of the body, prefigured by the German Körperkultur and also the Nacktkultur (cult of nudity), practiced, for example, in the "School of Light" run by a Dr. Fränzel, editor of an illustrated magazine significantly called *Soma* (The body).[33]

Beyond these criticisms, whether they are based on legitimate ideological suspicions or conservative reactions that the naturist rumor aroused, the fact remains that in its own time this tendency provoked a social and cultural shock, not only because its very possibility was "scandalous," but also because new images were circulated, images whose diffusion (at that time through clandestine or private channels) gradually spread the "curious" spectacle of a modified psychological relation to the body, to others, and to nature, one that actually transposed an Eden-like scenography of seaside leisure into reality.[34]

In *Aux îles Bienheureuses*, Théo Varlet, a real-life Robinson on the Île du Levant (although the first Fridays did not actually arrive until 1933), recorded his impressions of the periods he spent (between 1909 and 1914) on this "practically deserted island":

My wife and I spent five or six weeks each summer leading a primitive life, sleeping in hammocks, under pine trees, in a wood overlooking the sea; we were minimally dressed to make our way through the brush, but for ten hours a day we returned to the Edenic freedom of the beaches or the rocks of the deep narrow creeks. After such a sojourn, our skin color—which was shocking then!—would now be the envy of the most sumptuous of the "living bronzes."[35]

While literary nudism had little in common with the isolated provocations of the popular resorts, it nevertheless contributed to the banalization of nudity (and later to its popularization, just as erotic magazines do today). But, more important, such literary manifestations went beyond the visual, narrative, physical, and moral aspects of nudism to communicate the first reference points and testimonies of a truly Crusoean robinsonnade, in comparison with which Alexandre Dumas's 1831 Trouville version, for example, now seems quite tame.

Symptoms of their society, nudism and naturism were thus at the same time prefatory signs of the impending reversal and the break with nineteenth-century moralism. Historically, they were among the premises that opened the door in Europe to the free manifestation of hedonistic seaside practices, individual and collective practices that they rendered guilt-free by making the beach no longer a place of testing or violent redemption but of pleasure and peaceful reconciliation—a double reconciliation, between man and nature on the one hand, man and man on the other.

"We were created to live naked, just as we come into the world and as certain primitive races still live," Louis-Charles Royer wrote in *Let's Go Naked* in 1929; the work's original title, *Au pays des hommes nus* (In the land of naked men), could easily be mistaken for that of an ethnological narrative, in the style of "Terre humaine." "Primitivism," so feared among the ancients, was on the march. Still, if it were to exist, it would be of "high quality." Roger Salardenne points out that if naturism eventually triumphs, "it will not mean a return to the savage state; on the contrary, the entire ancestral and barbaric part of humankind will be stripped away along with clothing, and we shall see a Dionysiac joy take the place that is occupied today by the lowest and most abject instincts."[36]

The gods—or at least their names—were also invoked in the context of this reconciliation, and there were reminders of this when, some twenty years later, the first village of the future Club Med rose up out of the ground. As for the reconciliation of man with man, its achievement was announced in the following terms: "The habit of living naked on beaches during the summer would be, I am sure, the best way of teaching human beings, and especially young people, to know one another better, both physically and morally, and this custom would quickly bring about the disappearance of hypocrisy, which poisons the heart." A reversal with respect to dressing, nudism is also a moral (and not immoral) reversal that substitutes the ethics of purity and transparency for the ethics of sin and redemption. For what does one actually find in a nudist "tribe"? "Men, women, and children, in the attire of an earthly paradise, giving themselves over collectively to the joys of heliotherapy, physical culture, camping, and sports."[37]

What is nudism, in sum, whether in its integral form or in a modified version? Nothing, it would seem, but an "attempt at moralization—through the negation of modesty and habituation to nudity—along with an attempt at physical regeneration by exposing the body to the air and to the sun's rays."[38] Then what effects did this model have? With its irrepressible excesses, after the visible body, the image of the ardent body began to appear on beaches—the body that would burn in the sun by unclothing itself to an ever greater extent.

Like sea bathing, sunbathing was now no longer conceived as a medical aid to be administered, timed, and doled out in doses.[39] The therapeutic objective had been replaced by the symbolic. The dream of regeneration had won out over the perspective of mere treatment, and the body was no longer so much that of a sick person exposed to the sun's rays, the wind, or the waves in view of a cure as a body offered to the elements in view of a renaissance. Thus to the great dismay of hygienists and bourgeois citizens hostile to tawny skin tones, heliotherapy turned into sunbathing; no longer a remedy but a desire—heliotropism and even "heliolatry," sun-worshipping.

"The passion for the sun is irrational, and every beach offers colorful examples of this," Jean Viard has written.[40] In fact—for every schism lights its own sacrificial fires—in its day the naturist cult of the sun consumed some of its own practitioners, for example, Nicolas Dragoumis, "the true precursor of naturism in France and also its first victim, since he died of sunstroke."[41] But nothing could stop it. The "naked monkeys" also loved to warm themselves in the sun, even at the risk of sunburn. The naturist model thus spread, although rather slowly. In 1944 Albert Lecoq's Sun Club made nudism, which had been more or less the preserve of aristocrats up to then, accessible to people of all classes and conditions. And if Paul Morand attests in 1960 to the striking triumph of the model on beaches ("the new generations are avid for sun at any price, even that of frightful burns, hideous peeling, and voluntary incineration"), sunbathing as a fashionable activity really took hold only after the war.[42]

Why this lag, a clear sign of resistance to the spread of the model? Perhaps because life is a novel, and things happen in reality the way they do in fiction. Robinson has his shipwreck in the early pages of his adventures, and only discovers his "tan" companion midway through his account. Similarly, Théo Varlet got a tan on the Île du Levant in 1909, but only starting about 1945 was it "a real act of snobbery" to come back from a stay at the beach with a tan.[43] The hedonistic, balneophilic, and heliotropic inversion was sketched out before the First World War, asserted in the period between the wars, and diffused beyond the territory of the "naked monkeys" only after the Second World War.

In the wake of the Crusoe of the Île du Levant, let us note that nudity did not bear sole responsibility for the lag. Nakedness was to be condemned, but so was tanning, the epidermic corollary of taking off one's clothes. A dark "skin tone" was shocking, as Théo Varlet says. It shocked bourgeois citizens and health professionals alike because "medical discourse on the whiteness of the skin, a sign of health, perpetuates in particular the aristocratic morality of ostentatious leisure," a morality that "fears tanned skin for all the degrading physical activity it can evoke." Under these conditions, tanned skin is an illness.[44] To get a tan is to regress, not only socially but also in human terms. A living bronze, the individual with a tan is fantasized as the scandalous bastard offspring of the "naked monkey" and the sun, a degraded being whose skin, the object of an inverted pigmentation, evokes all the hideous animality associated with the "black man," the regression and savagery to which immodest exposure of the body to light will lead. The excessive consumption of the sun's rays taints the vacationer with the colors of the native, the fisherman, the proletarian, and other imaginary Savages.

For at the origin of heliophobia and the scandal of tanning—the tanning that made it possible, as Michelet said as early as 1861, to become "dark as an African"—there was also, beyond its sociological connotations, a real phantasm of racial metamorphosis that is cast by some in positive terms as a symbol of regeneration, of a change of skin and thus of resurrection, but that is always deciphered by others as the morbid sign of a primitive fall.[45]

From the experimental robinsonnades of the period between the wars to the mass robinsonnade that came later, it took several decades of reflection on the part of seaside vacationers for the hedonist, naturist, and heliophilist reversal to be truly accomplished, for it to be accepted and spread, adapted and translated in reality. The "naked monkey," with or without a genital covering, would then leave his island, and the "black man" would finally invade our vacation shores.

Scandal at Eden-Roc, or the Exotic Invasion

It needs to be made clear here that the onshore landing of the "naked monkey" and the "black man" corresponded to a genuine mutation in the very identity of seaside vacationing. This mutation, pertaining to the bather's personality, presupposes a total psychological reversal in the concept of residential seaside vacationing. This activity is no longer conceptualized, along with the therapeutic and social imperatives that justified it initially, as a simple extension of the social universe to the waves and beyond, but as a different world, or, more precisely, as a counterworld opposed to the "internal" norms of sociability. In fact, it is envisioned as a world in a state of rupture, explicitly valorizing reversal, and, at least in appearance, the rejection of taboos, inequalities, and other obligatory and coerced behaviors generated by urban society.

Contrary to a too-commonly-held assumption according to which in 1936 all of France suddenly began to take to the roads and headed to beaches in particular, the extension of beach vacations to the masses really began in the 1950s. Earlier, though, around the edges, we find a few signs "in the air" that point in a common direction, toward restoration of "wildness" to the shore. By means of various simulacra and simulations, these signs too translate and pave the way for the "reprimitivization" of the seaside.

Shortly before the First World War, in Coutainville, for example, a cabin of a new sort rented for twice as much as an ordinary one (fifteen francs for a month compared to eight in Houlgate). It must be said that these cabins were actually "grass shacks" made of local rye or wheat straw—"shacks" whose success (hence the higher rent) seemed to announce the birth of a new desire for rusticity or primitiveness on the part of bathers.[46]

Another sign, in the period between the wars: in 1935, on the Côte d'Azur, Dimitri Philipoff (who was to be a Club Med village chief in the 1950s) created the White Bear Club. This club, which operated until the war broke out, was open all summer long. Patronized by Marcel L'Herbier, who was its honorary president, and Danielle Darrieux, the club was a place where people "of course practiced sports, *but in particular they took off their clothes:* they left their constricting city clothing in the cloakroom and lived in bathing trunks."[47] This worldly robinsonnade took the form of a ponderous naturism that did not embrace full nudity but that nevertheless anticipated the "landing" of undressed vacationers; it paved the way for a more complete reversal through the adoption of tribal behavior marked by the symbolic abandonment of clothes. In this context, the rite of undressing signified at once a radical rejection of a dominant, urbanized, "civilized" mode of sociability, and a communitarian integration into a different form of conviviality, that of a simplified, "primitive" universe.

Beyond a new vacation market, we also have here the unmistakable outline of a new way of imagining a seaside sojourn, along with myths of origin and Crusoean ideas that still remained unformulated, except for the occasional nudist on his island, like Théo Varlet. After the war this imagined idyll began to be translated into real vacation opportunities, just when seaside vacationing was beginning to acquire the means suited to its dreams by establishing the first leisure communities, enclaves or artificial "islands" that were clearly conceived as small inverted worlds and thus as exotic stages well suited to blocking out the surrounding sociocultural realities.

Among the first of these small worlds, the villages of the Club Méditerranée come immediately to mind.[48] The first "village" (still only a campground with canvas tents) was opened at Calvi in 1949 under the name Club Olympique. The Crusoean Olympia in the Club Med version was just beginning to take shape. In 1950 a village of 200 tents opened in Alcudia Bay on Majorca. Next came Corfu, Djerba, where villages were propagated by "clustering." This concept, which is quite well known today, soon spread from Cefalù to Tahiti, from the Mediterranean to Polynesia.[49] Conforming in this respect to the geographic archetype of the robinsonnade, it spread most often from island to island: the French West Indies, the Baleares, Bali, the Caribbean, Corsica, Corfu, Djerba, the Falklands, New Caledonia, and Sicily.

Still, the important factor in this redefinition of the seaside sojourn as an exotic break with society is not so much the remarkable expansion of the Club over three or four decades (which is only a consequence attesting to the success of a new vacation dream) as the symbolic material that its invention summons up, namely, a Polynesian restructuring of the site. This expansion has had the effect not only of introducing Tahitian signs into Greece and elsewhere, but also—hence the appropriateness of Henri Raymond's expression, "concrete utopia"—of decontextualizing the summer vacation locale.

Decontextualization (the absence of reference to the local context) is a characteristic feature of the seaside universe. It has already been evoked twice—in connection with souvenir objects and in connection with the evolution of the thematic content of postcards, which today have very little to do with the indigenous world (see chapter 1). We find it again here as a formal project, in the framework of the Club at its birth. The Club's founder, Gérard Blitz, and his wife, Claudine, decided to introduce the Tahitian grass shack into Corfu in 1953. By the end of that year, five huts had been built, and at the end of the winter of 1954 advertising copy could make the following claims: "Some 500 huts have been built in place of tents. The hour of revelation is approaching. There will be no disappointments. An entirely new village awaits you, with its throng of fresh, cozy round huts that seem to be growing here in the Temari gardens, with a friendly boldness, under the hairy cone of their roofs of blond straw."[50]

It is important to understand clearly what was happening here. It might be said that decontextualization was already at work during the construction of the first seaside resorts in the nineteenth century, which replaced the fishermen's village with the model of the "modern city," imitating Paris in particular.[51] Indeed, the term "bathing city" was used. But this initial decontextualization brought about just the opposite of an exotic break: what was reproduced was the dominant social model, the urban universe. Far from instituting a break, the early builders extended the familiar environment of aristocratic or bourgeois summer vacationers to the seashore. And if, later on, from Deauville to Biarritz, people set about building anachronistic chalets, "Moorish or Persian villages, iron palaces and zinc minarets," the "exoticization" remained superficial.[52] It entailed an architectural simulation that scarcely transformed the vacationer's inner life or residential lifestyle at all. In the Club Med, on the contrary, in passing from simulacrum to simulation (that is, from trompe-l'oeil to reconstitution) with the Tahitian huts, the builders were appealing to the primitive sense of the hut and to the life of the tribe, in contact with nature,[53] to a minimal and egalitarian material and ecological ecology that blends or obscures social classes, to a generalized paring down of seaside life, "thus harmonizing the architecture of bodies with that of the village":[54] minimally undressed bodies on the one hand, architectural simplicity on the other.

However exemplary it may be, we must not let the Club Méditerranée become the tree that hides the forest; it must not be allowed to obscure the scope of the "exotic invasion" that triggered the "rewilding" of the seaside universe. The Club is indeed a phenomenon of its time and not isolated historically in terms of its symbolic principle. Its strategy of rupture, its "Polynesianism," could be found elsewhere during the same period, in other forms—less spectacular, perhaps, and more localized, or, on the contrary, more widely diffused, and more ephemeral in certain cases; today, absorbed into the everyday life of the beach, they tend to pass unnoticed. In any event, the desire for rupture, for the seashore as a privileged place for a decontextualizing experience, has nevertheless been expressed again and again, attesting here and there to the scope of the transformation of collective mentalities and sensibilities.

Paul Morand recalls "divine May evenings" where "a Polynesian calm presided over the Greek islands, from Crete to the Sporades, from Milos to Mykonos, bringing to mind the poems of Robert Louis Stevenson": and further on he reproaches the beach at Arcachon for being "too elegant, too 'yachting cap'"—in short, for not breaking with social convention and entering into the game of "going native."[55] Similarly, another writer recalls Saint-Tropez in the late 1940s and early 1950s in the following terms: "Prévert's poems, bare feet, love on the sand, liberty, equality, all those post-war ideas that ought to have died in two or three years and on which we lived until 1975—the sort of Rousseauist truth we thought we had achieved in Saint-Tropez."[56] Is it a coincidence that, in that era, "the owner of the Sphinx—the biggest brothel of the day— . . . had reconstituted a Polynesian village at Bastide Blanche"?[57] Polynesia (here too), bare feet, Rousseau, equality:

in short, the myth of the noble savage that saw a new Robinson appearing on French coasts, looking at Friday—and even at the other Savages—in a different way.

The signs of this feverish exoticization of the seaside sojourn multiplied, along the shore and in discourse, leaving their mark along the way on leading sites of luxury seaside living; these too were compelled for a time to sacrifice to the fashion for "going native" and for Polynesianism. Thus in 1951, at Eden-Roc, a sumptuous hotel built at the tip of the Antibes cape, one could "pay a lot to spend the day in the austerity of a little hut village," for each guest at Eden-Roc could rent "a hut on the water's edge where, as the Figaro article says, you will be able to live like a Polynesian all day long." The cartoon by Senep accompanying the article says a good deal about the conservative perception of this exotic innovation: a new guest at the village asks the director if "renting a bum's costume costs extra"! In other words, seen through the filter of a reactionary interpretation, this exoticization is essentially perceived as a way of turning the vacationer into a bum, that is (the old fantasy of going backward!), as a social—and even human—regression. One comes here not only to play at being poor, but also to play at being an outcast, a "nigger." The article in fact describes the misadventure of a South American billionaire, Enrico Canning, who, before fleeing to the United States (where he made a fortune), lived to the age of seventeen in a favella, that is (according to the author of the article), in "one of those villages of straw huts and shacks where idle Negroes live as they please, going down to the city to work only one day out of three." And what happened to the billionaire? While "Canning was taking a nap under the awning of his hut . . ., he suddenly sat up and shouted. He had just had a horrible nightmare as he dozed. He thought he had returned to the favella of his adolescence. A samba tune on the radio of a nearby hut had suddenly brought home to him how much the two locales had in common."[58]

Here, the exoticization of the shore and of seaside vacationing is shocking. Still, it is not the scandalized attitude that is important, but rather the accompanying feeling of decadence or perversion, betrayed by the humorous reaction and the dubious commentary in the face of the novelty of this "bum's" Polynesia. Yet what is an era of decadence if not "an era in which history is speeding up, as Daniel Halévy put it, one in which signs of the passage from one civilization to another proliferate, one in which the opposition between two structures stands out to the naked eye"?[59] In this context, where the eye is not the only thing that is naked, moreover, this is exactly what is taking place before our eyes: the passage from one seaside civilization to another, where a new vacation structure is organizing a "newly native" universe and is thus countering the one that had been established in the nineteenth century.

From then on, what structure and what universe are in question? And what collective project justifies the historical production of the one and the other? These questions are at the center of this study, but it would be premature to answer them now. However, we can already see the outlines if not of an explanation then at least of an interpretation, through systems of indices and the retrospective coherence of an evolution.

THE SCANDAL OF SEASIDE INDIFFERENCE

To go back to the last point mentioned, it seems first of all, in the context of the contemporary seaside mutation, that one must not overestimate in ethnological terms the "Polynesian" revolution of the 1940s and 1950s by perceiving it naively as the trace of acculturation or of real contact, as the sign of the objective penetration of one culture by another. "Polynesianism"—the habitat and lifestyle that it introduced into the vacation universe—must be evaluated in symbolic terms. "Polynesianism" was above all a symbol, a symptom, and a simulacrum: the emblematic image of another world—a counterworld—and not the result of an authentic ethnological transference. It refers not so much to a specific foreign cultural reality as to an idea—along the lines of the vacation resort called "Club Polynésie" which, in 1957, in an advertisement published in a magazine called *Nous Deux* [The two of us], offered Corsica, Spain, and Yugoslavia as destinations—that is, it offered "Polynesianism" without Polynesia!

Coming to fill the beachfront stage, "Polynesianism" appears to be chiefly an imported décor destined not to enable vacationers to discover a different culture but to facilitate the inversion of certain codes of sociability, the restoration of inhibited human relations and attitudes, and thus to favor play and the stylized expression of roles, behaviors, and relationships that were ordinarily inhibited by social norms. Historically, the Polynesian simulacrum, from Calvi to Saint-Tropez and from Corfu to Eden-Roc, thus fulfilled the dual function of revealer and symbolic accelerator at the end of a general process of hedonistic transformation and naturist banalization of the shore, an evolution that had already been announced by the betrayal of beach-wear, and even before that by the dissident emergence of balneophilia.

We must get used to this "scandalous" idea, at least from the stand-point of a certain vacation ethic: the leisure universe taking shape here has nothing cultural or touristic about it. In connection with con-temporary seaside resort life, one cannot properly speak of "cultural tourism"—where is the mobility? Where is the element of explora-tion, and the traveler's curiosity about the wide world?—nor even of cultural vacationing, in the sense of discovering through "immersion" a "typical" site and indigenous customs. A different sort of immersion is at work here. Let us recapitulate the major stages in the creation of this new universe.

1. It all begins with a politics of the void: the colonization of the shore, the capture of the Savages (fishermen and other seaside popu-lations), and an appropriation of shorefront real estate that left, be-tween people and the water, a long desert-like fringe to be traversed, dry-shod, by "crowds of pleasant folk" and other Robinsons in frock coats. The separation between land and water, the disappearance and folklorization of the natives, and the reproduction of city life on the seashore were the marking events of this episode, which was complet-ed by the cultural decontextualization of the shore with the establish-ment of major resorts. There remained a vast empty stage, battered by waves and the sea's fierce foam.

2. Next the bather came forward, at first cautiously defying the swells, warmly dressed, moored to the shore, and limited in his ac-tions by a medical authority that applied treatment methods to the sea. Then Robinson "got used to the sea," abandoned his frock coat, took off more clothes, learned to swim, and exposed more and more of his skin to the sun, going well beyond the usual prescriptions for healthy living. He asserted his autonomy. In other words, by shedding his clothes he threw off not only the mooring lines that had kept him on shore, but also the signs that had attached him physically to the social realm. He gradually rid himself of worldly symbols, became a visible body, created a scandal by becoming a nudist and an even greater one when the color of his suntanned skin made him look like Friday. This was the moment of reversal: the bather turned Savage. This led to great confusion in people's minds—especially with the naturist clamor in the period between the two world wars.

3. Next, some critical assistance made it possible to move beyond the troubled period on which the second episode ended: the Polynesian model, the picturesque stratagem and encoding of place and practices, the symbolic accelerator owing to which the Man of the Beach achieved reversal, the definitive rewilding of the shorefront according to his dreams, the total decontextualization of the site. For this site no longer had anything in common (this was its founding convention) with either the past or the present, or with local society, ancient or native, or with modern society, on the spot or in the vicinity. Here the beach was born, psychologically and materially, as a world apart, a third universe.

Seen retrospectively, the invention of the contemporary beach is the history of a detachment, a separation. The marginal territory to which this separation gave rise first "exoticized" the native population the better to exclude it, then gradually "exoticized" itself in order to exclude itself from the world in turn. This leisure territory was decontextualized in such a way that it was no longer fundamentally perceived and experienced by its user either as an "authentic" site or as a reproduction of the social universe from which the user came: it functioned neither as a foreign land nor as a conservatory nor as a mirror society. The new beach was a place to which one did not go to discover a world or to find one's own world again, whether present or past, modern or traditional. Moreover (and this is a significant index), whether they dressed "up" or "down," visitors donned costumes here that belonged neither to the city-dweller nor to the native—even if during a transitional period the so-called marine costume was adopted. (We shall return to this question in chapter 8.) The beach was thus a closed space, the theater of a strange quest that was guided neither by the goal of discovering the Other nor by the desire to reconquer some roots of one's own identity. Utilized neither for defamiliarization nor for refamiliarization,[60] this world was located on the margins of two complementary undertakings, cultural decentering and cultural self-renewal. In fact, as a totally decontextualized space of simulation, the beach world was a world in and of itself, an island in psychological terms: a world behind closed doors, indifferent to the world outside.

Of course, it is not because Robinson and Friday abandon casinos and other fortresses along the banks and prefer straw huts to bathing cabins or bathing trunks to shorts that the seaside coastline is suddenly nothing more than a bead on a string of villages. During the turning point of the 1940s and '50s, it was almost as if there were two Robinsons on the same island, but on different banks. Certain zones along the shore were conservative, ideologically and structurally still very close to traditional bourgeois vacation resorts; others, such as nudist camps, seemed to be set aside for the latest "shipwreck victims." Neither Saint-Tropez nor Corfu abolished Deauville or Biarritz; and at Eden-Roc, between the hut and the hotel, the time had come for the two trends to coexist, as we have just seen.

Let us make no mistake about it: the Polynesian village was only one model. It can doubtless be viewed as the emblematic figure of this "third universe," but it was nevertheless only a symptom, not a general pattern—just as the nudist movement, itself a sign of the times from the 1910s and '20s on, did not imply the widespread acceptance of nudity on beaches. From this standpoint, the resort village was thus only a spectacular and obvious expression of a new way of imagining seaside leisure. As compared to the overall mass of vacation practices, it is in fact a relatively minor phenomenon. In France today, all destinations included, only 5 percent of the French opt for the resort village structure for their summer vacation.[61]

But the important point is that the vacation village is, precisely, a model. Like the idea of nudity, the image of the village captures the imagination. An archetype, a place of condensation, a reference, it crystallizes, attests, and diffuses the idea of a vacation sociability haunted by a "primitive" communitarian dream—an active dream that, independently of the first villages that synthesized it, now leaves many traces on vacationers' bodies, beaches, clothing, manners, and customs. A dream without which the contemporary seaside universe, with its promiscuities, the density of its nudity, its wandering gazes, its authorized and exhibited stripping-down, its simplified sociability, and its minimalist or provocative dress would doubtless not have become what it is today.

Then, too, this village and its genesis allow us to approach more intimately—from the "Polynesian" end of the telescope, as it were—a vacation mentality and sensibility that are still not very well known, lost to view owing to the current vagueness of anthropological definitions of the so-called touristic practices. Even so, Alain Ehrenberg tells a story that touches on the very origin of the village concept in the Club Méditerranée and is worth recalling here.[62]

In 1945 Gérard Blitz, the Club's future founder, was charged by the Belgian government with the task of reinserting former concentration-camp inmates into society. To carry out this assignment he rented a hotel in Haute-Savoie. In this place cut off from the world, everything was made available to the survivors in view of their "deconditioning." "The prehistory of the Club," Blitz says, "was right here" in that experience of therapeutic insularity. The experience came back to mind immediately when he visited the Club's first village in Calvi in 1949. "It was in teaching survivors [like Robinson] how to live again," Alain Ehrenberg comments, "that Blitz invented the Club's special niche, as it were: human relations."

We shall return to this anecdote later on, for it bears traces of the idea that people sometimes require a small transitional world in order to relearn to live in the larger world; they need to inhabit an intermediate refuge of conviviality, an island, rather than to crisscross the planet. The anecdote is troubling. And if it is still too soon to draw its full lesson, the comparison of Club Med clients to concentration-camp victims leads us to begin to envisage the existence of a vacationer of a different sort, one who eludes the classical exploratory categories of discovery or return to roots. What is central to the preoccupations of this type of vacationer is neither the exploration of the world in its vastness nor the problem of his own origins, but rather the social bond that is lacking, like the famous missing link, in the space-time of his life.

What this vacationer's imagination demands is not that he remember the antipodes or recollect the traditional sources of life, not that he encounter the geographical Other or the historical Other, but rather that he forget, by going to places where self-consciousness and the feeling of being someone are lost. Indifference to the world here is thus not an immoral or meaningless attitude. It fully justifies on its own account the invention of a "third universe."

One woman evoked her stay at the Club Med in Corfu in 1960 in the following terms: "I was twenty and I had practically never traveled. It was a stunning revelation to live with my body in the sun." In short, "well before the obsession with one's figure and one's look, it was the discovery of one's own body."[63]

"Man is a social animal; set him apart from the community, isolate him, and his mind goes to pieces, his character deteriorates, his heart becomes full of ridiculous emotions. As many wild notions take root in his head as weeds on a patch of barren soil."[64] This is true of prisoners, concentration-camp victims, solitary recluses, all isolated beings, people shut in, like Robinson on his island—until Friday shows up. And it is still true in a society like ours, so ready to get along without solitude.

So? Well, there is always the beach—where so many fools are getting a tan!

PART II

At the Beach

It was their quietness that made me lean toward them fascinated the first time I saw the axolotls. Obscurely I seemed to understand their secret will, to abolish space and time with an indifferent immobility. I knew better later.

—Julio Cortázar, "Axolotl" (1963)

The late 1940s, the early 1950s: was this period indeed the great turning point in seaside vacationing, it too liberated and triumphant? Or, in the wake of scandal, social upheaval, and war, was it not rather a period of reaction, reconstruction, and return to order, all of which were sources of normalization, fracture, and division, factors that visibly separated the conformist majority from eccentric minorities at this critical juncture in the history of the beach?

Denizens of popular beaches or bourgeois shores, wonderstruck travelers on paid vacations or blasé dignitaries, vacationers on busmen's holidays or zealous watchdogs of the aristocratic seaside tradition, the former still novices and the latter forever reticent in the face of always-too-rapid progress in the direction of undressing: above and beyond their differences and the social segmentation of the territory, from Nice to Fort-Mahon, from Golf-Juan to La Baule or Saint-Brévin-les-Pins to Trouville, all these figures regrouped on family beaches, among themselves, class by social class, but in a single moral universe based on a "reasonable" approach to undressing and the sociability of leisure. From one shore to another little changed materially but the quality of the bathing suits (wool for Friday, silk for Robinson), along with the accompanying distinctions in the conditions of the stay. In psychological terms, everyone had the identical resort experience of seminudity in his or her own home: the experience of half-measures, between conventions and their overturning.

During this period of "shrunken" naturism, imperturbable nudists still haunted the pine groves of the Levant like wild children, while others, of indistinct origin, Polynesians from the operetta, beach bums for a summer or depraved Scouts, gathered and mingled in exotic villages. The worst rumors circulated about these places of damnation and their inhabitants' strange customs.

Does this mean that from this point on there were at least two Robinsons—and thus as many Fridays—on vacation islands? And if so, were there not at least one or two too many? In the immediate aftermath of the Second World War, mass seaside leisure seemed to shatter into enemy strategies, into morally incompatible models of conviviality, into robinsonnades whose contrasting forms illustrate such different styles of summer gregariousness that they seem irreconcilable.

Some people condemned, others mocked, while still others affected indifference. In fact, if "all that breathes of a casual, carefree state," as André Gide had already written with reference to a stopover in Calvi in the 1930s, and if "the atmosphere invites one to summary physical pleasures, to games, to debaucheries," among naked and half-naked people, Polynesians and conformists, suits and pareos, people looked upon one another rather as if they were ceramic dogs.[1] The provocations of one group were met by the troubled observations of the others, with the equivocal curiosity of the wise about the mad.

To put the question another way, could one Robinson have been hiding another? Could there have been a second shipwreck on the island, unnoticed by the survivor of the first disaster? An incredible discovery! Could it be that the other side of the island was inhabited by debauched doubles of Crusoe and Friday? This novelistic metaphor, intended to sum up a social situation, is worth exploring.

In fact, and this is what history has retained through its multiple literary avatars, there was first of all the emblematic image from the novel, the lawmaking and organizing Robinson, the one Defoe himself was glorifying: the world-making Robinson (see Introduction). This dominating Robinson drove away the Savages, or at least kept them at a respectful distance. If he could have done so, he would have locked them up or wiped them out. A demigod, he reconstructed space and life according to his own principles; then he saved Friday and educated him, bending him to his own values, customs, and norms. As it happens, he sent some of the Savages abroad or into ports, and he subjected the others to his own aesthetic, worldly, therapeutic, or technological models, making himself by turns an artist, an aristocrat, a doctor, or a hotel-builder. He pacified. This was the obsessive Robinson whom Michel Tournier describes in *Friday* as a rational monster: the maniacal Robinson, law become man. He was the *superego* of beach vacations, at once canon, policy, and rule.

And then there was the other Robinson, the occult, sentimental, and weak Robinson who sometimes experienced waves of melancholy, the one who felt drawn to Friday and thus to the Savages from whose clutches Robinson had pried him loose. Defoe carefully avoids exploring the relationship that forms here, in this rescue, this adoption, this friendship; he refrains from expressing clearly the dimension of desire in Crusoe, avoids lifting the veil over the impulses of this hero who has been suffering up to now from being "divided from Mankind, . . . banish'd from humane Society."[2] But Michel Gall in *La vie sexuelle de Robinson Crusoé* has dared to take a few indiscreet steps into this obscure region of the myth, conjuring up a passionate Robinson who, like Flaubert admiring the bathers' bodies, looks at Friday's with terror and fascination and discovers on the sand, terrified and fascinated, "the imprint of wild threatening forces that symbolize desire. This is where cannibals indulge in their orgies as Robinson watches, entranced, a voyeur threatened by the animality of collective rejoicing."[3] Here is the *id* of the beach: the shore as space of desire, instinct, and love, not of authority, a space of invitation to "voluptuous interludes"—the "evil" genius of the place, in a sense, that haunts and attracts Crusoe.

Thus we encounter the "reasonable" summer vacationer of the 1950s, a "voyeur threatened" but attracted, who lets himself be tempted by an excursion to the Île du Levant and embarks at Lavandou.

He behaves like the second Robinson. He gives in to the desire to see, to approach naked bodies—to go, as it were, to the other side of the island, to go beyond the law, or at least to go halfway toward breaking it by approaching what is taboo. Far from his "textile" beach, this voyeur-vacationer, his heart beating fast, now finds himself approaching "the island of naked men." Ill at ease, an anxious explorer, he disembarks. Photographs are forbidden. Already, during the crossing, he felt somehow threatened in his guilty clandestinity as he understood that around him there were clothed nudists who were awaiting only the arrival in port to get undressed.

Here he is in the village. With its shops and its bars, it is an airlock: a universe of transition between the dressed and the undressed, in which nudists wear the bare minimum required by the rules. With his hat, his shirt, his shorts, and his spy's sunglasses, he has never felt so dressed, or, finally, so much an intruder. The useless eye of his camera is miserably slung over his shoulder like a sign of evil intentions. He feels out of place rubbing shoulders in this way, at the same counter or in the same shop, with these primitive folk in loincloths, bare-breasted. All the embarrassment is on his side. And where there is embarrassment . . .

At the end of the village, isolating the beach, making it an island on the island, there is a high barrier. This is the frontier beyond which the real territory of naked men begins. Through the chainlink fencing, "one can see a little." But if the visitor's indiscreet gaze crosses it "a little," his body stops here, impotent, on this Maginot line of denuded seaside leisure. Already shocked by so much quasi-nudity, he cannot go farther. The "law," his morality, his model of the robinsonnade forbid him to cross the line. There was an eye in the fence looking mockingly at the summer visitor who had deserted the ordinary beaches. There is worse: during his visit to the island, he had to undergo a veritable assault. When the visitor passed a property in which a man was sunbathing in his garden, "the man got up from behind the fence in order to show us that he was really naked!" This militant exhibitionism was for its time a provocation that surpassed the threshold of tolerance of our semivoyeur. Between attraction and reprobation, Friday is caught off guard.

Forty years later, this explorer, now retired, remembers. He smiles and indulges in retrospective irony over the ridiculousness of the escapade, the discourse of his scandalized companions, and the customs of those days—customs in terms of which "bare breasts were really something!" Still, he adds, as an excuse or a justification: "You have to put it in context." For all that, even with hindsight, he did not become a nudist. No, really, he didn't go that far! From the desire to see a nude body to the desire to be one, there is a long way to go. But at age seventy he nevertheless dared to buy himself an "unthinkable" mini bathing suit, which shocked his wife. Unquestionably, since his shameful escapade on the Île du Levant, something has happened in the mind of this postwar conformist Friday. A question of "context" indeed.

Communitarian and naturist, destroying the civilizing world of the first Robinson, is it a second Robinson who is appearing here? He is no less a demigod than the other. One always recognizes him as the pioneer tinkerer, instigator of opinions and communities, builder of huts and village chief, from Varlet to Blitz. An inventor of robinsonnades, he is the ordering mind behind new practices. But by totally substituting hedonist emulation for social conventions, sharing for domination, the cult of the body for modesty, and an egalitarian tribalism for class divisions, he has modified the earlier contractual relations between Crusoe and Friday. From this point on, between himself and his double, he prefers exchange to education. Robinson has identified with the image of the Savage, with the simple life and happy naïveté of the naked Indian, innocent of any social stigmata.

Under these conditions, in the light of this tale of an escapade on the Île du Levant, an excursion characteristic of the transitional period in which all the ambiguity of Crusoean psychology is reproduced in the vacationer's gaze, we may revisit the metaphor and change our hypothesis, in order to account for a new situation.

In fact, there are not now, like enemy brothers, two Robinsons on the vacation island, but still only one and the same. It is just that the shipwreck survivor has changed sides. He has gone over to the other side of the island, to the side of pleasure, leaving behind on the first beaches, as if released in his own custody, the docile and well-behaved Friday of the early stage of seaside vacationing, the Friday that he had taken care to tame, to dress, and to instruct—the bathers of the first generation. From now on, Robinson is going to save a different Friday, the victim of other Savages who go by the names of War and Society and no longer Stupor and Illness. This Friday is Blitz and his fellow survivors; and before that the prophets of nudity at war against social hypocrisy and the ideology of bathing trunks. Robinson has changed shores and adopted a different pedagogy.

In other words, Robinson has vanished. Friday is lost and goes off looking for him. He goes to the Île du Levant (later, he will go to the Club Méditerranée) and finds his master. From a respectful distance he observes him and discovers, astounded, as Crusoe earlier discovered the imprint on the sand, that he is living there in the company of new Fridays, free men living in the same huts and on intimate terms with the master, who like them is undressed! It is as if Robinson had changed his mind. Friday remembers that at the end of his first night in the grotto where he had slept naked, Robinson's first concern was to give him clothes.[4] Here it is just the opposite; the model has been reversed:

> They lived in bathing suits, they didn't even get dressed for meals. Later, the pareo "imported" from Tahiti (along with an ethic of farniente) was introduced by Claudine Blitz, Gérard's wife, who had lived there in the 1940s.[5]

A certain beach society, dressed and conformist, has come to an end. Friday has just seen this; and when he returns to Lavandou, disturbed, he is haunted by the image. Even if he still finds it strange, from now on it is part of him; he talks about it and thus diffuses it, as many others have done before and since.

The rest, over the years of excursions and experiences, tales and testimony, fashions and influences, was nothing more than a matter of acculturation, recognition, and progressive transfer of the new seaside universe onto ordinary beaches following the slow rhythm of the rise of the desire to be part of it. A mixed desire, a cautious desire: the transmission and popularization of the discovery of this new World, of the other side of the island, on the beach of Mr. Everyman.

The seaside assimilation of the rudiments of this new universe, with certain adaptations, filtrations, or rebalancings of the model,[6] was accomplished only with the help of a certain number of supporting factors: Polynesianism was one of them, children were another.[7] Our curious postwar fellow, as we have seen, did not become a nudist for all that, and during the transfer onto "textile" beaches, one cannot deny that certain choices were made that soften the reference somewhat. But by the time this hedonist robinsonnade was finally imported onto the "Friday" beaches, the customs that had been established were in fact modified ones. A new seaside landscape appeared, one whose center of gravity was henceforth explicit:

> The cult of the body is at the heart of this new way of life. A body that one dreams of strengthening through sport, of awakening through a summertime sexuality, of tanning to a golden hue and putting on stage by means of a variety of costumes. A body that is loved, cleansed, healthy and purified. Suffering bodies are far away. The leisure body has taken over.[8]

The body. The body as idol. Portrait and landscape, the body is the luminous center, the vanishing point, once blind or blinded (see chapter 3) but now radiant, from which and around which contemporary seaside theatricality is orchestrated, the genius of the beach, where the setting amplifies the expression of these dreamlike physical properties of the vacationing ego. Pure water, golden sand, a site that has been "cleansed," purified of the world, in the image of the unclothed body.

4. The Dream of the Shore

*(or, How Robinson,
after cleaning up his beach,
found himself under the spell
of strange dreams and suddenly
experienced a bizarre feeling
of weightlessness)*

Often have I experienced this intimate love of man for shelter, on any
shore, however solitary, unknown, or desert.
—Alphonse de Lamartine, *A Pilgrimage to the Holy Land* (May 23, 1833)

Through his character Roger Sheldrake, presented as a leisure special-
ist doing field studies in Hawaii, the novelist David Lodge sums up the
way anthropologists of "tourism" perceive vacations as follows:

Two basic types of holiday may be discriminated, according to whether
they emphasize exposure to culture or nature: the holiday as pilgrimage and the holiday as paradise. The former is typically represented
by the bussed sightseeing tour of famous cities, museums, châteaux,
etc. (Sheldrake, 1984); the latter by the beach resort holiday, in which
the subject strives to get back to a state of nature, or prelapsarian
innocence.[1]

After spending a certain amount of time myself in this world of specialists, by attending conferences and reading, I am obliged to note
that this way of seeing things indeed largely prevails today.

This new and sharply dualist vacation typology leads scholars to
distribute the diversity of vacation practices along an axis whose extreme points, presented as opposite poles, are "nature" and "culture."
Between the two we find a space accommodating more or less balanced mixtures.

In the universe of leisure travel, there really are, at opposite poles, lovers of cathedrals and lovers of unspoiled nature. In Nelson H. H. Graburn's typology (which is probably the clearest synthesis of this approach), the first group, under the heading of *cultural tourism,* is classified as "historical tourism," while the second group, under the heading of *nature tourism,* is classified as "ecological tourism." Still according to Graburn, the ideally balanced mixture would be achieved in "ethnic tourism," oriented equally toward natural sites and the traditional societies that inhabit them.[2]

And where does the beach fit in? For Graburn, this vacation destination falls in the category of "recreational tourism," under the heading of *nature tourism*—the vacation as paradise, in Sheldrake's terms. Let us note for our part, first of all, that since beach vacations are immobile and residential, and are indeed sometimes labeled "passive," whether they are focused on relaxation or sports, they do not come under the heading of tourism at all; they belong rather to the summer-resort type of vacations—seaside resorts, in our case.[3]

But let us focus for a moment on the singular persistence of the prejudice that consists in stubbornly situating the seaside universe within the sphere of *nature* vacations. What nature is in question, then? And what "innocence"?

While we can acknowledge nature's insistent presence in the experiences of discovery, exploration, or renewal offered by ethnic or ecological tourism or by certain "green" resorts (crisscrossed by unspoiled sites, offering hiking paths, "agrotourism," or isolated stays deep in the countryside), the presence of the natural as such has a certain tendency to evaporate at the beach, to dissipate as a primordial factor, and, finally, like the cultural signs that formerly marked the shore (see chapter 1), to disappear in the framework of the empty stage the seaside space has become.

Among the various aesthetic procedures that contribute to the conditions of possibility of the contemporary dream of the shore, one in particular is of crucial importance, although it is too often ignored: the denaturing of the shore itself, its methodical falsification as a natural site.

Seaweedophobes and Beachophiles

Historically, we began by chasing various Savages away from our shores. For the beach stage to become a great empty theater definitively favorable to the unfurling of a multicolored forest of umbrellas, we had to get rid of yet another wildness, after the ethnic form: natural wildness, the ultimate savagery in contact with which the genius of the beach could not be fully expressed.

For we are obliged to recognize that the contemporary "beach person" is anything but a naturalist. If he still practices (a little) fishing for mussels or shrimp along the beach, almost no one but children continue to observe and tease the animals that live at the bottom of the sea and in pools along the shore. At the very most, our swimmer will appreciate these holes containing seawater outside of the sea as natural bathtubs, for their warm water. Likewise the sand: "Today, we settle onto the hot sand of a beach with a cozy pleasure, somewhat similar to the satisfaction afforded by a comfortable bed. Mud has lost its appeal. Whereas just about any photograph from between the wars shows it still there, present, dried, ready to spread with the first rain. These things, obvious and so quickly forgotten, characterize a way of life."[4] The same can be said of seaweed, whose destiny in itself condenses the entire contemporary attitude toward the seaside, in virtually perfect symmetry, on the side of nature, with the disappearance of the fisherman on the side of culture.

The domestication of the shore by seaside resort life is not merely a social and cultural phenomenon. It is also physical, having to do not only with the body but also with the setting. As early as 1927 a doctor could write that "for most bathers, the true beaches are the ones with a gentle slope, with solid sand resting on a deep layer of stone, with a sea that is sometimes calm, sometimes moderately agitated." In other words, the "real" beaches are "beaches sheltered from the wind, with fine sand" that are not disturbed by more violent or more obtrusive natural realities.[5]

Well before this recent period—in 1794, as Alain Corbin points out—a debate had already arisen "between partisans of the Baltic and those of the North Sea." The first group won the day, by promoting a sea that was more accessible, calmer, warmer, and with weaker tides. This victory and the physical requirements on which it was based allow us to see the emergence of a model beach definable as "a magnificently fine and unified sandy zone, wide open at low tide [where there is a tide], without reefs or pebbles," opening onto calm and gentle waters. This situation appears to prefigure, more than a century in advance, the reasons for the triumph of the southern beaches

(French, Italian, and later Spanish) where the "water temperature is always very pleasant" and the sand is hot.[6]

In short, if nature is still at issue here, it is already a chosen, selected nature. Not nature for nature's sake, but a particular version of nature: comfortable, welcoming, predisposed to human habitation, inflicting on visitors neither aggression nor challenge, and even supplying them with "the illusion of discovering some remote unknown shore, [so] exceptional [are] the quality of the silence, the purity and transparency of the water, the softness of the sandy beaches, the beauty of colors and forms."[7]

Coveting a space in harmony with a desire for a serene robinsonnade, one does not seek seaside nature in itself, but rather an idyllic, peaceful site defined by a certain number of preferences in the framework of which the raw, natural phenomenon is not always worth having. The seeker will choose a gentle slope as opposed to a cliff, a dune rather than a rock formation, sand instead of gravel—a paradigm of preferences that leads someone like Paul Morand, for example, to say that he avoided the Bay of Angels, "fleeing Nice and its horrible stony shore."[8] A desire for what, finally?

As one of Michel Tournier's characters says,

> the Pays de Caux region doesn't recognize the word beach, with all its connotations of soft sand and hordes of summer visitors. Tall chalk cliffs, permanently assaulted by the waves and the elements which tear rocky strips from them, shores covered in pebbles which get churned up by the undertow and come crashing down like thunder—that is the nature of our entire coastline. I am not ashamed to admit that I can't swim, even though I have spent years at sea.[9]

Whereas the summer vacationer, quite to the contrary, knows only the word *beach* and the gentleness it evokes. He is there to swim, not to navigate and cross the sea. As the photographer Elliott Erwitt, a great lover of beaches, put it: "I do not share [my father's] dream [of going away to sea], but I share the dream. I keep looking at the sea." And the contemporary summer vacationer is not there, either, to confront the fury of the waves that undermine the cliffs and break up the rocks. If he has come to the beach, it is because the shore is peaceful. He comes here to dream, far from nature's turmoil and turbulence, and far from everyday historical, social, and cultural realities. He wants the shore, his beach, to be sheltered from everything, and he wants the sea to be calm, shimmering, at most slightly agitated (inviting play), but not wild or stormy. Otherwise, the vacationer's dreams would go the way of the waves: they would break up on shore. "The only important thing," Doctor James wrote, "is to find enough water, a sea calm enough and a beach gentle enough to make bathing easy and pleasant."[10] Here is where the seaside history of seaweed comes into play. Seaweed belongs to the category of signs that are a priori minor ones and most often neglected, but that once analyzed reveal the dimension of repressed dreaming in everyone.[11] Seaweed is among these disdained symptoms, "obvious and rapidly forgotten," whose destiny nevertheless sums up an entire vision of the world.

Contemporary seaside vacationers have a phobia about seaweed. We have to face the evidence: especially when they are found on shore, kelp, seaweed, wrack, and other sea grasses generally inspire profound disgust in today's swimmer. How are we to interpret so seemingly anodyne a phenomenon? It is not a new one, as a late nineteenth-century description by Mme de Lalaing attests: "The beach at Arcachon is convenient and safe, but less beautiful than I would have imagined. The sand is fine and expansive; but when we saw it for the first time, it was covered with decomposing kelp, which gave it an unpleasant aspect, and we were assured that this was its habitual state."[12]

But the perception of seaweed in its various forms has noticeably altered over the years; attitudes have shifted from disappointment to disgust. Though it is a natural occurrence, the appearance of seaweed on shore is now perceived as a form of pollution. Seaweed is dirty; its green and brown spots sully the model shore, dirty the dreamed-of beach. Even tourist literature is not left untouched: it does not contradict but rather incorporates this henceforth conventional interpretation of the facts. In the introduction to one guide, we learn that "at low tide, the exposed stretches of beach, spotted with seaweed and marine grasses, often dirty, may be disappointing."[13]

Thus the advice to lymphatics from the *Larousse médical* in 1929— "All patients need to do is lie down in the kelp at low tide"—would appear totally incongruous today. But as Jean Viard notes, "suffering bodies" and the spectacle of their treatment are in fact no longer welcome in the seaside universe.[14] Sufferers are expected to turn over the beach to healthy, tanned, purified bodies; the infirm can bathe elsewhere, sign up for "thalassotherapy," get back in shape with seaweed therapy.

Still, all this explains nothing. What is the significance of seaweed phobia in relation to the vacation dream—this recognized aversion that summer vacationers evince when confronted with any beach that has been "dirtied" by fucus or posidonia?[15] This repugnance now incites municipalities to clean up their beaches every year before summer comes, by removing the seaweed accumulated over the winter and even by bringing in "clean" sand from the bay, as is done in Arcachon, in order to eliminate any trace and to give the shore a "good" appearance.

Much more than hygiene is at stake in such cosmetic treatments of the site. There is also a certain denial of reality, a desire for an unnatural purity that is inscribed in the continuity of a symbolic program of extermination of wildness so that the beach can be the ideal desert, the empty stage, the naked shore, mirroring the unclothed body (see chapter 8): a site henceforth exempt from nature and culture alike, a theater held in suspension for social play that is itself detached from the world and its contingencies. This is the very foundation of the seaside dream, a spatial imaginary whose general psychological orientation is confirmed and made explicit by the story of seaweed.

Pierre Jakez Hélias, referring to the ordinary seaweed phobia of today's vacationer, underlines the following paradox: "As for beach lovers, they complain about the dirtiness of the sand when tides or storms have brought up rolls of kelp from the deep and no one has cleaned them up. Afterward, as souvenirs, they buy little pictures made of seaweed, stretched out on a base of silk paper; these are astonishing even though quite common."[16] In fact, the paradox is only superficial; it disappears as soon as it is resituated in the framework of seaside aesthetics.

There is a certain symmetry at work: what happens with fishermen also happens with seaweed. Rejected, expelled, or eliminated from the shore, these elements are reintroduced into the vacation universe only when they have been transformed into exotic curiosities, that is, literally, into external realities (from the Greek exô, "outside of"). These realities are henceforth foreign to the beach world; they are no longer natural but naturalized, turned folkloric in one case, dried in the other, sweetened in all cases,[17] like the varnished seashell whose inhabitant has been expropriated.

Thus, if we want to understand the meaning of contemporary seaside vacationing, is it reasonable to continue to speak about it in terms of a collective search for contact with nature? Some imperturbable scholars continue to do so; piling on the contradictions, they assert that the "general desire is to benefit from a beach that is free and wild and nevertheless comfortable."[18] The term *nevertheless* says it all: seeking to reconcile comfort and wildness, it refers us directly to the seaside utopia and its apparent paradox, one that depends entirely on the persistence of the reference to "nature."

Summer vacationers are neither naturalists nor ethnologists. What are they seeking then? Not indigenous realities, which have been or are being removed from their universe,[19] but a stage, a setting, roles and symbols—in fact, a cultic site and a "prayer rug" for the performance of a ritual.[20]

Yet this ritual, which is mocked or condemned all the more readily to the extent that it is not understood, has yet to be fully deciphered in terms of its meaning and value. The mystery of seaside idleness remains intact, especially in the eyes of partisans of active leisure and "intelligent" vacations. In August 1980 *Le Nouvel Observateur* raised the following question: "Why, for one month each year, do millions of human beings flock together in the south of France?"—a question that has yet to be answered. Today, people are generally content to note that this opaque phenomenon persists and is growing.

> "Do the French spend their vacation time the same way they did ten years ago?"
>
> "Here again, many entertain vacation fantasies. They would like to be hyperactive; they plan a program full of sports or cultural activities. But these desires run up against the constraints of daily life. Have they stopped their idiotic tanning? When we examine the practices of French people who go to the shore (meaning nearly half of all French vacationers), they have no occupation but the beach."[21]

Are the "constraints of daily life" the explanation? Like the itinerary in the realm of tourism, the beach is a ritual, but it has not been adequately studied or seriously examined from that standpoint. Such an examination presupposes in fact attributing a project and an imaginary construct to beach people, granting a meaning to their idleness—no rite is possible without goals and representations—rather than implying that this "occupation" denotes a failure or a renunciation, an absence of rules or "planning," or else a failure of intentions, even impotence, apraxia, or collective numbness.

At the end of the nineteenth century, discovering an "admirable" beach across from the Île de Ré, one traveler wrote, "I understand that, when one cannot travel, one might spend an entire vacation on this beach without tiring of it."[22] The traveler thus seems to comprehend seaside idleness, but a correction immediately counterbalances this "comprehension"; this form of leisure is interpreted as what is left to those who are unable to travel, implying that beach people are only frustrated tourists or voyagers deprived of movement.

But for the seashore to impose itself as the dominant attraction, ahead of the country and the mountains, much more was needed than resignation or economic impotence on the part of a few frustrated nomads. A dream had to take hold of the place, had to incite vacationers to select the gentlest shores and to avoid natural asperities as they avoided the moral principles once dictated by science or social tradition.

The beach, the theater of a "concrete utopia," is a product of history. It is not a natural site; and except as alibi or illusion, its "naturalness" is not what ultimately underlies its attraction. The proof lies in the fact that the site had to be transformed, denatured, and rendered artificial, under threat of disaffection. Gabriel Désert remarks that "the [Normandy] region is not [or rather, is no longer] representative of the seaside milieu considered ideal in our day. It is true that the shore does not always consist of fine sand and that stones cover considerable stretches of beach."[23]

The beach is an ideal, a dream land[24] improved for summer vacationers who now prefer sand to stones, a calm sea to an angry ocean, and the warm caresses of the sea to the icy flagellations of the waves of yesteryear. The beach-lover has become the true native of this domesticated, depopulated, and sanitized world.

THE BEACH AND DREAMS OF REPOSE

So what are the first dreams of the new "native"? What desires and primordial fantasies mysteriously bring together hordes of dreamy Robinsons along the warm and limpid shores of the south of France and elsewhere?

Through the intermediary of Major Thompson, Pierre Daninos notes that the English have a way of "living six days a week and dying on Sundays."[25] This is also what beach people do every summer. They go to the beach to die: symbolically, socially, and sometimes literally. After all, in *Pierrot le fou* Jean-Luc Godard's Ferdinand Griffon commits suicide on the beach, with dynamite; and Christian Giudicelli's José too, hurtling himself into the void in a final dive from the balcony of his hotel room on the eighth floor.[26] José's companion in flight and despair, Marie, also contemplates dying at the beach, in the sea: "In Nice, I'll find a taxi at the station and head for the sea, I'll tell the driver to drop me off near the beach. I'll walk along the sand or the stones right toward the water, and I'll go right in, carrying my suitcase; the sea will be nice and cool and it'll close over me, I'll forget everything, it won't be so bad."[27]

Paroxystic, novelistic deaths like this one are nevertheless model acts. They all convey the same suicidal notion: leave the world behind, forget it, forget oneself, get rid of world and self in one way or another—and always on the seashore. Literature is rife with this sort of ending:

TO LIFE

TO THE SEA

This slogan is from a 1992–93 advertising campaign for Les Sables-d'Olonne. With the help of beach photos, it evokes the oath "to life, to death," and thus expresses, curiously enough (in the context of vacation advertising), an essential ambivalence: that of the symbolic relation to the sea for the summer resident from the end of the earth who is a seaside vacationer, a vacationer on the edge of the void, on the edge of nothingness. "No trees here, just flat sand, the flat sea,"[28] an imaginary, dream-like relation, unconscious or feigned, but a relation nevertheless, to nothingness and immobility, in the framework of which contemplation, swimming, sleep, and other ordinary behaviors of seaside indolence take on particular value: meaning is imparted to behaviors that can no longer be reduced to routine and idleness.

Life, sea, death. In its incessant coming and going, the sea lies between the two—and the swimmer as well. We may recall the fright of the balneophobe of earlier generations; let us imagine what the ablutions of today's balneophile may hide. "The silence of death was only broken by the throbbing of the sea."[29] And what breaks the silence of the sea? Here, between earth and water, on the liquid ground of this soft place,[30] the beach is the prefatory space of a strange encounter between man and the elements. It appears as the forestage of a kind of Orphic rite.

"To contemplate water is to slip away, dissolve, and die," Bachelard wrote. And to sleep? To nod off, close one's eyes, hear the waves, and doze on the sand? "Lying back with closed eyes, I lost count of time."[31] And swimming?

> In coaches, chaises, caravans and hoys
> Fly to the coast for daily, nightly joys,
> And all, impatient of Nylond, agree,
> With one consent, to rush into the sea.[32]

To rush into the sea, go under and drown—and then come back out, return and be reborn. Mortal and regenerating at once: the symbolics of the act is powerful and its meaning widely attested. Under the heading of mortification (see chapter 2), but also under that of regression to the womb or initiation, amniotic fluid for some, baptism for others—a great deal has already been said on this subject.

> By voluntary consent to immersion—which is a kind of burial—one accepts a moment of oblivion, of an abdication of responsibility, of sitting on the sidelines, of emptiness. Hence countless therapeutic uses of immersion. It breaks the thread of existence as an interval or a gap in the continuum and this automatically gives it an important role in rites of initiation.[33]

From acceptance to demand, from renunciation to desire (the desire for emptiness or hiatus), there is just one short step. With the addition of pleasure, the contemporary bather has taken that step, turned toward "little deaths," rites of forgetting the body, losing the self, through immersion, suspension, purification, the sense of dissolution. "It is in the sea that she forgets those things that she doesn't like about herself. The water bears her body. The water conceals her body. The salt baptizes her body."[34] So many Ophelian dreams, sacramental dreams, or mermaid dreams like these characterize an entire facet, probably the most intimate one, of the contemporary seaside dream. "Thus man thinks he goes to the sea only because it is too hot on land; but may he not be going to swim impelled by deeper appeals, those of the maternal breast and the fetal state, his only paradise?"[35] Is he seeking to recapture the prenatal nothingness? Is he nostalgic for limbo?

Thus the psychological substratum of the seaside no-man's land becomes clearer: this world may not be without attraction but it is at least without gravity, or rather without weight. It is a universe in which death itself is only a game, merely a pretended move into the nothingness of the waves. And life too is slowed down, lightened, as if suspended here and then begun again, freed in this soft flat landscape from ordinary existence with its rough spots, its rhythms, its weight, and its tragedy.

Rhythms

At the beach, to all intents and purposes, no tempo is imposed. There are motions, to be sure, but no events. There are repeated gestures, but no accidents. The beach can be defined first of all by a certain quality of the ambiance: its culminating point is reached in the afternoon, when the late arrivals are in place and those who prefer calm mornings or twilight swimming have left. It is a magical, luminous instant, feverish and vibrant, in which everything seems to stop, as if immobilized somewhere between life and death. "The noise of the waves was even lazier, more drawn out than at noon. It was the same sun, the same light still shining on the same sand as before. For two hours the day had stood still; for two hours it had been anchored in a sea of molten lead."[36]

Weight

Similarly, whether inert or active, the body seems to elude the laws of classical physics here. It is light, slippery, gleaming. It floats on the sand as it floats in the water, serenely. "I live on Brazzaville Beach. Brazzaville Beach on the edge of Africa. This is where I have washed up, you might say, deposited myself like a spar of driftwood."[37] The body floats so well that it even seems to levitate. Many images attest to this magical, idyllic, or miraculous perception.

In June 1993, accompanying a photo of a waterskier, the text of an advertisement read, "At Tiberias, walking on water is an old custom." Another example: some dozen years earlier, an ad for the Club Méditerranée (including the instruction: "Take one") depicted a woman floating a few yards away from a deserted, sunny beach, in a sea so transparent that the shadow of the woman's body could be seen below, on the clear sand, at the bottom of limpid water. To the suspension of time corresponds a body suspended in space, a general effect of weightlessness that is noted in passing from a distance by Lodge's Bernard Walsh as he takes his father to the hospital: "The tinted windows of the ambulance turned the whole world blue, as if the vehicle were a submarine, and Waikiki built on the seabed. The palm trees waved to and fro like seaweed in the tide and shoals of tourists swam by, goggling and gaping."[38] In the sea and out, there is a swimming pool ambiance: aquarium below and pond above, with the understanding that the two are mixed, like sand and water.

Tragedy

At the opposite pole from the Romantic view of shipwrecks, the contemporary beach does not tolerate tragedy any better than heaviness. Marine catastrophes—drownings or groundings—do not belong to the seaside universe, any more than fishermen or seaweed do, because they signify death, actual death, whereas the beach is a place where everything undergoes a loss of gravity. We may recall Ilya telling the stories of Medea and Oedipus in the film *Never on Sunday*. For her, these terrible stories all end with the same sentence: "And they all went to the beach"—a pacifying episode par excellence, in which existence and its dramas are abolished, rejected, and dissolved. Death is like the sea; here it is pacified, tamed. Gentle and inoffensive, it resembles life, in a place where "Neptune never takes himself too seriously," where, as Brassens wrote, "the eternal summer vacationer, going out to dream on the waves in a pedal-boat, spends his death on vacation."[39]

Here dreams of rest are inscribed on the sands and the tides. We are in the kingdom of "water dreamed in its everyday life, the water of a pond 'opheliaized' on its own, that is covered naturally with sleeping beings who abandon themselves and float, beings who die quietly," on waves of sand and a desert of water, sheltered from storms.[40]

THE SEASIDE UNIVERSE AND DREAMS OF ETERNITY

But since in this baptismal universe death is a game and swimming a rite of passage (now a dream rite, once a nightmare, always an initiation), dying is only one stage.[41] After immersion comes emergence, like awakening after sleep or resurrection after death. This is the second phase of the primordial seaside ritual. After "the sinful creature [vanishes] in the waters of death," there is "purification by lustration and the revitalization of that creature from the source of life. Emersion reveals the purified being in a state of grace, united with a divine stream of new life."[42] Upon its emergence from the water, that being is awaited on shore: hoped for, observed, and soon put on stage.

Even in the era of the balneopaths (see chapter 2), after the nightmare of trial by bathing, what people looked forward to was the "miraculous" reaction of flesh to water; and what they observed closely was the returning flow of blood that restored the colors of life to the cadaverous body of the poor bather, turned pale and bluish by the glacial lash of the breakers—truly the "waters of death."[43] Thus, for Michelet, the sea—the North Sea, at the time—could "recal[l] one from the grave. You may see there perfectly incredible recoveries." The sea is just a temporary tomb for fleeting burials: baths and the beach are a theater for happy funerals, since the dead are resurrected at the end of the ceremony. What is more, when René Quinton compared blood plasma to seawater in the early twentieth century, the "revivalist" dream drew upon this discovery, going beyond Dr. Russell's intuitions for yet another argument in favor of its propagation.[44]

On the beach, then, it is not simply a matter of calming nerves, cleansing wounds, or easing rheumatic pains, but also of resuscitating the dead, revitalizing the weak, strengthening the anemic, fortifying the young, and rejuvenating the old. "Luc's fresh kelp, like a fountain of youth, rejuvenates old age and fortifies childhood," according to a nineteenth-century advertising slogan.[45] This legend went on to increase in power: the myth of restored youth, the dream of regeneration, which, linked to the cult of the sun, continues even today to inform people's thinking as if it were supremely self-evident.[46]

Discovering the Mediterranean, Théo Varlet, a Robinson of the Île du Levant, wrote in 1905: "I had never before felt so clearly the marvelous attraction, the grandeur of the sun's kiss. I had yet to experience in my flesh, to live for myself, what were still just literary notions: the sea as creator of primordial life, the sun as father of life on our planet."[47] Thus above and beyond the amalgam of sun and water, a mythic certainty is gradually imposed: "She will surely be 'regenerated.' She offers the sea to herself as she did to her child."[48] A solar kiss, a marine kiss: death, sea, life. Eternal youth, regeneration. The magical annihilation of the effects of time and, at the origin of this recurrent fantasy, nothing less than an ancient dream of eternity.

The dream is everywhere, endlessly reiterated. The Dead Sea, for example, is one of the prime sites for its expression. A sea with lunar banks for stillborn fishermen (since it contains neither seaweed nor fish) on which the body floats better than anywhere else (its saline density is ten times that of the Mediterranean), this therapeutic sea is the balneary stage par excellence of the myth of eternal youth. The sea, death, life. A theater of the void, a restorative inland sea, an Ophelian pond combating chronic dermatitis and thus guaranteeing its bathers a genuine change of skin, a resurrection: the Dead Sea is full of life.

Advertising has not failed to exploit this theme, moreover. In 1984 a promotional campaign for a multiproperty residence in Saint-Raphaël on the Mediterranean coast used a picture of a transparent capsule containing a view of the residence alongside a swimming pool—the Ophelian pond once again, instead of and in place of the sea itself! The caption: "Vacation vitamins." In 1993 a television advertisement announced that "the Bay of Angels Marina now has its Olympus, with BIOVIMER, a health and fitness spa." This time there is no beating around the bush: the Olympian dream is the dream of eternal life.

The poet from the Côte d'Azur cited earlier, Général Matton, produced the following verses on sunbathing in 1933:

> In your eyes one sees a new brightness shining
> Through the patiently colored fiery rays,
> Your limbs, skillfully gilded under the sun,
> Seem to be alive with a new flame.[49]

Today, we no longer speak of "flames." We have given up this somewhat outmoded "pyrotechnic" metaphor in favor of more "electric" ones, shored up by images of laughing summer residents frolicking on a sunswept beach: "recharge your batteries" on vacation, or "store up energy" so as to have enough "to sell back all year long."[50] As if life were no longer a matter of irreversible time and wear but an expenditure of energy compensated by a restocking that would quickly abolish the effects of the one and the traces of the other. "Flames" may no longer be mentioned, but the fantasy appears basically unchanged. Another magazine expresses the same idea without resorting to figures of speech, instructing its readers to "grow younger on vacation," with a happy beach scene as usual to illustrate this fascinating piece of advice.[51] Grow younger? How? By relearning how to sleep, eat, breathe, and swim. The beach is an initiatory site.

Then why the sea, always the sea, the beaches and waves whose images inundate newspapers and magazines from May to September? It is because "the sea is ageless; covered with wrinkles, it loses them right away; it is a country without corners; it has a childlike turbulence." In contrast to the immobile majesty of the mountains, those geographic folds that look their age and offer us a "wooden face," the sea constitutes the most propitious context we have today for

Olympian dreams.[52] The gods no longer dwell on mountaintops but on the crests of waves; they no longer occupy the heights but the seashores; and whoever plunges into these waters is not only purified but absorbs their qualities, like a dry sponge that is immersed, an always magical image of regeneration. "'And why not be thus permeated?' some German physicians wonder. 'If when you first enter the water you contract and close up your pores, reaction brings almost immediately a warmth that reopens them, dilates the skin and renders it very capable of absorbing the life of the sea.'"[53]

True or false? It hardly matters! The essential factor is not so much the sea itself as the image one constructs of it, the meaning or value one gives it. A single anodyne sentence can suffice to induce the dream: "You could say that the same wave is always being reborn"—and the same can be said about someone coming back out of the sea.[54] In the collective imaginary, the aquatic origin of life has by and large supplanted the reference to the heavens, and dreams of eternity have shifted from the clouds to the tides. Earthly paradise is now located at the seashore. It is on the beach, not in the mountains, that the shepherd Endymion henceforth has his wish fulfilled.[55]

This is how the ablutions of the hippies of Ibiza were perceived in their day, according to the echoes we find in the press: "One of the finest spectacles one can witness is their morning bath, which resembles a rite. Whoever sees them inevitably thinks that this is how our ancestors must have awakened in Paradise."[56]

Adam's nakedness, Endymion's eternal rest, the fountain of youth, a world without wrinkles, the innocence of childhood—a scene of paradise or an Olympian reverie (let us not forget that the Club Méditerranée was originally called the Club Olympique): all these legendary references and idyllic images form a linked bundle of symbols. Under a sky that is always blue, facing a sea that is never angry, they weave the fabric of a model, a canvas on which today's atemporal seaside universe is drawn—a perfectly smooth, autarchic space for an extraworldly consciousness:

> If World War Three broke out, you'd probably find it on an inside page
> of the *Honolulu Advertiser,* and the lead story would be about a hike in
> local taxes. It makes you feel out of time, somehow, as if you've fallen
> asleep and woken up in a kind of dreamy lotus land, where every day
> is the same as the one before. Perhaps that's why so many people retire

to Hawaii. It gives them the illusion that they won't die, because they're kind of dead already, just by being here. It's the same with the absence of seasons. We have a lot of weather, a lot of climate, but no seasons, not so you'd notice. Seasons remind you that time is passing.[57]

Here it is, the site by the sea as a unique destination, with its specific promises, its seductive arguments. A local, hyperlocal world, from Ibiza to Matala, from Cannes to Hawaii, it attracts hippies and retirees alike, because it is a refuge. In the strong sense, it is a place of retreat for "emigrés from real life,"[58] a bubble for escapees from the hinterlands that guarantees access—illusory or simulated—to a preconflictual state, outside of history—an Edenic, Peslagian[59] state that antedates sin, the Father, the Law, a state outside the Law that precedes the reality principle and its confining turbulence. If this is where Ferdinand Griffon and José went to commit suicide, the beach is also where François Truffaut's Antoine Doinel went to escape Institutions in Truffaut's *Les quatre cents coups*.

It is thus against this background of lived utopia that we need to understand and interpret the seaside from here on: contemporary seaside mores and customs are structured in such a way that our most precious memories of beach vacations are in fact focused, as Daniel Pennac writes, "on those short weeks of eternity when nothing happen[s], really, nothing but the most tenuous, infinitesimal, intimate, and repetitive events, nothing but ourselves face to face with ourselves, without the prosthesis of work."[60] In this narcissistic search for the void, the absence of events, the eternal present, oblivion, atemporality, time without end or purpose,[61] with no goal beyond being there and "floating," the "scandalous" seaside indifference sinks its roots and finds its reason for being (see chapter 3).

DON'T LOSE
ANY TIME
Do you want to forget reality
and have wonderful adventures?
Enchanting, exotically perfumed sites
and sundrenched lagoons
are no longer a figment of your imagination

—this according to a "preface" systematically included in the frontmatter of every book in a well-known collection of romance novels,

Harlequin. "Forget reality": here is the message in a nutshell. And the romantic fictions in the series are set in an "enchanted" universe where references to islands and their corollaries—seas, beaches, waves, sand, blue waters, or the tropics—are frequent. The very titles of some of these works (not to mention the iconography found on the covers) make the point, even in translation: *The Isle of the Blue Lagoon, The Nymph of Blue Waters, The Patience of the Waves, Quadrille in the Bahamas, Two Huts on the Beach, An Island Sheltered from Storms, The Waves of Love, Under the Rustling Palms, Steps on the Sand, A Week in the Caribbean, The Island of Passions, Alone on a Deserted Island, At the Edge of the Pacific*...

One Olympus jumbled together with another, beaches or islands, these are the privileged sites of a fantasy of solitude in which undying love is won for all time, but that also satisfy an essential need to forget the world in the framework of an intimate if limited dramaturgy, the one that stages "nothing but ourselves, face to face with ourselves"— that of summer vacationing, the ideal robinsonnade, which has nothing to do with tourism.

The vacation expression of this other need, this desire for retreat, withdrawal, amnesia, distancing, turning inward, turns up everywhere. "Before plunging back in for a year, disappear without a trace," suggests a 1993 Irish National Tourist Office advertisement for an island destination. A great deal of evidence points in the same direction. "The wonderful summer of 1949! Finally, we could relax! A shared desire brought everyone together there [in Calvi, outside of time, at the end of the world]: to be done with all the old concerns, to stretch out on the seashore without doing a thing, or to dive in as if to wash ourselves of the old world, to dream of nothing but eating, drinking, and making merry."[62] "So he got undressed and relaxed in the sun. . . . The peace of the whole world seemed to be gathered on that beach, on that deserted island."[63] An anecdote: the singer Julien Clerc once described how he got his start, in Calvi, actually, in a nightclub called World's End, and he specified that this club was located at the end of the beach.

The desire to go to the end of the world—"at the very end of Portugal, between sea and sun, the Algarve" (Portuguese National Tourist Bureau, 1991)—betrays a need for extremes, the irresistible attraction of limits, to which the tourist succumbs too, but which are experienced quite differently by the summer vacationer, not in the mode of "I went there, I saw, I left," but in the mode of "I went there, I saw, and

I stayed."[64] "And this is why I like the beach—blobs of tar notwith-standing. Living on the extremity of a continent, facing the two great simple spaces of sea and sky."[65] Thus time is suspended and fabricates eternity: in the cessation of movement, not in motion or mere pas-sage; not in the stopover but in the "shipwreck"; not in the visit but in the installation, in conformity with the Crusoe model.

> To leave, a right earned by hard struggle, to leave for as long as pos-sible, to go as far away as possible. To the end of things, to the end of the world, to go where everything ends, finis terrae, as if the earth were still flat, not Copernician, still not Galilean, as if, all at once, one had to stop, using all one's cunning, one foot on the edge of the void, on the fringe, the edge, the bank. On the edge of the sea, on the shore.[66]

In this psychological universe that proscribes itineraries, tours, jour-neys, and that encourages the simulacrum of the one-way voyage, the traveler's race is interrupted, for the space of a summer. Here begins the sojourn of the "gods," feet in the water.

THE DREAMED-OF SHORE

Even if for now it remains somewhat abstract, the portrait of a dif-ferent vacationer is beginning to take shape here. This one is also a traveler—he does have to get as far as the shore—but not a tourist. He does not project himself into the world: he is not an explorer. He withdraws from the world, seeks to have nothing more to do with it. "It's so comfortable in the village that you hardly ever want to leave. If you go on an excursion to explore Spain, the bus is likely to break down, and if you decide to go see a bullfight, when you get back you swear you'll never set foot out of the camp again."[67]

Signs of an era, provocative mixed messages that defy a certain va-cation ideology but condense the spirit of the times, the testimony and petitions that come out of the historiography of the Club Méditerranée serve as a magnifying glass in this context (see chapter 3). They make it easier to decipher the major psychological features of a mentality by making them larger than life. Refusing to set foot outside the village or the beach: do not seaside vacationers make the same response to the external world?

A tourist or not a tourist? This question has already been raised elsewhere,[68] but here, raised again in the very different context of seaside vacationing, it can be answered very quickly, with Robinson's answer to Phileas: "The objects that are of so much interest to the abominable tourists are exposed to contempt: the old stones are rejected along with crosswalks and ties, and, of course, newspapers and telephones."[69]

The summer resident responds here with a flat rejection; and the tourist, who looks at beach people with such disdain (see chapter 5), finds that the summer resident returns the compliment. Fogg is a great fan of means of communication, while Crusoe is unaware of them: "The island will always remain what it is: an asylum of peace, a retreat where one will continue to be oblivious to automobiles and telephones."[70] And if Passepartout is interested in the surrounding world, Friday, like his master, is suspicious of it. That is where one encounters Savages, whether cannibals or the urban variety, so-called civilized folk: "They wanted to break with civilized life, with the disguises people wear in town."[71] Rejecting clothing, newspapers, and the telephone, the Club Med's Crusoean tandem Gracious Organizers/ Gracious Members reject not only conventions but also even contact with the outside world. This attitude on the part of the inhabitants of the "Polynesian" villages of Majorca and elsewhere attests to and sums up the essence of a certain psychology.

So why the beach? Why especially the beach, the seashore, its sandy stretches and its "rustling palms," rather than other sites? The answer is that a beach is really a space like no other. "Hardly anything comes between you and your children on the beach," Elliott Erwitt notes. "No telephone [precisely!], no distractions, just you and your kids. They will remember these days [as Pennac does!]. The sea and clouds and surf are there, but they don't impinge. Nothing interferes . . . except the occasional picture."[72]

Alain Laurent for his part emphasizes what may be another specificity of the place. "The sites of the 'cult' of the sun demigod are first and foremost beaches, which impose 'ritual' behavior: the naked body, a horizontal, immobile position." But do beaches impose this ritual, or rather are they chosen and arranged specially for it? In fact, with regard to this heliophilic justification of the beach, Laurent himself immediately weighs this argument, adding: "but high mountains and especially cruises are also appreciated."[73]

The sun, today an indispensable ecological parameter of vacations, is not a sufficient reason for the preference given to beaches—no more so than is the economic factor (the countryside remains the most competitive destination) or the presence of water as such (lakes and rivers also provide sites for swimming). There is something more Ophelian, more Olympian, an empty space, a borderline territory detached from the world, favorable to withdrawal into the self as well as to the expression of many different forms of conviviality (see the introduction to part 3): the summer vacation beach has the particular characteristic of escaping the classic triad of spaces, Desert, City, Countryside.[74] It is neither a natural place like the Sahara and other allegedly unspoiled sites nor a culturalized space like the City, a space constructed in total isolation from nature; and yet it is not the blend of nature and culture synthesized by the countryside, that "necessary disfiguring of nature by social humankind."[75]

The ideal vacation shore, the one corresponding to the seaside dream that comes out of the contemporary seaside utopia, is defined in the margins of all that. It proceeds from a paradox, quite similar to the one Mr. Palomar notes in connection with his meadow:

> Around Mr. Palomar's house there is a lawn. This is not a place a lawn should exist naturally: so the lawn is an artificial object, composed from natural objects, namely grasses. The lawn's purpose is to represent nature, and this representation occurs as the substitution, for the nature proper to the area, of a nature in itself natural but artificial for this area.[76]

Likewise the beach. This tongue of clean golden sand, without seaweed, stones, or fishermen, is an artificial object composed of natural objects, that is, grains of sand. Its purpose is to represent nature (that is why certain authors include it in the category of "nature tourism"), but it is not nature, following the example of "the introduction of a fantasmatic botany" on its fringes during the twentieth century: palm trees, agaves, or banana trees, which are not native to the locale.[77]

To address the question of its symbolic value, and the better to circumscribe the concept, we can connect the beach of dreams with the place where Grenouille takes refuge, Grenouille being the hero of a novel by Patrick Süskind, a boy afflicted with olfactory hypersensitivity. Seeking "the point that was the farthest away from men in the entire kingdom," at the summit of the Plomb du Cantal he discovers a place so ideally situated that no human odor reaches his nostrils. This place is so inodorous that Grenouille settles in, "for he had made up his mind that he would not be leaving this blessed region any time soon."[78] Similarly, the beach is defined fantasmatically as a place that is sheltered, not from human odors (although to some extent it is), but from all the external realities that might be impediments to the ideal existence that attempts to establish itself each summer in that "blessed country," the self-contained seaside community.

For those who might consider this interpretation of the contemporary seaside universe somewhat venturesome, let us use the Club Med magnifying glass once again. Alain Ehrenberg puts it clearly: the Club's philosophy is based on two fundamental principles. It would bring individuals together in a single community and on the seashore—thus on the margin of the world—without regard to their "class origin and their level of wealth, that is, their genealogy (eradication of the past) and their place in society (eradication of everything beyond the villages). The promoters of the Club Méditerranée were seeking, in short, to be only individuals, to create an existence for themselves without a past,"[79] in a place far away from everything, an "odorless point," a sort of decompression chamber conceived in view of an ideal experience of sociocultural weightlessness: an artificial, atemporal, and utopian sojourn, in an anachronic, self-contained village, always on the seashore.

Thus if we note in opinion surveys that "cultural and historical characteristics are fairly rare in positive images [of the seashore],"[80] we should not be astonished. The shore's sociological role and symbolic function for vacationers is in fact located apart from these typical, temporal concrete reference points.

So what is the ultimate aesthetic and dramatic register of the beach of dreams, a site that seems to attract its "migrants" by a tacit promise of "complete happiness away from society"?[81] Since it is in this framework, on this dreamed-of shore, that beach society comes to be inscribed, the answer to the question is important.

Cut off from the world, isolated, the beach is nevertheless not wholly unreal, not wholly artificial. In aesthetic terms, it is surreal, or rather hyperreal—in the manner of the picture of the beach at Santa Monica painted by Paul Staiger.[82] It is a sort of desert in vitro or in laboratorio, an idealized site, a minimalist setting, a scene in a vacuum, under glass, with no background but the changing monochromy of the sea and the transparency of the sky that extends it to infinity. A refuge for an intimist spectacle in the open air, the beach is a fantastic, paradoxical space. Honoré de Balzac noted this quality in his own day:

> This landscape, which has only three distinct colors, the brilliant yellow of the sands, the azure blue of the sky, and the uniform green of the sea, is large without being wild; it is immense without being deserted; it is monotone without being tiring; it has only three elements, [yet] it is varied.[83]

This space is neither realistic nor marvelous, neither authentic nor fantastic. It is neither totally closed nor totally open. In dramaturgic terms, it is an immense enclosed space, a public theater of private life or a private desert for public use. It is an intimate world that I enjoy without being its owner, and in which I take refuge under an invisible glass bell; a place from which I can see and hear everything around me even though nothing can penetrate through to me from the outside, as is said—coincidentally?—in a book on life in concentration camps.[84] Translated literally, the French expression être en villégiature means "to be staying in the country." But it is also used metaphorically to mean "to be in prison." An architecture of the void, open and yet self-enclosed, is this not the ultimate beach of dreams, a soft cell, with no doors or windows because it has no walls (at least no visible walls), a bubble or a bell jar? And what do we do there? We give ourselves over to farniente; we do nothing at all. So what does this mean? "The pursued hopes to be given up as dead, to be left lying on the ground while his enemy goes away. This transformation is the one which is nearest to the centre of the circle, the point which is still. The subject renounces all movement, as though he were actually dead, until the other creature goes away."[85] Through this ruse, the other moves away from me, and the other is the outside: the world, society. Here on the shore, a theater of forgetting is thus put in place.

In the evening, when the oblique lights of restaurants illuminate it or when the streetlights on the promenade bathe it in a soft glow, this space reveals its true nature. Like a tropical beach in moonlight, it takes on "an air of unreality like a deserted theater or a public garden at midnight,"[86] or like that of a Zen garden in which, instead of rocks and traces of raking, there remain only a few forgotten umbrellas, abandoned sand castles, and the dark mass of a breakwater, like a beached whale, dead on shore, its sides gently caressed by the surf; and then, here and there, still readable, prints of vanished feet and bodies.

In the morning, the castles will have been destroyed by the waves; the breakwater will still be there, and the man with the rake will come by—not a Zen monk, of course, but a municipal employee who will wipe out the last traces and remnants of the previous day. Then it will begin all over again. Robinson and Friday will return to their prison cell of golden sand.

5. The Overcrowded Desert

*(or, How an oil-blackened Robinson
had a nightmare in which he imagined
Friday whitened by polluted waters
and discovered new Savages)*

If I had been content with reading Stevenson I should still believe in the
paradisical charm of a coral reef and a coconut tree. Now the one is a
thing that stinks like Billingsgate market and knocks nasty holes in ex-
pensive boats, while the other is the produce of 1/100th of a ton of copra
which also stinks. Even the rags of romance that still fluttered round the
South Sea pirates disappear when one has seen them vomit in their soup
and go to sleep with their heads in it. No, it was foolishness ever to come
to the S. Seas. So goodbye to one more poor little dream.

—Robert Fletcher, *Isles of Illusion* (1923)

What remains of the dream, then, when the crowds come jostling
onto the shore? What becomes of the little corner of the world where,
normally, like the Little Mermaid in the foam, all the conflicts of life
are dissolved, along with its collisions, noises, dirt, and wounds?
Once the vacationer is drowned in a heap of bodies, what becomes
of the dreams of the summer resident who is "naked, idle, lying out
fetally, fatally, and letting himself be invaded by the elementary, the
primordial, the primary, the three colors at the root of Everything,
the chrome yellow of the sand, the vermilion red of the setting sun,
the deep blue of the waters, colors that by themselves repaint life,
cauterize the wounds of eleven months of hysterical urbanity"?[1]
What happens to the theater of oblivion under these conditions? To
its self-contained world? To the gilded "cell"? To the deserted island,

once it is offered to all and sundry? Goodbye to one more poor little dream?

Let there be no mistake about the meaning of these questions. They suggest that making vacation consumption of the seashore widely available inevitably entails the very impossibility of realizing the dream; and they imply that, above and beyond all the variants on the Crusoe myth found on contemporary beaches, what is really at stake here, among models and practices of seaside leisure, is the social and historical pulverization of that myth. What becomes of the character and his moral code—of Crusoe and Crusoeism, as it were—once the pleasures of seaside sedentarity become popular? On the horizon of vacations the specter of a devastated seaside theater is taking shape—the specter of a landscape disfigured in the way a pleasant countryside can be after a volcano has erupted and covered it with ash.

The painters of this sinister landscape are numerous. They either privilege the mobility of leisure and condemn the immobility of seaside vacationing (which certain critics, as we know, deem "passive"),[2] or they require that the sojourn be of such exceptional quality that, since the daily realities of popular beaches cannot meet their expectations, they denigrate these sites and avoid them. In short, we have on the one hand nomads, "active" travelers, explorers, that is, tourists, and on the other hand state-of-the-art summer vacationers, experimenters, fully fleshed-out Robinsons, whose most intimate convictions resist and oppose the contemporary extension of the robinsonnade to the masses.

We have already encountered both of these types, the first in the figure of Mrs. McKisco at the beginning of Fitzgerald's novel,[3] and the second, on several occasions, in the figure of Paul Morand in particular, but especially in the persona of the "summer resident on the verge of a nervous breakdown" (see Introduction). In fact, these are merely the earliest representatives of a very widespread critical attitude with respect to seaside vacationing: it is time to explore the themes and arguments of their discourse more fully. Why? Because this discourse, which is certainly not devoid of good sense and truth, is also an obstacle to the observation and analysis of the phenomenon, which it obscures with caricatures, stereotypes, prejudices, and misunderstandings. From this standpoint, it thus fulfills the same ideological function in the sphere of seaside vacationing that anti-tourist discourse fulfills in the sphere of tourism.[4]

If the popular beach, seen from afar, is still bearable, and even sometimes acknowledged as beautiful by its critical observers, this perception of the place quickly deteriorates in their eyes as soon as they approach. When Pierre, Maupassant's unhappy hero, went to the beach at Trouville, here is how he saw it at first:

> From a distance it looked like a garden full of gaudy flowers. All along the stretch of yellow sand, from the pier as far as the Roches Noires, sun-shades of every hue, hats of every shape, dresses of every colour, in groups outside the bathing huts, in long rows by the margin of the waves, or scattered here and there, really looked like immense bouquets on a vast meadow. And the Babel of sounds—voices near and far ringing thin in the light atmosphere, shouts and cries of children being bathed, clear laughter of women—all made a pleasant, continuous din, mingling with the unheeding breeze, and breathed with the air itself.[5]

At that moment, the beach was beautiful. Then Pierre drew nearer, entered the picture, moved around within it, and saw things differently:

> All these many-hued dresses which covered the sands like nosegays, these pretty stuffs, those showy parasols, the fictitious grace of tightened waists, all the ingenious devices of fashion from the smart little shoe to the extravagant hat, the seductive charm of gesture, voice, and smile, all the coquettish airs in short displayed on this seashore, suddenly struck him as stupendous efflorescences of female depravity. . . . All these women thought only of one thing, to make their bodies desirable—bodies already given, sold, or promised to other men. And he reflected that it was everywhere the same, all the world over. (116–17)

To be sure, there are reasons why Pierre's view of the place changes in this way (I recommend the novel to anyone who has not yet read it), but certain major arguments of the "classic" denigration are already expressed here: the artificiality of practices, the exhibition of desires and the display of flesh that make the beach (we are still in the nineteenth century, of course) not a world apart from the world but a caricature of the world, whose hidden obscenities it reveals to the light of day.

Later, in 1960, in Jean-René Huguenin's *The Other Side of Summer,* we find a similar narrative relating this perceptual experience in which suddenly, as with a cruel zoom lens, the observer's gaze shifts from admiration to scorn:

Balloons, red parasols, the sound of waves, sand castles.... Olivier, walking ahead of Anne and Peter on the road, stared down at the beach whose activity was suggested only by the distant sound—shouts, children calling, waves breaking, the sea speckled with bright boats, the slender stems of girls' legs in their flowered bathing suits,

but as they approached, climbing down the dunes, walking across the sand, all he could see were skins scorched by the sun, the tiny limp heap of a naked baby, a varicose vein on a women's leg, vaccination scars, armpits—

beaches! Sand castles, the sound of waves, red parasols, balloons ... the summer when he was five: he had spent in Touraine with his mother, and he was in love with the woods.[6]

At the end of the path, at the farthest reaches of this promenade of the gaze, whether in the nineteenth century or the twentieth, what the close observer experiences is disgust, a sudden repulsion at the sight of skin, flesh, bodies—their grotesque or sordid details and their idle or provocative postures.

BEACH MORALISTS

To be sure, things do not always reach this point. The discourse critical of beach people, like antitourist discourse, includes nuances or degrees of intensity of feeling, from irony to aversion. Confronted with piled-up bodies, some observers are content with simple mockery; they deride rather than condemn outright. In such cases, just as images of dogs, sheep, fowl, or ants have been used to characterize tourists, other metaphors are used to characterize seaside vacationers:[7] the reptilian image of a lizard, to depict the vacationer's heliophilic apathy; the image of a chicken cooked on an assembly line (in Morand), or marine images like that of a sea bream to make fun of the flirt who (like the fish in warm waters) spends his time roaming the beach and its environs in order to seduce girls by showing off his tan, or seals beached in whole colonies on the shore, or bright red lobsters who stand for the glaring victims of the sun, or even the less familiar but attested images of mussels and crabs: "On the rocks, on the seashore, near the beaches, one sees blissful mussels and agile crabs practicing heliotherapy side by side ... As for me, I'm for the crabs ..."[8]

Still, as with antitourist discourse, as soon as we get beyond these first images, the tone hardens perceptibly and other, more virulent comparisons come into play:

> The Ligurian side, as far as Genoa (interminable Genoa), is so populated, so stifled with busses and trucks (oh the black suburbs of Sampierdarena!), so sticky with families clumped on its Albaro beach and with madreporic colonies that you have to go all the way to Rapallo and Portofino to find a bit of nature.[9]

Robinson is disgusted, and flees to other beaches, other islands. The flabby baby flesh discovered by one observer has its counterpart here in the familial stickiness seen by another, gregariousness perceived as glue: viscous, soft, and tenacious. As for "madreporic," the term refers us to the equally zoological image of a metazoan (a multicelled animal) whose polyps colonize, forming coral reefs and atolls. By virtue of its poetic intensity, this metaphor denigrates seaside vacationers as Gerhard Nebel's image of swarms of giant bacteria disparages tourists.[10]

However, this aggressiveness and scorn toward beach people are by no means the monopoly of our contemporaries. Once again, as was true in the context of antitourist discourse, critics did not wait for 1936 or, more generally, for the expansion of seaside vacationing to the masses in order to manifest themselves. Alain Corbin notes that this form of vacationing, even when it was still only "foreshadowed," aroused criticism, scorn, and revulsion even before 1840."[11]

We can indeed find stupefying declarations from the nineteenth century, for example the following, by the Goncourt brothers, on the verge of nausea; for them "beaches unquestionably offer the most horrifying image of women, who are perceived in terms of genitalia and the reproductive function." "Trouville. July 23, 1864. Maternity is on display here, a sort of animal, chicken-like maternity. One feels that sea baths are some sort of undisguised and disgusting site of reproductivity, a place where one brings one's wife in order to proliferate. The sea is a little like the water bucket under mares' tails."[12]

What disgust and scorn in these lines! What a gaze! And what an interpretation, too, crudely applied to beach sociability, which was only beginning to be organized around sea bathing! After evoking this sordid literary passage nearly a century later, Paul Morand takes it a step further. Even while denying that he is "condemning his fellow men," and while purporting to speak out against these "popular poisons," stating forcefully and clearly what, according to him, "everyone celebrates out loud and curses under his breath"—and without ever asking himself why people gather in this particular place in such numbers, Morand actually writes "that one would like to bring Goncourt back [to the Trouville beach] on August 15 in the 1960s, on one of those teeming mornings when there isn't even enough room to write your name in the sand."[13]

After the first thrusts of these moralists on the warpath against mass vacationing, the door was wide open to every sort of inquisitorial, reactionary, and sectarian delirium. Closer to our own day, we can cite for example a Montesquieu of the beach, very popular in his time, whose "theory of climates" applied to sites by the sea deserves our attention. The name of this "philosopher," the author of forgettable novels and an imitator of Pierre Loti, is Claude Farrère. And here is what he dared to write about the beach in 1925—in a footnote, to be sure:

It would be of more philosophical than frivolous interest to establish, according to the laws of logic, the necessary and sufficient conditions for the creation of a first-class luxury beach destined for continuous and complete success. Like Deauville in Normandy, like La Baule in Brittany. Well, in the first place, the choice of site is not as unimportant as one might think. Look at all our Norman coastline, so fresh, savory, and truculent, and all our thorny Brittany, half granite and half shipwreck: could anyone have invented anything more banal, more ordinary, more mediocre, than La Baule and Deauville, a pair of abandoned swamps? And yet swimmers flock there by the tens of thousands and more. Crowding like this cannot be attributed to chance. The successful beach thus has to be established on a perfectly ugly coast, or even worse: one without any originality or character. It is clear that in their unconscious exodus toward the west, the summer tribes have sought landscapes in mysterious harmony with their own mindset, that of newly-rich, freshly-laundered war merchants, avid for anything second-rate. Similarly, on the beaches where the diminutives of the true grand dukes and great lords cavort, few people require the wherewithal to bathe every day or to satisfy their hunger regularly either in hotels or villas, so long as their automobile is of a striking brand and so long as there are flowers at dinner at the Casino every Saturday night.[14]

To be sure, in concluding these prolegomena to an aesthetic philosophy of the beach that focus on practices of ostentation and their hypocrisy, I have invoked a social criticism that unquestionably has some merit. But we find something more serious underlying and antedating this criticism, namely, the hypothesis that an essential relation exists between the mediocrity of a site and the mediocrity of the people who populate it. If people "are therefore more vigorous in cold climates" and if "in warmer climates, [love] is liked for itself,"[15] what can be said of the character and passions of people who have chosen to settle on abandoned swamps? Here again we find disgust that is not concealed but rather rationalized by a morphopsychological "theory" of the beach.

As for the Belgian explorer Anne de Mishaegen, who arrived in the late 1930s in the seaside city of Avalon, on Catalina Island, across from San Pedro (the port of Los Angeles), a city whose site, casino, and ideal climate made it "an enchanting place to stay," she could not keep from comparing the summer vacationers on the California beach she had discovered with those of Europe: "This crowd is very different from the pitiful display of vanities clustered on the Côte d'Azur, quite different too from the family groups vacationing on the beautiful Flemish beaches [a bit of obligatory chauvinism]: it is good-natured, joyful, rather boisterous, young and healthy-looking."[16] This amounts to saying that on the shores of the Old World, and in its likeness, the "stale" vacationer has lost his freshness and his joie de vivre—that he is calm or even melancholic, that he is old and ill. Here is yet another "climate theory," a comparative anthropology of the beach in which regret now vies with doubt.

Claude Lévi-Strauss expressed a similar sentiment some fifteen years later. Even before declaring that beaches "are now trodden by hordes of people and serve only for the arrangement and display of nondescript rubbish," he wrote, "Such charms as I find in the sea are denied us in the modern world. Like some ageing animal whose thickening hide has formed an impermeable crust around his body and, by no longer allowing the skin to breathe, is hastening the ageing process, the majority of European countries are letting their coasts become cluttered with villas, hotels and casinos."[17]

From this starting point, extending the anthropologist's metaphor, when the crust not only thickens but is afflicted with eczema and infections, when the animal is not only asphyxiated but is covered with an excess of parasites—"blissful mussels or agile crabs," it hardly matters which!—and when pus full of germs and other cellular and necrotic debris begin to ooze from it, we have a nightmare. This vision haunts our era and prolongs the disgust inspired by vacationers' colonization of the seashore: the nightmare of total and irreversible pollution owing to overpopulation, the disfigurement and poisoning of the coastal regions.

VISIONS OF APOCALYPSE

It would be pointless to deny that this polymorphic nightmare—demographic, aesthetic, and chemical—is proceeding full steam ahead today or that prophets of the beach apocalypse have produced enough colorful commentaries on this hypothesis for us to be in a position to have a fairly clear idea of it at present.

Overpopulation

Paul Morand, who compared bathers to "sand fleas," offers the following apocalyptic image, in a commentary on his visits to campgrounds: "For my sins, I wander through these canvas cities which now hem the fringes of every European shore, as in a world after the Bomb." He continues: "Property owners along the shore post feeble notices—Private Road, No Hunting—in vain; the signs are carried away (and, on borders, so are the customs-officers) by the tide of nudists on vacation." And he adds: "This is the inflation of universal pleasure in the nightmare of a permanent boat show. The inflatable rubber canoes and plastic rafts add to the impression of a planetary shipwreck."[18]

Philippe Simonnot for his part invokes neither the tragic figure of a shipwreck nor that of a nuclear cataclysm to describe the phenomenon of overpopulation; instead, he draws on a laborious and repetitive working-class imagery coupled with the rigor of a mathematical proof. Let us follow his argument:

> In a quarter of a century, the number of stays at [French] beaches during the four summer months has increased tenfold, reaching the enormous figure of five million, owing chiefly to the influx of Northern Europeans. According to the experts, the 180 kilometers of the Languedoc-Roussillon beaches can accommodate 750,000 people at a time, based on an allotment of twelve square meters per person

(three meters by four). Let us suppose, during the high season, the presence of five million tourists on the coast. In order to maintain the minimum space of twelve square meters, there would have to be a rotation of three groups of bathers each day—the equivalent of three eight-hour shifts in a factory, but spread out over a maximum of twelve hours.[19]

This calculation is clearly farfetched. But, as mathematics is a language and not a science, we have long since learned to reason correctly about incorrect data. The calculation does not take into account either the variable degree of gregariousness of the summer people (even in low season), nor, quite simply, the surface area of the beaches. The supposition consists here in conceiving of the beach (as we may imagine the self-styled "experts" do) as a theoretical, perfectly linear linking of regulation chessboards twelve meters square along the shore. We need only go to Argelès or Saint-Cyprien-Plage to observe that the area available to summer vacationers does not have this longitudinal form. In short, Simonnot's arithmetic is not of much value; but it does attest after its own "ecolometric" fashion to the powerful presence of the demographic nightmare in public opinion.

Let us note that the caricaturist Serre goes even further in this direction, imagining a beach with, for each beachgoer, a space with a parking meter scrupulously controlled by the beach police, metermaids clad in bikinis with blue, white, and red tops calmly writing up tickets for every summer resident who has failed to pay for the right to park.[20]

Disfigurement

Here again, let us let Paul Morand have the floor first. He is speaking of Venice. "When the Lido offered just a lagoon like any other, it was a touching, funereal desert where little waves came soundlessly to lap at ground that lay scarcely above water. The first mushroom to rise up from the ground was the Excelsior Hotel . . . and everything else followed. The Palace of the Doges disappeared behind the new buildings."[21]

Mushroom hotels, coastal dermatitis, shoreline psoriasis! "'The beach is just back of these hotels,' she said, waving to her right. . . . 'When we first came here, you could see the ocean between the hotels, but not any more. You wouldn't believe the construction that's gone on since then.'"[22] The sky is still above the rooftops, but the sea now lies behind the houses. The earliest arrivals, the Robinsons of the Lido or Honolulu, were the happy ones; they could still see the water from their windows or at least, a bit later, between the hotels.

"What have we done to our coastline? Are there still any perfect beaches?" The question was raised by a magazine that published "all the maps of hell-holes to avoid and paradises to preserve." In addition to crowds, concrete is also now taking over the shore in epidemic fashion. "Massacre by concrete" is the title of another magazine article in the context of a special report titled "SOS Bretagne"—Brittany, with its oversized artificial ports, giant parking lots, Mickey Mouse beach clubs, and, as elsewhere, marinas. "Seashore: stop the massacre," a weekly newsmagazine demanded in 1991.[23] Now, as if on the eve of a catastrophe, we seem to have a state of alert, a unanimous state of emergency, supported by opinion surveys, in the face of a prophecy about to be accomplished: the denaturing of the shore by urban pollution!

Denaturing?

But has this not been true for a long time? From the beginning of the refurbishing of coastal regions for vacation purposes, the death of the fisherman, the construction of the earliest promenades and jetties, the first casinos and hotels? The massacre of the shore dates back a century or more. But now, at least in discourse, the feeling is coming to the surface: nature and landscape are going to disappear completely under concrete! Disfigurement, disappearance—the nightmare. Still, to the question: "What shoreline do you want?" while 81 percent of the French respondents answered that "nature should be preserved," only 28 percent said that "it should be less urbanized."[24] In other words, 72 percent had the opportunity to express a wish for deurbanization and did not do so. And yet according to an official statistic of the Ministry of the Environment in 1993, "20 percent of the linear coastline has been permanently urbanized."[25]

In short, we encounter a peculiar abstention, and a strange nightmare that seems to exonerate summer vacationers from responsibility for an inadmissible dream of a synthetic utopia. There is an ecological morality and there is a religion of seaside vacationing. People say one thing and do another—an eternal gap between attitudes and behaviors. On the one hand there is tradition, and the small fishermen who must not be allowed to die, and on the other hand there is the irresistible expansion of the joys and spectacle of yachting. On the one hand there are unspoiled landscapes that we want to be certain to protect, and on the other hand there are the palaces in Nice or Miami that we admire and photograph, bordered by the "prayer rugs" of their beaches, the fine imported sand on which we stretch out without compunction. We may as well get a bit of a tan while waiting to die. There is, finally, the natural shore as opposed to the perfect shore, the beach of our dreams and its artificial commodities, which have arisen precisely out of the historical repression of the former: Robinson's triumph over the Savages and savagery (see chapter 1 and the beginning of chapter 4).

Intoxication, Finally: The Poisoned Sea

The other "state of emergency," this time chemical or biological. Even ahead of crowds and concrete, this third aspect of the nightmare probably generates the most apocalyptic visions, the most sordid metaphors, the crudest parables. We can only call it anguish, for it exceeds disgust, mere condemnation, or nostalgia; here it is not simply a matter of the setting, the environment, but a matter of the body: my body.

As Roger Sheldrake puts it, "[t]he Mediterranean is like a toilet without a chain: you have a one in six chance of getting an infection if you swim in it."[26] Here is a terrible probability that one is inclined to acknowledge, owing to the various maritime pollutions, well known and dreaded today, whether clandestine or manifest, surreptitious or spectacular: household garbage and industrial byproducts, dirty water or black tides, "red mud," tar, oil, gasoline, pesticides, and even nitrogen of agricultural origin, which has stimulated the proliferation of algae in the English Channel and the Atlantic in a phenomenon known as eutrophication. And, finally, there are nuclear power plants, giving rise to fantasies far worse than dirt or sickness.

Thus the sea, a space of multiple excretions, a public convenience, and the beach, contaminated by floating or submarine evacuations, become objects of grim, repulsive evocations and representations. To Sheldrake's image of the Mediterranean as a toilet that cannot be flushed, the cartoonist Serre prefers that of the sea as gutter, with a beach across from a sidewalk-horizon where the setting sun is the black hole of a sewer outlet. Among the characters depicted on this beach, we see a man getting out of the water, his body dripping with a black substance that has stained his arms and legs.[27]

Let us turn again to Mr. Palomar, who has left his meadow behind. We find him on his trashcan beach, still philosophical:

> The wave flows, a solitary breaker, until it crashes on the shore; and where there seemed to be only sand, gravel, seaweed, and minute shells, the withdrawal of the water now reveals a margin of beach dotted with cans, peanuts, condoms, dead fish, plastic bottles, broken clogs, syringes, twigs black with oil.
>
> Lifted also by the motorboat's wave, swept off by the tide of residue, Mr. Palomar suddenly feels like flotsam amid flotsam, a corpse rolling on the garbage-beaches of the cemetery-continents.[28]

The nightmare, already well advanced with the toilet and gutter metaphors, takes on increased intensity here. Filth and illness are not all that lurk in this picture of the end of the world. There is also death, supported by a biological dream of generalized decomposition.

And beyond that? Clearly, I cannot catalog here all the nightmarish or apocalyptic landscapes of the beach and classify them according to a dramatic scale extending from suspicion to horror. But I can mention one last fantasy, one situated beyond those of filth, illness, and even death: the fantasy, linked to the fear of nuclear catastrophe, of a monstrous mutation of the earth's fauna and flora, as if poisoned nature, having gone mad from overindustrialization, suddenly took its revenge on the seaside colonization of the shore by devouring swimmers. Traces of this fantasy of an environment out of control and of uncontrollable metamorphoses of life can be found, for example, in a small piece of science fiction by Pierre Ziegelmeyer:

> "Have you heard the news? The little So-and-So girl was eaten by a sea monster only 50 yards from the beach!"
>
> "Another sea serpent farce!"
>
> "Don't joke, it's serious. Near all the nuclear power plants there seem to be mutations everywhere: plants, animals, people."
>
> "Come on, now. We already had to look high and low to find a spot that wasn't too polluted, between the acid piss of the chemical factories and the tar turds put out by the oil tankers. Not to mention the vaginal discharges of the nuclear submarines on patrol (the *Redoubtable,* the *Terrible,* the *Lightning!*). . . . If crabs and shrimp and eels are getting as big as elephants and whales, now, where are we headed, my good sir, where are we headed?! . . ."

"We must be there already! . . ."

"It's soon going to be unbearable! . . ."

"Still, the monster must have had a hard time, with the little So-and-So girl—she was a native of The Hague, a certified mutant, covered with razor-sharp bones and scales!"[29]

Apocalypse now! This is the great fear, if not of the end of time, at least of the end of the century, a fear all the greater in that it is inscribed in the imminence of catastrophe. The time has come for nature's revolt against man, for monstrous inversions and hybridizations, for Gulliver's passage from Lilliput to Brobdingnag, for invasion, for a very old fear (see chapter 9)—now enriched (like uranium, with the specter of technological delirium)—which Theodore Monod mocked deliciously in the 1950s:

I should still not like to stir up unnecessary panic and prophesy for next year an invasion of giant octopuses: the Cephalopodes are still aquatic animals, breathing through brachia. That gives us some breathing room. . . .

But the day when the forty-two-ton squid decides he wants some natural or artificial lungs so he can go walking in the open air, *Homo sapiens* had better watch out—including of course the representatives of the "generally-well-informed circles."

In the meanwhile, if I were in the government, I'd put lookouts on the beaches: fifteen minutes gained, the day of Operation Squid, could mean lives saved, it's as simple as that.[30]

In the meanwhile, the ancestral fear is there, always present in the imagination of the ordinary bather as it is in the collective consciousness, maintained and indeed fanned by the permanent state of ecological emergency that characterizes our era.

Moreover, isn't nature itself getting involved? While I don't really know what is happening with octopi and other mutating fauna, things are becoming clearer on the flora side, aren't they? There is eutrophication, but now there is also *Caulerpa taxifolia* (from the Latin *folium*, "leaf," but which in French at least sounds like *folie*, folly, madness!), an algae that has been described in newspapers as the "green cancer" of the Mediterranean; just a small fragment sufficed "for the monster to begin colonizing the Big Blue"; it is "diabolically beautiful"; it suffocates the shoreline, driving off fish and shellfish alike.[31]

So? Well, we may suppose that if Ulysses were to come back, he would feel pretty much at home; after all, after nearly drowning so many times, and after surviving so many shipwrecks, he "no longer approaches the shore without apprehension; for him, all beaches are like those where the Sirens lie in wait for him [fish-women, mutants before their time], sinister spots covered with wreckage and bones."[32]

There is no need to darken the picture further. Fantasies and prejudices have been identified. Paradise-beaches, beaches of illusions? Between fear and disgust, the shoreline of every nightmare, is the beach of our dreams gone forever? In fact, from nineteenth-century moralism to twentieth-century ecologism, what we discover in the shadow of the excesses of the former and the phantoms of the latter is that the image of the beach, so disparaged today, arises out of the telescoping of two discourses—one on the body and quantity, the other on the environment and quality. Making a sandwich of seaside reality, these discourses blur its interpretation, reducing its features to caricatures and denigrating its meaning. Without taking the analysis any further, let us say that the site of residential seaside vacationing, far from resembling an Ophelian pond, can then indeed appear as a sort of "swamp": a "crust" on the bank, where "stale vanities" are on pitiful display, emerging from the fatal encounter between two pollutions—one social in nature and the other biological.

The Shore Scorned

Seaside vacationers are the new Savages—or at least are perceived as such. We are now aware of the violent reactions of those who discovered them, condemned them, and finally could not repress either their massive taste for beaches and bathing nor their appetite for nudity (see end of chapter 2 and chapter 4). Before this, the aristocrats among summer vacationers, on their own, that is, alone among themselves in their new resorts, or, better yet, in their modest fishing villages still undiscovered by the hoi polloi, felt themselves to be safe, like Robinson midway through his adventures: "I found no ravenous Beast, no furious Wolves or Tygers to threaten my Life, no venomous Creatures or poisonous, which I might feed on to my Hurt, no Savages to murther and devour me" (104). It was later that everything shifted, with the discovery of "nine naked Savages, sitting round a small Fire," who soon started to dance, "stark naked" (142–43). As everything is called into question at the spectacle of this indecent festivity, safety for Robinson and the social order for moralists, suspicion, scorn, and then hatred take over their minds.

The Savage is the Other—and he is not good. What is this Other? In the case we are considering, the Other is first of all a body, naked or at least unclothed, and thus obscene; and then, in addition, it is a quantity: nine for Robinson, a crowd for the others. An ugly crowd for Léautaud, in Pornic in 1923, when he wrote, "[They] circulate throughout the country half naked, their female companions also; the men are ugly, like all naked men; the women are bulky, their bodies ruined, their skin baked."[33] The crowd is dirty and hypocritical in Farrère's eyes, stale and vain in Mishaegen's, full of sensuality for Maupassant's Pierre, bestial in addition for the Goncourt brothers. In the last analysis, this crowd seems to come to the sea like dumb beasts to the slaughter, impelled simply by their instincts—an image that remains firmly anchored in the popular mind. "'Where are they going? Honolulu. Honolulu! . . . Must be mad. They're all mad, if you ask me. . . . Look at 'em! Like lemmings. Lemmings.' He smacks his lips on the word, though in truth he isn't entirely sure what a lemming is. Some kind of small animal, isn't it, that moves in a mindless pack and throws itself into the sea?"[34]

The crowd is mad, impulsive, and noisy. Always bothersome, it ultimately inspires hatred. This feeling is not a new one, even among the most "democratic" commentators: "I love the people, but I hate a mob; especially a noisy mob of fast livers who come to sadden the great Sea with their noise, their fashions, and their absurdities," writes Michelet, who is eager to reserve the beach for the sick, but who also has a clear picture of "the sadness of the lady who, in July, suffers under the invasion of a mob of these fops, fools, and gossips."[35] So what becomes of Crusoean solitude, caught up in this hysterical quantity?

We find the same discourse in Paul Morand. He is not thinking about sick people (there aren't any more, or they are elsewhere); where the Goncourts attacked women, Morand prefers to focus on children: "Let's hear it for collectivities, health to the masses, fine, but not on the seashore! Silence, except for the water! The mewing of the waves brings fulfillment, but not the squawking of children disemboweling the sand the way a gastronome disembowels a pâté!"[36] The crowd, in its idiocy: what a relief when it is gone! It is like Robinson after the horrible cannibal festivities, when he sees the savages get into their canoes and head back to their continent.

I love this somewhat shaky mid-season, when the little resort [Sainte-Maxime] is still feeding on the surge of tourists, on the movement that is slowing down, coming to a stop. . . . And this September light, finally so clear, so frank, so cold, once the dubious August heat has been forgotten, the fog that obliterates shapes, the stale smell of sun-tan lotion and the howling stupidity spilling out of the parking lots marked "full."[37]

So there it is: the crowd. It is the social pollutant of the shore, with its primary attributes that make it the ever-so-hatable Other: its mass, its flesh, its noise, its odors. . . . Moreover, much as Laurence Sterne enumerates types of travelers,[38] Reiser lists the attributes of the seaside crowd, as noted by an irritated summer resident:

> They're ugly.
> They're pitiful.
> They're dumb.
> They're ridiculous.
> They're grotesque.
> They're obscene.
> They're smelly.
> They're scared.
> They're noisy.
> They're dangerous.
> They're repressed.
> They're bad.
> They're numerous. . . .

And as he is leaving the beach, spotting a perplexed dog reading a notice that says, "No dogs allowed on the beach," this summer vacationer says to him, "Hey, you're not missing a thing."[39]

Is this all? Of course not! Other criteria, other arguments, carrying a supplement of scorn and hatred, are also part of the malediction on the seaside vacationer. They refine his otherness, which is also cultural. Not only are beach people vulgar (ugly, pitiful, stupid, numerous), but they're also ignorant: "In Paestum," says one music professor, "there are very beautiful Greek temples, and they [the vacationers] have retained only the fact that five kilometers from Paestum there is an extraordinary beach with sand and a fabulous sun." Here we see the resurgence of an old fracture, the one separating the tourist from the summer resident, distinguishing the traveler presumed to be intelligent from the fool who lingers at the shore.[40]

And then there is alterity in the social sphere. "Clerks, employees, self-made tradesmen. A pretty spectacle. Here are human stupidity and vulgarity in full measure. . . . You have to see them planted at the far end of the pier, looking out from under their visors at the horizon of the sea, with an air of connoisseurs." White collar versus blue collar. Provincials versus city-dwellers. Locals versus vacationers. Here is one fisherman's observation: "Bathing, sunbathing, and other summer frolics, as well as the bric-a-brac of so-called underwater fishing with its masks, flippers, wetsuits, guns and oxygen bottles—all that is for Parisians, for rich idlers who come to play with the ocean for a few days. We seamen don't know how to play with the ocean."[41]

As for the workers, let us recall that they have been called "bastards in hard hats." Profiting from their first paid holidays, they were turned away by hotel managers on the pretext that they would lower the tone! From the Côte d'Azur, on August 27, 1936, Thomasson cabled the following report to the newspaper *Candide:* "On the whole, quantity can be said to be winning the day over quality." Pierre Rocher, writing in *L'Oeuvre* on August 18, 1936, corrects the aim in a few lines about the "bastards" in question.

> They hide their game so well that they could be mistaken for good folk here for the weekend. They don't eat salami on the beach, they don't sing "La carmagnole," they don't insult friends, they don't spit on cars. All day long, you see them in bathing suits. They go swimming, they work on their tans, they read newspapers. The "bastards" wear shorts, pajamas, underwear just like that of the Marquise de Breuteuil, who, under the name of Moussia, shows a good deal more of it; and when they walk in front of you, clacking the wooden soles of their sandals, you are obliged to observe that nothing resembles the bare back of a financier's wife more than the bare back of a Billancourt metal-worker's wife. . . .
>
> This is naturally worrying to those who want to reserve the Côte d'Azur for unemployed kings, heavily-made-up old ladies, and gigolos in evening dress. "Aren't you afraid," they whisper under the awnings, "that these people, dazzled by our sun, will end up taking over the country?"[42]

In short, the fear of invasion, the fear of the Savage, again and always, but a fear subtended now by the anguish of a loss of social identity:

the hell of mixing and confusion of classes, in place of Olympus or the aristocratic summer Paradise.

Is all this fear naïve and outmoded? Not necessarily. In a dictionary published in 1980, under "Holiday" we find the following: "Paid holidays: paid vacations to which a salaried worker has a right each year. Pejor. The persons who have the right to paid holidays. A beach invaded by paid holidays"[43]—an illustration of the definition that proves the persistence of social fear in this arena. The beach is so attentive to homogeneity that it becomes sectarian and xenophobic. When Crusoeism turns into leisure, it becomes a matter of classes and clans (see chapter 7).

In fact, not all that long ago, in the April 1982 issue of the *Journal du Touquet,* with reference to motorcycle races on the beach and the dunes, the well-known "enduro," we read that the "luxury [of the resort town] is out of harmony with that of the cyclists, who were a majority of those present that day." This is the moment when hatred of the other becomes shame for oneself, a moment when certain resort towns such as Le Touquet deny their seaside origin and turn their backs on "the beach, a terrain for popular maneuvers." For here the fear of motorcyclists is still the fear of Savages, people who bring in scandal, to wit, the social fracture of homogeneity, the cracking of the mirror—precisely the rift that breaks up the ideal being-together of "nothing but ourselves face to face with ourselves." All that is left is denegation or flight: one can turn one's back on the beach or take to one's boat, as Paul Morand does, rediscovering a decidedly profound truth: "Life would be too easy, if we didn't have 'the others.'"[44]

SCENES OF ORDINARY POLLUTION

And then, since bad things always come in clusters, social pollution— the massive return of the Other, or rather the arrival of new Savages on the beach—is compounded by biological pollution—the return not of Savages themselves but of savagery, wildness, the parasite invasion, the infectious and filthy irruption of the great outside world in the seaside cocoon, a supplementary soiling that entails the superposition of the proliferating stigmata of an out-of-control shoreline ecology onto the proliferation of women, babies' flabby flesh, squalling children, madreporic families, and other excessive popular agglutinations. From hatred of the other to repugnance for the environment, from aversion to bodies to aversion to the décor, this extension of disgust can of course only aggravate the negative perception of the place. After the quantitative phobia, here is the qualitative one.

Like the aristocratic summer resident's xenophobia, this other pollution of the site is not new. It can even be said to have been an ordinary aspect of beach life for decades, as the following advertisement from 1973 attests:

> Ah! The tar on the beaches . . . What an eyesore! No use complaining. Defend yourself. You have an ally: SCARLET WATER, a liquid spot remover. But don't wait! Go after the spots right away with SCARLET WATER. Better still, take a bottle with you in your beach bag. You'll save your skin and you'll save your bathing suit. A detail worth knowing: SCARLET WATER smells good.[45]

From the late 1950s on, long summer vacations on the Belgian coast taught me how to get rid of the tar blobs I stepped on—a common pollutant owing to the intensity of maritime traffic in the narrows of the North Sea. What seems striking, from this distance, is that this pollution was not openly denounced or even challenged at the time. Moreover, as the advertisement just cited indicates, defense was the approach of the day, not attack. Pollution was there and had to be dealt with—one came armed with a bottle of Scarlet Water, of course—and that was all there was to it. At the risk of shocking some readers, I shall venture to say that it was even, in a certain way, folkloric, an integral part of learning the joys of the beach, and it occasionally lent itself to comic scenes, something like this: "Jean-Paul, armed with a scoop, went off to poke around in the zone where the boy had been without retrieving anything but a used condom and three bubblegum wrappers."[46]

But attitudes have unquestionably changed. Before, when a child got tar on his feet, his parents turned to him and told him to be careful; now, they turn to the local authorities and protest. Pollution is no longer an accident, it is an act of aggression. "For some reason, my thoughts were full of Amilcar and his mad moral certainties. I was distracted from them, fairly ruthlessly, when I trod on a fat blob of tar the size of a plum. It squashed between three toes of my left foot, clotted and viscous like treacle."[47]

It is not a matter of challenging the scope and the seriousness of this broadly endemic phenomenon, nor of denying the realities of the dangers it hides. Tied to the industrialization of the coast, to the increase in worldwide maritime traffic, and to the unending growth of the summer migration of citizens toward the sea,[48] the pollution of the shoreline, making a spreading oil stain (this is the term for it!), has taken on unprecedented proportions on the international level. "'Maybe I'll go swimming.' 'Good idea,' he said. 'We have the best beach in the world' [in Veracruz]. It is called Mocambo; I paid it a visit the next morning. The beach itself was clean and uncluttered; the water, chromatic with oil slick."[49]

Nor is it a question of denying that pollution exists (that would be absurd) but of noting, above and beyond its objective traces (which in a way legitimize the nightmare visions evoked above), what happens to pollution on the symbolic level, in collective attitudes, behaviors, and representations.

It would seem, first of all, under the combined aegis of the hygienist discourse that has been revived by current events, a greatly magnified aesthetics of cleanliness, and an increased ecological sensibility, that the perception of the phenomenon has been sharply dramatized and that certain beach spectacles have become intolerable. "That afternoon there was a party of tourists at the Terrace . . . looking down in the water among the empty beer cans and dead barracudas."[50]

What is at stake is the defense of Paradise, or its corruption. For the human overpopulation of the beach is now coupled with that of sand and water, overpopulated with heavy metals, bacteria, streptococci and other infectious germs "capable of producing all sorts of harmful effects (mycoses, for example)," germs whose count is multiplied at least sixfold in the summer: from 3,000 per gram the proportion mounts to 20,000! People have begun to ask where they can go swimming in Europe. And in a great fervor of sanitation, the struggle is organized, the beach is remedicalized. Paradise today must be clean or it will not be. "'The history of Hawaii is the history of loss.' 'Paradise lost?' I said. 'Paradise stolen. Paradise raped. Paradise infected.'"[51]

In the water, bubble screens rise up to protect the beach from effluent coming from the great world beyond. On land near the beach, ditches are dug all around to prevent cars from getting too close: there are no automobiles in Paradise. No dogs, either; dogs are banned. And on "the island," with its shores already cleared of seaweed, a layer of clean sand over the dirty sand is no longer enough. Now, the sand is washed[52]—for safety reasons, of course (science has spoken), but also because this site has to remain, in its very substance (and here the imaginary is speaking), a world outside of this world, one from which dirt is driven away like impurity from the Garden of Eden. Finally, around the slogan "Vacances propres" (Clean vacations), which adorns the biodegradable plastic bags lining trash receptacles along the beach, the summer residents themselves (it really happens) take the symbolic operation to its peak. They move to the offensive. For example some people in Corsica, "summer residents at the Arinella Bianca campground who mobilized under a broiling sun for an entire afternoon, working all the way up to the Calzarellu tower, to eliminate all the trash from the beach, most of it debris thrown up by the sea that was dirtying the shore."[53] An anecdote in the form of a parable reminding us that Paradise has to be earned.

6. Borderland

*(or, How Robinson finally managed
to forget the interior of his island
for good and made Friday one of his
favorite spectacles)*

All societies in fact have to deal with area: that is, all societies are situated
in space, in a space that they particularize and that particularizes them.
—Françoise Paul-Lévy and Marion Segaud,
Anthropologie de l'espace (1983)

The ethnology of the beach is now beginning to take shape on the horizon of this study. A world is being sketched in, and the time has come to situate it more precisely in space, on the map of leisure and vacations. A certain distance is required so that we can observe this universe without its knowledge and as outsiders, as if we ourselves did not belong to it,[1] as if we were now situating our gaze on an island located fairly close by but invisible, a few leagues away from Robinson's, so we could spy on the inhabitants' doings: "Today she had been completely happy. They had bathed in a creek, they had swum and dived and played, and when they got tired they climbed up on a rock at the water's edge, an islet, but such a small one they could barely sit down. From there they could see the crowded beach and hear the swimmers' shouts."[2]

Between the Olympus promised by some and the apocalypse prophesied by others, between the soothing discourse of the hedonists and the catastrophic discourse of the guardians of Paradise, between weightlessness and gravity, at the crossroads between idyllic images and ecological catastrophes, between utopia and disgust, it is time to ask a crucial question. What is this place, really, or rather this scene, this paradoxical theater of a religion held in contempt, "this beach affair, this love affair with the sea, sprawling bodies and perfumed waves, right at the bottom of roasted France"?[3] For in public opinion, both popular and scholarly, the beach is indeed an "affair." It inspires so many contradictory landscapes and discourses, so many incompatible dreams and feelings, that the instinctive attraction to beaches becomes even more enigmatic. How can one account for the mass frivolity, teeming for some, the stuff of dreams for others, that brings a crowd back every year to the refuge of the shore?

After reading what the Goncourt brothers, Claude Farrère, Paul Morand, and many others have had to say, what are we to make, for example, of the following enthusiastic evocation of the earliest popular vacations: "For the first time, thousands of men, women, and children discovered nature, the mountains, the sea. Henri de Turenne's film, *1936, le grand tournant* (1936, the great turning point), made up of newsreels from the period, shows whole families sitting in city clothes on sandy beaches. Some people are wading; others are swimming; many are just sitting there dreaming"? And what can we make of this other proclamation: "The sea lends itself to crowds, to the masses, to collective dreams; the sea is a democratic empire"? Morand, a jealous and resentful Robinson, wants the beach to himself, and even Michelet does not want to welcome every Friday who comes along. In his eyes, the beach is not for the leisure-seeking crowd, the worldly-wise, and the celebratory, but for wornout working people, the ill, women, and children: "Hither! Hither, worn and wearied nation, swinked laborer, failing woman, young child, fading because your parents sinned; hither! To the Sea, and the Sea shall cure you!"[4]

Nevertheless, between the repugnance, hatred, and jealousy of the elites and the limited opening of the hygienists to seaside leisure, caught up for more than a century in the turbulence of a storm of arguments that demanded its desertification in one place, its controlled occupation in another, our overpopulated Eden, a thousand times denounced and ridiculed, is still there! What, then, is the collective reverie that has allowed the beach to resist all assaults—those of yesterday's moralists and today's, as well as the onslaught of the masses?

A CONCENTRATION-CAMP DEMOCRACY?

If the beach has given rise to contradictory images and discourses, it has led to equally contradictory arrangements and behaviors. We dream of the desert and are submerged in a crowd. We want to be alone in the world and we cluster together on the beach. We imagine a hut, a cabin, a grotto, a tent on the shore, and we settle down in cities, in hotels or campgrounds. What has become of the Crusoean ethic? Attitudes and dreams are confronted with objectively contradictory gestures and facts, signs that confirm above all a mingling of dreams and realities. If "the function of myth is to empty reality," a good deal unquestionably remains to be done in this instance.[5]

Advertising tirelessly sells deserts, empty shorelines, coconut palms, and hammocks against the background of a blue lagoon: Adamic or Crusoean, always the same solitude, the blessed solitude of the time before sin and after the Savages. One advertisement says: "If you see Footprints on some of our Beaches, they are surely Your Own"—thus footprints that cannot frighten Robinson in the least. Another ad promises "immense beaches of fine sand," "hidden brooks," and "sheltered bays." Still another promises the moon: "Give yourself the moon at the edge of the Indian Ocean."[6] There is just one problem: with respect to daily life at the beach, the figures, cynically, tell a different story. Advertising offers resistance; so do the facts. The Crusoe myth is drawn and quartered, as it were, devoured by numbers, carried away by the crowd.

In the context of contemporary seaside ethics, as expressed in statements by national or local agencies dedicated to protecting the coasts, do we not get the impression that the beach is supposed to be a wild site and at the same time peopled with civilized beings, or at least with informed and responsible Savages, reasonable vacationers of sound body and mind? Numbers without conscience mean the ruin of a site.

From the perspective of a seashore under the aegis of a medical establishment focused on prevention or treatment, Michelet predicted that future summer vacationers would be produced by a veritable "Science of Emigration."[7] He could not have imagined that the movement toward the shore would attain the vast demographic proportions it has reached today. Nor could he have predicted the uneven distribution of the vacation population across the globe produced by this "emigration," so he could not have foreseen the effects of the phenomenon on coastal development.

Concentration, overpopulation, densification, and *disproportion* are the first words that come to mind when we look at the statistics. For more than twenty years now, the proportion of French vacationers whose destination is the seashore has fluctuated between 45 and 50 percent (see Introduction). In 1992 this meant that beaches accommodated about 19 percent of the entire French population, not counting all the summer residents of foreign origin. In all, as we have seen, more than 25 million vacationers now visit France's beaches every year—in contrast to 3 million in 1936, after the passage of the law mandating paid holidays, and 16 million in the summer of 1978.[8] But other statistics allow us to see a clearer picture of the seaside phenomenon and its consequences on both the national and international levels.

In 1989 more than 48 percent of summer residencies in France, but only 26 percent of the available lodgings, were concentrated on the coasts. This disproportion, which underlies "a very lively atmosphere of speculation," is further evidence of the power of the coastal tropism; we find the same phenomenon at the international level, in countries with attractive beaches whose capacity for housing vacationers is primarily concentrated on the shore. Thus, in Belgium, 53 percent of the hotel capacity is along the coast; in Bulgaria and Romania, 60–70 percent; in the former Yugoslavia, the proportion was 80 percent; in Tunisia, it is 83 percent; and in Greece, 90 percent. All this implies massive programs of coastal development. We saw the same phenomenon earlier in France, first along the Riviera and then later on, in the 1960s, in Languedoc. Elsewhere, we have seen the growth of Miami, Palma, Acapulco, and Waikiki. And we are seeing it still along the coasts of Brittany, in the Basque country, the Ivory Coast, Baja California, Malaysia, and—still—the Riviera.[9]

In France, despite the efforts of the Conservatoire du littoral, an agency created in 1975 which is responsible for protecting more than 500 kilometers of shoreline, the densification and urbanization of the seashore continues apace in France. It is estimated that "one percent of the natural space along the coasts has been urbanized each year for fifteen years in a row." If to the zones of concentrated urbanism we add zones characterized as "moth-eaten" (where there is at least one building every 500 meters), more than 50 percent of the French coast has been built up, "that is, 2,800 kilometers of shoreline [are] already filled in; this proportion exceeds 75 percent in four departments and 90 percent in the Alpes-Maritimes and the Pyrénées-Atlantiques!"[10]

So what can be said about the coastal vacation population? Its excesses—with its sudden increases, the resultant lack of space, and

the attendant unregulated development—have been and still are frequently denounced by the press. The point hardly needs belaboring;
a few local examples will suffice. In Canet, in the Pyrénées-Orientales,
the population increases from 10,000 inhabitants in winter to 70,000
in summer. Not far away, in Argelès-sur-Mer, there are 30,000 campsites, that is, six times as many as there are permanent residents![11]
In Sables-d'Olonne, in the Vendée region, there are 17,000 winter
residents and 100,000 in the summertime. The Riviera, a short portion of the coastline that extends from the Estérel mountains to the
Italian border, receives 8 million vacationers each year (not counting
short-term tourists), in relation to 1 million year-round residents; this
region by itself represents 1 percent of worldwide "tourism."[12]

Here, then, in broad terms, is the ordinary seaside landscape of the
French, far removed from luxurious Pacific Island sites. Thus we can
readily understand that discourses expressing alarm have been legiti-
mately developed on the basis of the statistical evidence and have led
to condemnations of this form of coastal leisure. But condemnation is
not enough. On the margins of the economic interests that lie behind
its expansion, we must also attempt to grasp the psychological dimensions of the phenomenon, balancing the way it is perceived from the
outside, globally, against the way it is perceived from the inside by
residential seaside vacationers.

We might suppose, a priori, that the perception of seaside vacations by vacationers themselves would be fairly close if not identical
to the critical opinion that condemns them. We might expect that the
dissatisfaction of one group would find a favorable echo in the other,
corroborating their negative view. Yet this is not at all the case, as we
learn from a survey cited earlier, according to which 92 percent of the
respondents said they were satisfied with the beauty of the site, 88
percent with the available services, 84.7 percent with the price/quality
relation, 83.4 percent with the cleanliness of the beaches, and 83.2 percent with the quality of the accommodations. We might imagine that
these individuals had only stayed briefly on the beaches and did not
have time to suffer the inconveniences of the site. But this is not the
case either: the respondents' satisfaction increased with the length of
stay. And 80 percent of these vacationers even said they were ready to
return to the same spot within the next three years.[13]

This testimony, which goes against the grain of well-established
judgments and widespread criticism, can only lead us to weigh the

interpretation of the facts—or, more precisely, to interrogate these facts anew. What are they really after, these more or less satisfied people who spend their vacations on the beach or nearby?

"The beach endures, I think as I wander along its length, as well as changing all the time. What is its invariant?"[14] Denatured, over-crowded, urbanized, the beach indeed changes and remains. Its power of attraction thus appears to resist all evils. From the therapeutic beach of yesteryear to the hedonistic beach of today, the collectiviza-tion of the shore by way of seaside leisure seems for the most part not to have marred its capacity to seduce. What is the constant motive that accounts for the lasting success of this fringe of earth, separate from the world and full of people, in which society is concentrated?

THE PORCUPINE PARADOX

First of all, we must not persist in thinking that the summer vaca-tioner is drawn by nature, by a coastal rusticity that would inevitably be accompanied by a certain precariousness of the material arrange-ments. Neither naturalness nor precariousness corresponds to the tastes of this topophile—even if he frequents campgrounds, drives a motorhome, or stays in a Club Med "village" (see chapter 7). This is confirmed by another previously cited survey detailing what sea-side vacationers look for in rental units: "Vacation renters expect to find the same comfort they have at home [and perhaps even more]: dishwasher, color television, telephone, microwave, washing machine, swimming pool, tennis, child care, bicycle rental, etc."[15]

However much the proponents of a certain vacation morality may argue the merits of a "savage" way of life, they seek to be as comfort-able as possible in their summer residency, no matter what type of lodging they select. In this they resemble Robinson, the consummate tinkerer who never stopped improving the comfort of his residence during the long years of his sojourn. From this viewpoint, there is only one difference between Crusoe and the renter: the former's so-journ is experimental, while the latter's is initiatory.[16]

In contrast, what this summer resident seeks—and finds—is prox-imity to the sea and the beach: 54 percent of the clientele along the French coast stay less then 500 meters from the shore, and two-thirds stay less than one kilometer away. The quest for proximity attests to a choice of periphery, a desire for a border strip, even for narrow-ness. In this preference for proximity, contemporary vacationers are not in harmony with Paul Morand, who criticized the Ligurian coast (and others) for being too shallow: "I am not fond of this supervised shore, still very Belle-Époque, long on façades and short on depth. A plywood Brazil; this lack of thickness is what keeps one from believing in San Remo and Bordighera, or in Nice and Menton; they are not real beaches."[17]

But the summer vacationer, a temporary inhabitant of a world apart, is not seeking depth or thickness any more than he is seeking a "real" beach. He comes from the borderland, and the world's depth is precisely what he wants to leave behind, to forget. Each of the two studies cited above attests in its own way to the prevalence of this attitude—one by emphasizing that "cultural and historical characteristics are fairly rare in positive images" of a seaside area,[18] the other by indicating that among the elements viewed as factors in the success of a seaside stay, cultural activities come in next to last.[19] For the summer vacationer is not looking for a "real" beach, but a real stage: it must be clean, first of all, but also beautiful and peaceful, a place conducive to the game of detaching oneself from the world and forgetting all about it.

As for peace and quiet, in the vast majority of cases, and contrary to expectations, vacationers claim to have found them—with more than 84 percent satisfied; of these, 38 percent are very satisfied and 46 percent rather satisfied. At issue here is precisely "peace and quiet," and not the absolute solitude and emptiness sought by Paul Morand, a Robinson decidedly lacking a Friday, who prefers the deserted shores of Boulonnais, Berk, or the mouth of the Somme to the overcrowded beaches along the English coast. The words *peace* and *quiet* refer to a very different reality, that is, to a collective universe without anxiety or stress, a world without worries, without too much agitation or noise. There should be no more than a low rumble, the commotion characteristic of the seaside, produced by a crowd on land: background noise that seems to consist in murmurs and whispers and is only punctuated by the shouts—muffled by the water—of swimmers and children, the coming and going of naked bodies in motion slowed by the sand, and the "stifled flight of conversations."[20]

The beach in question is peaceful, then: not a desert but a site of tranquil sociability. It does not offer emptiness and solitude, but people together in a calm state, that is, calmed down, relaxed, and content because they are on vacation. They are not concentrated or clumped together but regrouped and gathered on the shore, away from the turbulence and conflict of daily life, ready to replay happy social scenes, restore loosened ties, establish new ones, or recover sensations of neighborliness and familiarity that have been lost in the city, the feeling of belonging to a community. We should bear in mind that in France, seaside vacationers come for the most part from the Paris and Lyon regions and from urban areas with 100,000 inhabitants or more.[21]

Given the sociological realities and the ritual function of the beach, we need to relativize certain images or received ideas—overpopulation, for instance, and the notion that the ideal robinsonnade consists in solitary enjoyment. The latter point in particular needs to be stressed. Robinson does not have any particular liking for solitude. Once he has settled into his island and is protected from all danger, this utopian villager, "divided from Mankind, . . . banish'd from humane Society," finds that he is subject to "Despondency" and "Miseries," to such an extent that it is he who reaches out to Friday by saving him, in order to have company. The vacationer likewise goes to the beach to find companionship, "being-together," living with or alongside others and mingling with them, a little like the "man of the crowd" who refuses to be alone and desperately seeks ultimate sites of sociability in the four corners of a city and in the depths of night.[22] Robinson, isolated by accident, is at bottom a community member homesick for society—a feature that Jules Verne highlighted in *Two Years' Holiday* by transforming the solitary figure of the Crusoe character into a "boarding-house" grouping of Robinsons.

As for overpopulation (without denying the reality of excessive density on certain beaches, where neighbor-to-neighbor relations deteriorate into unbearable promiscuity), what are the actual facts? Is the problem not simply the result of concentration? The anthropologist Edward T. Hall would tell us that overpopulation is actually an ambiguous notion having to do with the relative nature of its assessment in space and time.[23] A given neighborhood, in a city, may strike one person as "overcrowded" and another as simply "animated" or "lively." Similarly, the beach, seen from afar (often from too great a distance), may look like a frightful agglomeration, while from close up or from within it may be perceived as the site of pleasant conviviality or even as the euphoric space of rediscovered community. What is at stake here, to use Hall's term, is the issue of "sensory input" in human relations.

From this perspective, the notions of *peace* and *quiet* are eminently relative and largely fantasmatic, based on aesthetic models that are not widely respected, such as silence or immobility—just as people criticize a crowd and its hubbub even while unconsciously appreciating its presence. Phyllis Passariello has demonstrated this ambivalence in situ, in an observation of Mexicans during a weekend at the beach.[24] She found nothing but noise, piles of empty bottles, music from countless radios and tape-players, dancing, racket all around. And yet the protagonists of this festive sojourn said they had come to the site because it was typical, natural, and quiet!

In short, between the beach of one's dreams and hell on shore, it seems that the human practice of clustering together at the seaside, with all the attendant cacophony and concentrations, conceals more than the classic criteria reveal, namely, a desire to agglomerate—with specific rules, rites, and customs—governed by complementary strategies of proximity and distance, aggregation and division, imitation and differentiation.

Philippe Perrot notes that "in seaside promiscuity, the mechanisms of physical distance and gestural control function with a quite puritanical rigor." In fact, between transparence and opacity, everything is established here via an interplay of ambivalent installation, made up of contact and separation, exhibitionism and modesty, toleration for visual palpation of bodies and vigilant protection of bodies and of personal privacy, which are on offer but untouchable. A society of naked men emerges here in its constitutive complexity and contradictions, inherited from the hedonistic conquest of the shore; it functions according to a mode of sociability that brings to mind the paradox of the porcupine in winter.[25]

In freezing temperatures porcupines tend to gather together to get warm, but then they prick one another. Thus they cannot live either completely alone or completely in common. They are together without being together even while being together. Similarly, on the beach, the "agglomeration" of vacationers—who in this case are seeking the warmth of a community—reflects this universal social paradox, identifiable everywhere but particularly readable in this place, where people are seeking not only to unwind but also to establish new bonds or reestablish bonds that have come undone.

This is why the beach also deserves analysis, despite the customary disdain in which it is held, and notwithstanding the inquisitional gaze of the moralists, who depict the seaside phenomenon as one that observers "neglect to explain, the better to display its scandalousness" and thus supply the weapons for its condemnation.[26]

SEASIDE TOPOPHILIA

Then the man of the beach is an idiot and proud of it? Not at all! Taking into account the activist, cultural, and sports-oriented discourses that press in on him, we may suppose that he is ashamed to be so classified. In the final analysis, he is almost ashamed to stay at the beach—even though it feels good to him to be there. This summer vacationer is almost compelled to go through his stay wearing a mask, cloaking his "passivity" in pretexts and excuses—hence his alibis full of always-abandoned touristic projects and never-kept athletic promises. He manages ultimately—and surreptitiously—to satisfy his reveries of repose and his dreams of eternity only by lying (see chapter 4).

For, once he has reached his destination, this traveler does not resemble the tourist targeted by travel agencies that "invite you to visit the five continents, to climb the highest mountains, to explore the depths of the seas. To restore historical monuments, to learn to weave or throw pots. To photograph animals in their natural environment. To go horseback riding, skiing, sailing." Sailing and yachting do not tempt seaside vacationers any more than cultural events do (these account for 2.4 percent of their activities)—it is as if they did not want to distance themselves from the beach! They want simply to stay put, nothing more, remembering perhaps that Robinson, wanting to make a tour of his "dear island" in his little boat, was nearly carried off by the currents to the open sea, and this painful experience of distancing left him with a feeling of such overpowering despair that he resolved never to go out in a boat again.[27]

Thus, during their stay, only 2.8 percent of vacationers go out in motorboats, and only 3.7 percent use sailboats or sailboards. The statistics confirm the taste for sedentary consumption of the coast, in an environment that is excursionist but not maritime. Despite the development of yachting (see chapter 1), boating is virtually absent among beach vacationers; and if the port is a desired destination, it is "as a spectacle and an element of animation, but never as a place to tie up boats."[28] Thus contemplation clearly wins out over mobility.

But what about hunting and fishing? Only 4.6 percent of vacationers make these their primary activities. And sports? Tennis is played by 3 percent, while 62.2 percent concentrate on swimming and the beach, and 13.3 percent acknowledge that they engage in no activity in particular.[29] We can only conclude that these vacationers are genuine topophiles; their attachment to the place presupposes that they require few, if any, auxiliary or external features in order to settle and stay there.

These vacationers seem to have taken literally the philosophy expressed in one advertisement, which says simply, alongside a picture of a beach:

> YOU ARE AT HOME HERE.
> It may not be the Spain of the Alhambra or the "paradores," but this is what Spain looks like for many of us. The Spain that reminds us of our youth and our first moments of independence, or our first family vacations abroad. Well, some things don't change. In Spain, you can still spend whole days on the beach.[30]

Stirring, moving about, expending energy, paying visits, getting out and about—this is not what our vacationers want to do. What do they do, then? Seemingly, nothing at all! Over and beyond the picturesque, the typical or the natural, they appear to have succumbed to one major argument: comfort.

> But it's really the incomparable comfort found on Spanish beaches that brings people back. You feel truly at home, except perhaps for the sun that is always shining and the Mediterranean that is right there at the edge of your garden.[31]

As if they were at home here, Robinson and Friday are out of all danger; they are satisfied, looked after, protected, reassured. They don't need the five continents. Their island—this beach—belongs to them; it is enough for them. They have set up housekeeping in utopia. They shut themselves away, as long as their vacation lasts, and they don't want to leave. So why climb mountains, engage in underwater explorations, or take pictures of animals? All nature, with its crudeness, its rough spots and its dangers, is abolished here in this theater of sand with its Ophelian dreams. Look for lost civilizations and forgotten people? But at the beach the point is to forget everything, including the forgotten peoples; and if there is rediscovery of lost civilizations, it is a fleeting moment, the span of a stroll to the old port.

Restore ruins? Such shoulder-rubbing with history is inconceivable in the framework of this Olympian scene! Learn to weave, try pottery? Why reintroduce images of work into a Crusoean universe that is so well arranged that there is nothing more to do?

> What other distractions are found in the summer at La Nartelle, except for the beach, the baths, the siesta, the meals, reading sometimes, and the beach again, the sand that burns your feet, that gets into everything, your books, under the soles of your shoes, on the mats, in the cars, slipping and endless sliding through the hourglass of motionless summers.[32]

Except for swimming, sleeping, eating, and reading, one does nothing at all in this static universe, in this kingdom of nonevents and nondiscoveries, where days flow by sheltered from everything.

Reading? Reading is very important—and very revealing as well. Unlike the tourist who is constantly on the move and does not have time to read, except for his guidebooks, while walking, riding in cars, trains, planes, or in his hotel room in the evening, the summer vacationer has time and sometimes reads a good deal. He even comes to the beach with books that he has accumulated during the year for vacation reading, the way others stock up jars of jam for the winter. In general, these books are novels,[33] that is, fictional, imaginary worlds, into which, between two swims, the vacationer plunges for hours, closing himself off from the rest of the world, as in a sort of narrative apnea (see chapter 9). In so doing, he is isolating himself even further from the outside world.

Current events are much less appreciated and sought-after. They are always intrusions of history into Paradise, blemishes, like stones thrown into a still pond or the return of gravity to a weightless world. Vacationers do buy periodicals, but mainly magazines dealing with vacations (so as not to change the subject), collections of crossword puzzles (to pass the time), or local newspapers (a matter of getting a bit of news from the interior of the island, or incidental information about the beach). But in general, the relation of vacationers to stories about the serious realities of the outside world (economics, politics, society) is rather casual, distant, even negative; this is manifested by some in a refusal to read newspapers, listen to the radio, or watch television, at least as sources of information.[34] Through this practice of reading and information, seaside topophilia positions itself psychologically more and more outside of the world. It thereby reinforces its own autonomy, that is, its isolation and indifference.

But then what is summer vacationing, this being-together or living-with, which from afar resembles nothing but a disorganized crowd concentrated along a shore?

> The recipe is simple and tested. You take a blue sea, preferably warm and silky. You edge it with a sandy beach, preferably white and soft. You shade it with a fringe of coconut palms wafting over the water. And you sprinkle sun over it all. Generously. Especially if the consumer spends most of his time under a desperately gray sky. Here, defamiliarization is often limited to the blue overhead.[35]

The recipe is easy to follow, and it can be simplified even further. Most beaches attest to this; the ingredient "coconut palms wafting over the water" is not indispensable. Nevertheless, the reasons for the recipe's success are more complex: they stem from a more sophisticated "physiology of taste."

And in the first place, who is talking about defamiliarization? Here, as we have seen, we have the land of "nothing but ourselves face to face with ourselves"—in other words, a living-together on the order of among-ourselves, thus of Sameness. On the beach, everything having to do with Elsewhere and the Other is abolished: all contact, every disturbing dialogue with the outside, whether cultural, social, or even natural. Here, homogeneity and resemblance reign—individual and group narcissism (at the water's edge, this is basically quite obvious), a collective egotism with several levels: individual, family, and class.

On the beach, people are thus looking neither for defamiliarization nor for "refamiliarization"—experiences of lag, decentering, or revitalization that are provided precisely by tourism or vacations in the country. The beach is not "the country," not a region with its own territorial traditions. It is rootless, lacking in inhabitants and in history. It is without identity, as it were—or rather, like Robinson's island, it has no pre-established identity except the one it is given by the individual who appropriates it for herself, the one who takes it over and rebuilds her world on it.[36]

What world, then? And for what experience? The world here really does belong to you—at least within the spatio-temporal framework of the simulacrum of moving in. Like an empty room, it will be what you make of it, you and your fellow topophiles, at the outset of your vacation—and at the solemn hour of dividing it up, as well (see chapter 7). The beach is the theater of an experience that derives neither from defamiliarization nor from refamiliarization, but from a particular kind of familiarization, one that might be called *paysement* in French: the act of bringing all or part of one's own hometown or region along in one's baggage, as it were, and transplanting its signs, customs, values, and dreams into a space that is vacant or perceived as such. Without question, such transplantations have some affinity with colonial migration—but here the vacation "colonies" are ephemeral entities, regularly dissolved by summer's end.

What does the summer vacationer proceed to do at the beach, then, if not—on the basis of units of reference such as the family or a group of friends—to transplant a model of simplified sociability, in which the material and moral constraints of daily life are noticeably lessened? With its decorum and its emphatic conviviality, the Polynesianism of the Club Méditerranée appears from this standpoint like nothing so much as a rite exaggerating the characteristics of the model. Always within the framework of a provisional, "performed" sociability, is not the heart of the matter above all, and in all cases, despite proclamations of a total break with the society from which one comes, the conservation of the best of the world left behind—the world in which people talk to one another?[37]

The seaside imaginary thus situates the beach neither Elsewhere nor with the Other. It is a collective being-at-home, deported onto the border, onto the side of the World (as the English terms *seaboard* and *seaside* suggest), and retained for a vast ceremony that is not one of discovery but of social and emotional reaggregation, of cocooning on a mass scale impossible in cities. As opposed to the happiness of the private sphere, "the tiny individual sphere that had a stale odor about it," happiness can be conceived "as a social force, which means that individual happiness has dignity only if it is obtained within the framework of a collective happiness." If the beach is indeed a place where this force is delivered and expressed, can we continue to refer to it as a site of "passive vacations"?[38]

Unlike the tourist who, unable to change the world, changes worlds[39] and goes off into the extraordinary, the summer vacationer neither changes the world nor changes worlds. He starts the world anew; he reifies it, restoring the infraordinary features of his life for the span of a few weeks, following the rhythm of his desires: that is, the eminently common but profound realities of gregariousness, exchange, play, or seduction, the banal desire to appear and to please. A naked man, he manifests in various ways, in the crowd freed from city garb, the limpid necessity of that desire.

"It is not in novelty," Raymond Radiguet wrote, "it is in habits that we find the greatest pleasures."[40] After many scandals, today's beach offers an excellent illustration of this reflection. It is a place where habits, reproduced and lived in an ideal form, become king; they are aestheticized and stylized as they become rites. A place between land and sea where images of a repetitive and unsullied conviviality are staged and exhibited in the homogeneity of a self-contained space on the margins of any confrontation with the Other—historical, natural, cultural, or social. This is also the function of the seaside ghettos, popular or "deluxe," that isolate social classes from one another (see chapter 7). Thus, like that of the Nambikwara as seen by Lévi-Strauss, beach society may appear as the space of simulation and representation of "a society reduced to its simplest expression"—a space in which the essential relationships and bonds of emotional, private, and collective life can be read in purified form.[41]

What about defamiliarization and refamiliarization in this autarchic universe? It is a self-sufficient world, without roots (or at least it imagines itself as such), a territory without soil or folklore—a bubble, a full fortress particularly well suited to a sort of "group autism"[42]—the beach is not a space of defamiliarization or refamiliarization. Culturally, there is neither defamiliarization nor refamiliarization in utopia. One does not become reacculturated on an "island" with no past, marked by no trace of origins; and one does not experience culture shock, either, on a shore with no Savages, without the foreigners whose presence so disturbed Robinson. This is why it can be said that "defamiliarization is often limited to the blue sky overhead," and nothing else.

Still, to the extent that *paysement*, the transplantation of models of sociability, introduces the return or rediscovery of a convivial logic that is obscured during the rest of the year, we can speak of a social refamiliarization, of a return to fundamental social bonds. And, correlatively, of a possible defamiliarization, also in the social sphere, when, owing to the nakedness that erases marks of belonging, the summer resident, a social migrant, slips from one class to another, wiping out his difference. A sensation of effacement experienced by one sixteen-year-old boy of modest origins when he encountered the daughter of a wealthy family: "On this terrain, Chantal escaped from the world of wealth; she thus became more accessible, and he dreamed once again about the texture of her skin."[43]

Nevertheless, this transmigration, this social game, as quest and as experience, soon comes up against its limits in space and time. Signs in the form of fierce opposition to any defamiliarization arise and oppose transplanted worlds to the confusion of universes. In Portugal, the agglomeration of Santa Bara de Nexe has become a

> true English colony to which our neighbors from across the Channel have imported their life style, created real estate agencies, a nursing school, cottages surrounded by lush lawns where one can sometimes find bed-and-breakfast establishments, authentically British restaurants and pubs like Sue's Bar in the village center. Without any doubt, at the extreme edge of Europe, the height of defamiliarization . . . and of snobbery![44]

I would call it, rather, for the well-to-do Englishman (Birmingham metalworkers do not take their vacations here), the height of paysement—the robinsonnade carried to its pinnacle. And in Greece, in Rhodes, along the same lines, one can find a Danish zone, with restaurants scrupulously reproducing the dinner hour observed in Denmark. Well sheltered from local rhythms, here the soup and shrimp cocktail are served at 6 P.M.

THE BORDERLAND AND ITS BACKWATER

Unlike the tourist universe, the seaside vacationer's universe thus does not manifest, on the beach and its surroundings, a desire on the part of its inhabitants to get outside themselves, to modify their own rituals or reference points. Instead, quite to the contrary, the inhabitants of this universe manifest a desire to be totally themselves, to remain themselves or to become themselves anew. Here we are touching on an essential difference in goals and behaviors. There has probably been too facile an agreement that the "tourist" in general—that is, the vacationer—had one and only one goal during his vacation: "to be someone else, somewhere else."[45]

The formula is ambiguous, especially when the somewhere else in question is experienced as a home and thus not conceived as a genuine "elsewhere." To be someone else, under the circumstances, can mean to identify with someone else, to forget oneself in the face of the other and perhaps proceed from there to a transfer of identity by the adoption of all or some of the other's characteristics, clothing, customs, rhythm of life, or language—to play at being a peasant in the Quercy, or an Indian in the Andes, for example. Or it can mean to affirm oneself and put the internal other on display, that is, take off the mask, let down one's guard and allow one's true identity—or at least what one imagines is one's true identity—to come to light. In the first case, "being another" stems from identification, an operation of projection; in the second, it stems from a cathartic operation that falls under the heading of revelation. To be "other" may mean dressing or undressing: replacing one's own clothes with someone else's, or simply taking them off, as the seaside vacationer does. In the first case, one plays at being what one is not—one becomes other—and in the second, one plays instead at what one thinks one is—one becomes oneself.

Without underestimating the degree of illusion that feeds these two strategies of identity (re)formation (in each case there is reference to models, and thus imitation), the distinction is nevertheless decisive. It separates two radically opposed vacation mentalities and appears indispensable to the understanding of residential seaside vacation psychology. To varying degrees, what characterizes the tourist, but also the fusional seaside vacationer, the ethnologist, the neorural of the late 1960s[46] or the emigré in pursuit of assimilation, all eager to be integrated into a cultural environment, is the refusal of Sameness, and, correlatively, the desire to escape one's fellows, people like oneself. What characterizes the seaside summer vacationer, like Robinson, on the contrary, is the rejection of the Other and the simultaneous desire to reconnect with one's fellows. It is on the basis of this rejection and this desire that the seaside microcosm is constituted as a "system of signs and behavioral norms in which the gaze and appearances prevail."[47]

This system, which presupposes the rejection of the environment[48] and of all contact with the outside world in order to function, is characteristic of a society that reflects itself in its identity and not of a society that experiences itself in its difference. On the beach, society puts itself on display, looks at itself as a whole and in parts, and stages itself for itself, outside of any context. The beach site is a decontextualized theater structured by the narcissistic dialectics of seeing and being seen. If, as Yves Lacoste notes, the tourist "has difficulty imagining that he is being looked at," the seaside vacationer on the contrary accepts this quite readily.[49] When a "beach person" looks at another "beach person," what is he looking at but himself or those close to him, for better or for worse? We compare; we judge: the varicose vein on a neighbor's thigh belongs to the same story as the mote in a neighbor's eye.

What comes into play here, decisively (defining the theatrical convention of the place), between the inside (the territory of local society) and the beach properly speaking, is the creation of the backwater of the borderland: a frontier in the form of dunes, pine forest, or promenades that serves at once as demarcation line and observation point. Whether natural or artificial, the separation is an ambivalent one that gives the beach both its specular quality and its autonomy.

If we may suppose that promenades and piers were initially built so that people could contemplate the sea and breathe in the salt air, and that later (at a time when swimming was still fairly uncommon) they became a corridor for strollers seeking to meet others and put themselves on display, in "a new parade," especially for the aristocracy, we note that they quickly became a privileged site of observation for walkers examining not the maritime or worldly spectacle but that of the beach.[50] If there was a time when the promenade indeed allowed the walker to turn his gaze toward the horizon, and later toward the nearby parade of worldly personalities, there was another when the spectators' glance was directed downward, toward the intermediate landscape outlined by swimmers' bodies in ever-increasing numbers.

In the period between the two world wars, this tacit agreement about seeing and being seen was definitively adopted among summer residents. As Liselotte wrote in her 1931 manual, "One comes to see, to be seen, to gossip, and to dress up."[51] And even before that, starting in the late nineteenth century, this collective voyeurism became part of the unwritten behavioral code. It is a frequent and unremarkable distraction, as Mme de Lalaing's account attests. At Sables-d'Olonne, Biarritz, or Pornichet, her travelers never fail to stroll along the promenade at each stop and observe the bathers with amusement or admiration: "It was just the time for bathing, and the little beach struck us as quite animated. The bathers were numerous, and many spectators were also present to watch the joyful frolicking, as well as the exploits of some very skilled swimmers." Thus, the traveler goes on, "[having sat down] with the intent simply to rest a few moments, we stayed to watch for more than an hour, participating in the admiration of their usual public."[52]

From the promenade to the sand, from the dunes to the cabins,[53] close up or far away, the game is played everywhere: everyone scrutinizes everyone else in the vicinity. Far from the protocols of modesty commended by Michelet, but already quite close to the troubling confrontation between visitors and nudists on the Île du Levant (see chapters 2–3), this permissiveness became a custom that was gradually integrated into the order of the beach. Our poet of the Riviera described this distracting spectacle in 1933 with almost entomological scrutiny:

> The beach is made up of very fine sand.
> There one can see all humankind,
> In a very small space,
> In bathing suits, almost nude, piling up.
> Tanning one's skin in the sun
> Is all the rage. In addition, one darkens it
> With "oil the color of bronze."
> Ten or eleven varieties can be counted,
> From light to black.
> What happiness, to be able
> To turn oneself thus into a Redskin, a Negro![54]

Thus the gaze follows a trajectory determined by the stroller's gaze. Shifting from traveling mode to panoramic, then from panoramic to zoom, it finally freezes to count the color of skin tones and to contemplate the bodies gathered in a circle around a beach umbrella. Note is taken of this visual practice—and the backwater of the borderland decks itself out appropriately. In addition to the promenades sprinkled with benches and chairs, there are terraces and restaurants where the "voyeur" can settle down and observe the beach at his leisure, while enjoying a cold drink or a bowl of fish soup.

In the early 1920s, in San Feliu, Spain, when bathers had become numerous enough to warrant the construction of a new bathing facility, a more elaborate structure was built for the purpose, "with a raised gallery from which one could admire the bathers while having a drink and listening to Catalan dance music."[55] Since then, countless "beach cafés" have been built in the background of beach landscapes.[56] These are ritual places for observation, but also for meeting, for exchanges and blending between the dressed and undressed worlds—channels in a sense linking decency and indecency, reserved for social interplay on the frontiers of modesty.

In the course of these installations, the specular function of the beach site, like that of a theater, with its actors and its spectators, has been gradually confirmed. The beach has taken on the force and form of a narcissistic stage, and the borderland has won its unity and independence, imposing itself as a closed system of representation. At the heart of the system, the vacationer, playing on the dialectics of gaze and appearance, is by turns spectator and actor, a curious onlooker and a curiosity himself.

Earlier, as we read in the 1897 *Guide des familles aux bains de mer*, photography—that is, the gaze of the other—could still pose a problem on beaches. "It is quite obvious that a husband, a father, or a governor would be perfectly justified in lodging a complaint against an indiscreet amateur who photographed his wife, daughter, or ward in a bathing costume without her prior consent."[57] This is no longer the case. Without any prior consent, Claude Nori in Rimini, Bernard Descamps on the beaches of Picardy, or Elliott Erwitt on all the world's shores, from Saint-Tropez to Blackpool and from Miami to Rio, have surprised swimmers, stolen their images and published them.[58] No scandals ensued; no charges were pressed.

Today, all this goes without saying. It no longer astonishes us. And yet, when we think about it, it is quite a strange spectacle—for example, on the Croisette at Cannes in midsummer, where thousands of dressed vacationers lean over the promenade to look at thousands of undressed vacationers, who are actors indifferent to the crowd of voyeurs, allowing themselves to be observed acting out "primitive" scenes of topophilia. They are there, before our eyes, and yet far away, as if they were on the shore of an island, separate from the world, installed in a sheltered spot, on the other side of an invisible mirror.

"In the modern world we have stages; we see people everywhere who are there to be admired, but we do not see admirers anywhere," writes Jean-Pierre Dupuy.[59] This is unmistakably true, almost everywhere. And yet there is still the beach, where people do not necessarily admire one another, but where at least they still look at one another.

Let us now move to the other side of that invisible mirror.

PART III

In the Land of Naked Men

The place held in common by the ethnologist and those he talks about is simply a place: the one occupied by the indigenous inhabitants who live in it, cultivate it, defend it, mark its strong points and keep its frontiers under surveillance, but who also detect in it the traces of chthonian or celestial powers, ancestors or spirits which populate and animate its private geography.

—Marc Augé, *Non-Places* (1995)

If we used a scale of merit to compare an Africanist with twenty years in the bush to a "beach person" with twenty years on the beach, the latter would clearly not stand up very well to the former. Taking into account the dangers faced and the hard-to-reach cultures explored by the Africanist, the beach person's ethnology can only provoke a smile. Still, are the object sought and the approach taken by these two groups of explorers so very different? The question is worth raising.

"We know," Claude Lévi-Strauss writes, "that among most primitive peoples it is very difficult to obtain a moral justification or a rational explanation for any custom or institution. When he is questioned, the native merely answers that things have always been this way, that such was the command of the gods or the teaching of the ancestors." What, then, is the difference between these primitive peoples and beach people? "Even when interpretations are offered, they always have the aspect of rationalizations or secondary elaborations. There is rarely any doubt that the unconscious reasons for practicing a custom or sharing a belief are remote from the reasons given to justify them."[1]

So how much is the medical justification of sea bathing actually worth, in relation to the rites and games to which the success of this practice has led? The anthropologist adds, "Even in our own society, table manners, social etiquette, fashions of dress, and many of our moral, political, and religious attitudes are observed scrupulously by everyone, although their real origin and function are not often critically examined."[2] The same thing can be said about the beach, a space where both formal and informal codes apply. The former are based on considerations of health, safety, or morality, and they stem precisely from "rationalizations or secondary elaborations"; the latter, which may be customary, ritualistic, or ludic in nature, stem on the contrary from "unconscious reasons."

In the superimposition of formal and informal rules, explicit and unconscious codes that govern this place, "the land of naked men" is solidified as a cultural reality in its own right, a worthy object for ethnology. There is a great deal more than ad hoc scientific or political discourse at the origin of the seaside phenomenon. More obscure powers—chthonian, celestial, aquatic, or other—also drive people to the shore and determine how they behave there.

Whereas Fitzgerald describes the beach as a "prayer rug," Morand declares that "the gulf of Porto and the deep rocky inlets of Piana constitute the most famous temple of the seaside religion." Just as there is a Club Med "spirit," there is something sacred in all this—or at least a force, an impulse that exceeds the utilitarian definition of seaside practices. At the sight of beaches in California, Edgar Morin wonders: "But what *elohim* drives these young people by the thousands onto the beaches, the shores at the ocean's edge, as if in the expectation of a fabulous voyage, as if to find something that symbolizes the freedom and original confusion of all things, the mother sea, the free sea?"[3] This question can be extended to all beaches and to all who seek them out and settle down beside them. A reason of a different order inspires the scrupulous obedience of this migrant crowd.

Krzysztof Pomian notes the following phenomenon:

France has taken the rite of the summer interruption to a degree
unknown in the rest of the world. In his *Seasonal Variations of the
Eskimo*, published in 1908, the sociologist Marcel Mauss pointed out
that Eskimos move to the edge of the sea to hunt in the summer;
in the winter, they huddle in igloos, protected from the elements.
Mauss's text was at once descriptive and prophetic. Parisian intellec-
tuals today behave no differently. Concentrated quite promiscuously
in the winter in two arrondissements, they disperse in the summer,
spreading themselves out among the Lot, the Lubéron, and the hinterlands of the Côte d'Azur.[4]

Similarly, large numbers of people who are concentrated in cities in
the winter, like the Eskimos in their igloos, prefer the front lines to
the hinterlands and go no less ritually to the seaside in the summer.
But for what hunt? To play what games and follow what rules? Seaside
conviviality is, like most leisure convivialities, whether nomadic or
sedentary, a space for "playing at life."[5]

Beneath the norms of behavior imposed by the formal codes that
govern its organization, divide up its space, define its arrangements,
and establish the limits within which the vacation practices housed
there are to be exercised, the sense that rites and games are inscribed
here is the fundamental issue that a beach ethnology, oriented by
definition toward decoding the "unconscious foundations" of social
life, has to address.[6] Understanding that games "precipitate the flavor
of the times the way a chemical agent precipitates out bodies dissolved in a liquid,"[7] the goal of this ethnology will be to identify and
interpret the signs of the "flavor of the times" whose manifestation is
prompted by the critical property of games we know as precipitation.

Dissolved and dispersed in the prevailing social milieu, bodies in
fact deposit themselves on the beach. They gather there and experience one another as they do nowhere else, "precipitated" as they are
onto the shore by the unconscious quest for the great seaside game.
What is this game? In the mode of the provisional morality of "as if,"
it is a game played apart from and outside of the world; it induces
simulacra by virtue of which each individual, returning to forgotten
knowledge, freedoms, and gestures, claims ritual roles and powers
that have become inaccessible elsewhere. It is no doubt in this respect
or for this reason that there is an element of the sacred on the beach,
if it is true that "sacred things are things protected and isolated by

prohibitions."[8] The beach, as we shall see, indeed protects and isolates this ritual demand. Thus it enables the restoration of elementary physical and social relations, based on sensory experiences, primitive coenesthesias, and convivialities. These latter make the beach a special place of initiation, one that "no teaching can ever communicate to us."[9]

In the context of the seaside game, in theory nothing existed prior to the place itself. Even if this is an imaginary condition, a fantasy, or merely a pretense, it is the essential quality of the beach, its function, and its primary law. As the result of a tacit or unconscious convention, everything here is to be created or re-created. We find nothing of the old internal, real, or past world—or at least we act as if this were the case. We invent everything in the framework of a system that starts from zero in social relations, where everyone is reduced to being only what he or she appears to be, "having only a face, a gaze, and the unaccustomed length of a stripped-down body to display."[10] As soon as they arrive at the beach, as if leaving the world behind in the borderlands, in the wings, or in the cloakroom of their everyday identity, summer residents are peers, equals: "naked folk." In the strict sense, they are undifferentiated; their status is in principle symbolized not only by their nudity but also by the empty stage of the beach, a space without social or cultural reference points, a minimalist setting for a vacation on the edge, where anyone at all, armed with substitute signs of distinction, can reestablish or invent a personality whose expression can be controlled at the whim of the individual, depending on how he or she wishes to be perceived.

Moreover, some people may find the beach unbearable for this very reason. What makes the beach intolerable to them is not so much the idleness of its occupants or the vacuousness of their own occupations as the ritual effacement or loss of one's preexisting identity that is presupposed by one's arrival at the beach. Not only does the beach strip away the body's garb, but it also robs individuals and groups of the social masks that singularize and categorize them. Once this sign is lost, it has to be won back. People have to "put on a good face," as the saying goes. This is essentially what our beach "Eskimos" are seeking. Their prey, the object of their hunt, is their own identity; they are engaged in a quest for a self-image, an effort to reappropriate and reaffirm themselves and their loved ones. Here, with the help of rites, games, and protocols, one has to produce signs and meanings in order to reinstall oneself as an individual, in one's unity and difference.

In fact, once on the beach, lost among our fellows like fugitives in the crowd, we are indistinguishable.[11] Separated, orphans with respect to the outside world, we are now dispossessed, emptied of our social substance, just like the semiological emptiness of our unclothed flesh, our bodies washed, purged of the signs that ordinarily distinguish them. Unless the pallor of our skin, white "like an aspirin tablet," an ultimate trace of the exterior, should still give us away as "foreign bodies"—an involuntary difference, an embarrassing epidermic lapse that betrays us, reveals and exposes our weakness, our helplessness, to the gaze of others, like ridiculous novices, sick people, or intruders caught in the act of interfering. But this is all part of the seaside game.

We have to assimilate, find a place for ourselves, mark it as ours, defend it, and win acceptance; we have to win recognition and be forgotten at the same time; we have to become part of the setting, making sure that we both stand out from and blend into the order of the collectivity that is always already in place, always already there before we arrive. The seaside game begins with a rite of aggregation. We have to integrate ourselves into the community, into its habits, its rules, its space, and at the same time we have to preserve our own autonomy, "establish a little colony, as it were," like Gordon, the orphaned leader of a band of children shipwrecked on a desert island, whose only goal is to restore networks of lost sociability at the heart of this robinsonnade.[12]

The next step entails simulacra of moving in that have everything to do with the primordial act destined to restore a center and an environment to existence, to restore a place and a milieu to the individual, that is, an identity and a network to the person. This rite of refounding is sometimes so highly developed that the game almost goes unrecognized as such, passing from simulacrum to simulation, from imitation to trompe-l'oeil, from reconstitution to reproduction or, better still, from copy to counterfeit. After all, the French word for beach, *plage,* has among its derivatives the premonitory terms *plagiat,* "plagiarism," and *plagiaire,* "plagiarist," terms that seem tailor-made to designate the beach as a space for simulation favorable to the accomplishment of this game which is more serious than it seems.

Thus the rite rejects the simple and ephemeral gesture of moving in, the everyday or even seasonal act, in favor of a permanent Crusoean habitat, close to the illusion of a definitive social interruption. This is the case of the Club Méditerranée, as soon as it abandons the formula of canvas tents in favor of Polynesian villages, creating an isolated, durable, and autonomous mode of living, with its own currency (bar beads), its specific form of dress (pareos), its philosophy of independence ("if you could, you'd be naturalized as a Polynesian!"), and its setting in the form of a primordial hamlet, a mythical village: "the one that slumbers in each of us, the one that reappears in every child's drawing"[13]—the one, at bottom, that fascinated the ethnologists of the South Seas.

> As the dawn begins to fall among the soft brown roofs and the slender palm trees stand out against a colourless, gleaming sea, lovers slip home from trysts beneath the palm trees or in the shadow of beached canoes. . . . Restless little children roll out of their sheets and wander drowsily down to the beach to freshen their faces in the sea. . . . The whole village, sheeted and frowsy, stirs, rubs its eyes, and stumbles toward the beach.[14]

This is a description of the awakening of a "real" village. And yet it could apply to an early morning at the Club, so closely does the original resemble its "copy."

Beyond the confusion of places and references that this hedonistic search for an exotic illusion institutes, the fact remains that the Club's village, in a spectacular trace of the installation rite, at bottom simply attests to the strength of a common imaginary, the summer vacationer's "intimate geography": the fervent topophilia inherent in any robinsonnade. This being the case, after the "huge furnished tents" set up on the beaches of Normandy in the nineteenth century[15] that already foreshadowed it, this symptom-village only brings to light the meaning of the game: to demonstrate the importance of the symbolic function of the first of the seaside rituals, installation.

We now need to examine *in situ* the strategic variants, that is, from umbrellas to hotels via tents, grass shacks or little huts; we need to recognize on the ground the practices and their variations, the adaptations and the ruses, for they all have to do with the application of the Crusoe mythology that inspires this pleasurable sedentarity—a diversity under which the model of the robinsonnade sometimes seems to dissolve and disappear.

7. Tribes and Territories

*(or, How Robinson and Friday
declare war, build walls, and
divide up the shore of their island)*

We learn that there are also beggar communities of fifteen-year-old
children gathered under tents along Ocean Beach and Pacific Beach—
fraternities of misery and love, heat, and cold, addicted to smoking and
drugs...

—Edgar Morin, *Journal de Californie* (1970)

Like Icarus, attracted by the sun and then plunging into the waters,
an angel hovers over the beach: the angel of communism. All seaside
summer vacationers have come together in a Sacred Holiday to ensure the support of his tutelary power. Still, this angel has his work cut
out for him, too much work to rest on his laurels: he has to figure out
how to satisfy the communitarian dream for one and all, simultaneously, without compromise or distortion of the ideal. It is all very well
to say in song:

> Shine on our systems
> The desire for everyone to love one another
> The sun gives
>
> That excellent old desire
> That we'd all be more or less brothers
> The sun gives
> The sun gives
> Intelligent gold

The sun gives
The same color to people
The same color
Nicely[1]

To be sure, everyone gets tan; and the resulting chromatic equalization of epiderma encourages the dream of abolishing racial, social, or personal differences. It is the same egalitarian utopia that inspired the proselytizing discourse of one naturist writer in the late 1920s: "Every class of society communes with its superiors and inferiors in the same ideal of nakedness: there are factory workers, bank clerks, telephone operators, rich Berlin merchants, Hamburg ship owners, and even clergymen."[2] Later, the Club Med philosophy incorporated its own version of this ideal of social confusion. Once the ideal "3S" (Sea, Sand, and Sun) site has been discovered, here is the recipe for a successful vacation: "Mix in doctors, mechanics, journalists, students, some young people at loose ends, and viscountesses. Stir well. Gild under a beautiful sun from late May to late September."[3]

Nevertheless, this cheerful principle of blending races, classes, cultures, and identities has its limits. If the search for Sameness and not Otherness is what lies behind residential summer vacationing, a quest whose success is by definition measured by the yardstick of a certain anthropological homogeneity, that of "nothing but ourselves face to face with ourselves," the move toward a concrete utopia implies some practical arrangements. Just as Narcissus could not bear to have someone else's reflection compete with his own, or as Endymion could not bear to be awakened and dragged from sleep by noises from outside, the summer vacationer does not want to go on confronting too many differences of external origin or noting their persistence on the beach. The consequence: logics of concentration and dispersion gather and distribute groups of "fellows" according to the degree to which they resemble one another.

The photographer Elliott Erwitt notes simply that "[p]eople at the beach act pretty much the way they do in their daily lives, but the contrasts are clearer. They segregate themselves." Why is this? Because here, by choice or by necessity, the vacationer is reconnecting with a fundamental fraternity, with the tribal schema—"the ideology of traditional society," which prescribes "an absolute identity between man and the soil."[4] To the same soil, the same type of human being must correspond. As soon as an individual is different, he must be on another soil, apart from the tribe, outside its world. He is a savage.

Claude Lévi-Strauss writes:

> Mankind stops at the frontiers of the tribe, of the linguistic group, and sometimes even of the village, to the extent that a great many of the peoples called primitive call themselves by a name which means "men" (or sometimes—shall we say with more discretion—the "good ones," the "excellent ones," the "complete ones"), thus implying that the other tribes, groups, and villages have no part in virtues or even human nature, but are at the most made up of "bad people," "nasty people," "land monkeys," or "lice eggs." One often goes so far as to deprive the stranger of this last shred of reality by making him a "ghost" or an "apparition."[5]

Populations of seaside vacationers seem in many respects to be governed by analogous if not identical schemas of thought and behavior as betrayed by the facts. To identify with savages is out of the question: doesn't Robinson do everything in his power to recreate Friday in his own image so that Crusoean cohabitation will be possible?

The fact remains that the myth of community haunts the seaside imaginary; it is not dismantled at the beach. Instead, the various segregations that sharply divide up the space splinter, scatter, and multiply its applications in the name of homogeneity. The myth is actually realized only in the framework of an archipelago consisting of watertight isolation chambers in which a limited form of communism prevails. This is a communism *weighed down* by class consciousness (which is never totally abolished in the best of cases), a communism in which nudity itself becomes a mask rather than the sign of authentic equalization. Moreover, it is a temporary communism, along the lines of the Club Med, which has been said to offer vacationers a "weeklong version of a classless society, without money or work," in "the mini-socialist atmosphere of a seaside campground."[6]

The potential seductive utopia of seaside socialism, conceived as a stage of social purification and fraternization, is in fact multiply limited in space and time: geographically, seasonally, and also historically. If residential seaside vacationing is indeed the place of relational conquests, interpersonal contacts relieved of everyday constraints, these rites and games are nevertheless inscribed in an interval that is overdetermined by more or less obvious social boundaries. Is the robinsonnade a form of communism? Let us not forget that one of Robinson's first gestures with regard to Friday was one of discrimination: he ordered his companion to call him "Master"! The famous shipwreck victim manifests a will to power and prestige just as clearly as he does a desire for companionship.

The contemporary beach is the theater of an "oblique" society, one that deceives its world in that it does not inscribe itself definitively either in an extension of external society or in a total break with that society.[7] It is less the exotic scene of a total inversion than the scene of a tribal inflection of values and models of sociability that are transported to the seaside and installed there. The rest is nothing but a (serious) matter of simulacra and ritual behaviors producing the illusion of "shipwreck" and the magic of oblivion.

THE ISLAND DIVIDED

Goodbye to one more poor little dream? The old dream of community destroyed yet again? The fact is that the seashore is much more than a seat of "figures from elsewhere, figures of adventure."[8] The shore today is a territory invested by vacationers not only as a place to be at home, but also as a place where everyone is to be in his or her own home. Of course, it is possible, almost, to dream of the absolute: one can offer moral resistance to the facts and refuse to recognize the objective limits of the seaside robinsonnade. Edifying examples can be brought to bear in justification of this attitude. Thus the process of breaking down ghettos and dissolving apartheid in South Africa began to manifest itself with the opening of beaches to Whites and Blacks together. But many counterexamples quickly come to mind, challenging this utopian vision. Ophelian, Olympian, overpopulated, democratic, the beach is also sectorial, and it echoes in its space the discriminations of the dominant ideology. On the beach, the possibilities for social defamiliarization and confusion of status are limited: whatever the nature of one's otherness (physical, cultural, economic, or sexual), each group excludes every other in the name of the homogeneity that is indispensable to the success of the topophilic rite (see chapter 6).

This is true in crisis situations—for example on an Algerian beach, in the summer of 1955, on the eve of the war of independence. "We were vacationing in Fouka Marine, a little village on the coast. I was on the beach and the guard came to tell me that I was no longer allowed to swim there. The mayor of Fouka had decided to close the beach to

Arabs. From then on, nothing was the same as before. In the months that followed, I saw the war take hold."[9] If this is how things were, someone will argue, it is because Franco-Arab coexistence had already deteriorated; this social exclusion by municipal decree, shattering a state of social peace, simply announced the coming confrontation. So be it. The discriminating gesture has the value of a symptom in this instance. But in other more or less pronounced forms, and on different levels, the strategy of separation has also been verifiable in daily life, in peacetime, for a long time. Homogenizing the summer populations at the shore, it is at the origin of a double process of distribution and concentration of seaside vacationers.

As early as about 1840, in England, as the proximity of London made it easy for new social categories to frequent Brighton Beach, the aristocrats clustered together farther away, on the beaches at Ramsgate, Hastings, or Devonshire.[10] Direct exclusion (by prohibition) is converted here into an avoidance tactic, but the result is the same: to each his own beach. During the same period, and later on the continental beaches of northern Europe, especially in Germany, we find seaside sites in which partitioning not just between sexes but between classes was scrupulously observed (see the beginning of chapter 3). And today, in France, Italy, and elsewhere, the institution of private fee-charging beaches or of official policies authorizing the commercial exploitation of certain parts of the shore simply uses economic selectivity to reintroduce an age-old territorial discrimination that is explicitly or implicitly attentive to the preservation of social cleavages.[11]

Despite the naturist tendency of the period between the wars, and despite the postwar Polynesianism—each renewing the communitarian utopia in its own way—or, more recently, despite the bulldozer offensive launched by a socialist minister against private beaches in France, the rejection of mixing or the conscious or unconscious search for homogeneity seems to be an unfailing constant of the seaside world.[12]

The phenomenon of rejection that partitions the seashore is found everywhere. It was embodied in the 1830s in a story by Charles Dickens, where a grocer who has inherited a great deal of money takes his family on vacation to Ramsgate in order to avoid mingling with the shopkeepers of Gravesend or even Margate. One cannot "jump into the water in the middle of so much poverty and ugliness."[13]

This sort of discrimination is not only territorial but also temporal. And here, too, there is nothing new under the sun at the beach.

Following a strategy of avoidance, seasonal and daily scheduling make it possible to avoid the looming collision of classes. In Brighton, in the nineteenth century, summertime was left to the lower classes; September and October belonged to the upper crust. And today? "In Brazil," Elliott Erwitt notes, "the Beautiful People never get to the beach before 2:00 p.m. That's a worldwide standard." This rule seems to govern a social choreography of nonencounter, a division of space and time that tacitly preserves the principle of exclusion. Similarly, in France, a municipal official from Étretat describes the rites of alternating occupation of the beach.[14] In the morning, until 1:00 p.m., the beach is full of temporary summer residents staying at the hotel, in rented quarters, or in the campground. From one to two o'clock, while these beachgoers have "retreated among themselves" to eat lunch, the "regulars," owners of vacation homes, take their turn. The temporary visitors come out again at two, remaining on the beach until five or six o'clock. During this period, the regulars "retire" into their residences. At six, they come back out to find themselves among their own kind on the beach.

The socioeconomic categorization of the seaside population that can be observed on an everyday basis at the regional and seasonal levels is also attested at the national level. The "popular" Adriatic coast in Italy has its counterpart along the coast of Languedoc in France; symmetrically, the Riviera corresponds to the Ligurian coast. Recent statistics attest with greater precision to the force of this social logic.[15] On the banks of the eastern Mediterranean, the dominant socio-professional category is that of upper-level management; on the western shores, the middle classes predominate; and along the English Channel, the working classes are in the majority. In Brittany and in the Atlantic region, the classes appear more evenly distributed, at least seen from a distance.

By choice or by obligation, then, seaside conviviality (and thus the communitarian experience it offers), overdetermined as it is by direct or indirect, local or global socioeconomic discriminations, is a form of collective leisure that is inscribed within the boundaries of a certain social homogeneity. Selected by some, tolerated by others, this homogeneity may well correspond to an individual or familial desire to turn inward; however, at an even more fundamental level it emanates from a vacation discourse of division and segregation that first invites or summons the summer vacationer to a sociological retreat.

Among its practical arrangements, the great ritual of summer gatherings is thus specified in this context as a system of flow that divides and redistributes social classes in coastal space, regrouping individuals who belong to similar or adjacent social classes, sector by sector. Unable to achieve a classless society, summer vacationers at least manage to create "mono-class" zones of sociability.

Still, even if this is its most obvious manifestation, sorting by socio-economic class is not the only form of discrimination and exclusion that contributes to the creation of the homogeneous milieu the seaside robinsonnade requires. In order to bring like together with like, other forms of difference have to be eliminated. Thus there is a time-honored distinction between family-oriented beaches and beaches oriented toward social life and/or entertainment, and, more recently, between "textile" beaches (where people wear clothing) and nudist beaches; "resort" beaches are also distinguished from "residential" or "family" beaches.[16]

But above and beyond these social, economic, vestimentary, or environmental discriminations, the seaside "island" is further subdivided on the basis of segregations of another order, beginning with cultural segregation, which often approaches xenophobia. Paul Morand announces that he does not like the Spanish beaches on which families of British officers have settled, "washed up like carp collapsing under the sun in great chintz armchairs," or "French refugees from North Africa," or "colonies of Israelites in retreat from Morocco."[17] And even today, certain discourses and commercial strategies echo this tendency to reject, and flee from, the cultural Other.

For example, in the summer of 1991 one newspaper article commented on the success of a newly opened boat service offering summer vacationers regular transportation from the Saint-Florent beach to the beach of Lodu, in the Agriates desert:

> From Saint-Florent, where guttural accents from the other side of the Rhine or from Tuscany are heard more often than Corsican speech, in thirty minutes you can forget civilization for a few hours or for a day, as you prefer, and find yourself on a beach where the water, sky, and sea are somehow reminiscent of faraway Pacific isles. . . . There are hundreds, thousands of them every week: candidates for communion with Mother Nature, delighted to play Robinson. (*Corse-Matin,* Aug. 31, 1991)

In passing, we should note the distortion of the Crusoe myth, for that shipwrecked tinkerer does not commune with nature; his sole concern is to transform nature to his own benefit. But it is true that Robinson is content to speak only his own language; he is not prepared to learn either the savages' language or Friday's.

As for commercial strategies corresponding to this misanthropy vis-à-vis the social or cultural Other, the evolution of the Club Med's prospectuses is not the least astonishing example.

> The time when Gilbert Trigano touted a single product where social classes mingled is long past.... From now on, people stay with their own kind ... and for those who prefer to stick to veal stew, spaghetti, or sauerkraut, the Aquarius Clubs in France, Valtur in Italy, and soon Calypso in Germany will welcome only citizens of those countries. "For at least ten more years," Gilbert asserts, "we still have to have villages where only the guests' own language is spoken."[18]

Here, unquestionably, the formula of the robinsonnade is well understood and applied in the form of an offer of summer residency based on a triple homogeneity: social, cultural, and linguistic.

And then, above and beyond this fundamental triad, there are still other segregations, harder to discern because they are veiled or unconscious but real nonetheless: they entail discrimination on the basis of age or sex. What can be said about the age of the seaside population? Olympian, fashioned by dreams of eternity (see chapter 6), the fantasmatic background of the seashore designates the ideal beach as a site populated with "divine" individuals: perfect, ageless, and in full possession of their faculties. In principle, then, there is no room here for the weak, "land monkeys" or "lice eggs"—nor for the elderly, with their bent, wrinkled bodies, variously altered and deformed by history, nor for children, who are unfinished and immature beings. At Saint-Tropez, there is one beach, La Voile Rouge, where the owner reportedly denies access to "dogs, kids, and old folks"![19]

Fortunately, this is not quite the situation encountered in reality—except perhaps for dogs.[20] The beach is a prime spot for family vacations, which at least saves children from exclusion. Still, generally speaking, although in variable proportions, summer sounds the tocsin for the presence of "senior citizens" on the shore. At the end of the low season, the elderly head for home. Departing by the trainload from Biarritz or Cannes, these retired "Eskimos" go in the opposite direction from the younger folk: they head north, or else withdraw into the interior.[21] During the summer of 1992 65 percent of those who spent their vacations at the seaside were under age forty-five, whereas the national average is 56.1 percent; along the Mediterranean and Atlantic coasts, people under thirty-five represented more than 40 percent of the vacation population, and people under fifty-five represented more than 75 percent.[22] Unquestionably, the underrepresentation of that last age group attests to something like the unconscious search for a form of homogeneity now signifying that to remain among one's fellows is also to remain among active young people, "thus implying that the other tribes" do not share in the virtues that can be required of seaside humanity.[23]

What about sexual discrimination on beaches? The sexes are no longer kept apart, as they once were; men, women, and couples are not assigned to different swimming zones.[24] Instead, bathers are segregated by sexual practices and orientations: distinct territories are allocated to the various forms of sexuality, in a sort of Balkanization of mores. This phenomenon of sexual territoriality is practiced in the United States, as Erwitt attests:

> Near my house in Amagansett in the late 1960s, the age of the singles, there was a spot called Asparagus Beach because the girls and boys were packed so tightly, looking for each other. They ignored the other hundred or so miles of Long Island beach. With AIDS, that's changed, so that stretch has become a family beach. Then there's a homosexual beach and a lesbian beach, evenly divided by a road—tight little neighborhoods, just like back in the city.[25]

In France the phenomenon is not very well known, or, rather, not very widely recognized. Still, in France as elsewhere, between rumors and information, word-of-mouth communication does its work and allows us to suppose that a sexual geography also collaborates in the structuring of the seaside vacation archipelago. Thus not long ago a weekly magazine attempted to map out the "hot beaches" in terms of vacationers' preferences: hetero- or homosexual, voyeurs or exhibitionists, swappers or Don Juans, nudists or not—a whole gamut of variations is spelled out along the coasts in separate sites that seem to be ritually homogeneous.[26]

At the origin of the "divided island," we can thus now suppose a whole combinatorial of discriminations that determine the summer vacationer's choice of destination and lodging. But instead of lining up terms in order to produce a sentence, this syntax of seaside vacationing orchestrates social, economic, cultural, linguistic, generational, and sexual preferences—a series of selections and combinations that ultimately delineate typical beaches, like "protected zones." In theory, there could be a residential family beach for homosexual working-class senior citizens; why not? Without probing too deeply, we may well conclude that this is the way anthropologically differentiated seaside universes come into being and isolate themselves from others, above and beyond the specifics of climate, geology, and aesthetics.

MOVING-IN RITES

Once these criteria for discrimination of place have been posited, the great seaside vacation game can begin: the topophilic game of sedentary conviviality and indifference to the world, withdrawal into oneself and one's own group. To be fully understood, the game requires that we set biases and moral issues aside, and that we refrain from crediting the vacationer with cultural, athletic, exploratory, discovery-oriented, or social projects that he has not chosen. The beach is such a "self-centered" gregarious universe that the relation between indigenous and intruder populations is reversed. The summer residents dread Saturdays and Sundays, because the locals "invade" the beach (their beach) on weekends, disturbing the order of the outsiders' installation. This aspect of the vacation experience, which turns natives into interlopers, is widespread, and it points to a collective psychological framework in which the permutation of the status of native and outsider is complete. This may shock vacation moralists, but it is a sociological fact.

From this standpoint, what is true of tourists is all too often true of summer residents as well: they are understood less often than one would suppose by observers who proffer normative discourses on what should be rather than describing what is.[27] In the early 1980s, the weekly magazine *L'Express* published a ranking of French beaches in which those of the south, especially along the Mediterranean coast, came out well ahead of the rest. Appended to this survey were assorted comments by well-known personalities, including Roland Dumas, then a deputy from the Department of Dordogne. Dumas made an unambiguous statement countering the opinions expressed in the study: "This classification is absurd: the sites at the bottom of the list ought to be on top. It's so much better to be on the shores of the Channel, or the Atlantic! Never mind the cold water! After a swim, you can walk along the sand for miles, and behind the beach, at Cap-Ferret, you have real countryside for cycling."[28]

If we stick with this peremptory judgment, we can only conclude that those who stay on the beach are behaving mindlessly. From Dumas's perspective, after a good cold swim, the beach is there only to be walked on or abandoned in favor of cycling excursions inland. In other words, if you go to the sea, it's really to be in the country! Viewed in these terms, the behavior of millions of individuals becomes incomprehensible. Jacques Barrot, the president of the Conseil général of the Department of Haute-Loire, applauds the "Mediterranean score" but then goes on: "That said, I am sorry that the beaches of the Basque Country do not have a higher ranking. They offer the best possible combination for vacations: sea and mountains."

After the countryside, here are the mountains! But the geographical combination that attributes excursion plans to the seaside vacationer continues to underestimate the autonomy of the beach, its specific human dimension, and the symbolic function of the shore linked to its topophilic use.

The writer Paul Guimard weighs in as a sailor who despises beach "crawlers," seaside resorts, and summer residents: "This ranking? It is consistent with France's seaside vacation outlook: France is proud of swimming in the sea, but lacks any maritime vision. As for me, I love fishing ports with no beaches and no hotels. When I spot a beach from my boat, I head the other way."

When Guimard laments—in a tone that recalls Gerbault, Morand, or any other purist (see Introduction)—the lack of "maritime vision" among those who share the "seaside vacation outlook," his critique is more than a sign of personal incompatibility; it reflects a total misunderstanding of the phenomenon. It betrays the intolerance of an elitist vagabond who, like many others skilled in long-range navigation or perhaps merely in a form of coastal yachting that plays to the gallery, is unable to acknowledge that, for many of us, the seaside is not a point of departure but a destination, not a site of mobility but of settlement.

On the beach, the practice of settling in is not a matter of mere agglutination or haphazard clustering. Between dispersal and concentration, proximity and distance, the practice is in fact structured by a variety of ritual behaviors: strategies of occupation of the ground, territorial logics, primordial relations, roles and gestures that are repeated on a daily basis. These behaviors set up borders, institute zones of conviviality or rivalry that are sources of alliances, tacit agreements, or, on the contrary, open conflicts. For what we are witnessing at bottom here is one of the earliest episodes of human history being played out yet again: the dividing up of space.

To be sure, there are the "teeming beaches on which it is impossible to unroll an air mattress without waiting for a neighbor to move his leg."[29] In such an environment, it goes without saying that neighborhood agreements are broken more easily, that border incidents proliferate, and that rites of sharing or aggregation often degenerate into confrontations. But there are many intermediate positions between this extreme demographic situation and the opposite pole, in which vacationers turn their backs on beaches and shun crowds entirely.

We must not allow crowding to be an obstacle to our decoding of beachgoers' ritual strategies. The crowd is the beach. Its strategies define the internal rules of the seaside game and give the game its meaning. Despite all the caricatures lampooning its density, the ordinary overpopulation of beaches must not prevent us from identifying the essential protocols of demarcation and contact. Whether spontaneous or conventional, institutionalized or negotiated, these protocols constitute the beach. Furtive dialogues, glances, smiles, overt movements, or lack thereof—all these beach exchanges are based on politeness, seduction, or intimidation, codes of access to community life that help determine whether tacit contracts of proximity sealing temporary boundary-sharings are accepted or not. These languages of installation simultaneously construct both the scenic unity and the complexity of a place in which the typical forms of social exclusion and integration, assimilation, autonomy, marginalization, or recognition are inscribed, interpreted, and experienced.

The defensive attitude manifested by summer residents toward natives who come to the beach on weekends attests to this unity and complexity, as does the summer residents' attitude when "newcomers" show up on beaches full of "regulars." As in hazing, a rite of passage, the newcomers are traditionally marginalized for a time and subjected to some initiatory bullying, a prelude to their eventual integration. "Farther up, where the beach was strewn with pebbles and dead sea-weed, sat a group with flesh as white as her own. They lay under small hand-parasols instead of beach umbrellas and were obviously less indigenous to the place. Between the dark people and the light, Rosemary found room and spread out her peignoir on the sand."[30]

To translate this ritual and tactical dimension of seaside customs, we may also make use of geopolitical, diplomatic, and military vocabulary.[31] Can we not say that the "palefaces" are located in a zone of retreat situated at a respectable distance from an occupied zone, that of the "natives"? Rosemary for her part opts for a median position that can be characterized as an outpost, well situated for triggering hostilities or, on the contrary, for the establishment of cordial relations with the locals. Such is the theater of operations whose future will be constituted, according to circumstances, by conquests or defeats, nonaggression pacts, treaties, or offensive strikes. So is this trench warfare, or a blitzkrieg? Some people take over a little more territory every day, in an irredentist approach; others adopt a strategy of annexation, preferring to skip the declaration of war and launch an early morning surprise attack, before the other has arrived on the scene; still others use guerrilla tactics and move their own encampment from place to place. In this way, bases and fronts are established. In this area as in others, there are strategists and desperadoes, federators and nationalists, invaders, terrorists, and deserters demanding asylum and protection.

The Birth of Territories

We have been watching from a remote observation post; let us now move closer. Here is a man arriving on the beach, armed with a folded umbrella in his right hand, an ice bucket in the other: the booty. This man is a scout leading a commando that follows close on his heels. He advances among the group that has settled in, inspects the site; he evaluates the situation, spies on the enemy, and collects data. Suddenly, in a foundational gesture, he plants his umbrella like a flag in conquered territory and thereby establishes a center. He unfurls the umbrella, and his territory now extends to the length of its shadow. The rest of the troops arrive, armed with beach towels and mats that are quickly positioned all around the standard, broadening the extent of the bastion and giving its boundaries material form. Some people play the role of hussars to achieve their territorial demands; others, more diplomatic, are negotiators or mediators and, in cases of conflict, call upon higher authorities: the mayor, the office of social services, or the prefecture. As with war, there is nothing new about these tactics:

In 1911, a Parisian swimmer came into conflict with the adjudicator of the beach at Lion-sur-Mer, after the latter ordered him to remove a tent that he had set up about ten yards in front of the row of cabins. The swimmer appealed directly to the prefect, explaining that he was within his rights, since the regulations allowed any swimmer, if he so wished, to set up "a shelter against the sun," provided that he put it up in the morning and took it down the same evening. When the chief engineer of Ponts et Chaussées was consulted, he agreed with the swimmer, given that moveable chairs and shelters are freely authorized for everyone on the beaches in the department of Calvados.[32]

At stake here in every instance is not only the creation of a territory or refuge but also the defense and preservation of that space from aggressors—both common space, which must be protected against autochthonic "invasions" or illicit privatizations (in which case one has to appeal to official regulations and to municipal authorities) and private space (where one has to appeal to good will). It is in the latter circumstance that volunteers or sacrificers emerge, that is, those who remain on watch in the "camp," like sentinels, while others go swimming. There was a time, during raids by moralists on "wild" nudist camps, when these terms were not in the least metaphorical.

Tribal Space Rediscovered

Here, where collective life indefatigably rewrites its segregations, its strategies of gathering and dispersal, on a map of sand whose contours and lines are washed away every day, the beach may thus first be observed from a slight distance, the way Georges Perec observed Place Saint-Sulpice in Paris.[33]

Beach: Île-Rousse, Corsica.
Date: August 13, 1992.
Weather: beautiful, as usual.
Air temperature: 31° C at 11:00 A.M.
Water temperature: 25° C at the same hour.
Wind: 20/30 knots, south-southwest.
Observation point: the promenade.

8:00. A city employee finishes cleaning the beach with the help of a large wire mesh rake. Below the promenade, hikers are still asleep in their sleeping bags, using their backpacks as pillows.

8:15. Arrival of the first vacationers. They set themselves up in the center of the crescent formed by the beach, at the water's edge. First umbrella. Arrival of a group of teenagers.

8:30. Several groups of vacationers, still somewhat scattered, but spread out all along the water's edge, outlining a beach front. The teenagers have taken up a position a little toward the rear. Stretched out in a star shape on the sand, they are asleep. An umbrella is carried off by the wind. A man and woman rub suntan lotion on each other. A fisherman with his rod is an object of attraction.

9:00. The sea front is established. On this first line, groups of vacationers, two or three yards apart, form a string of beads at the water's edge along the entire length of the beach.

9:15. Installation of the first "entrenched camp" behind the front line.

10:00. The fisherman has disappeared. Families are arriving in large numbers, quickly filling up the second line. The hikers are gradually leaving the beach. The teenagers, in full sun, without umbrellas, are still asleep: no one in the group has budged since they arrived.

10:30. The first front line of the "entrenched camps" in the rear has been constituted. A third line is taking shape.

11:00. The beach is full. The crowd has by now wiped out most of the previously readable traces of the successive "waves" of installation. While other vacationers are still arriving, groups from the first and second lines are leaving, triggering furtive migrations toward the water by people from the third and fourth lines.

11:15. As in a jigsaw puzzle, the intervals of a few yards left vacant by the first occupants have been infiltrated, filled in or converted into passageways through which the occupants of the rear lines come and go, especially the children. Lost in the mass, surrounded and then merged with the crowd, the once-distinct group of teenagers has become indistinguishable.

There is nothing astonishing, then, in the fact that the installation rites are sometimes converted into military or warlike tactics. For it is a matter of maintaining the unity of the group, the sign of its existence, and its closed nature. If the umbrella, as the totemic symbol of a tribe or clan, is a semaphore that resists external aggressions, the borders, susceptible to surreptitious modifications, must on the other hand be the object of vigilant surveillance and maintenance: they must constantly be re-marked by the redeployment of a beach towel and other signaling objects that can warn, head off, or at least slow down the attempts at expansion that threaten the integrity of the territory. The sand pile molded with an overturned bucket is a fragile but effective sign of demarcation. It usually incites newcomers and passersby to keep their distance or go around it. About 11:00, worn out by the increasingly frequent incursions of people from the interior, some of those on the front line lift the blockade definitively and leave.

Still, we must not let ourselves be overwhelmed by the military metaphor. There is no point in blackening the picture further, as so many others have done, by reducing the beach to a battlefield. Taken literally, such a reading would underscore the strategic and conflictual aspects of the beach, but it would only be a caricature of the place and could only lead to forgetting its fundamental dimensions, which are convivial, ludic, and ritual. This "theater of operations" is a place of leisure before it is a battleground; and its conflictual aspect, although it may sometimes get out of control, is primarily just a game during which the proxemic schema of each individual is tested, with naked bodies and without major impediments: the need for proximity is measured against the threshold of intolerance for the other. Between flight and aggression, evasion and encounter, self-protection and openness to others, group autism and exchange, between the defense of intimacy and the quest for contact, beachgoers are flirting here with critical distance.[34]

Let us recall that the robinsonnade does not entail a rejection of companionship. And the empty or only slightly occupied beach is not the most attractive of beaches for everyone. A woman who deems the beaches at Mandelieu or Bandol "unlivable in summer" and says she prefers to take her children to Corsica, in the Gulf of Propriano, where "there are still beaches where the nearest neighbor is 100 yards away,"[35] is only expressing a maternal proxemic schema, evidence of a tribalism that radically privileges the defense of intimacy, the desire for isolation, and the rejection of contact. What do the children think about this? It is true that the autarchic aesthetic of seaside living focused on couples and families is widely credited as the ideal image of the beach sojourn, especially in advertising. But in reality, for many children and single adults, a deserted beach is synonymous with solitude and boredom. It is the place of a melancholy Crusoeism: the period before Friday appeared.

If it is true, as Alain Corbin has emphasized, that the "rush" toward beaches from the eighteenth century on can be explained as the counterpart of an urban pathology, the various aspects of that pathology that are manifested today must still be considered. To escape the city may mean to escape crowds. But it may also mean to escape a network of social discriminations, or to escape isolation, for the urban universe today is a formidable generator of solitudes. In that case, will the lonely city-dweller, if he does not go to a vacation village, seek a beach where the nearest neighbor is a hundred yards away? His installation rite will in all likelihood be inspired by a desire for contact and conviviality.

Edward Hall, who developed the notion of "proxemics" with reference to the individual's sense of territoriality, proposes distinguishing among four categories of interpersonal distance. From zero to eighteen inches, we are in a relation of intimacy; from eighteen inches to four feet, the relation is personal in nature; from four to twelve feet, the relation is one of social distance; beyond twelve feet comes public distance.[36] In fact, every summer beach vacationer, consciously or not, uses this interpersonal code, this language of space, and carries out her installation rite in terms of the proxemic relations that she intends to establish with her environment.

The mother cited above chose public distance: the most distant distance. In contrast, a Robinson longing for company, arriving on the beach with the hope of creating a situation favorable to encounters, may initially opt for a social distance of five or six feet—an intermediate distance in the framework of a protocol aiming to establish, in a second phase, a personal relationship with neighbors.

Beginning with this elementary level of installation, then, the beach appears as a complex and variable ritual space. In function of his or her own desires, whether alone, accompanied, or in a group, each individual beachgoer plays on this code of relations.

FAMILIES AND FRIENDS

Unlike the way it appears when it is perceived globally, with the crowd observable only as an undifferentiated mass (in which case the terms *agglutination* or *piling-up* are used), the beach now appears not only as a field for maneuvers but also as a sort of magnetic field whose poles are the alternative forms of topophilia, positive or negative depending on whether they produce attraction or dispersal. Fluids circulate among the bodies, bringing them closer together or pushing them further apart. Each group or individual expresses a sense of territoriality through simulacra of sedentarity that isolate, federate, fuse, or Balkanize. The outcome depends on the size and degree of impermeability of the bubbles of sociability instituted by these simulacra, these installation games.

Given this relational complexity, it follows that the very notion of promiscuity with respect to the "players" is eminently relative. Everyone establishes a center upon settling in; but the territorial estimation of the required periphery varies. For one mother, as we have seen, the mere passage from public distance to social distance can be perceived as a threat, a weakening of the tribal bubble, or even as a break in the group's field of protection. She will then view the proxemic transformation as a sign of the end of a nonaggression pact, and as the negative index announcing the imminent degradation of proximity into an "unlivable" promiscuity: "It's becoming painful. Every year there are more and more people on this beach! We have trouble now finding a quiet spot." But for someone else who is looking for company, the same transformation may on the contrary be interpreted as a positive sign of a burgeoning convivial dynamics that may be a prelude to the formation of a communitarian sphere: "I really like this beach. It's lively. I'm going to be able to meet people here, make friends here, find a boyfriend or girlfriend, start a new relationship."

Between communion and protection, the beach is a field of forces made up of bubbles of sociability whose magnetisms are complementary or incompatible. Even during peak periods, when the crowd makes this system of bubbles unreadable, the field of forces remains, notwithstanding personal or intimate proximities that do not arise from family ties, friendships, or conquests but are rather provoked— that is, imposed—by the density of the occupation of the territory and thus tolerated. In this case there is an extreme promiscuity that abolishes the intermediate distances of the proxemic code and thus tends to reduce the territory of each individual to the limits of his or own body; the situation becomes in fact explosive.

Nevertheless, in the absence of such demographic extremes, we have to take note of the structuring and particularly obvious presence of two contrary forces on the beach. One is "sociofugal," the other "sociopetal," that is, one favors the spreading out and dispersal of social life, while the other encourages its grouping and concentration.[37] Seaside existence, at once isolating and collective, is at the crossroads between these two forces. The first provokes the tribal dissemination of vacationers along the shore, and the second leads to encounters and intertribal relations among them.

How are these forces distributed? As we have seen, the seaside population is young. More precisely, "the propensity to vacation on a French coast is strongest" between the ages of twenty-five and forty-four, one of the reasons "probably" being "the presence of children in households of average age." These households alone represent 45.6 percent of the coastal clientele in France; another 20 percent come from the age group between fifteen and twenty-four. Thus, as Hubert Macé noted as early as 1967, "two types of groups can be distinguished [on French beaches]: families that are friends, and bands of adolescents," the former being more frequent than the latter.[38]

These two types of gregariousness represent two different forms of tribalism. They do not manage the simulacrum of sedentarity and group life in the same way. Their installation rites attest to different practices and representations that associate no less different meanings with their topophilia.[39]

> The beach was not crowded. A dozen teenagers were scattered about in their ritual rows. A few couples lay dozing—motionless as corpses, as if to move would disrupt the cosmic rhythms that generated a tan. A family was gathered around a charcoal fire in the sand.[40]

Whether the family is nuclear, extended, or augmented with friends, groups of the first type generally have a strong, solid tribal structure, that of the clan, based on bonds of kinship, stable friendship relations, a well-established organization, and well-understood roles. Even if this structure sometimes brings together ten or twenty people, it is fundamentally sociofugal. A self-sufficient, unitary microsociety, it excludes new individuals from its community. A closed society, it defends itself first of all against the external world and encloses its own members within its circle. As F. Scott Fitzgerald wrote with reference to this type of vacation party, "they obviously formed a self-sufficient little group, and once their umbrellas, bamboo rugs, dogs, and children were set out in place the part of the plage was literally fenced in." Only afterward, if this clan happens to establish contact with another clan during its sojourn, will the drawbridge of the "fortress" be lowered—and only the drawbridge, for a few polite exchanges of mutual recognition among regulars, or some pleasant chitchat about children who play well together. In any event, nothing will happen that might call into question the unity of the group, that might destabilize its structure or threaten the self-contained nature of the bubble. Instead, we encounter a protocol of clan affiliation that further reinforces the exclusion of all others. The literary model for this robinsonnade, even more than Defoe's, is that of Johan Wyss: "Obviously each family possessed the strip of sand immediately in front of its umbrella; besides there was much visiting and talking back and forth—the atmosphere of a community upon which it would be presumptuous to intrude."[41]

"Adolescent gangs" are thus the opposite of these powerful, compact, and well-organized tribes with their "jealous possession of happiness."[42] Made up of "runaways" from family groups, unless they are Scouts, they generally have a weaker tribal structure, that of the horde, based on few or nonexistent bonds of kinship and still-fragile friendships. Although more communitarian than families, it would seem, in terms of willingness to share their lodgings,[43] these tribes of teenage campers, open to adventure, sociopetal but errant and weakly ritualized, are frequently shaken by internal rivalries, emotional revolutions, reversals of alliances, or encounters that reconfigure their system of sociability. Exposed to the outside world, an experimental form of tribalism with a happenstance hold on territory, without protection or umbrellas, these are open, temporary, and unstable structures that last for a summer and rapidly dissipate; they sometimes split apart even before their summer sojourn is over.[44]

For some, this dispersal signifies solitude or the end of vacation, for others a change of group or an attempt to live as part of a couple, for still others a return to a unit belonging to the first type of gregariousness, the family tribe, which is unquestionably the dominant form or "social unit" (Durkheim) on beaches. Why is this the case? First of all because family tribalism is a micro-universe of sociability based on a "focused interaction" in which people group together and cooperate openly in order to maintain a single object, the unity and intimacy of the group or the defense of the clan—whereas adolescent tribalism, breaking with parental or clan logic, is based on a "diffused" or "unfocused interaction" that in the absence of solidly preestablished ties only serves to achieve a physical copresence of individuals.[45] The durability of this type of "atomic" association is thus largely dependent on circumstances, changing affective parameters, peripheral influences, and other internal and external variables that may disturb the group's organization and spatial integrity at any time, bringing its installation into question.[46]

Highly ritualized, as if overdetermined by a species consciousness, the family tribe excludes the unexpected, cutting itself off or at least protecting itself from the context. Everything from its developed sense of territoriality to the smallest details of its installation attests to this. The adolescent tribe, on the contrary, seeks the unexpected, or at least is open to it.

And then, psychologically, the predominance of family tribalism can be explained by the fact that it corresponds to a desire for the symbolic restoration of solidarity, of a group identity whose homogeneity is fragmented or dispersed during the rest of the year. Jean Viard notes that "the dominant wish of the French to spend vacations with their families is also a project to reunify a private territory that is more and more fragmented during the year"; and the beach came to be perceived very early as an ideal place to bring about such a reunification. Even in the nineteenth century, it was thought that "the sands and rocks of the beach were an occasion to recreate the primordial circle of family or friends."[47]

Adolescent tribalism is a form of gregariousness that is self-seeking, self-inventing, and self-producing; family tribalism is a form of gregariousness that is self-rediscovering and self-reproducing. If the former is an invention, the latter is actually a reconstitution, based on the complementary logics of repetition and exclusion. What governs the ritual of family installation on the beach, what this ritual reenacts every day, is basically nothing but the imaginary reconstruction of the primordial hut. The spatial marking of this reconstruction and its defense, the need to be constantly on guard against "territorial offenses," have as an immutable value "the concentration of intimacy in the refuge."[48]

Within this ritual framework, a territorial offense may be either human—that is, social—or natural. What is at stake is the intimacy of the group versus the entire outside world. I recall late afternoons on the Belgian coast when, as the rising tide threatened the various families' installations, children undertook the ritual erection of walls of sand—walls repeatedly rebuilt, since they were repeatedly knocked down by the waves—in order to protect the peace and quiet of the "old folks" in their lounge chairs as long as possible. Toward the end, caught up in the game of desperate resistance to the encroaching waters, the fathers came to lend the children a hand, until the fatal moment when the sea triumphed, breaking through the rampart and suddenly washing over the grandmothers' feet. Only then, after so valiantly defending the imaginary hut, did we finally "break camp."

"The hut [is] centralized solitude, for in the land of legend, there exists no adjoining hut. And although geographers may bring back photographs of hut villages from their travels in distant lands, our legendary past transcends everything that has been seen." The imaginary hut associated with seaside family vacationing is also a centered solitude. This sort of vacation practice thus remains fundamentally faithful to the Crusoe experience, even on an overcrowded beach. It repeats the mythical figure of the "real" robinsonnade. As Daniel Pennac writes: "Repetition is reassuring. It is proof of intimacy, the very breath of intimacy."[49]

As for exclusion, which is already expressed *in situ*, through proxemic, polymorphic, sociofugal, and xenophobic strategies, it is also expressed afterward, as memories are formed, via certain details that leave no room for doubt. For example: "The ones we'd put in the album?" says a father commenting on photos of his children at the beach taken during a vacation at Royan. "That one isn't bad, but there's a boy in it we don't know, somebody we'll never see again, so I don't think we'll use it." Above and beyond the Crusoe experience of the sojourn itself, photographs have to correspond to it, coincide with it, bear witness to it, confirm or reinforce it. Moreover, as this father explains: "That child was really there by chance; he was always around; but we usually just take pictures of our own children, not many of the others." The others, outsiders, "Savages," the anonymous "they," are mercilessly excluded from the album, driven away from the tribe, from its "legendary past," from memory and its traces, from the selective archives that this imaginary universe requires. There must be archives that only portray and recount the self and the group to which it belongs. Similarly, a mother who has returned from a stay at Argelès-sur-Mer says she likes a particular photograph "because I have my husband and my son swimming together, far out; I think that's terrific." To each her island, to each his minimal society, with its Robinson and its Friday on the horizon.[50]

Thus "the individual, fragmented and often desocialized by his work, attempts to reconstitute an absent unit through his dreams and vacation practices."[51] The fact remains, however, that families and friends have their respective cultures, and that their tribalism is transposed onto beaches in different ways as a function of these differences. Some accounts point to important ritual contrasts. According to Erwitt,

> The British go to the beach only to put it in its place. They fight it, putting on their best white shirts and ties. They stake out their territory and bring out their baked-bean sandwiches, or whatever they are, and then they sit. They engage in the sport of "paddling": you roll up the cuffs of your Sunday suit about three inches or so and place your feet in the water; then you stand immobile, communing with nature.[52]

Calm and contemplative, this beach practice clearly contrasts markedly with the one Phyllis Passariello observes in Mexico.[53] Mexicans also appropriate the beach, but they do not mark off the tribe's space with a windbreaker physically denoting the boundary. They manifest their presence and isolate themselves from their neighbors through noise, by turning the volume of their radios or tape-players way up. Thus they create a field that is not visual but acoustic, signaling the extent of their territory in a different mode. Their neighbors do the same. The message changes, but the language is the same.

There is material here for a comparative ethnology of seaside ritual practices and at the same time an opportunity for an ethnologist to undertake a new study of the meaning of the family in contemporary society on little-explored terrain. While we wait for such a study, we can already anticipate that it will demonstrate the fundamental function and universality of the rite that the beach, more than any other locale, has been inviting people to perform since the nineteenth century. In this liminary place, the rite of installation, by reconstituting an "absent unit," restores primordially the dividing line between intimacy and the outside world, between private and public space. It is both a rite of separation and a rite of aggregation, anticollective and communitarian.[54] It is sociofugal with respect to global society, but sociopetal with respect to a world of restricted sociability. And if we are to believe recent statistics, it is not about to disappear. During a recent ten-year period, in a trend running counter to the increase in the divorce rate, the importance of the family unit paradoxically regained strength.[55] This development may represent either a reversal of the trend or a symptomatic compensation in the form of a perverse effect[56] that—in the face of a social order increasingly destructive of families—appears to manifest an endemic and restorative withdrawal into themselves of family tribes on the beach.[57]

TETRALOGY OF SEASIDE VACATIONING

Finally, our human geography of the seaside, above and beyond the evocation of tribal units that atomize the vacationing "masses" populating the seashore, would be incomplete without a discussion of its immediate surroundings, lodging sites contiguous to the beach or nearby, on the periphery, that echo, specify, or underscore the signs and meanings of the topophilia in question while multiplying and enlarging them: campgrounds (for both tents and mobile homes), rental units (houses, apartments, rooms), vacation villages (bungalows, cabins, or "huts"), and hotels. On the margins of family-owned properties (principal or secondary residences), places known collectively in France as "commercial housing" accommodate the majority of seaside vacationers (more than 60 percent), in the following proportions: camping 24.2 percent, rental units 23.9 percent, vacation villages 5.2 percent, and hotels 4.1 percent.[58]

It is not the disparity in frequentation but the symbolic value of these structures that calls for our attention here. Right up to the edge of the seaside universe, they prolong and confirm the ritual logic of the beach. When Fitzgerald writes that "the hotel and its bright tan prayer rug of a beach are one," he pinpoints the essential continuity and homogeneity that make these places the amplified signs of nostalgia for island living.[59] We find it again in a letter by François Truffaut dated Sunday, August 11, 1958, with reference to a hotel:

> A little outside Concarneau, we spotted La Belle Etoile, a bourgeois paradise but a paradise nevertheless, a place of rest and meditation where you are quickly relieved of all the money that is weighing you down, in exchange for all sorts of soft touches and attention. Madeleine insists on "doing Brittany," however; we are leaving this quasi-Hawaiian retreat Tuesday morning to go deeper into the Finistère and beyond.[60]

After the installation, there is the desire to stay put: the topophilia of the frustrated seaside vacationer François is pitted against the exploratory whims of the tourist Madeleine.

One particular form of hostelry, like a connecting link set up between the wide world and the beach refuge, has answered this sedentary desire better than any other. I am speaking of the family boardinghouse: the Family Hotel (and not the Travelers' Hotel), the Pension Bon Repos, the Waves or Parks and Beaches.[61] Owing to the proximity of the water, the immensity and emptiness of the sea, the seaside boardinghouse seems to be a more self-enclosed universe. With its ocean views and its end-of-the-world atmosphere, it is a sort of Nautilus washed up on the shore—an "emblem of closure" that corresponds to "the bliss of . . . closure."[62] Only a Hulot could disrupt the order of this island, the self-contained perfection of this peaceful enclosure. The family boarding-house is the tribe of tribes. Crusoe in spirit, Swiss Family Robinson in form, with its "full room and board," it seals off the utopia of a complete and repetitive atemporal world in which, through table-to-table conversations or the establishment of common tables for the evening meal, the intertribal relations of the archaic beach world are prolonged, contractualized, and solidified.

Even if Alain Ehrenberg claims that "hotels are the counter-model for the Club," this latent nostalgia for an insular experience has been exploited by the Club Méditerranée and in its wake by an entire industry of vacation villages. By first displacing or extending this feeling to the realm of friendly relations crossed with amorous en-counters, then by refocusing it on the "rediscovered sense of family," these places do nothing so much as exacerbate the Crusoean taste for self-contained territoriality that is already at work in the family boardinghouse.[63] Alain Laurent notes this in the course of his survey in the Club Med village in Cefalù, Sicily: those who indicate a desire for excursions, and thus an interest in the outside world, are treated pejoratively as "tourists" in this world of "pure" summer vacationers. When one goes to Cefalù, one does not go to Sicily: one goes to the Club. The same holds true for Greece, Morocco, and Spain. "It's so comfortable in the village" that if, for example, "we decide to go off to see a bullfight, we swear when we get back that we'll never again set foot outside the camp."[64]

Thus, with respect to this nostalgia, if "the vacation village pre-sents a sort of unexpected perfection"[65] in comparison to the family boarding house, it is only the end result of an exotic exaggeration of the isolation of the tribe—with its chief,[66] the abolition of cash, the use of first names (and, in French, familiar pronouns), the pareo, the conversion of rooms into "grass shacks," huts, and bungalows, and even a welcoming rite that Rackam describes ironically, saying that it is a "traditional dance from the remote past, the time when the first tribes of the Club sought to communicate their sense of hospitality to the first 'Gracious Members.'"[67] From this standpoint, on a different scale and with a specific symbolics, the Club simply goes further in affirming and manifesting the meaning of a vacation practice that is essentially based on a desire for withdrawal and enclosure.

As Christiane Peyre and Yves Raynouard observe, there is something mythical in the insular strategy of the original Club that evokes the island of the Lotophages, the hospitable people who welcomed Ulysses and his companions and invited them to eat a fruit (of the lotus plant) that caused them to lose their memory, to such an extent that the sailor's companions lost all desire to go back to Ithaca. From this point of view, the Club takes the Crusoe experience one step further. At no point does Crusoe himself ever give up the idea of going home—even if over the years the memory of the female body retained by Michel Gall's Robinson in his erotic dreams is increasingly vague. For that matter, is forgetting even a real possibility—especially in our world, in which information pursues the vacationer right onto the beach? At most, one's memories may become imperfect, blurred by artificial means.[68] This blurring is one function of the rites, games, and enclosed spaces characteristic of the seaside universe, which temporarily obscure the recollection of the outside world. Since complete forgetting is impossible, we have to distinguish here between loss of memories and loss of memory. Seaside residency, despite its indifference to the world and notwithstanding the stratagems it uses to shed the world, can produce no more than partial amnesia.

And then, between yesterday's hotels or boardinghouses, today's vacation villages, grass shacks or huts, and campgrounds for tents or campers, even before the massive urbanization of the shore, we find the modular spaces of pavilions and villas. From the late nineteenth century to the beginning of the twentieth, from the dunes of Normandy to those of Aquitaine, the implantation and architectural fantasies of these residences, over and beyond their value of ostentation, already signify the dream of withdrawal and enclosure. In Arcachon, in the late 1880s, "the pine woods that crown the dune hide coquettish villas, leisure homes of every style, Russian chalets, Gothic manors, Moorish or Chinese pavillions." It is not yet the era of Polynesianism, but the exoticism found here prefigures the contemporary seaside utopia. By introducing Arab, Asian, or Scandinavian styles, Persian palaces or Swiss chalets, in places where they do not belong, the voluntary anachronisms of the heteroclite architecture erected behind promenades and dunes confirm the break between the shoreline and the rest of the world. They are the ultimate frontier, the demarcation of a separate universe, and not merely the sign of social competition. Unlike the lodgings that "green" vacationers seek out in the countryside in the form of manors, abbeys, mills, or old farmhouses, traces of a "world rooted in the truth of the soil," these exotic beach edifices do not present themselves "as products of history and the region."[69] They are totally artificial and display their inauthenticity with pride.

The discourse held by this architectural language through a simulated chaos of styles is still, in relation to the sea, a discourse of extratemporal tribalization, of the extraction of a group from history and the correlative institution of a micro-universe of sociability detached from the cultural context and from the inland world. To each family its façade, as to each tribe its totem, symbolizing the cultural identity and unity of the clan. The variety of these architectural fantasies has been explored in detail by Dominique Rouillard, who even mentions a design for a house with a rounded foundation that makes explicit reference to a ship's hull, a vacation spot on earth for Nemo corresponding to his desire for isolation: an imaginary ship for a motionless cruise that is not the index of nostalgia for exploration but a "privileged locus of . . . closure," of protection.[70] Not a ship for navigation but a ship in which to enclose oneself. Not a boat but an ark—a hut floating on the surface of the world.

From this perspective, the scandal of coastal urbanization in the form of seaside Manhattans and "Costa Brava" high-rises is not only ecological and aesthetic; it is also symbolic. If certain residences— former hotels from the early twentieth century converted into apartments, such as we still find clinging to the lofty slopes of Vallauris and elsewhere—evoke the image of passenger ships transported inland, this recent urbanization destroys all the signs of the dream, those through which the feeling of the hut and the taste for refuge can be expressed. Away from the beach, Robinson is no longer anything but a tenant or co-owner lost in an apartment building, with his grotto merely a studio on some upper floor. For the mythic value of the villa in the dunes (and thus its symbolic function), which is also that of the vacation village and the family boardinghouse, is in many respects comparable to that of Robinson's cave—or to that of the blockhouses of France's northern beaches, where children and lovers creep in despite the "no entry" signs. It refers to the image of the grotto, a uterine space, a place of first refuge. "'This is exciting,' said George. 'Caves— and more caves—and yet more caves!'"[71]

There is still the campground. In 1942 Francis Ponge wrote: "I wish that—instead of those enormous monuments which only testify to the grotesque exaggeration of his imagination and his body . . .—man sculpted some kind of niches or shells to his proportion (in this respect I find African huts fairly satisfactory)." The Club Med had not yet been invented, but campgrounds, essentially linked to forests and the countryside at first, were already in place; tents and trailers responded to this desire with the canvas architecture and folding trailers that appeared at the end of the First World War.[72]

A reputation for nomadism is still attached to mobile-home camping. However, with the exception of the camping trailer designed for itinerant use and thus for tourism, summer residency has to a large extent taken hold of this means of setting up housekeeping. The mobile home has become a privileged tool of vacation topophilia, especially in seaside settings. In 1984 63 percent of the nights spent in tents in France were spent in municipalities along the shore, and today, as we have seen, camping accounts for 24.2 percent of seaside lodgings, against a national average of 18 percent.[73] In other words, going against the grain of the mobility for which they were invented (for economic reasons they can even substitute for second homes), tents and trailers or mobile homes have become precious auxiliaries of leisure sedentarity and of the seaside robinsonnade in particular.

A great deal has been said and shown and written about camping: the universe of *Dupont Lajoie* (a film by Yves Boisset), the space of a teeming "cabinism."[74] In the best of cases people speak of "poor campers" as they would of "poor dirt farmers": with pity. Condescending critics say that they are "so crushed by the banality of their existence that they are unable to escape it, even once a year." But are they really fleeing? No, they are starting life over and improving it, on the margins of everyday life, just as Robinson is constantly improving his circumstances. In a welcome shift of perspective, Agnès Varda has good things to say about campers in *Du côté de la côte* (1958), for example: "Camping was the freshest form of liberty, and the most incredibly ceremonial; you can live a good life with the majesty of ancient chieftains retiring into their tents." Similarly, in *Les gens de peu* Pierre Sansot explains the genius of a campground by detailing the customs that organize it, its actors, their moving-in strategies (choice of neighbors, orientation of the tent, interplay of sympathies and cooperation) or their distended management of time and space. In conclusion, he writes: "one can take pleasure in 'not disrupting one's habits,' in reliving different scenes under the same light, away from the constraints of work and bosses."[75]

We shall not linger over the description of this universe except for one point, where Sansot remarks that campers "aspire to responsibilities that daily life does not allow them. Hence they are sometimes tempted to take over a portion of the campground and mark it visibly, by putting in borders, planting flowers, granting themselves authority to oversee their path and encroaching on it. Given the opportunity, they would pour concrete, they would install fences and gates." And some mobile-home campers do just that, in the huge "trailer parks" set up behind the dunes on the northern beaches of France or Belgium, for example between Wenduine and Blankenberghe, in New Venne Park (with room for 850 vehicles); there the desire for something "solid" and durable, for gates and concrete, can be not only glimpsed but satisfied.[76]

In this campground, one discovers an astonishing bivouac consisting of trailers and mobile homes in which everyone pretends to camp without really camping; people play at leading a nomadic life by setting up housekeeping in a temporary framework made to last. The rudimentary nature of the installation is only superficial, the minimum required to produce the feeling of a "self-made home." For the rest, these huts have every comfort: electricity, heat, shower, refrigerator, sewage, television (cable, in the best parks). And external signs of installation, territoriality, and topophilia abound. Trailer wheels and mobile-home supports are hidden by boards or brick walls that simulate foundations. Somewhat along the lines of the workers' gardens of an earlier era, the borders of each lot are marked by fences, hedges, or bushes, and the entry gate is framed by wooden or stone posts. All around, between the enclosure and the residence, the remaining surface, covered with grass and paving stones, is set up like a little garden, invaded by the ornamental symbols of leisure sedentarity such as statues, basins, ceramic dwarves, permanent windbreaks for barbecues, and even fake wells, sometimes decorated with fake pumps.

Like a caravan that has halted at the entrance to a desert (for behind the dunes there lies the sea), a petrified vacation oasis from which the nomad's tent has disappeared forever, replaced by trailers that no longer trail behind cars and mobile homes that are now immobile, everything here betrays a denegation of mobility, a desire to live in this place, to eliminate the signs of the itinerant life for which these lightweight residences were intended and to load up the surroundings with signs of an immutable domesticity. The functional deviation of the nomadic material and the topophilic reinscription of the site tell us a good deal about the Crusoean desire for retreat into the self that inspires such makeshift arrangements. What we see is all the work of a tinkerer "who builds his house like a myth because it is one." It is the language of a ritual of refoundation, implantation, and protection, reminiscent of the excessive fortifications Robinson installed around his cave.[77]

Completing the tetralogy, underneath the disparity of places, habitats, actors, social classes, and practices, a common meaning arises here: a series of symbolic equivalences that traverse the various domains of vacation residency but proceed from a single code. The juxtaposition of these equivalences manifests a collective imaginary from which properly touristic dreams are banished.[78] Here we are at home among ourselves and nowhere else. No outsiders, no savages, no real exoticism; only neighbors, friends, families, people like ourselves living in the same way within the ritual limits of a closed universe.

From shelter to beach and back again, whether the shelter is a comfortable hotel, a cozy boardinghouse, a fortified village, an isolated villa, or an entrenched camp with thousands of tribes (the New Venne Park is adjacent to three camps of similar capacity, which in principle means an ephemeral summer city of 10,000 inhabitants or more), what is important is not that these residences are there "on display thirty or sixty days per year, and that is all,"[79] nor that these villages lack basements and attics. In its dreams, the seaside vacation world sees itself as primordial, emergent. It believes or wants to believe that it has no historical, social, or cultural memory. It is a suspended, floating world, like a cruise hotel, a houseboat, or, washed up at the foot of the dunes, an Armada-campground, a place about which it has been said that "the demand for internal animation . . . can be compared, all other things being equal, to that of a cruise ship."[80]

8. Beach Society

(or, How Robinson, observing Friday,
Girl Friday, and little Sunday
on the beach, discreetly noted their
customs in his diary)

"I shall call you Sunday," said Robinson. "It is the day of the resurrection,
of the youth of all things, and the day of our master, the Sun."

—Michel Tournier, *Friday*

Once the summer vacationers have marked off their territories and
established their regular paths between the beach and their shelters,
boardinghouses, villas, villages, or campgrounds, the self-enclosed
world of seaside life proper commences. The tribes have settled in;
individuals, couples, and groups sporadically break away or rejoin the
others, some to swim, some to dry off. Still others take walks, play,
or jog between the surf and the dry sand, looking at their immobile
counterparts who are seated or stretched out, face down or face up,
keeping their eyes closed or observing the parade of voyeurs. In short,
people look at one another and put themselves on display. People pass
by and watch others pass. They are being observed and they know it.
Daily life is being reinvented. Everyone observes everyone else. Each
deciphers the others, recognizing, commenting on, and judging body
language, gestures, and objects. Individuals circulate, exchanging and
manipulating one another like signs. This communication, which de-
fines a way of being together, is social life itself.[1]

But what sort of "being together"? Jean Viard writes: "Tourism is a
courtly practice, without kings or royalty."[2] Does this apply to seaside
summer vacationing as well? If there is a seaside "kingdom" in the

world of leisure, there is no king on the "partitioned island"; or rather there are many kings—far too many. At the beach, there is at least one per tribe, and there are countless tribes. Within the framework of primitive seaside sociability, no monarch federates the fiefdoms. There are no suzerains here. Whether conjugal, familial, or based on friendship, hordes or clans, these microscopic fiefdoms resemble independent states: they constitute integral parts of a common space that has the shape of a shattered kingdom with haphazard diplomatic ties, yet they are not integrated into that space.

Only in specific places away from the beach, as was once the case, for example, in fashionable resorts, can a court be maintained or reconstructed.[3] People stay at different hotels; they come from different clubs or villages; they set up housekeeping in different campgrounds. And within each of these domains, individual "courtiers" may receive different privileges from the "king." It is not unusual for people to return, voluntarily or not, to the practices of a developed and structured feudalism dominated by a single leader, a powerful organizer who distributes privileges and punishments: the best-located hut in the village; a room with "a view"; the out-of-the-way table in the dining room, far from the kitchen or the noisy entrance; "friendship prizes," or the shadiest spot in the campground.

> The management of humanity on vacation is further complicated by the fact that space within the campground is anything but homogeneous. Between sites next to the bathrooms—zero degree in the hierarchy of campsites—and beachfront sites, which are obviously the most valued, there is an entire subtle gradation that the clients of the Tamaris campground (on the coast near Bordeaux) understand perfectly. Promotion along this scale is organized by Jean-Mi in terms of seniority. The newest clients begin their careers near the toilets and showers. As the years go by, they get closer to the beachfront sites; these are reserved for the clients who have been coming the longest. Progress toward the sea is irreversible; no client agrees to go in the other direction. Thus the surest way to get rid of a family that has become undesirable for one reason or another is to offer it a place whose "value" is inferior to that of the place won the previous year. Wounded in its camper's honor, the family will refuse every time.[4]

This Jean-Mi is a little like Robinson: an absolute monarch on his island. He decides where Friday will live and assigns him a hut at some distance from the castle.[5] But farther away, on the beach, an open stage (unless an admission fee is charged, and reserved spots are assigned), the power to command weakens and tends to dissipate. On this narrow fringe of ground, Friday is liberated. The robinsonnade is out of Robinson's control, freed from his laws, from his anointings, from the dictates of his inegalitarian divisions. Still hierarchical at the shore's edge, humanity on vacation atomizes on the sand. A number of its conventions and other segregations come undone. Its society is emancipated and reconfigured; it pretends to shed the cleavages that always stigmatize its surroundings.

The closer one gets to the sea, the more the rules of the social game are blurred and seem to be abolished, as if they were water-soluble. Here there are only bathers, bodies whose nudity expresses an apparent equality and conspires to eradicate hierarchies, to confuse roles and statuses or at least to diminish the readability of the social privileges acquired and maintained by certain bathers up to the threshold of the beach. If the seaside universe is a world apart, a floating universe for a weightless society, the beach is precisely the spot where the loss of gravity may seem to reach its peak. And it hardly matters then that this social flotation is only a superficial egalitarian effect—an illusion.[6] Without this illusion, the seaside game would be impossible.

In an earlier day, the manifestation of social discriminations extended to the beach, via bathing cabins in particular. Bertail had this to say on the subject in 1876: "Seeing all these unequal silhouettes erected above the beach with forms that seek to distinguish themselves from one another by their effect or their exaggeration, one thinks of family vaults, the last refuge of human pretentions."[7]

But today, the massive access to beaches and swimming has made commonplace a once-forbidden practice: unconcealed undressing.[8] People now take their clothes off on the beach. Moving beyond obligatory use of the private transition points that filtered the passage from the clothed world to the bathers' universe, this contemporary "indecency" has largely made obsolete the seaside structures in which signs of modesty were blended with signs of ostentation. Thus in a context that has become immodest, bathing cabins are no longer what they were. They either serve as simple cloakrooms or sheds intended for the storage of beach equipment, or else, preserved and restored by the local community as part of its heritage, featured on postcards from Deauville to Pornic, from Binic to Bernières-sur-Mer, they give the seaside site an old-fashioned charm that contributes to the distinctive image of the place. Utilitarian or decorative, mere closets or archaeological gems, they are now just vestiges of an outdated vacation morality and order in terms of which they possessed a quite specific higher value: they were "dark chambers," objects of every sort of curiosity, because they were special, secret places concealing nude bodies.

Cabins are no longer what they were, and the long lines of beach tents at Biarritz and elsewhere are disappearing. A whole architecture of canvas and boards is fading away, and with it an entire social tradition. Today on the beach the actors are often "homeless," without prosthetic furnishings, reduced to the signs of their own bodies and a few portable accessories. The historical "expulsion" of nudity out of cabins and tents attests not only to the end of a form of modesty based on a protectionist ideology vis-à-vis the "fair sex," but also to the establishment of a new strategy of ostentation, focused, unlike the earlier one, on body image. The body is no longer concealed by means of an opaque opulence; instead, it is put on public display.

Contemporary beach society is characterized by this reversal, this displacement of ostentation toward transparency. In a sense, the body is substituted for the social element (or the subject substituted for its economic attributes); in place of "external signs of wealth," the body becomes the initial sign of valorization and recognition. A ritual *corps-à-corps* is the first rule of a new collective game. Played without screens or prostheses, without masks or other extracorporeal intermediaries, this game is based on the immediate aesthetics of flesh, the instantaneous discourse of skin, appearance, the beauty of forms, volume, or gesture, and the henceforth ambivalent "speech" of a costume whose purpose is no longer so much to hide as to reveal. A change in costume, in custom, and in setting as well: "Dress *(habit)* and habit *(habitude)*: the relationship is obvious and significant. Clothing can only vary in a time when customs vary, when habits are broken."[9]

If the costume is made to correspond to a simultaneous desire for protection, for modesty, and for ornamentation, the contemporary swimming suit, the product of an evolution that presupposes the transgression and abandonment of a certain number of models and attitudes, can be said to result from the questioning of this triple motivation. Between ornamentation and protection, today's bathing costume bears witness to a choice that very clearly privileges the former, and its success attests to the consecration of a new social imaginary of seaside leisure. Here is the symbolic key to contemporary beach society, the "society of the twelfth month, living on the margin of the eleven others," but also—and especially—a society of the unclothed par excellence.[10] What sort of "unclothing"? Let us take a closer look.

CUSTOMS AND COSTUMES

Here, as with the moving-in rites, seaside reality has to be observed close at hand, closer than ever: we move past the atomic stage of the tribe to the anatomic stage of the individual. While bodily signs may well be "unsuited for extended discursive messages, in contrast to speech, they do seem well designed to convey information about the actor's social attributes and about his conception of himself, of the others present, and of the setting." The body speaks through its epidermic, vestimentary, pigmentary, plastic, and textile encodings, along with its choreography. It speaks of itself, of what it is and what it wants to be, for itself and for others. Beyond that, it condenses a vision of the world or at the very least a way of being in the world and of dreaming the world. In this sense, the body writes itself in function of situations; it inscribes itself (and "inscribe" is the right word for it) in a tissue of relations and representations. A symbol and a symptom, the body recounts, reflects, and summarizes dreams. Although more or less under control, the body is a semaphore put on stage by each individual according to common rules of representation, expression, and substance; it is a premeditated sign whose silhouette is a pictogram. It takes shape in space like a signature, a print, a proof, or a declaration of intent. Clothed or unclothed, the swimmer's body is always dressed, costumed, if only in signs—intentional or not. Paul Morand, summing up this complex paradox of seaside nudity in his own way, wrote, "The all-weather clothing now in vogue here on our shores is the tanned skin of the athlete." More than ever "here," the skin itself is a form of clothing—just as an article of clothing can be in turn a second skin.[11]

Since the time of the earliest scandals and transgressions, beach mores and manners have obviously undergone considerable change. We need not revisit the adventures and misadventures of swimming suits. The outcome of these tribulations (called "fashions") is that the swimmer's body is no longer either a shadowy image or an encrypted reality. Formerly surreptitious, more imagined than seen, a masked object, a furtive apparition dimly glimpsed by the curious, today a swimmer's body is durably exposed to the gaze of others. At the point when heliophilic idleness has triumphed, the body is not only on display, it is emphasized; it now asserts its corporal presence and its sexual readability by way of a language accepted by all. A system of signs made up of constraints and prohibitions but also of tolerances and innovative infractions, this language has a history, of course, but it also has a meaning, a raison d'être, a motive. The latter has been powerful enough to elude a social vigilance resistant to nudity, and correlatively to give signs for self-expression and means of satisfaction to a collective desire for inversion. But just what is this language? What does it mean? And in particular, around the edges of its scandals, by what detours has it finally succeeded in imposing itself?

On the fringes of the nudist world (which has from the beginning advocated a complete break with the clothed world), the invention of the contemporary bathing suit (which, however minimalist it may be, does not break with clothing) presupposes a gradual emancipation with respect to other dress codes. The process of invention entailed a series of compromises, and it progressed slowly, reaching its successful conclusion quite late. Jacques Laurent explains that "the second half of the twentieth century, by inventing nudity for the beach, invented a new form of clothing: the state of undress. Conscious nudity."[12] In other words, whether total or partial, nudity was now clearly intended, perceived, and experienced as a fact, an act or a state contrary to the social norm. Prefiguring this later invention, transparent, clinging, short, and open garments had prepared the way (see chapter 3). But still other innovations, detours in the form of deviations, also announced the reversal in their own way. For example, the use of beach pajamas: clothing intended to be worn at night and indoors was recycled as daytime outdoor clothing. The use of boxer shorts was similarly significant; here, too, a private sign was transferred to public space. In other words, what had been inside, underneath, was now outside, on top: the image of reversal could hardly be clearer.

Still, we cannot account for the meaning of these vestimentary languages of inversion without evoking a significant historical subterfuge that underlies the minimalist aesthetic of the contemporary bathing suit. In the process through which the seaside vacationer conquered the unclothed state, this subterfuge was socially decisive and symbolically revealing: I am referring to the emancipatory use of children. In the history of leisure, the child in fact appears at several points as a privileged intermediary between the adult world and the world of nudity or the unclothed state. Children have in effect served as experimental models, prototypes, or guinea pigs. It is as if adults used children as scouts assigned to investigate the morally uncertain terrain of denudation, as explorers or adventurers unwittingly testing a new vestimentary practice destined to become widespread if the experiment were a success.

Benigno Cacérès once noted that workers discovering outdoor leisure would "go back to wearing shorts, as if they were schoolboys again." For his part, Paul Morand offers ironic observations about "false Brigitte Bardots with ponytails and overalls from Dior," and "old ladies in pirate pants."[13] Child-women, they seem to be disguised *as* children or else *like* children wearing costumes. More seriously, Michel Pastoureau notes that the striped clothing worn at the seaside, corresponding as much to nineteenth-century pajama stripes as to those of sailors or health advocates, has finally become vacation clothing; it has taken over "the world of leisure, of games and sports, of childhood and youth. Once healthful, fashionable, and maritime, it has become playful, athletic, and cheerful"; adults have adopted striped clothing on this basis as a kind of inheritance from children's attire. Jacques Laurent observes more specifically that "before the First World War little girls wore fairly short skirts, and it was customary to let pantaloons show underneath; these got shorter, and became little underpants prefiguring the ones women wore under short dresses in 1925."[14] As earlier with pajamas and boxer shorts, inside wear was moved to the outside; little girls could now go to the beach wearing little underpants, ancestors of the bikini bottom, and they were soon imitated by their mothers, who, until the late 1930s, covered their torsos with overblouses and their underpants with short skirts. Later, after the war, two-piece suits appeared, replacing the overblouse or the whalebone-corseted one-piece suit[15] with a brassiere top, to be followed by the Bikini (a brand name registered in 1946)—"bathing costume for women, in two pieces reduced to the minimum," as the *Dictionnaire Hachette* says. There were similar developments on the men's side:

> While the great Victor was strutting about in the first fitted "bathing trunks," the triangular ones that show off your advantages. With a comb stuck into the elastic. The cousins looked at him as if he were Tarzan the Monkey Man!

They were in bikinis, the cousins; they'd turned into two-piece
cousins, with little steering wheels in the balcony, quite an effect!

Papa was shocked to see them riding their bikes "dressed like that!"

And Mama said: "It's the way things are today, George, it's the way
things are going."[16]

In short, where transgressions in apparel are concerned, changes in
customs and costumes or progress in undressing, adults find precious
allies in children and adolescents. Jacques Laurent also pointed this
out, confirming the objective alliance in the form of an unconscious
symbiosis: "Shorts had to be worn first by children, then by adults."[17]
Similarly, between bare skin and the two-piece suit, we can imagine
that the concept of the monokini, "topless" attire, leaving breasts bare
(a fashion that began to appear on beaches at Saint-Tropez after 1968),
was first inaugurated by preadolescents with breasts in the bud stage
who were still wearing only bottoms, as younger children do.

In the history of beachwear, it is thus finally as though children
were innocent front-line soldiers leading the way in the undressing
and bathing-suit wars, with their parents following the operations
from a distance like prudent generals, before imitating them in case
of victory. For if you can win without risk, you avoid a lot of trouble.
There are sometimes defeats, like the one described by Dr. Pierre
Vachet in the late 1920s:

> On an uncrowded beach in Brittany, some parents didn't think there
> was anything wrong with letting their three pretty little girls, aged 3,
> 4, and 8, go swimming in the nude; the sun and the water revitalized
> the wan little Parisians, and no one had any objections. One day, a
> local country squire showed up in the company of a tutor-priest and a
> couple of cloddish children aged 12 and 13. The gentleman was indig-
> nant, and went over to order the Parisians to put bathing suits on the
> innocent girls; these polite people agreed. Does it not take a singularly
> perverse mind to object to nudity in children that young?[18]

But the defeat Dr. Vachet observed was only incidental. Many victories followed, from nudist guerrilla actions to fashion revolutions.
Via the "dissident" use of nudity in toddlers and children, all these
victories led to the contemporary beach: an autonomous, undressed,
and visually permissive society whose establishment is also indebted
to another inversion, that of the mimetic relation between children

and adults. Roger Caillois emphasized this point in a book on play: with costumes, masks, mimes, and miniature toys representing the tools, weapons, or machines used by grownups, an entire category of play activities is based on the principle of the imitation of adults by children.[19] On the beach, what happens is just the opposite.

So why do adults copy children? There are many reasons, even if naturists have a simple answer: if the child is father to the man, he is also the first nudist. "We were created to live nude, just as we came into the world, the way certain primitive races still live," Dr. Vachet wrote at the beginning of his reflections on nudity.[20] But it is also because adults perceive children as wild beings, only weakly socialized if at all. Convention does not yet inhibit their behavior, and that is why they serve as models for the Crusoean utopia. They are brand-new Fridays whom Robinson fears and envies. Robinson dominates his child Friday, but also plays with him and projects himself onto him. And then the child, far removed from the Freudian definition of "polymorphous perversity," enjoys an intangible reputation for innocence: he is at once like Friday and like Adam. Finally, he is the image of eternal youth and of origins, and by this token his naked or unclothed body incarnates the most positive of seaside daydreams, that of regeneration, of liberation from history (see chapter 4).

The child is an archetype. He is an "initial and terminal creature," a symbol of beginning and recreation. He is the image of the beginning and the triumphant end, expressing in ancient mythology the entity of man reappearing "in the child-like frolics of a new life, surrounded by the sea-forms of dolphins and tritons."[21] In other words, the child may well be the one who introduces scandal, but he is above all the one owing to whom the break with the society of "sewed-up man" and his traditions is made possible. His nudity and even his bathing trunks are symbols of the negation of the clothed world, a model for the "simple accouterments" on the basis of which the bourgeois on vacation will toss out first his city clothes, next his oversized bathing costume and the darkness of the bathing cabin, and then, little by little, the "blue tee-shirt and faded red pants" that he had donned "to imitate the local fishermen"—and other marine emblems.[22] There are no more fishermen in this utopian universe (see chapter 1), and, moving from indigenist imitation to mythographic mimeticism, changing from one dream to another, it is the child-god who comes to be imitated, an atemporal being with a pure, unalienated body, a veritable model of the contemporary seaside robinsonnade. The child gives rise to the creation of a dress code in his own image.

That is why we would be mistaken to see this history of the bathing suit merely as the shrinking of an article of clothing during which "skin rediscovers contact with the atmosphere over an ever-increasing surface area."[23] Such a functional history would neglect the imaginary dimension of customs and costumes; its ineluctable outcome would be, like an announced textile void, purely and simply the disappearance of clothing. The reality of practices is more complex, and the evolution of the bathing suit cannot be reduced to that of a *shagreen*, a shrinking rag. Taboos remain, resistant to the dream, limiting or endlessly redefining the frontiers of undress, focusing on certain parts of the body or displacing its signs. For nudity is not only a state, it is a message: it is expressed quite as much as it is exhibited. The dream of Eden thus continues, but it borrows other paths of dress and custom.

For example, as evidence of the "resistible ascension" of denudation and the impact of taboos, we can look to Brazil. There, "where women cunningly appear more naked than anywhere else, all attempts to go topless have provoked disaster: hissing, booing, and occasional Bronx cheers. Nipples must never be seen on the beach . . . everything else," Elliott Erwitt comments, "but not the symbol of motherhood to a macho society." And then, between ostentation and protection, as Philippe Perrot quite rightly notes, "as nakedness is gradually devalued by the inflation of its extensive practice, as the zones of modesty and desire are gradually diminished, those of sanitary surveillance, anatomical control, hygienic vigilance, and cosmetic restrictiveness are gradually increased."[24] A different aesthetic policy, that of denudation, is established, between prescription and proscription, imposing different rules, different limits, different customs, and thus, finally, different costumes.

THE HAIRLESS UNIVERSE

It would be a mistake to believe that the abandonment of references to indigenous clothing (replaced by Polynesianism, the Brazilian "string," or California fluorescence), or the shrinking of bathing suits or even their disappearance, are signs of access to or even an evolution toward absolute transparency. Not only is the naked individual still marked socially by his way of speaking, the ideas communicated by his discourse, or his ways of doing things, but he also still lives within the shelter of the ultimate "fabric" constituted by his own skin. Skin, the first protection and the first clothing, is also the first "parchment." In the history of human societies, through scarification, tattoos, makeup and other artificial, natural, ritual, or accidental imprints, skin dresses the body. It narrates, signals affiliation with a group, betrays, or encrypts the person wearing it.

Even if bathing suits were to disappear entirely from all the world's beaches, this would not spell the end of bathing costumes. In the framework of a seaside futurology, it is all very well to predict, jokingly, "the timid appearance of bathing trunks that 'show it all,'" but this would actually change nothing. The bathing suit's focused, exhibitionist encoding still belongs to the order of clothing, and feigned, displayed transparency is a new form of mask. One might think that this is because a bathing suit is still involved, but no: nudism does little better when the indices of encoding persist. "Trimmed along straight lines in an impeccable V, pubic hair itself is transmuted into a cache-sexe that hides nothing."[25] Moreover, even without a technical intervention of this sort, does man not continue to convert his body into a sign and a system of signs by his way of using and displaying it? The clothing may be gone, but the sign remains; between encoding and decoding, the play of masks continues. Beach society, however unclothed it may be, is intimately nourished by this oscillation, the corporal rhetoric of hide-and-display.

Whence, advocating display and protection simultaneously, today's highly ambivalent discourse about seaside undress, which probably stems from the ambiguity of the image of the nude body itself—an ambiguity highlighted by both Paul Morand and Jacques Laurent. "Clothing says a lot about a man: naked, he will hide his secrets more jealously," as the former puts it. And the latter raises the following question: "But can we even say of these men and women swimming or sunbathing on the sand whether they have shed all their clothing when they are nude?" This is because in fact "as soon as appearances cease to wear an obvious mask, they become an enigma to be deciphered."[26] In the decontextualized universe of the beach, the swimmer's appearance seems not to be defined by any particular function, nor is his role determined in any way: he is a vacationer, an actor at rest, whose undressed body no longer has—and this is the point—the self-evident semiotic value of a mask, as it did when he was costumed for society. However, although it is more discreetly covered with signs, the nude body is still a mask, and its function is primarily to express not a role but values such as cleanliness, health, purity, youth, and beauty (if possible), and above all a certain image of "naturalness."

Cosmetic discourse on sunbathing ("How to get a good tan" was the title of one advertisement disguised as a report), in which there are many references to combating wrinkles, free radicals, infrared rays, and to total screening, is highly revealing of this equivalence between makeup and clothing. The terms *care, makeup,* and *protection* are used, but "invisible" clothing is actually at stake. "You can tell the difference," a well-known magazine says, "between tanning 'fanatics' and those who simply like to look healthy. For women in the second category, tinted cream is still ideal. It operates on two levels: skin care (it is remarkably effective, and it vanishes completely) and makeup (it comes in any number of colors, its coverage is precise, and it's easy to use)," and it thus allows women to acquire "an entirely new and natural skin tone."[27] How one "looks" is the key. Body image is indeed what is at stake here: a tinted body, covered with a "vanishing" cream, to be sure, but covered nonetheless. Colored cutaneous "clothing" does the job. One weaves for oneself "a golden tone." Once naked, one clothes oneself with a "fluid texture," a self-tanning product that "gives you the healthy look of being on vacation." Sublitan, by Guerlain, offers "skin care like sunshine." Here we have "naturalness" indeed!

People play games, and they cheat. They tan without sunshine. At bottom, what counts is the surface. Appearances. Naturalness is not what we find at the heart of all this, but its idyllic, Edenic figure, imaginary or stylized. The body is only a sign for a nudity that is sometimes difficult to achieve. The body needs help, then, if it is to deceive and do it well, if it is to succeed in expressing the reigning values in a "striking" way (this term is widely used). Cleanliness: "I sand off the rough spots (knees and elbows, otherwise they look dirty) and I make sure to rub the product into the wrinkled spots to avoid leaving lines." Youth: "Tinted Oenobiol Anti-Age Cream gives you the optimum dose of anti-radical vitamins and essential oligo-elements that are indispensable for the youthfulness of your skin and the sparkle of its tone."[28] We can take note of the cosmetological jargon, in passing: to create an impression of simplicity, of "naturalness," the expression has to be complicated, scientific. Beauty: deception can be quite crude when it is a matter not only of skin color or tone but of the flesh and its forms: "Fool everybody . . . by putting your flat eggs into a suit with shells"; or turn to some magic ointment that develops and firms up, as people have been doing for at least forty years: "I am thirty-five years old. Three years ago, I applied the beauty treatment STAR-SEIN for a few weeks. It was a really magical fountain of youth for my breasts. Again this year, on my vacation, I astonished the people I was with by the fullness and firmness of my bust."[29] The important thing is to deceive, to put one's nudity on stage, not so much finally to display it as to hide the truth about it—which can even include using false tattoos. These were the "latest thing" during the summer of 1993: removable decals that restored, for the duration of a swimming party, a factitious parchment body, clothed in words and pictures.

But the imaginary dimension of the seaside body, its trompe-l'oeil "naturalness," in harmony with the aesthetics of the place, is unquestionably the most clearly expressed in the ritual of hair removal. For this is now a ritual scrupulously followed and carried out with the beach in mind. The period just before summer begins is high season in this realm for sales of depilatory creams and appointments in beauty salons. Philippe Perrot has done a good job of describing the rising importance of this "pilophobic fervor" in the nineteenth and twentieth centuries; after tackling the head (hair, forehead) and the face (eyebrows, lip area, chin), women turned toward legs, armpits, and finally the pubic area, the ultimate zone of unvanquished hairiness whose final conquest appears indispensable if a smooth and unified body with sunlit skin is to replace a female corporal geography overly invaded by that "wild" and shadowy vegetation. Body hair is now no longer perceived as a superfluity: "These grenadiers' charms repel desire and are a mistake of nature," as one man puts it. Nature herself has made a mistake, and the retention of these "charms," when they are too dense, stems henceforth from bodily negligence: body hair can be seen as the sign of uncultivated zones that escape the social order. A great many women, says another man, "are happy to show us the black forest, without any traveling, just by lifting . . . their arms."[30] Thus the idea that the female body must be deforested was imposed gradually: it had to be defoliated, cleared of brush, or at least of a certain amount of substantial kindling in order to domesticate the corporeal landscape just as the landscapes of the countryside and the seashore had been cleared and tamed. Let us have the bush in place of brush, grass in place of weeds, and sand instead of seaweed!

A disturbing metaphorical unity. To the clearing of land corresponds the "de-seaweeding" of beaches and the removal of body hair from women bathers. Depilatory cosmetology is to bodies what "de-seaweedology" is to seaside sites—which confers a very specific symbolic meaning on a vacation attitude evoked earlier, seaweed phobia (see chapter 4). Catherine Carlson is mistaken when she writes that "in the great process of deodorization, there's an obstacle that none of our sociologists had foreseen: body hair!" Sociologists have been observing it and fighting it for some time now, and with the help of progress in the cosmetic industry, the obstacle, on the beach, is being conquered, eliminated or reduced to next to nothing. "A woman is an island. Fiji is her perfume," one advertisement used to say a few years ago. Today, another advertisement (also for perfume) tells us that a woman is a dune, with the help of a landscape-portrait: a profile whose hairiness (eyebrows and eyelashes) resembles dwarf vegetation—brush, bushes, grassy clumps, or closely cut grass.[31]

Under these circumstances, what is the status of nudity and naturalness on today's beaches? People are not in fact seeking naturalness; nature is full of mistakes. From body to setting and vice versa, what they are seeking is a corrected body image; this is attested by the triumph of the feminine ritual of hair removal as the leitmotif of the "clean beach." The beach is feminine, by gender, sex, form, and usage. And nudity, then, once it has been put through the filter of this pilophobic ritual? Is it nuder than ever? More authentic? More real? Not at all! Instead, it is surreal, more figurative than veritable—since on the beach being bare-skinned (*être à poil*) means having hairless skin (*être sans poil*).

In the nineteenth century, Eugène Chapus wrote, "A woman in a corset is a lie, a fiction, but for the rest of us [men], this fiction is better than the reality." A depilatoried woman, like a seaweed-free beach, is also a lie, a fiction, and the aesthetic fiction is her new costume. Speaking of stockings, Jacques Laurent notes (and the influence of the child model is also clear here) that where the "old ones were white, black, or sometimes colored, the new ones are flesh-tinted; they tend to imitate nudity, to relate women's legs to those of young girls."[32] In other words, if the old stockings could serve to hide hair, the new ones are designed, among other things, to show that there is none. The same thing holds true for body hair removal, which is the ostentatious sign of an absence. By this token, hair removal is nothing less than a new variant of undressing, and not nudity itself. It is a form of clothing, invisible, like cosmetic creams, perfumes, and self-tanning pills. Depilatories are masks. Rather than making something appear, they make it disappear.

What do they mask? Nature, of course, with the understanding that nature refers historically quite as much to the idea of a wild environment as to that of a human constitution, whether physical or psychic, genital or instinctive.[33] Philippe Perrot reminds us that this is a very old rule: pubic hair has always been erased from sculptural, pictorial, and photographic representations of the female nude. He adds: "This is because that particular form of hairiness is the last region of wounded modesty, an overly violent vision, a sign too powerful to be depicted, and one which, like excretion, perhaps brings us to the most animal level of our animality, which is at once threatening and fascinating."[34] Beach society applies this aesthetic rule to the letter, hiding or effacing the hairiness of armpits, whose metaphoric value no longer needs to be demonstrated. The fact that a given beach is nudist does not alter the rule. Here, too, hair is removed from the underarms and the figuration of sex is removed to the realm of abstraction—by geometrizing its hairiness (as we have already seen) or even by reducing it to the size of a tuft.

In short, we have a body that, if not perfect, has at least been perfected; we have the waxed and the peeled alongside the fresh, the young, the supple, the smooth, the tan, or the unified, enriching a paradigm of qualities that make the body watertight, immaculate, homogeneous, and impervious, as if exempt from the consequences of biological excretion, from the traces of aging, from signs of wear and tear, internal or external: a body liberated from time, from decomposition, from the vulgar vegetative realm, a body dreamed as autarchic, a pure sign of itself. These qualities, according to Jean Baudrillard, are "qualities of closure." They ensure in fact a sort of "vitrification of nudity [that] is related to the obsessional function of the protective wax or plastic coating of objects and to the labour of scrubbing and cleaning intended to keep them in a constant state of propriety, of flawless abstraction . . . and [to maintain] them in a sort of abstract immortality."[35] And still other signs contribute to making this fantasy concrete: swimming suits made of "lycra" may dress bodies, but they also encase them in plastic; indelible makeup specially designed for swimming turns faces into unalterable images; there are even shampoos that not only wash the hair but also make it waterproof. A whole world is summed up through this corporeal semiology—the discourse of a closed body for a closed world.

GAMES AND CEREMONIES

On the sand at the beach, illuminated by the single projector of the summer sun, the play can thus begin. Happy and jealous gregariousness, eternal youth or immaculate cleanliness, the values embodied by tribes and "costumed" bodies now come to life, all in quest of roles that will prolong their images. Between concern for oneself and the presence of others, one must now play the game, that is, simultaneously regroup—for people play together—and isolate oneself—for people play against one another, face to face, or side by side. The game is the encounter between individuals and society. It presupposes rules, and calls for stereotyped scenes and scenarios: actors' gestures, theatrical conventions, protocols for entrances and exits, ruses and mysteries. Quite often, these theatrical artifices entail a shift from play to ceremony, or from simulacrum to simulation, so great is the extent to which they confer on everyone's behaviors, acts, and movements not just a ritual quality but also a real solemnity, even a certain gravity. A seriousness that, without making the player lose all consciousness of ordinary reality, brings him close to believing that he "really is" a tribal leader, in the case of an adult, or a castle-builder, in the case of a child.[36]

I do not propose to draw up some sort of exhaustive scenographic catalog of the beach that would begin with the installation rites already mentioned and end with a description of the sandcastle ceremony and other contests or competitions. That would be pure description and pure ethnography—whereas in fact the details of these customs, their variety and their enumeration, are less meaningful than their function and their repetition. I have thus retained just a few "typical" accounts or representative anecdotes in which most of us will be able to recognize ourselves or our neighbors; these will suffice to bring to light the ludic dimension of beach society and its essential aims.

Has pilosity, for all that, like seaweed, completely disappeared from the shore? Not at all! But if it is maintained in this depilated universe, it is no longer as unwelcome vegetation or a universal trace of animality, but rather as a specific sign. A differential mark, on the beach, even if it occasionally approaches hirsutism, body hair is the distinguishing characteristic of males. Abhorred in women, it is flaunted in men. It is no longer body hair, it is wool; no longer a weed, but a sign, a herald, a coat of mail: that of Man himself, his emblem, his poster, and his certificate, it "symbolizes virility and is benign if it grows only upon parts of the body such as a man's chest, chin, arms or legs" and the lower torso, whence a certain ostentatious practice, commonplace and virtually a form of advertising in some instances, in which pubic hair spills over the edges of mini-trunks like a flowering beard.[37] In this undressed universe, the eradication of women's body hair thus has a corollary heraldic function, that of underscoring sexual difference: the smooth versus the rough. Among other corporeal contrasts, this difference is one of the "rules" that "determine what 'holds' in the temporary world circumscribed by play."[38]

But beyond these well-known contrasts (tanning, slenderness, or musculature), which still belong to the realm of costume, other codes regulate the seaside game. These arise not only from the individual's self-image but also from its interpretation. Here we pass from the static and private symbolics of dress to the dynamic and public symbolics of the role an individual plays, from the ornamented and decorated body to the strategic and operational body. For an initial example, we can turn to literature, to a passage in which novelist William Sansom describes a man arriving on a beach:

> [H]e took care to avoid catching anyone's eye. First of all, he had to make it clear to those potential companions of his holiday that they were of no concern to him whatsoever. . . . The beach might have been empty. If by chance a ball was thrown his way, he looked surprised; then let a smile of amusement lighten his face (Kindly Preedy), looked round dazed to see that there were people on the beach, tossed it back with a smile to himself and not a smile at the people, and then resumed carelessly his nonchalant survey of space.

Courageous exploration, scouting, is the first sequence in the game. Then comes the installation sequence, the figure of conquering sedentarity:

> But it was time to institute a little parade, the parade of the Ideal Preedy. By devious handlings, he gave any who wanted to look a chance to see the title of his book . . . and then gathered together his beach-wrap and bag into a neat sand-resistant pile (Methodical and Sensible Preedy),

rose slowly to stretch at ease his huge frame (Big-Cat Preedy), and tossed aside his sandals (Carefree Preedy, after all).

Here is the moment of the first integration pact, the first social contract entered into with the people nearby, who watch the newcomer take his place among the others.

Next comes the rite of immersion: a test of aptitude, in a way. Through the exhibition of aquatic competence, this ceremony ratifies the newcomer's "naturalization" as a member of seaside society; the quality of the gesture, the familiarity with the element to which it bears witness let everyone watching know that he belongs:

> The marriage of Preedy and the sea! There were alternative rituals. The first involved the stroll that turns into a run and a dive straight into the water, thereafter smoothing into a strong splashless crawl. . . . Quite suddenly he would turn on to his back and thrash great white splashes with his legs, somehow thus showing that he could have swum even further had he wanted to, and then would stand up a quarter out of water for all to see who it was.[39]

This last sequence is unquestionably one of the best known and most often repeated. Who can claim never to have indulged in a little bit of theatricality under the circumstances, under the real or imaginary pressure of the others' gaze? "As Rosemary came onto the beach a boy of twelve ran past her and dashed into the sea with exultant cries. Feeling the impactive scrutiny of strange faces, she took off her bathrobe and followed."[40]

The gaze is there. You pay, or appear to be paying, more or less attention. It pays more or less attention to you, in return. But you certainly intend to remain in control of the impression that communicates the spectacle of your body to the people in the vicinity.

> The alternative course was simpler, it avoided the cold-water shock and it avoided the risk of appearing too high-spirited. . . . It involved a slow stroll down and into the edge of the water—not even noticing his toes were wet, land and water all the same to him—with his eyes up at the sky gravely surveying portents, invisible to others, of the weather (Local Fisherman Preedy).[41]

Here the ante has been upped, in a shift from display to particularizing consecration, from simple self-affirmation to self-legitimization via the simulacrum of a native, in this instance. "For we want at one and the same time to be entirely self-made and yet be descended from someone."[42] If Preedy embarks upon this game of differentiation in the meteorological mode, by summoning up the image of the knowledgeable native, another fictional character does the same thing in the mythological mode, playing Venus emerging from the waters.

> She knew, but didn't verify in any way, that the young German had been looking at her all along, that he was still staring at her from a distance.
> She dove in and swam about twenty meters using the very suitable crawl stroke that she had been taught every Wednesday morning for five years at the Racing Club; then she turned onto her back, in no hurry, and undertook her customary and carefully-planned "exit" from the water.
> It was hard not to watch her, from head to toe; there was nothing to criticize. Nymph-like hips, a narrow back contrasting (this is an absolute rule) with an ample bust, situated high up, with dark little points; long, slender, muscular thighs, hair black as ink and a face with regular features rather than beautiful, but illuminated by the sparkle of green eyes; Chris was exactly what she wanted to be.[43]

The game is not a new one. Gabriel Désert described the way it was routinely played in 1900. To be sure, people went into the water, but only for a brief moment, essentially "for appearances' sake, especially so that one's elegant manners upon emerging from the water could be admired."[44]

Lord of the sea or nymph of the foam from the beginning of the world: in the margins of that fundamental dyad, other roles can continually be deciphered on the beach. They have in common the fact that they are immediately readable; they are "the intelligible representation of moral situations."[45] For example, when the man is a "responsible" father, he becomes Preedy the Great Initiator. He becomes priest and professor, taking charge of the baptism and apprenticeship in the water of the smallest or most fearful children—a familiar childhood scene:

> Dad suddenly tosses the big ball in the water and yells:
> "See who can get it first . . ."
> He rushes out right away, followed by Jack, Nelly, and Mom. Only Bob has stayed motionless on the beach. He's terrified, watching his

whole family playing in the water. . . . Suddenly his mouth opens wide, his eyes fill with tears, he bursts out sobbing. Dad rushes over to him.

"Aren't you ashamed, my little man, to be scared of the water?"

He takes his son in his arms and goes back into the sea. Bob has stopped crying, but he doesn't yet feel very safe. He clings to Dad, holding him tight around the neck. And yet Dad doesn't want to scare him.[46]

We do not need to inventory all the actors and the multiple "dramatic situations"[47] that they can interpret for the function of the seaside "theater" to become clear here. It is a microcosm owing to which a return is accomplished and played out: the symbolic return from a society of jobs—a society that generates anonymity, relational dislocations and divisions—to a society of roles that restore identities, a society of foundational differences and bonds.[48] In a framework of immediate intelligibility, from body to mind, from gesture to meaning, everything stems here from the order of the fundamental. One is born, one appears, conquers, triumphs, moves in, baptizes, initiates, orders, protects, divinizes, purifies, builds with others:

"Lend me your shovel; we'll make a nice castle."

Jack and his sister get to work. Dad himself joins the play. The sand piles up. The walls come up, nice and straight, with round towers and a dungeon.[49]

One invents. One reinvents. One rediscovers and reappropriates a paradigm of essential experiences and actions. As at the beginning of time, one also names, with the help of a rudimentary vocabulary that attributes to unknown beings not a real identity but the signs of their roles.

"These healthy bodies lying around," Paul Morand notes, "who call one another by their first names, know nothing about one another, not even last names." But what is important here is not really knowing one another. It is being together, remaining together in the framework of a contract of sociability, for a limited period of time. Under these circumstances, first names or nicknames are perfectly adequate. They suffice for the convivial transparency that is sought in the heart of this ephemeral universe situated apart from the world. So we'll call that good-looking dark fellow Perkins, because he looks like the actor; we'll call those two regulars Harold and Maude, because of their age difference; we'll call the old American woman the "Treasurer of Saint-Marc": she always sits on her folding stool and never goes in the water, so the other summer people have gotten into the habit of entrusting her with their jewelry while they go swimming. These ephemeral creations and conventions also share in the definition of a universe peopled with stereotypical characters and relationships.[50]

Finally, because in this symbolic, Ophelian, and baptismal spot, individuals die and are born, they are also immortalized. For nearly a century now, the democratizing practice of photography has been the cause of major ceremonies on the beach, in which individuals get together, as for a class photo or a wedding picture, united forever as they pose in the surf. "Sometimes you wonder: is it really worth it to take a picture? We take more on the beach, we're all there."[51]

We don't capture just anything on film for all eternity. Above all, we capture images of childhood, youth, love, family, repose, and friendship. This aesthetic preoccupation, the choice of subject, belongs not so much to a documentary biographer as to an idolatrous archivist reporting on Paradise. The Olympian dream is what inspires the photographic ritual (see chapter 4). The ritual fulfills a game of idealization, of divinization. Faced with the infinitude of the sea, it expresses a pure affirmation of the self and of loved ones, an absolute desire for existence that owes nothing to the world.

WORLDS COLLIDING

Through this new evocation of seaside practices, the coherence of a marginal universe is thus confirmed. Still, the ethnological deciphering of this closed society and its rituals must not—lest it fall into the trap of its own utopia—make us forget its context.

To constitute itself, this hedonist society of "pure existence" called from the outset upon a sort of magical revocation of the real: of local reality and its traditions first, of inland—especially urban—reality and its standards second. This double abolition, necessary for the invention of the seaside utopia,[52] brought some problems in its wake that have not yet been resolved. Thus we cannot fail to look at the peripheral effects of this invention, and the concrete questions raised by the existence and the development of this Imaginary Country on the fringes of yesterday's society and—even more so—of today's.

The contemporary seaside world is a complete paradox. Open and closed, both far away and close at hand, it is the paradox of every bubble-society that excludes itself from the world but nevertheless remains within it. Although in the world, the beach dreams of being outside it, like an island lost in the ocean but moored to the shore. It is the distant proximity, the indifferent or ferocious nearness of this Epicurean hermitage that makes beach society a problematic universe. And the more signs of this rupture there are, the more difficult the cohabitation of worlds becomes, with open resistances and numerous conflicts, all in a climate of noncomprehension.

This climate is, of course, not a new one. Nineteenth-century moralists were already making their own lack of comprehension known. By greeting the invention of undress with disgust (and, for the hygienists, with modesty), they raised the problem of the ethical cohabitation of dressed and undressed worlds: the clash of mores (see chapters 3–4). It would be a mistake to believe that this problem has been definitively resolved in the contemporary world—that nudity is no longer an issue. The following alarmist passage will suffice to prove the contrary: "In Quebec, the law does not allow women to expose their breasts on beaches. In contrast, the situation is quite different in certain countries where this fashion is more and more widespread. In Guadeloupe, for example, the proportion is increasing every year at an *alarming* rate. *A professional aesthetician agreed to share her thoughts on this new frenzy.*"53

Then, with the help of the masses, with the appearance of "dirty bastards in baseball caps" and "people on paid holiday" on the beaches announcing the overpopulation to come, there was the problem of clashes between social classes, the challenge of cohabitation, that took hold of seaside leisure. This problem has not been resolved either, except perhaps superficially. Let us say, rather, significant as we know the communitarian dream to be, that the problem has been sidestepped, in particular owing to the socioeconomic sectorization of the shore (see chapter 7).

And today there is the further problem of cultural cohabitation, which raises the question of the relation of seaside vacationers to local society: the clash of summer people with the natives. It is not the problem that is new—think of Robinson, earlier, with the Savages— but the fact that it is finally being confronted, rather as if, through their descendants, through the intermediary of local dignitaries or officials, the exiled fishermen of yesteryear were coming back to the shores to reclaim their rights, in particular the right to be recognized (see chapter 1).

Yet all conditions seem to be ripe for a dialogue of the deaf. The summer people complain about their lukewarm reception, and even of the natives' aggressiveness.[54] As for the locals, they complain about the lack of respect shown them by the visitors.

On the Costa Brava, Yvette Barbaza notes that while the first reaction of the local people when summer residents began to arrive in large numbers was rather welcoming, "curiosity mingled with interest, for the foreigner benefited from a favorable predisposition," this sentiment deteriorated "given the attitude of some of these strangers, daily direct contact with whom robbed them of their prestige." Thus "curiosity quickly gave way to disapproval mixed with scorn or irony." Barbaza cites the invitation offered in 1964 by *Tramuntana,* a magazine from Lloret: "See for yourself the get-ups of the summer tourists who visit us, and see if you don't feel like laughing!" The laughter is hollow, under the circumstances, for it is "actually a defensive reaction" in the face of the impact of seaside vacation society on the natives, especially the youngest, who abandon their own dress and traditions to adopt "modern dances, songs by 'idols' of every nationality, and bikinis."[55]

If the seaside vacation world, a "closed society," does not allow itself to be penetrated by features of the surrounding world, it appears in contrast to be an influential model, a source of acculturation and loss of local identity. The debate arises from the fact that this leisure world seduces the natives and "swallows them up" into the abstract universe of a utopia that destroys regional human characteristics. The reversal of the situation is then complete: Robinson and Friday triumph fully over the Savages, not only by taking over part of their space, but also by dispossessing the survivors of their cultural difference.

And then, as the protection of identity is displaced from people to the landscape, the problem of ecological cohabitation arises: the clash of summer vacationers with the natural milieu, which means that the original cultural cannibalism is now coupled with the territorial cannibalism of contemporary seaside life. A closed world, the seaside vacation universe is nonetheless an expanding world, a phenomenon in the face of which the locals, their elected representatives, and institutionally responsible parties do not hesitate to use harsh terms such as *artifact, dumping ground,* or *third world of the Atlantic.*[56]

We have already examined the urbanization of the seashore, its galloping demography, its hyperconcentrations, and the privatization of beaches. New modes of temporary occupation of the shore are also manifested on occasion, for example in vans equipped for camping, which inspire a veritable phobia among the local population. Some elected officials in Brittany call them "a real scourge, worse than gypsies and their caravans." As a result, camping vans are subject to a sort of "witch hunt," going from simple expulsion to open aggression.[57]

A symptom of the increasingly difficult cohabitation between local society and beach society, the problem of camping vans is undoubtedly related to a deeper problem, that of the collision between two incompatible readings of space. If for the natives "the coastline is a feature of their identity" (as the place where they live and work, it belongs to collective memory),[58] for the vacationers, it is experienced chiefly as virgin territory, an extracultural expanse, devoid of memory, and thus favorable to the symbolic consumption of a zero-degree sociability, devoid of history or tradition.

Another aspect of the territorial cannibalism of the seaside vacation universe has to do with the development of naturism. Badly received in certain regions, this type of coastal vacationing is "an enormous consumer of space. The multiplication of enclaves that it is obliged to create is bound to cause problems at all levels," as the president for the development of tourism in Corsica declared in 1975; speaking of nudists, he added that "there are too many of them. It's not normal, and it's dangerous."[59]

Beyond the examples of camping vans and naturism, at all events, in the way natives look at the seaside vacation phenomenon, especially on sites that are said to be "in flux," "under pressure," or "mythical,"[60] in the face of ecological and economic stakes that are difficult to reconcile, there is not only a fear of saturation and overflow, but also a fear of physical and cultural absorption and collapse. This fear emanates from a sense of territory and identity reactivated by the spectacle of a confrontation that can no longer be controlled by the strategy according to which each world ignores the other.[61] In reaction to the expansion of beach society, a feeling of "ancestral" belonging comes to the surface, reinterpreting the growth of the seaside vacation world as a threat of destabilization, dispossession, and uprooting, both geographical and human.

This fear of devastation finds supplementary arguments in the de-

velopment or emergence of leisure practices that are objectively preda-
tory, like the use of all-terrain bicycles, motorcycles, or all-wheel-drive
vehicles on the dunes or the backcountry, beach buggies and spitzers
on the shore, and waterskiing, windsurfing, surfboarding, the use of
waterscooters, jet-skis, and pleasure boats along the coast. According to
some, "pleasure craft pollute the shore and destroy underwater grasses";
according to others, "sailboards can be killers"; as for all-terrain bikes,
they "destroy the environment" and "are a public menace."[62]

And this evolution of beach society in the realm of sports is not
merely a source of incompatibility with local society. Invasive at the
very least, the shift of coastal leisure toward "fun" sports, toward activities requiring specialized equipment and the aesthetic of (highly
mediatized) technical prowess, also sows discord within the vacation
microcosm itself, raising a problem of internal cohabitation. Beaches
today are encumbered with assorted equipment, and swimming is
disrupted by the endless comings and goings of sailboarders and other
motorized spoilsports. What becomes then of the traditional tranquil
beach activities, such as bathing, walking, fishing, sunbathing, or even
diving, once these new disturbances have been introduced?

Just like risk-taking and performance, display practices that have
replaced exploration and discovery in the universe of tourism,[63]
this neoaristocratic approach to sports replaces individual figures
of contemplation and being-together with those of competition and
exploits in the summer vacation world. Is a symbolic contract not
broken here, along with a certain idea of the seaside sojourn and the
Crusoean dream of detachment from the world and of conviviality
that is associated with it?

Making rules to control access to the open sea by vacationers with
specialized equipment in order to protect mere swimmers, whether
or not this is done in the name of the perennial emphasis on safety,
does not solve the problem. One does not play at being Robinson in
the same way if one is facing a sea studded with increasing numbers
of buoys marking off a labyrinth of reserved channels, including a few
swimming areas. The city now extends into the water, with its pedes-
trian zones, its roads and lanes for specific vehicles. When traffic is
thus regulated, we are confronted with city life and no longer life on
an island. To be sure, quarrels and accidents are avoided. But a seashore utopia is betrayed, because its image is marred.

The fact remains that the fears of the local world, whose causes we can now grasp, as well as the growing instrumentalization of a sporting population—a minority,[64] but one whose negative effects on the environment cannot be denied—must not become an obstacle to our understanding of the seaside world. Behind the sociocultural and technological disturbances that stigmatize the phenomenon today, there is still, at the origin, a dream. Hence the need to go further in deciphering the founding myths of this closed society—the imaginary dimension of this vacation universe whose place and symbolic function in the general system of leisure are still not entirely clear.

As in the realm of tourism, the time for criticism is past. Denouncing the detrimental effects of seaside vacationing is no doubt morally satisfying, but it will not reduce the tensions. On the contrary, it will intensify the clash between worlds and will add by that very token to the reigning lack of understanding. Instead of regretting the time of deserted beaches and summer aristocrats, instead of fleeing from popular shores and declaring what good summer residents once were or ought to be, we must first know who they are and what determines their behavior.[65] Between local society and beach society, it is not the time for criticism, it would seem, but for mediation; and mediation "cannot do without an understanding of the symbolic systems to which the participants in the debate refer."[66]

9. The Naked and the Raw

*(or, How Robinson, after discovering
that Friday was still a cannibal and
Robinsonetta unfaithful, had a delicious
dream during which he would have been
drowned if he had not been awakened
by Sunday shouting as he was being
swallowed by a sea monster)*

So I try to ignore civil time on Brazzaville Beach and instead measure
my days by the clock-like systems in my own body, whatever they are. I
am pleased with this idea: if I can ignore civil time, as I age, and as my
nervous system slows, the sense of the passing of my life will become
ever more attenuated.

—William Boyd, *Brazzaville Beach*

The most delicate moment of this study has finally arrived, namely,
the one in which we have to break into the vacationer's intimate space
and approach his psychology no longer just from the standpoint of
tribes, costumes, rites, or games, but also from the standpoint of emotions, tastes, passions, and sensations.

We are still looking at the beach, but this time from the inside,
through the eyes of the vacationer himself, starting with his body,
which is at the heart of this luminous affair. We keep coming back to
this. The body in itself, for itself, or for the other; the body cared for,
prepared, protected, and displayed; the body of desires and phobias,
impulses and repulsions. The lived body. The body felt, experienced,
rediscovered, exchanged. The manipulated body, whose practices and
pleasures, attractions and rejections tell the tale of—and are metaphors for—an entire world.

The seaside body is a constructed body. It is a specific sign. Its nudity, as we have seen, is not a defect of encoding. It is, on the contrary,

a fact of language. It is a complex message. In the framework of this communication, hair removal, not as simple absence but as negation, is just one symbolic element of this corporeal rhetoric. At the beach, we strive to do away with all asperities, to eliminate, domesticate, or turn away anatomical resistances and any other stubborn natural heaviness reminding us that we are still in the world and physically subject to its laws. Nature is obstinate, and so are human beings, in wanting to get beyond nature's wild manifestations.

Thus losing weight is an expression that, in view of the beach and above and beyond its usual medical justifications, takes on a quite particular meaning. It invokes a fantasy of lightness—of doing away with the all too human gravity that distorts our figures, softens our flesh, and makes us beasts of burden lugging our own bodies around.

36 17
SLIMMING
Get back in shape
Before the beach

This was the message of a poster on all the newspaper kiosks in France in June 1992. June, and not October or November. One would have to be particularly inattentive to the environment not to notice the ritual increase, starting in April or May, of such instances of blackmail in the media with reference to weight loss, promises of delivery from heaviness, as if all human beings, at this precise moment of the year, owed it to themselves to think about acquiring the means to escape earth's attraction. Posters, magazines, news reports. Special issues devoted to "getting thin" proliferate when spring comes—a kind of harassment by the media, whose denunciation ("watch out for worthless diets") is part and parcel of the advertising campaign, designed to make it really "take off": "The battle against pounds is on. As happens every year with the approach of warm weather, people think about losing weight. No more down jackets, heavy sweaters, or love handles. You attack life with a slender new look, you feel good about your body, you're happy to be alive."[1]

Inform yourself about the latest nutritional techniques, the latest slimming products. Run, drink, eliminate: the beach is coming. "Choose your slimming aids," discover "anti-snacking tricks," and, already, "think about what comes after your diet." Your buns are drooping? It's because of your weight! Because time is passing, too! They have to get back in line: "Take your buns in hand!" Life begins again on the shore, provided that you have made the right purchases. "The buns of your dreams? Here's where it hurts! You envy Brazilian beauties, with the loveliest buns in the world, so firm, with their unmatched muscle tone? Don't spend your summer just complaining about your own. Today, Medical Research has a little technological marvel for you: an Undeniable Novelty."[2]

No more weeping over your behind. What is this "marvel"? "Simple, fast, effective, reliable: only eight applications": UP LIFT, thanks to which "your buns will be firmer, higher."[3] Everything has to be lighter, uplifted, before you enter the "light-land"[4] of the August islands: buns, busts, abs, facial features—body shape and figure in general. Everything has to slim down, grow thin, weigh little, less, or nothing at all; everything has to become youthful, taut and firm, smooth and impeccable, without body hair or fat, like a new suit of clothing—and this is true for men and women alike. "Thinning is (also) man's business."[5] To reach the goal, anything goes, from a simple diet based on appetite suppressants to lymphatic drainage via ionization, electrotherapy, or medicinal plants in the form of powders, creams, gels, or tablets.

The move toward weightlessness in the beach world begins at that moment, in the aesthetic, dietetic, and cosmetic antechamber, the place where one can take in ultraviolet rays, self-tanning "potions," and other purifying operations that destroy all the "imperfections discovered by our modernity."[6]

What had been identified up to this point only in the mode of impressions and images (see chapter 4) is now spelled out as a veritable mystique of lightness, a faith manifested concretely by a ritual practice of the body whose symbolic coherence is expressed through a series of characteristic negations: neither weight nor hair nor folds nor pallor on the beach. Like the world within which it is housed, the body clock at the beach is a stopped clock. An abstract world for an abstract body; both are liberated from nature.

And yet are there not "fat" people on the beach, obese people, people with wrinkles, body hair, or pale skin? Indeed! But these are only monsters who have wandered into Paradise, confirming the triumph of the mythology of "lightness." Noticed as "wrecks," they offend against the required aesthetic; they are different, and they are "failures," glimpsed out of the corner of the eye as aberrations—curiosities that denote a new norm.[7] After all, these people are not playing the game; they have not adopted the obligatory signs of seduction and conformity that the utopia of this narcissistic world demands. They are tolerated but not accepted in view of a somatic imperative with the same message to everyone: "Get rid of your pallid look, your hideous cellulite, your unwanted hair, your inconvenient perspiration."[8]

THE PARADIGM OF RAWNESS

Beyond the rites and customs we have already identified, connected with territoriality or nudity, eating habits on the beach attest to, prolong, and at the same time condense a fantasy, a multifaceted one that inspires not only treatments applied to the body but also physical activities and affective strategies: the fantasy of rawness.

After all, is it a coincidence that, in good weather, the culinary art of raw food always experiences a comeback that is redeployed every time, in the same climate of surprise, as if people were making a fantastic discovery of the vital simplicity of fresh food? To be sure, there are rhythms of consumption: in winter, we consume on a deferred basis, owing to conservation techniques, and in summer, breaking with the frustration inherent in hibernation, we consume foods directly. But there is more to it than this, unless of course we ignore the fact that an imaginary dimension has always played a considerable and essential role in human nutrition. "To absorb caviar or simply a tomato," as Claude Fischler points out, "is to take into one's body not only nutritional substance, but also imaginary substance, a tissue of evocations, connotations, and significations that go from dietetics to poetics via 'standing' and festivities"—to such an extent, as we learn from the anthropology of food, that "not everything that is biologically consumable is culturally edible."[9]

The beach calls forth its own share of alimentary evocations. Seaside vacation society has its own culinary ideology, which privileges cooking based on raw ingredients (or at least the image of such cooking), because cooking based on raw ingredients is first of all fantasized as a return to the primordial: to alimentation in its elementary state. Beneath the categories of the simple and the natural, it offers itself as belonging to an "originary" gastronomy, which provides the consumer with a gustatory experience that is not only restorative but reminiscent of the Garden of Eden experience, as one advertisement indicates: "Here I'll get the memory and the taste of happiness back.

Every taste: salt on my lips, the fried bread that we used to devour on the beach, every plunge into the sea like a mouthful of freshness."[10]

Drinking, savoring sea salt—a symbol of incorruptibility and purification[11]—then devouring the emblematic fried bread: a lot of images packed into a couple of lines! If oysters had their Francis Ponge, and walnuts their Charles Trenet, fried bread still awaits a poet to unlock its secrets. This little bread, round like a breast and golden like tanned skin, soft with olive oil inside, contains a treasure of freshness that sums up the meeting of land and sea: bits of tuna mixed with lettuce, tomato, and fresh onion with the yellow and white solar orb of a hard-boiled egg perched on top.

If eating birds makes one flighty and is for that reason forbidden in certain African societies, eating raw food makes one raw, in all innocence, that is, fresh, uncorrupted, and thus pure. This "magical" idea is not new. Was it a coincidence that "the first naturists associated nakedness with rawness and were themselves most often vegetarians who feasted on plain water, raw vegetables, and wind"? And in the late 1920s, one of them asked, "Would you like a glass of milk? It is thoroughly pure, just as we are."[12]

An entire Edenic semantics of food takes shape here, quickly enriched by numerous auxiliary ingredients with similar psychological value. "If I happen to catch some small fish or sand eels, I copy the Japanese and eat them raw. I believe in the virtues of plankton."[13] For swimmers inclined to hunt and gather, responding to "seaside instinctotherapy," there are also oysters, sea urchins, mussels, shrimp, lances, limpets, and other shellfish;[14] in restaurants, there are raw sardines, anchovies marinated in lime juice, carpaccio of salmon, or scorpion fish tartar. And today, in addition to shellfish, fresh fish, salt-water plants, and various salads, in this season, "with no danger of hypervitaminosis," you are encouraged to indulge "in orgies of carrots, raw tomatoes, and red peppers" as well as peaches, melons, kiwis, and citrus fruit. Why? "Not only will this diet help you tan beautifully, it will also help your skin combat premature aging."[15]

It is not really an accident that the consumption of raw food, even if it is more imaginary than practiced, more metaphoric than real, is at the heart of seaside eating. As an "authentic" and inverted form of ordinary nutrition, it convokes and concentrates dreams of regression and atemporality. "This is an openly dream-like cookery"[16] whose difference corresponds to a desire not only for social but also for natural marginalization. To return here to Claude Lévi-Strauss's celebrated analysis, a substance is in its ideal state when it is raw, as opposed to cooked or rotten; the latter states result respectively from cultural or natural degradation.[17] If you are what you eat, then eating raw food means breaking magically with these degrading determinations, social on the one hand and biological on the other.

Thus we understand better the symbolic value of raw food in the seaside vacation context, and the function of rawness in the vacation imaginary. The raw state at the nutritional level is the counterpart to nudity at the corporeal level—with its correlatives, which are the cooked and the dressed states on the side of culture, the rotten and the old, wrinkled, wornout, or hairy states on the side of nature.[18] The consumption of raw foods plays a fantasmatic role, in that it operates a double denegation—of the cultural and the natural—that will be validated by thinness and tanning (for raw foods help people lose weight and get a better tan), as opposed to the bodily deformities and various depigmentations generated by the social and biological order of things.

Since raw substances are henceforth identified as foods that typify the break with the surrounding world and its laws and constraints, the mythology of rawness has a considerable effect on attitudes and behaviors.[19] The resident summer vacationer, who on various occasions has already discovered that he himself possesses the soul of a Robinson (via the simplicity of his quarters on the beach or in the campground),[20] now finds that he also has the soul of a Friday, that is, of Robinson's "cannibal" double, a desiring, instinctual, and impulsive being. Jean Viard notes that "the desire on the part of the French to spend vacations as a family" with the goal of "reunifying a private territory" is also "often mingled with dreams of amorous encounters."[21] The dreams may be more or less obvious, more or less manifested, more or less conscious, but the desire is right there on the surface.

From this perspective, we cannot fail to see rawness as something more than the object of a nutritional practice. A metaphor for a certain relation to the world, it is also a value, an archetype, and thus a model for the type of existence it induces. With it comes an entire sensory and emotional universe. We need only consider the figurative meanings of the word to realize that the term *raw*, in expressions such as a "raw response," a "raw deal," or "a raw performance," refers to the rejection of protocol, to the licentious, the inappropriate, the transgressive, the sensual, and in some contexts to exposed skin ("a raw wound") and the sphere of primary sensations. Rawness, which calls for the remobilization of culturally marginalized or deviant sensations, emblematizes the transparency of origins and elementary emotions.

An advertisement for fruit juice that summons up the seaside universe in the background (as if by chance) suffices to sum up this symbolic and existential affiliation between rawness and nudity. The picture features a young woman lying face down, completely naked, at the edge of a sunswept blue sea. She is holding a bottle of orange juice in her right hand, and smiling at the person who is looking at her—the consumer. The slogan: "Joker, the naked fruit!"[22]—that is, raw, the fruit without its peel, the undressed orange, nothing but its flesh, its pulp, and, as a metaphor of this native state of the substance, a woman also lacking a "peel," unclothed, sensual, and pulpy. A representation that appeals to all the senses and pleasures.

PLEASURE AND MOVEMENT

"No question about it, sexiness is an essential part of beachgoing." Voyeurism, exhibitionism, the interplay of seduction and amorous conquest find privileged terrain on the beach. But we must be careful not to reduce the sensual quality of the place to the stereotypical image of a commerce in glances and encounters that some are ready to caricature as horse-trading sessions. "The beach is a better pickup spot than any cocktail party," Elliott Erwitt also says. "There's always a lot of pawing going on. And you get the product properly displayed."[23]

As a place of pleasure and seduction, the beach is nevertheless more subtle and complex than this—even if it is raw. "They walked side by side in the little waves, making sure their arms often brushed against one another."[24] And then here, from "salt on my lips" to "orgies of carrots," everything is sensual, even the most anodyne—indeed, a priori insignificant—practices. Everything is sensualized, not only one's relation to other people but also one's relation to oneself and to the world: to time, space, the environment, and physical substances.

Paul Morand declares that he has "acquired the voluptuous habit of rubbing [him]self with hot sand," while Jacques Laurent confesses that he has rediscovered "that sand, that dream . . . at the seashore where the imaginary degenerated into orgasm."[25] As an autoerotic experience or the discreet voluptuousness of contact with the elements, pleasure is everywhere. It takes multiple paths, changes place, spreads out, and its signs can be read in the images that give meaning and an emotional and erotic charge to disturbingly unstable elements: sand, waves, and water. After lightness and rawness, mobility is the third parameter of seaside weightlessness.

The pleasure provided by shifting sands is not a new one. We know it was experienced by members of the ancient Roman elite, who enjoyed "the pleasure of treading the sand beneath their feet" at the water's edge.[26] But very few seem to have shared that experience at the time. A pleasure lost and then found again in the course of a forgotten history of sensations, its rediscovery in the nineteenth century was unquestionably the source of powerful emotions, so powerful that they sometimes led to catastrophe. For example, in the Biarritz region in 1920, "three ladies who were bathing in a group, frightened to feel the sand shifting underneath them, lost their footing and drowned, even though they were not exposed to any real danger."[27] This was at a time when the fantasy of being sucked under was still competing with anxiety about safety, when losing one's footing was not yet entirely a leisure activity, a source of enjoyment.

Since then, beach sands have lost the mysterious and disquieting imaginary power to swallow us up (that power has shifted to deep waters),[28] but they have kept an important symbolic and emotional potential. "If a ship floated on water, then it would also float on sand."[29] Sand is a strange substance, after all. Liquid when dry, solid when wet, quasi-volatile under water, it is soft on the beach and hard as cement in the surf. It is an undecidable form of matter, at once fluid and solid, in which the ephemeral and the eternal, traces and their absence, form and formlessness blend—for in it everything is erased. At bottom—at least this is how we may imagine it—sand is the very "earth" of utopia, ungraspable, nondegradable, lacking in humus and not subject to cultivation.[30] Sand is to earth what rawness is to food or nudity to the ideal body. Sand is like waves, "waves of dunes to stop the waves" when it is in giant heaps, and like waves and dunes even when it is nearly flat, seen at eye level by a swimmer lying on the ground.[31] Sand has neither memory nor scale. It resembles the universe that it carpets. It flows in and out. It is hot. It is soft. Its pliability gives pleasure: it can be touched, stroked, patted, picked up by the handful. Without distinction it bears traces of human bodies, seagulls' feet, and the wind—and it quickly loses all memory of those traces. It is the land of oblivion, the unstable ground of a world that confers on people who walk on it the aspect of astronauts or movie actors filmed in slow motion.

And then there is the sea, where the sand disappears: the sea and its waves. "'And what are those things that keep rising up to look at us and then falling over with a big splash?' 'They're only waves,'" Big-Ears explains to Noddy, who is seeing the ocean for the very first time. In fact, things are not so simple. For one thing, in phonetic terms, waves don't always make a "splashing" sound. For Fitzgerald, they sound like "wa-waa"; for Régis Franc, they make the sound "sschhh" or "schllooouffff."[32] It all depends on who is listening. But what is the sea really saying, with its waves? Or rather, what messages do humans attribute to it? This is a matter of interpretation. We can find a whole paradigm of images that humanize and sensualize the water's movement to varying degrees. These images, which transform the sea's slapping sound into "breath," its louder noises into "cries," its movements into "gestures" that invest the element with "intonations" and "behaviors," turn the sea into the observer's twin, a mirror for human emotions and feelings.

To begin with, through rustling lips, with a hushed voice, the sea murmurs, whispers, or sighs—unless it is shouting in anger. In that case it no longer offers caresses, but slaps in the face. This basic poetic imagery is then further complicated in a variety of ways. On Camus's beach, the sea no longer breathes, it gasps.[33] Mandiargues speaks of "waves lapping." Morand says that the sea uses "a soft and scratchy tongue like a panther's" to lick a shore that the waves "corrode with their foamy saliva." And, like Morand, who says that he likes "to look at the sea, its mossy waves on top of one another," Anne Philippe watches a rising tide and writes, "Everything is moving, palpitating within the movement of the tide. Later, [the novel's heroine] finds the same perpetual motion, the same alternation, in love." Finally, Claude Nori, as he is reluctantly leaving Rimini, confesses, "I would like to stop the taxi, get out and roll around in the water, go back to the very spot where the white foam is quivering like an erotic essence."[34]

This sensualization of the sea at the shoreline, of its foam and its tides, its ebb and flow, its movement in general, is expressed, as we know, in countless metaphors. As for the eroticism of waves, we need go no further than the metaphor of the "blade" (see chapter 2). Photographers and filmmakers have immortalized this encounter between bodies and waves time and time again—as sensuous, languid, or brutal; as caressing or masochistic.[35] Thus if the tide is a figure for the rise of desire,[36] the swimmer who plunges into the flow, mixing his flesh with the waves and exposing it to their stimulating pressure, shares in the fantasmatic sensuality of the element and of course derives pleasure from it. Motion seems to establish a relation of body to body here, a relation of carnal intimacy between swimmer and sea that makes of the sea not just a metaphor but an erotic partner. This theme is found in abundance in contemporary romance novels, where references to the seaside context are omnipresent, as we know (see chapter 4): "A wave pushed her against him. The sea became in one moment an ally, in the next an enemy: it united them and divided them by turns. Angela finally had to stop struggling simultaneously against the waves and against Kell. He took her under his arm and said in a somewhat uncertain voice . . ."[37]

What are the real facts behind the contemporary seaside sensuality that seems to contaminate the shifting totality of this light and raw world, waves and sand alike? For the time being, after all, we are still at the stage of impressions, the erogenous coenesthesia of bathing and its literary attestations. By its very nature, is the beach really the propitiatory framework for pleasures that it is said to be? Do actual seaside vacationers experience waves of desire and amorous tempests? Does lightness do away with taboos? Does rawness relieve people of their inhibitions? And what about the element of motion, the everyday inertia of bodies and persons who cross paths without seeing or touching one another on city streets?

What seems to be undeniable, at least as a first index, is the importance the media attribute to the beach as a privileged place for discovery, contact, and (possible) amorous happiness. Journals and magazines appropriate the theme in a variety of ways, through docufictions, practical and tactical articles, studies, and surveys. In May 1977 *Lui* offered a "report" on Robina, who was the model for the poster for Fellini's 1972 film *Roma*. We learn that Robina lives "on an island, an island that is hers alone. This daughter of Robinson has not yet found her Friday." On this island, "she has rediscovered the taste for freedom, and on the beaches a new art of living." "If Crusoe had known her, he would have called her—depending on the calendar— Mardi Gras, Sunday, or Holiday." In that presummer-vacation period, the eroticization of the seaside robinsonnade was at its height, as if by general agreement. "Practical" information, for the boys: "This summer, have them all." How? "Do a 'Grand-Bleu' scenario for her," or "Play the surfer"—all the more because "61 percent of women between the ages of 18 and 35 say they are 'ready for adventure.'" And for the girls: "The boys of summer. All the plans of attack," with the help of "swimsuits good enough to eat."[38]

Thus with seaside imagery omnipresent on covers and inside, the articles come on hard and fast: "Your Summer 1992: Love, Sex, and Seduction"; "The Erotic Summer: Six Brand New Stories by Women Writers"; "Love on the Beach"; "How to Change a Crush into a Love Story"; "Your Summer Flings: Whom to Seduce? Whom to Avoid Like the Plague?" And then there are "studies" looking into desire. "Sexuality: Love and the French"; "France's Beaches: The Hot Spots," followed by "Hot Nights in France: Le Touquet to Biarritz, Perpignan to Saint-Tropez," and copied the following year by another publication, "The Hit Parade of the SEXY Beaches."[39]

Finally, there are the opinion surveys. "Survey. 1 in 3 Frenchmen is experiencing it right now. Passion. Whom and How Does It Strike?" But let us look more closely at another one, undertaken in August 1991 for a report titled "The French, Summer, and Love."[40] What do we learn from this survey? First of all, that for 75 percent of the people interviewed, the beach at night is considered the most appealing place to make love, and that 80 percent of these same people think that men and women are more inclined to be on the make in the summer than during the rest of the year. A priori, taking this percentage into account (it significantly exceeds the percentage of unmarried individuals interviewed), are we to suppose that faithfulness in married couples is subjected to severe testing, that casual sex is the rule? Not at all: for 78 percent of the people interviewed, deceiving one's spouse while on vacation is out of the question.[41] So where is the famous flexibility of seaside mores? Where are the extramarital adventures and other erotic incidents that certain media urge upon their audience[42] and about which, in theory, vacationers dream? Between the dream and the reality, the difference is perceptible, to say the least; and if vacationers do practice a more active sexuality during the summer, nearly 50 percent of the time they do so by making love with their spouses or regular partners rather than with others. Exosexuality is rejected out of hand by 85 percent of the population studied.

The 1991 survey also reveals some very interesting contradictions that run counter to the interviewees' intentions and prejudices alike.

Dreams again. As for intentions, 47 percent of the people surveyed stated that a vacation love affair "is better if it lasts after the vacation is over." Yet 65 percent admit that they have never written love letters after returning from vacation. Between the eternal and the ephemeral, or at least between the lasting and the short-lived, it is clear that mobility wins out—so much so (and this despite "common knowledge" that vacations, summer vacations especially, are favorable to the discovery of the love of one's life) that 85 percent of the interviewees who lived with a spouse or partner gave negative answers to the question: "Did you fall in love with your spouse/partner while you were on vacation?" And this figure may even be lower than the actual percentage, if we can believe recent studies by the National Institute for Demographic Studies (INED) indicating that no more than 5 percent of French couples were constituted during vacation encounters.[43]

Here, then, is the story. As soon as we come back to couples or families, we discover that the mobility of mores, presumed to be considerable, does not exist, the erogenous stereotypes pertaining to beaches notwithstanding. Emotional fickleness and casual sex are more imagined than real. They belong to the order of simulacra, appearances, blackmail, or role-playing; they do not really challenge existing affective structures. The mobility in question here is symbolic.

People do not go astray at the beach; instead, they rediscover one another. They do not decenter; quite to the contrary, they recenter, refocus on their habits, their friendships, their loved ones, their partner's body, their own body. They allow a measure of doubt to arise, a possibility. But they ultimately reestablish, resettle, recenter themselves, even as they allow themselves, assisted by unexpected and ambiguous proximities, to take a few peripheral liberties in the realms of dreaming, gazing, seduction, playful contact, or friendly relations. In fact, such liberties and driftings are tacitly allowed, even uniformly expected, as if the better to test and enjoy the privilege of a rediscovered affective unity within a couple, a family, or a group of friends. Confronted with the sea's vast horizon, and with the vast horizon of humanity as well, people play with emotional interactions "whose importance the actors more or less confusedly suspect," testing both the dangerous charm of their attraction and the desire to remain safe by avoiding it—just as they simultaneously offer themselves to the waves and resist them.[44]

At the beach, mobility is comparable to rawness and lightness. It can no more be reduced to the love relation than pleasure can, or than raw food can be reduced to rawness, or lightness to thinness. The element of mobility has the value of a parable. Above and beyond its erotic meaning, it is the third dimension of seaside society. Mirrored in summer loves, this society is precisely a society of the ephemeral, of temporary sociability and haphazard relations, provisional contacts and the mobility of feelings, Marivaudage and badinage in all their forms, rather than a society of lasting encounters.

At the beach people also practice "social zapping."[45] Not only can they change sexual partners, for pleasure, but—even more easily, and in contrast to everyday life—they can change friends, acquaintances, neighbors, or buddies, as misunderstandings arise (the tribe can be moved) or, more trivially and more often, according to the rhythm of departures and arrivals that punctuate the intermittent geography of this shifting society. For at bottom, traversed by an endless coming and going on the part of the actors, it is the society itself that is mobile, not its mores and values; these latter, on the contrary, are reproduced, reconstituted, or consolidated, in particular via tribalization (see chapter 7).

Still, we must not deny the sensuality of the site by reducing it to a social game, although the game itself can be a source of pleasure. Its sensuality is what makes the place special: it belongs there, to the history and myth of the beach. On the historical side, we have noted some of the scandals (see chapter 3). On the mythical side, a great deal more could be said.[46] Venus emerging from the depths has been transformed here. The sensual Michelet, watching a woman bathing in the sea, had it right: "Venus, who was born of Ocean, is from Ocean reborn every moment, and not a sick, suffering, peevish, pale, and melancholy Venus, but the triumphant Venus full of passion and certain of fecundity."[47] Passion and desire belong to the beach.

Further away, beyond our own culture, in the Trobriand myth of incest, it is on a beach and in the water that a brother succumbs to a sister's advances.[48] The beach everywhere, as soon as it is pacified, appears erotic, as if this were its vocation. After painting, literature, photography, and film,[49] advertising frequently uses beach imagery to this end. The ambient sensuality of the beach stems from a material imagination. It probably has to do with the maternal and feminine nature of water[50] and, beyond that, with the liquidity common to the substances that make up the site—sand and sea, dunes and waves. Here is how the poet Jean Richepin portrays this sensuality:

First, a shiver on the green satin plain
With its blue reflections,
Then a great fold, wide and undulating,
Made to swell by a breath from below.[51]

Shiver and fold, breath and swell, sand and sea, dunes and waves are all soft, quasi-carnal realities, welcoming and protective, that seem to invite beings to self-abandonment and fusion through mimesis or osmosis. Referring to form and not substance, Michelet does not hesitate to see the shore as a product of the sea's "assiduous caresses," "the visible tenderness of a woman's breast, that which the infant finds so soft, shelter, warmth, and rest."[52]

The French word *mouvant*, "shifting," contains the word *mou*, "soft"; similarly, in *grève*, "shore," we find *rêve*, "dream," and also *ève*, "Eve." The beach is a sensual place, and it is experienced as such. Among other qualities, it is amorous.[53] From yesterday's Gustav d'Aschenbach, a passionate onlooker mutely admiring the young Tadzio's body on the beach in Venice, to today's triumphant pick-up artists, beach boys, and beach bums, via "the vacationer with a tormented libido and a drinking problem . . . who comes to Mexico in search of a lover," or any other sentimental Crusoe who wanders around the beach looking for his Friday, the Robinsons of love are certainly not phantoms.[54] But the sensual quality of the beach, like the summer adulteries whose frequency is more legendary than real, cannot be reduced to an "amorous disorder." The latter, like the social disorder presumed to be characteristic of the beach, is merely one aspect of seaside "zapping." The pleasure of mobility is more varied here, and the quest for it is subject to many behavioral transpositions that attest in multiple ways to its diffuse presence.

THE APNEIC STATE, THE WORLD OF CARTESIAN DIVERS

Between reveries of repose and dreams of eternity (see chapter 4), "zapping" implies a multiplication of contacts but also of denegations: breaks, abandonments, forgettings. To "zap" is simultaneously to disconnect, detach, and transport oneself from one universe to another: to change worlds and states. From the collective to the intimate, the beach thus invites vacationers to explore, to superimpose universes of varying dimensions. The beach is made up of spheres of relationships, experiences, and sensations through which individuals circulate and transform themselves.

Seaside tribalism, which deports the individual into the closed and centered universe of the clan, is one of these spheres (see chapter 7). It proceeds from social zapping. Marriage is another: the conjugal sphere is an affective state that is modified during vacations. It proceeds from emotional or sexual zapping. But floating on one's back also entails changing worlds and states. An anodyne activity a priori, floating is "a little death," an intimate experience of weightlessness for the swimmer in which, under the luminous orange of her eyelids, rolling on the surface in her body, her back turned to the depths like the hull of a ship and her ear hesitating between the sounds of the sea and the distant murmurs of the beach, she drifts, inert like a drowned woman or inanimate like a board.[55] The swimmer soon loses all sense of orientation and experiences a feeling of distancing, as if she were in a different space. "I emptied my mind and let the waves rock me as if I were a piece of flotsam."[56]

Diving is yet another form of zapping. "Diving is something else. And right away it's something else again. Going through the mirror of the water's surface is actually a way of flipping all at once into another world, a way of crossing the border of a country quite unlike our own, as quickly as the brutal and peremptory snap of some giant pair of scissors."[57] One yields to a concrete experience that is very much like dreaming.

Flaubert retained a similar dreamlike memory of the beach at Cancale, but on land: "There, lying flat on my back on the sand, my hat over my eyes, my arms spread straight out, I spent at least an hour and a half warming my carcass in the sun, being a lizard. You feel your body inert, drowsy, inanimate, almost inherent to the earth on which it is wallowing, while your soul on the contrary has drifted far, far away; it wafts about in space like a stray feather." Nearly a century and a half later, Marie Cardinal wrote: "Little by little you succumb to the charm of the sun, the wind, the strong aromas, the secret soul you sense through the whole exaggerated setting that is too overpowering to be just a façade. You let the beach take you in. . . . It is time to stretch out on the hot sand and forget everything, to become just an ember."[58]

What seaside zapping integrates beneath the social and affective shifts is thus also a zapping of sensations, an internal and external transport of the senses that reveals the deep zones of a collective imagination behind patterned behaviors. We generally take little notice of these ordinary behaviors, yet they constitute a language of their

own that warrants analysis. At the origin of a panoply of characteristic gestures and attitudes, games and practices, there is a code of
impressions, a source of images and emotions that open onto the
"intimate immensity" of seaside dreaming.[59] For, as a study undertaken some years ago showed, the seaside ambiance is a frequent
theme of dreams, the content of which corresponds to specific sensations. "Almost all the dreams of managerial-level workers and their
wives touch on vacation themes, as if the life they are leading now has
only these 'do-nothing' rest periods as a goal. Mountains and winter
sports appear less often in these dreams than the sea and the tropics."
One interviewee relates, "I was flying over a beach and I knew that
the people down below were watching and shouting to me." Another
recalls, "I let myself go ahead and glide on the sea, but I don't know
if it's a boat or something else." A third reports, "An airplane is cruising at a high altitude with me in it. It heads down toward a deserted
island where I know we are going to land. The island is tiny, too small
for the plane, but the pilot turns around and shouts that everything's
all right, he's going to manage. I feel very relaxed." Yet another interviewee says, "We're arriving in the islands, we're no longer thinking
about what came before, only about the beaches and the village we're
discovering." And here is one final account: "We're gliding over the
sea. There are islands more or less everywhere, but the dinghy seems
to know where it's going."[60]

In these dreams of beaches and islands, the image of a light, almost toneless body comes back over and over, that of a body flying,
floating, and letting itself go, as if it were caught up in a relaxing
movement originating somewhere outside itself. The serene descent
onto an island that is too small inevitably brings to mind the arrival
of Peter Pan and his friends in Never-Never Land. An irresponsible,
weightless body with no anxieties and no memories is at the heart
of these seaside dreams. In the course of such oneiric experiences,
centered on itself and its sensations, the body forgets the world. Cir-
culating within an indeterminate space made up of places without
reference points, it yields to the coenesthetic intoxication of floating,
gliding, and descending. Afterward, it is just a short step from dream
to bather, taking us, as it were, from the air of dreams to the water
(and sand) of daydreams, the remainder being only a matter of transposition, translation, or adaptation. The beach is there, with its material mobilities—all valid, as we know, from the strategy of playing the

lizard to that of playing the Cartesian diver (unless the sleeper is himself a Cartesian diver in his sleep, where he plunges in, emerges, and floats as he dozes off again)—to reconnect in various ways with these oneiric emotions and give the dreamed body the concrete means to realize its desire.[61]

But what desire? A desire for what? "Beyond the hills and the plains the sea was stretched out, welcoming, protecting, a huge warm uterus where life was made and unmade. Land, sky, time, space, all were in correspondence; only immobility did not exist." In all this, in the facts as well as in these dreams and this prose, we find a clear desire to regress, to return to earlier phases of one's existence: a return not to the historical past but to the sensual past, the intimate past in which primary emotions connected with gregariousness, eroticism, or proprioceptism arise anew.[62] Correlatively, this "return" presupposes a certain loss of consciousness. It is also a rite of separation that dissipates the memory of everyday reality—whose demands weigh on existence and constantly hinder both individuals and groups from satisfying the desire to regress.

This fundamental desire is manifested at all levels of seaside practices, including that of modest paddling about: "mouthpieces at our lips, face down in the water, we amused ourselves by sinking and then coming back up with the alternating contractions and dilations of our chest cavities."[63] This simple game epitomizes seaside psychology all by itself—just like lying down on the sand, it entails being no more than an "ember," or being "inherent to the earth," a body that floats and then sinks, swept away in a deep sleep. Similarly, when a swimmer floats on his back, plays at being a mere piece of driftwood, at being just a floating body lost at sea and vulnerable to the first big wave, he is playing the same game and evincing the same desire. At the heart of the seaside vacation reality, the recognition of this desire thus calls for a concrete phenomenology of seaside pleasures.

These pleasures are linked to behaviors that induce vertigo.[64] Whether real, oneiric, or simulated, externalized or internalized, active or contemplative, these behaviors all refer to dreams of flying, floating, or falling.[65] The windsurfer, for example, the most airborne of seaside Cartesian divers, is a sports figure who plays with surface agitations. He flies above them and sometimes even remains suspended for a moment in the air, flying up on the crests of the waves. He punctuates his performance by falling back down with a splendid splash. The surfboarder, another Cartesian diver, seeks the vertigo of falling from the outset, by gliding over the oblique or virtually vertical flanks of the waves as if on a playground slide.[66] "They go surfing by the hundreds of thousands, they go to play with the sea, and that becomes the most important thing in life." A far more innocuous pursuit than such spectacular exploits, the simple act of wading into the water may also be a vertigo-inducing behavior, just as apt to evoke the reveries associated with it: "The water comes up to our ankles; the current pulls the sand around our feet, it feels like it's pulling us under."[67] Vertigo and the dream of falling are both present here. The desire to let oneself be carried away can be experienced perfectly well with the help of a few dying waves.

"In the calm little creeks," says an advertisement for Spain in March 1991, "let yourself be carried away by an air mattress." Cradled by the sea, floating, dozing, and sinking gradually into sleep. A somnolent Cartesian diver now, suspended above the abyss: go ahead and sink into the water of dreams. The pleasure of falling is endlessly renewed. All this is implicit, not always clearly expressed. The dream is often manifested only between the lines, allusively, through the metaphor of games or sports; or it may be experienced "vicariously"[68]— spectacularly, as when people go off to admire the quebradistos who dive off the high cliffs of Acapulco, or perhaps more discreetly. What is that man doing leaning over the end of the wharf where the water is deep and clear? He has come like a child to toss in a shell and is now following its descent very attentively. Who has not indulged in this sort of exercise? At this precise moment, the man is inside the shell, like a crew in a bathyscaphe. Little Nemo, a tiny Professor Picard, Jacques Cousteau in a miniature diving platform, he is undertaking a vertiginous descent into an imaginary abyss by means of the shell.[69]

From the intoxication of sliding to the vertigo of the depths, by way of these actual or dreamed experiences of falling and immersion, events undergone in reality or vicariously, we thus always come back to the desire to escape the surface one way or another. This may well be the symbolic key to the various seaside behaviors, and, beyond them, to the vacation universe as a whole. But what surface? That of the water, of course, but also, metaphorically, that of the world, with its agitations, its disturbances, its waves of cold and discontent, its raucous assemblies, its social turmoil, its economic and military storms, all the shock waves that make life a chaotic and complex, heterogeneous and divided reality—of which the sea is the living metaphor. Beneath the surface, what will be found is ultimately the contrary: a calm, simple, homogeneous, elementary reality. There is room for reverie then. Are not swimming, diving, floating, and wading all to some extent means of slipping out of the world, with the beach being the designated air-lock that makes this fantasmatic operation possible?

In the seventeenth century Robert Boyle discovered "that even the most terrible storms could not upset the serenity of the sea's depths." And well before Boyle, in the fourth century, St. Ambrose taught that "the beasts that are horrible and cruel on earth are beautiful and gentle in the sea." The idea that makes the sea the immaculate inverse of dry land, "the invisible receptacle for the perfection of Creation and a repository for innocence," is thus hardly new. And the Little Mermaid's idea of leaving the undersea world behind was a bad one. And although this positive marine mythology was obscured for some time by the pathetic aspect of the shore with which we are acquainted, made up of shipwrecks, misery, drama, and savagery, it is alive and well today—as the success of *The Big Blue,* among others, has demonstrated.[70] This film was based on the life of Jacques Mayol, a deep-sea diver who went down nearly 350 feet without an oxygen tank.

This exemplary film warrants closer attention. In many respects, it can serve as the poetic figure, the ultimate metaphor for the contemporary seaside imaginary and the philosophy of leisure that this imaginary induces. It strikes me indeed as the purest model of the founding reverie that lies behind the seaside as we imagine it today.

The proteiform desire to escape somehow from the surface, from the external world and from awareness of that world, finds a symbolic expression of its logic and its meaning in *The Big Blue.* Beyond the theme of "abyssal impulse" (which is related in this instance to an attempt to break records) and the mystique of depth (the belief that there is "something" down there), what the film illustrates is not so much the search for limits or for a secret as nostalgia for the elemental. The bottom of the sea is imagined here not as a natural space but as an overturned celestial void, an ecstatic crevasse such that the more nearly one approaches the bottom, the closer one comes to Heaven. It is a pure solution, an amniotic liquid perhaps, but it is above all an atemporal and perfectly homogeneous milieu, without gravity or alterity.

The only beings that the hero, Jacques, meets in these serene depths are dolphins, that is, the most human of underwater animals, who have a significant legendary biography, from Apollo to Flipper.[71] Like those of Proust's young girls, dolphins' bodies are "polished and blue." They are sensual, communicative, and friendly mammals, familiar and even family-oriented: they live in groups, in tribes, as we do at the beach. Thus they are not figures of alterity; they are friends, fellow creatures, twins, partners. This is no longer the sea, but an immense swimming pool, a vast aquarium with selected fauna. There are no intruders here, no impurities. We are among ourselves (see chapter 4). Not so much as a single school of sardines traverses the blue sea of *The Big Blue:* we are in a closed container, an abstract, indefinite, selective milieu in which the denegation of external reality and its turbulence is successful. In objective terms, we are in a realm of absolute peace; thus we are in an internal, hyperreal milieu of contented and unfrightening vertigo procured by apnea, the place where everything—time as well as the heart—slows down and finally stops. In this space, the rhythm of ordinary life dilates and then fades away, and drowning is one of the avatars of successful fusion.[72] All that remains then—the final image—is the human being, his pleasure, his loved ones, and his loss of awareness of the outside world. Jacques goes down to the depths with the dolphins; in the end, he chooses the maternal sea over his own terrestrial paternity.[73]

In fact, for Jacques Mayol, it is "in the sea that everything becomes easy for him again; on land, time sometimes seems to drag." Here, there is no more time. Only what is essential. It is "on the surface [that Mayol] seems lost, tossed about by the waves. It is at this moment that his attraction to the depths is strongest."[74] Jacques is a vertical Ophelia who plunges like a great lily into the eternal blue. He is the ultimate Cartesian diver, the one who does not want to come back up again. He is the image of total zapping, of the definitive change of state. He is the ideal figure of oblivion, of the wholesale rejection of the world.

So what is the relation between the universe of *The Big Blue* and that of the beach? "The big blue" is an atemporal, homogeneous space, without gravity or alterity, that is inspired, via the desire for depths, by nostalgia for the elemental as opposed to the existential complexity of the outside: the surface world. Ideally, the beach meets this description as well. This is the "bottom" the beach aims toward, even if it does not quite get there. The beach universe, as if it has sunk to the bottom of a dream of unity, of primariness, is itself apneic. It is a slowed-down, frozen, suspended world, completely focused on the discovery or reappropriation of elementary contacts, at four levels. The first is the level of the individual, one's own body, and one's image of that body. The second is the level of the dyad, the couple, the interpersonal. The third is that of the group, the family, the tribe, and the territory. And the fourth is that of relations among similar groups, relations delimiting the maximum social extension of this world that wants to remove itself from external disturbances, that seeks shelter from storms.

Given all this, it is normal that the closed-off, psychologically insular world in which the search for vertigo is that of an inner fall should be perceived as a Crusoean utopia. It is the egocentric universe of withdrawal, the autarchic utopia, the denegation of the outside, the rejection of the Other. As a result, it can no longer be reasonably assimilated, in the strict sense, to any form of tourism, for tourism is oriented by definition toward the outside.[75] The impossible dream of Jacques Mayol, *Homo delphinus,* is to stay at the bottom of the sea. It is also the dream of seaside vacationers, after their fashion; by spending a few weeks camping on a fluid land lacking in memory (the sand, pounded by the waves of the big blue), they are seeking to forget the world, not to know it better.

A number of years ago, a satirical "newspaper," not really as stupid or ill-intentioned as it might appear, offered the following advice on its front page:

An endless vacation: DROWN YOURSELF.[76]

The newspaper had the right idea. The apneic state is that of the beach—a matter of breath, delicious drowning, atmospheric breathing interrupted by hyperventilation, hypocapnia,[77] closed-circuit oxygenation—just as tribal gregariousness and beach society are forms of closed-circuit sociability. Thus one can let oneself be drawn down toward the bottom, by ballast, like Jacques, or by sleep and the pleasure of being together.

We find this state in the amorous transports of Margery Hilton's Angela and Kell, as they lie intertwined on the beach: "Angela lost all notion of time. Her arms had fastened around sturdy shoulders; her whole body was melting, becoming a burning, aching entity. Now she was returning Kell's kisses, sharing his breath."[78] Described this way, Angela's ecstasy is virtually apneic. Likewise Flaubert's "contemplative effusion" in the course of his walk along the shore at Belle-Isle, where "the odor of the waves," "the softness of the grains of sand," "the fringe of waves, the breaks in the shore, the voice of the horizon," the passing breeze "like invisible kisses," produced in him such "boundless joy" that, as "in transports of love, one would like to have more hands to touch with, more lips for kissing, more eyes to see with, more soul for loving, spreading ourselves out onto nature in a transport full of delirium and joy," while regretting that "our eyes cannot go right into the heart of the rocks, down to the bottom of the sea, up the end of the sky." Beyond regret, here is what happens: "Together they were carried away by a wave from the bottom [just what is called for] and, when the tide had abandoned them on an isolated shore, they continued to cling together until the last traces of their passionate voyage had faded."[79]

After this "dive," whatever form it may take, it will be still more painful to come back to the surface. "But one has to think about returning to the land of turmoil, sun, and irritations; and yet it was really nice down there at the bottom."[80] "Returning to the land of turmoil." Metaphorically, this means returning to the outside world, to ordinary reality. Does the little death dream of growing up? "It's really nice down there at the bottom. That's the right place to be. Push me a bit so I can go back there." Back to the seaside on vacation? No. Enzo, the other hero of *The Big Blue*, is speaking; he is dying because he has gone down too far. He is speaking to Jacques. Might the suicidal individual be gnawing at the seaside vacationer? Every summer, when our vacation is coming to an end, when we take one last swim, when we get out of the water for the very last time and, already gripped by the anxieties of departure, complete our last return from the beach to the hotel or campground without a "decompression stage," are we not overcome by a wave of melancholy? Sometimes by a storm? The dream is followed by mourning—for a death that did not take place, the death of time and "all the rest." It is the end of our vertigo. The beach gods become mortal again, and their loves as well.

Ophelia Devoured

And then, up to a certain point, we have to be suspicious of still waters—of the water of dreams, of the sea as "comforter."[81] There are of course children in Never-Never Land, but there are also pirates. There is the Mermaid Lagoon, but there is also Cannibal Creek. In other words, as every myth gives rise to a complementary myth, an antimyth, we suddenly begin to realize that there are not only dolphins in the sea, but that some Leviathan is also sleeping in the depths and that when he is roused from sleep by manmade noise, he may surface and threaten whoever is bothering him. "In thirty-five feet of water, the great fish swam slowly, its tail waving just enough to maintain motion. It saw nothing, for the water was murky with motes of vegetation."[82]

The day will come, then, when an unforeseen monster, rising up from the dark bottom of the jar, will inevitably swallow up some stray Cartesian diver who has let himself get carried a little too far away from the shore—on an air mattress, for example:

> The boy was resting, his arms dangling down, his feet and ankles dipping in and out of the water with each small swell. His head was turned toward shore, and he noticed that he had been carried out beyond what his mother would consider safe. He could see her lying on her towel, and the man and child playing in the wash. He was not afraid, for the water was calm, and he wasn't really very far from shore—only forty yards or so. (57–58)

Here, the imaginary shifts: the depths are no longer dreamed in blue. They are murky. A dark, silent, and hostile universe inhabited by voracious monsters has superseded the idyllic sapphire of undersea paradise and haunts the swimmer's unconscious. Thus the vacationer who eats raw foods at the beach becomes in turn, by a cruel reversal, a sort of floating raw snack naively exposed to the appetites of an abyssal anthropophagus:

> The boy's last—only—thought was that he had been punched in the stomach. The breath was driven from him in a sudden rush. He had no time to cry out, nor, had he had the time, would he have known what to cry, for he could not see the fish. The fish's head drove the raft out of the water. The jaws smashed together, engulfing head, arms, shoulders, trunk, pelvis, and most of the raft. Nearly half the fish had come clear of the water, and it slid forward and down in a belly-flopping motion, grinding the mass of flesh and bone and rubber. The boy's legs were severed at the hips, and they sank, spinning slowly, to the bottom. (58–59)

In the mythographic lineage of the Leviathan, Jonah, and Moby-Dick, the seaside myth of *Jaws* answers that of *The Big Blue*. Like its predecessor, it allows for several interpretations.

Underneath paving stones, there are beaches; but underneath dreams, there are nightmares. Through the figure of a bestial intrusion into the seaside universe, *Jaws* is first of all the image of a violated reverie. As such, it exercises a certain fascination—which certain tabloid journalists do not hesitate to exploit on the eve of the vacation season. Sharks and diets are treated in a similar way. In July 1992, for example, the cover story of one magazine was titled "Alert on the Mediterranean. 'Jaws' on the Côte d'Azur: What They Don't Want to Tell Us." Inside, the alert in question becomes "red"; so do the accompanying photos. The report plays simultaneously on the registers of terror and safety; it denounces "the attacks kept secret by resort towns," lists all the more or less well-documented shark attacks since 1950 on Mediterranean beaches, specifies that "the favorite prey of the Great White are funboarders, divers, and windsurfers," and concludes with an injunction not to panic: "You're very unlikely to encounter a shark"! True or false? This is not really the question. The heart of the matter is the fantasy of being devoured that this sort of "reporting" stirs up.[83]

Beyond this ambiguous sensationalism, the myth of *Jaws* (and its success), taking on the figure of a violated reverie, is particularly interesting if we reconsider it as a metaphor, a vehicle for expressing the limits and the fragility of the seaside imaginary. For in psychoanalytic terms, cannot the shark in *Jaws,* swallowing up vacationers as it does, be said to embody the return of the repressed? Does it not figure in an allegory of vengeance? And, at the same time, does it not symbolize the contradiction of the pleasure principle by the reality principle? Does it not figure in the allegory of an impossibility?

Thus this myth can be interpreted on at least two levels. In a first stage, it is like a call to order. The shark that lurks near beaches is in a way a terrifying sign of revenge, a fantasy of nature getting even—nature once driven out with all its savagery and its savages, and now parodied, trivialized, and indeed totally repressed: fauna, flora, and humankind included (see chapters 1 and 4). This is the first message of the flesh-eating fish: if you don't want to be eaten, get out of the water. Stay on your island, as Robinson did. Remember that Robinson Crusoe almost died when he ventured far from shore. Maritime nature is not gentle and good; it is irredeemably savage. The liquid element is and remains a primitive milieu. Come back on land. Don't believe the ads that say, "In front of you, the sea, a vast heated pool that extends along the Atlantic, from the Canabrian corniche, the coasts of Galicia, the Costa de la Luz, to the Balearic Islands and the Costa Brava."[84] The sea hides monsters. The sea is suspect. The Mediterranean itself is neither a basin nor an aquarium; it is a giant pit, a menacing gulf from which jellyfish, octopuses, and sharks emerge—or else it is polluted or poisoned with pesticides and explosives.[85] Given all this, no wonder the sea takes its revenge!

The shark erupting in the peaceful waters of a seaside resort is, first of all, beyond the paroxystic image of the recollection of a dangerous natural reality, the reactualization of an age-old fear that sees the liquid element as an "enemy of happiness and life," and thus the manifestation of a phobic unconscious that can never be totally destroyed.[86] Beaches and waves are minefields of evil intentions, even where the water is shallow. Who among us, while swimming, has not stepped on a clump of seaweed or a tuft of posidonia and jumped up or shouted out in fright, as if some sticky monster had suddenly grabbed hold of our legs? Furthermore, the beach is a very fragile site for repose, subject as it is to the fury of weather and the sea. At the first storm, it clears away its inhabitants and recoats itself with seaweed. Nature reasserts itself. A red flag. No swimming. Now it is the breakers that kill, in place of the sharks. Now we have a beach submerged, as if sucked up and devoured by the waves, soon to be entirely annihilated; as for us, apart from a few daredevils, we are condemned to withdraw like survivors of Atlantis, to retreat to inland bivouacs. Farniente abolished, Ophelism proscribed, charm destroyed.

Suspicion, then. The sea is to be taken in moderation, with ever-increasing prudence, otherwise it is she who will consume us. The renewed phobia has been expressed for a number of years now through appeals to caution and vigilance, under the well-meaning aegis not of morality or health, but safety and ecology—during seaside stays abroad, for example,[87] but also in eating habits, in the form of a growing obsession with contaminated shellfish, mussels and oysters in particular; beyond their nutritional and symbolic virtues, these are subject to closer and closer scrutiny. One would think that the sea is always ready to trick us with its "fruits" the way the witch tricked Snow White. There is an underlying layer of anxiety close to superstition here, denoting the marked persistence of an ocean phobia. The big blue is also blue as cold fear.

From sharks to contaminated shellfish, from the beach to the table, we find the same anxiety toward what comes from the bottom of the sea—the same nightmare, too, which slips from rawness to cruelty. But after all, the word "oyster" comes from the Greek *ostrakon*, "shell," the root that also gives us "ostracism," referring to an attitude of hostility toward another person that leads to that person's banishment.[88] This etymology brings us to the second level at which the myth can be read.

For, on the one hand, the shark in *Jaws* embodies the myth of the sea that swallows men whole, a sea populated by "slimy savage things that rose from below and shredded ... flesh, by demons that cackled and moaned,"[89] suddenly terrorizing the "world of Cartesian divers": "A devious current like a chameleon's tongue grabbed hold of the swimmer and that was it! Neither hide nor hair of him left, all vanished into the immense guts of the depths: one tourist a day on the menu from the beginning of summer! It was so bad that the authorities ended up sending that cop to stand guard in front of the ogre's mouth."[90] On the other hand, as an image of a violated reverie, it also symbolizes the intrusion of alterity, the eruption of the Other into a closed world, a world that is in principle homogeneous and protected against every danger, including the sun.[91] This safety-conscious homogeneity is at once the strength—the raison d'être—and the Achilles' heel of this universe that accepts only Sameness and Likeness. Alterity is what shatters its unity, scrambles its code of sociability, and bursts the seaside bubble. This is indeed why "the island is partitioned," why the coast is sectored and segmented into socioeconomic zones (see chapter 7). In response to the myth of *The Big Blue*, the shark is to the dolphin what the Savages are to Robinson and Friday, or, in an earlier day, what the "dirty bastards in baseball caps" were to vacationing aristocrats and members of the bourgeoisie (see chapter 5). If a softening of the ostracism inherent to this society can be envisaged and even observed, in particular from the angle of an amorous integration—one with no future, however (let us call it a provisional pact of cordiality between the Robinsons and the Fridays), this moderation of exclusion goes no further.[92] For beyond this, given the image of panic that overwhelms the resort community of Amity in Benchley's novel when the shark's presence in its waters is announced, the seaside universe, faced with Otherness, collapses and is dislocated, emptied, transformed, or further divided. Worlds collide once again (see chapter 7), but this time they are seen from within.

Ophelia, in order to float, has no need for these "monsters" that come from other worlds, whether maritime, indigenous, or social. The happiness of weightlessness, of nude living, and the apneic state, on the margins of Polynesian mirages and other communitarian dreams of universal mixing or blending, always seems to come at such a price. The desire for withdrawal into the self precedes and determines modalities for forgetting the world.

Robinson Faces His Destiny

I am divided from Mankind, a Solitaire, one banish'd from humane Society.... But I am cast on an Island, where I see no wild Beasts to hurt me.

—Daniel Defoe, *Robinson Crusoe*

By introducing the term *residential seaside vacationing* in this study of seaside mores and customs, I intended first of all to call into question the contemporary extension of the notion of tourism. The overly broad sense in which this notion is used today confuses the analysis of the vacation phenomenon by crediting it with a symbolic and psychological unity that it does not possess. The debate is thus not merely etymological; the problem raised is more than a simple matter of wording. It is a conceptual problem, with reference to practices, motivations, and imaginary schemas of leisure activities that are fundamentally distinct, as I have sought to show here in detail by studying the case of the seaside sojourn. Just as Robinson Crusoe is the mirror image of Phileas Fogg, the robinsonnade is the opposite of tourism.

Between leisure sedentary and leisure mobility, between topophilia and itinerance (whether permanent or intermittent), there is a difference in nature and not merely of degree. We need to come to terms with this idea and learn its lessons. Is it still legitimate to speak of tourism with respect to the 62 percent of seaside vacationers whose chief activities are centered around swimming and the beach,[1] and especially those who shut themselves away within the enclosed space of a club-village? If not, is it not then contradictory to integrate these populations into the category labeled "long-stay tourism"? Where does the "tour" come in? The travel involved is most often limited to a simple round trip to a place of immobility, where the stay will be only occasionally "disturbed" by visits to nearby sites, excursions, or day trips.

Long-stay tourism: the expression reflects the typology that is currently in force, one whose terminology is a source of paradoxes and pleonasms. According to this "touristic" typology, developed by marketing specialists, the "tourist" category is subdivided into "sedentary," "sedentary-mobile," "itinerant," and "nomadic" tourists.[2] With the exception of "itinerant" (referring to the touristic itinerary or circuit), all these terms are subject to question, beginning with "sedentary."

The *sedentary* subcategory stems from an unjustified integration of topophilic vacationers, that is, practitioners of leisure immobility, into the category of leisure mobility. This is a paradox, a logical impossibility.

The *nomadic* subcategory, for its part, is based on a false anthropological analogy. The term is used to refer to the idea of improvised or adventurous mobility—wandering or vagabondage, as it were. Yet as a major cultural figure, the nomad is anything but a vagabond. Nomadic mobility is always planned, governed by traditional trajectories. It is at the very most only a customary variant of itinerance: it entails an itinerary that is planned or one undertaken by people familiar with the route, people who know where they are going or what they are looking for.

Finally, the *sedentary-mobile* subcategory, suggesting the pleonastic contrary "sedentary-immobile," is clearly the most unfortunate of the various designations applied to tourists. Given that it purports to designate tourists who divide their vacation time into phases of sojourn and displacement in variable proportions and rhythms, the term *semi-itinerant* seems more appropriate for characterizing a form of tourism in which mobility and pauses alternate. Strictly speaking, only cruise vacations, which offer the traveler the experience of a world in motion, make the notion of "sedentary-mobile" anything but absurd.[3] In short, it seems desirable to reform this terminology and to exclude from it the sedentary subcategory, elevating that grouping to a separate *residential vacationer* category parallel with tourism. Like tourism, this new category can be subdivided into experimental and initiatory types, depending on whether it is a pioneering or a ritualized activity (see Introduction). Residential seaside vacationing will have to be segmented into types in its turn.

ESSENCE AND AVATARS OF RESIDENTIAL SEASIDE VACATIONING

> The castles of the Comtesse de Ségur, like desert islands, are places where one lingers, and not, like those of Balzac and Stendhal, places that one passes through and leaves behind.
>
> —Marc Augé, *Domaines et châteaux* (1989)

"In vacations," as Gilbert Trigano has pointed out, "we note a desire to escape from anxiety, a dramatic search for security." Present among the requirements of tourists, what form do this desire and this quest take in the sphere of residential summer vacationing in general? How is the desire satisfied? To what conditions does the quest lead? As one thirty-two-year-old woman has indicated, "a vacation is a collection of reproducible events that are repeated and encountered over and over again in the course of a day, if things are going well." We are at the opposite pole here from exploration, adventure, and, a fortiori, defamiliarization, in a definition of happiness based on predictable, recurrent joys. The universe of residential summer vacationing is primordially a universe of repetition. "Repetition is reassuring. It is proof of intimacy, the very breath of intimacy," and in leisure topophilia it finds what may well be the "purest" space in which it can be practiced, that is, the space the farthest removed from the world's disturbances.[4]

For if it is true that "one of the paradoxes of tourism lies in the antagonistic pairing of a troubling defamiliarization and a return to reassuring habits," this defamiliarization is precisely what is abolished in the context of residential summer vacationing; thus the paradox in question is dissolved. These simultaneous disappearances give free rein to the expression of "reassuring habits" and make possible the "return to the only paradise that is worth anything: intimacy."[5] Whereas tourism entails circulation, residential vacationing always entails suspension. For the former, a stop is a stage; for the latter, it is a settling-in—even if, as Marc Augé rightly notes, Robinson thinks that he wants to go home; for the pleasure of residential vacationing is an ambiguous, anomic pleasure that cannot acknowledge itself as such, so passionately is it experienced, consciously or not, as a relationship of opposition to the world, the social world in particular.[6]

We are now at the crossroads between contrary vacation mystiques. Concerning the imaginary dimensions associated with travel, we are reminded, in a way, of the competition among theological interpretations of mobility. The association may be more than a coincidence: beginning in the early Middle Ages, these interpretations posited that man's salvation depended either on displacement—desert crossings, crusades, and pilgrimages—or on staying in one place—isolation and retreat.[7]

According to the first interpretation, human beings purify themselves by keeping on the move, eschewing comfort and fornication; according to the second, wandering is the wrong approach—traversing the world is tantamount to heading straight for temptation and the devil. From this second standpoint, purification is no longer achieved by evasion and a geographic quest, but by withdrawal and refuge. In fact, caught between centrifugal and centripetal forces, the modern vacation universe is similarly divided between tourists and summer residents, as measured by incompatible maxims such as "travel broadens the mind" and "we must cultivate our own garden"—the last words Voltaire put in the mouth of Candide at the end of a long trip. It is a question of choice, of sensibility, and of epoch as well, for in some periods people tend to be curious, inclined to search for novelty and otherness, while in others people are prone to getting "cold feet," inclined to search for what is already in place and for themselves, thus instituting, by a leisure practice of inward withdrawal, an artificial state that can indeed be labeled an "event strike."[8]

For is this not the essence of residential seaside vacationing: the absence of events? And from Robinson Crusoe to Paul and Virginia, do we not find the same temptation of emptiness and the same axis of sensibility in outline form, ready to be deciphered?

> Their sole study was how they could please and assist one another; for of all other things they were ignorant, and indeed could neither read nor write. They were never disturbed by inquiries about past times, nor did their curiosity extend beyond the bounds of their mountain. They believed the world ended at the shores of their own island, and all their ideas and all their affections were confined within its limits.[9]

From this point of view, the first avatar of residential seaside vacationing, as a choice among universes, is a matter of percentages or proportions. Sojourning and visiting are not the same. In studying the historical and geographical fluctuations of the choices made between these alternatives, the anthropology of leisure has everything to gain if it maintains this distinction as an analytical tool, that is, as a sign through which the options, orientations, or mutations of mentalities can be measured, depending on whether they are exploratory or Crusoean. The fact that international pleasure travel is increasing does not necessarily mean that international tourism as such is developing. One can cross a border to circulate elsewhere or to transplant oneself there. One can go to Senegal in order to discover exotic nature and traditions, or on the contrary in order to hole up on the shore in a vacation "shell" whose entire reality is encompassed between the hotel and the sea.[10]

The variations in the relation between tourism and residential summer vacationing unquestionably constitute a crucial indicator that warrants analysis. Without underestimating the influence on vacationers' behavior of the politics involved in the structures of housing and other amenities in the receiving countries, the avatars of this alternative also mirror collective sensibilities and reflect their evolution. Between an openness to what is foreign and a withdrawal focused on the self and loved ones, these variations translate the relative portion taken up in vacation space overall by the search for the Other and the desire for the Same. For example, how can we explain why, in Greece, after fifteen years of cultural tourism (from 1950 to 1965), the vacation industry suddenly shifted on a massive scale to residential seaside resorts,[11] if not by a transformation of vacation mentalities, a shift in what summer vacationers were seeking, and thus a change in the "spirit of the times," characterized by a loss of interest in local life, regional identity, and authenticity? For it is indeed this "spirit," with its desires, its fears, and its denials, that is expressed in the last analysis, like a symptom of society, through these oscillations between tourism and summer residency. Underlying these variations, there is the dialectic between the dreams of discovery and the dreams of seclusion that call the vacation tune, as it were. It is this dialectic between immensity and intimacy, between attraction to the wide world and a competing attraction to small children, that modulates decisions, modes, and strategies.

The fact remains that, if residential summer vacationing—as opposed to tourism—is defined and takes on its full value in vacation space as a quest for a microcosm, the beach itself is only one among various possibilities. Seaside topophilia, a "blue-water summer," is just one avatar of the robinsonnade. The structure can be transposed into other sites: in summer, the country or the mountains; in winter, the desert or even the city, the broiling refuge of an oasis or the privacy of a suburban estate. The "cocooning" that is so much discussed today stems basically, on the home front, from a common desire for insularity. One is at home, sheltered from storms, and that is what counts.

Still, this transference of sedentary leisure to other sites has its consequences. The shift modifies the quality of leisure. Whenever the leisure in question falls in the category of "green vacationing" (sojourns on a farm, vacations in one's summer home or other rural lodgings), for example, we can associate it with "refamiliarization." Symbolically, it is as if Robinson, turning his back on the sea, were to retrace his steps to the interior of his island, to his goats and his crops, thereby manifesting a desire to return to rusticity, to the soil, to the land. If the often-announced renewal of this form of residential country vacationing, of rural "retribalization," were to be confirmed in the years to come, if vacationers were to forsake the shore in favor of island villages, we would doubtless have to acknowledge a symptomatic inflection in the meaning of sedentary vacation practices. There is nevertheless a margin of difference that remains to be analyzed between an integrated neorural retreat[12] and a retreat to a beach enclave comparable to the one Tintin found in Captain Haddock's castle at Moulinsart.

In contrast, "white residential vacationing" (sojourns at winter resorts) seems to have a good deal in common with seaside vacationing, at the symbolic level. The two are symmetrical in terms of time and space, seasons and altitudes. In place of depth, there is height; in place of sand and sea, there is snow, which erases the world and invites us to forget it. It swallows up the world's signs under its surface and drives away flora, fauna, and indigenous populations. In a hard, immobile world, snow reintroduces softness and the pleasures of mobility. It is also a support for vertigo-inducing behaviors: gliding, falling, or jumping. We bury ourselves in snow. We let it carry us away. We surf on it as we do on the sea. We play with it the way we play with sand and water. At least one ski instructor rents out sailboards on the coast in the summer: a highly significant alternation of professional activity between sea and mountain. The dolphins of summer often become chamois in winter.

Blue, green, or white, summer or winter, residential vacationing is thus taking shape as an autonomous and specific vacation universe with its own typology. From this perspective, it is a universe that remains to be explored. In view of a more nuanced psychosociology of leisure sedentary that would not call the underlying concept into question, we are called to develop its definition, especially by way of specific studies that would identify constants and significant variations beneath the similarities and dissimilarities of genres and species.[13]

The Mutation of Topophiles?

I hate islands, the impression that you'll never ever be able to get away.
—Paul Morand, *Bains de mer* (1960)

Does Paul Morand speak for our contemporaries here? Does today's summer vacationer want to get away from his island? To abandon the beach? Has the desire for Crusoean confinement come to an end? Are we witnessing the demise of seaside enclaves with their autarchic sociability? Is beach society about to disintegrate? These questions need to be raised, not so much owing to the steady increase in international travel (which is not synonymous with tourism) as because sensitivity to the natural and cultural environment seems to be inducing new exploratory behaviors.

"Unfaithful" summer residents are indeed moving away from the shore. They are discovering that they are drawn to outings and excursions:

> The most general remark, formulated by most observers and corroborated by our investigation,[14] is that travel to the shore is no longer limited to the beach. During their stays, which are now shorter, summer vacationers are on the move. A desire to see the country is superimposed on the desire to go to the shore: there is greater interest in the historical, architectural, and ethnographic patrimony on the one hand, and in outings (on foot, on horseback, by bicycle) on the other hand. The diffusion and mediatization of ecological preoccupations, along with the work of local associations . . . are beginning to arouse an interest leading to outings—still very small-scale, but significant— focused on local flora and fauna.[15]

Does this mean that after detaching itself, isolating itself from everything, seaside summer vacationing may be embarking now on a return to the world? Is Robinson preparing to leave his island? Is Never-Never Land returning to reality—to History, to Nature? In the form of peripheral explorations manifesting a new interest for the outside, the practices described may prefigure a sort of "touristic" remobilization and thus a still more profound mutation in the map of residential vacationing. Veering from blue to green, the spatial mutation of seaside topophilia (which consists simply in reestablishing it elsewhere) may be supplemented by the possibility of a psychological mutation (one that transforms the island into a peninsula). Such a change would break residential seaside vacationing out of its isolation and repatriate it, relocating it in the margins of leisure mobility.

Although the practices just mentioned are significant, they are still minority practices, and too tenuous as indices to justify any pronouncements as to the real importance of the phenomenon. In addition, other signs seem to contradict this hypothetical evolution of residential seaside vacationing in cultural and ecological directions—a phenomenon that for the time being may announce only the emergence of a new division of the seaside vacation population, a partial mutation and not the end of a model of leisure.

The seaside universe, as we have seen, is much more inclined to condensation than to extension. It is not a universe through which people pass, but one in which they stay. It prefers concentration to dispersal, installation to circulation, retreat to evasion, and by definition, fringe areas to wide-open spaces. It corresponds in this respect to a need that itself corresponds only weakly, if at all, to appeals from the cultural or natural exterior: the backcountry on land, and the blue horizon at sea. Tribes, vacation villages, "shell hotels," and other jealous territorialities constantly remind us of this fact.[16] In 1967 Hubert Macé wrote: "The ultimate degree of seaside vacationing may well be yachting with stops for tourism."[17] But the resident vacationer is no more a navigator at heart than Robinson. Some three decades later, Macé's prognosis has been formally contradicted by the facts. Despite the increase in pleasure boating (see chapter 1), "90% of vacationers view the sea as a décor or use it as a swimming site, and are not prepared to consume products that use it as a support"—sailboats, sailboards, or motorboats.[18]

Real or imaginary, natural or artificial, insularity is and remains the characteristic feature of seaside topophilia. It is the emblem of this form of residential vacationing, so much so that the study cited above about the frequency of visits to the French coast proposes as a conclusion to its analyses, in view of the promotion of seaside France, a logo that "presents a stylized map of France looking like a desert island." For southern coasts, "the island harbors a palm tree"; for northern shores, the tree would be a pine.[19]

With this cartographic logo that stresses the imaginary detachment and emptiness of a country transformed into an island without natives, a symbol of the denegation of geographical, social, and cultural realities, the unconditional figure of the robinsonnade still carries the day, the image of a self-contained, virgin perimeter that serves "nothing but ourselves face to face with ourselves," where no external or internal sign of human life that would demarcate its borders or dwell in its space intervenes to blur the dream terrain.

In fact, if summer seaside vacationing has to undergo some mutation, in particular as a consequence of the saturation of the shoreline that may trigger a migration toward the interior, it can also be envisaged as operating in the other direction: not toward an ecological and social integration of seaside leisure but, on the contrary, toward its radical exclusion, in conformity in this respect with the requirements of myth and the resistance to reality that characterizes this form of residential vacationing. From this perspective, other signs, less significant, allow us to glimpse ultimate avatars of the Crusoean utopia that would provide equal justification for the reverse prognosis.

HYDROPONIC ISLANDS

> He raised his arms toward the sky: "Selling memory holes for leisure time! Nobody ever would have thought of that, and yet God knows there are plenty of ideas around. Their 366th day is a stupid utopian joke."
> —Max-André Rayjean, *La guerre des loisirs* (1986)

What signs? To begin with, this observation: "Vacationers are looking for a shore that is nearby, if not in the immediate vicinity; yet only 15 percent of our clients go to the sea, to Cap Estérel for example. These clients prefer artificial aquatic spaces as long as they can profit from the sea; a pool without a view of the sea is used much less often."[20] Here is the height of detachment and vicarious experience. It is rather like dipping one's finger in a hot cup of coffee while watching a volcano erupt in the distance. There is nothing to fear from here. The image of nature is being consumed, not nature itself. Robinson is terrified of savagery.

Another example, another sign. "In the middle of Paris, on the Seine, right by the heliport, Aquaboulevard, 5:00 p.m., a young mother with her two clean and delighted children says to her neighbor, who is fresh and dewy as a rose in the morning: 'What a day! Fabulous! Trouville without the sand, the cold water, and the highway!'"[21] At this stage, it is not even the image that is being consumed, but the idea—the idea as pure concept and pure product. One advertisement for Aquaboulevard in June 1991 got it just right:

> To get to the beach,
> Take the subway.

Métro Porte d'Auteuil: destination, the sea! If you aren't going to the beach, the beach will come to you. Here, "the sun shines all day long and there are waves every twenty minutes." Once again, this is not a new idea. At Luna Park in Berlin in the late 1920s, there were already "splendid baths with artificial waves."[22]

From Berlin to Paris, from yesterday's Luna Park to today's Aquaboulevard, in the absence of shores, we might think we are dealing only with compensatory simulacra, but this would be a mistake. After mimicking the sea, these simulacra now figure among the amenities of the shore itself. At Eilat, for example, "the hotels are clustered around a marina, with a pretext-beach tucked in somewhere and a host of swimming pools in compensation."[23] Pretext-beach, swimming-pool-as-sea, ocean-as-décor, all this leads us to believe that via the technological evolution that enlarges the values of the Crusoean model, far from opening itself up to and integrating itself with external realities, the contemporary seaside world is instead ever-increasingly closing itself off to those realities.

Gérard Blitz, the founder of the Club Méditerranée, stated in 1965 that "future vacations will take place in all seasons, in winter preferably under sunny skies, in all countries that equip themselves, starting now, to receive us. The race for the sun is a constant in human history"[24]—unless of course technology tackles the problem and interrupts the race in exchange for spaces of simulation.

Today, "funny warm bubbles"[25] are proliferating next to cities or seashores. Some offer thalassotherapy (there are some fifty of these in France alone), while others offer games or recreational activities for families. In any case, their classification in the category of "health tourism" or "nearby leisure activity" changes nothing. These are chiefly

islands, new islands set aside for shorter or longer robinsonnades—
sterilized, filtered, air-conditioned, and disconnected from the world.

From this viewpoint, Center Parcs are exemplary: a new type of
family boardinghouse, Robinson Clubs out in the country that bring
Crusoean reveries to fruition in the absence of the sea. For the seaside
public, which often cites these centers as an interesting alternative, is
not deceived, nor is the Center Parcs organization itself.[26] During its
1993 advertising campaign, Center Parcs presented itself explicitly as
a form of leisure competing with the beach by contrasting images of
overpopulated and urbanized shorelines with idyllic images of a serene tropicalism designed for conviviality in limited groups.

Just what is the Center Parcs universe?[27] It is first and foremost,
according to its advertising, "a Mediterranean microclimate under an
immense transparent vault." Totally artificial, it is a seaside universe
under a bubble, in which the tropical swimming pool (with palm
and banana trees, waterfalls, waves, and whirlpools) has replaced the
beach. This world is protected from all the influences of its surroundings, beginning with temperature variations. "29 C all year round!" is
one of the featured slogans in the promotional discourse. So much
for the weather. On a total area of 766 acres, only 156 are used; the
remaining land serves solely to isolate the center from the surrounding realities. This desert of protection is to the center what the vast
ocean is to Robinson's island. Since the model population intended
to fill the island is the family, bungalows are the basic hotel unit; these
have a lot in common, in spirit if not in form, with the "Indian huts"
of a Bernardin de Saint-Pierre. In 1990 80 percent of the visitors had
at least one child, and 56 percent had more than one child under the
age of fifteen.[28]

I have no intention of embarking here on a fantastic futurology
of leisure by prophesying the wholesale triumph of these seaside
"greenhouses." In the future, will they play the role of winter complements, relay stations between summer vacations and the drabness of
everyday life (thus corresponding on the home front to Gérard Blitz's
projections), or will they become spaces that substitute exclusively
for residential seaside vacationing? Robinsons are flocking to these
new islands, with a constantly increasing room occupancy rate: in
Verneuil, 75 percent in 1988, 82.5 percent in 1989, 90 percent in 1990.
In Great Britain room occupancy has been as high as 98 percent. Even
the Fridays, notwithstanding the economic forecasts that might keep

them away from this new product, are venturing in turn into the embrace of these tropical bubbles. Instead of spending three weeks at the beach, they are now choosing to invest their vacation budget in a week of hydroponic balnearity, sheltered from all storms.[29]

The significance of these "funny bubbles" must not be underestimated. They are at once synthetic metaphors for a leisure imaginary and, running counter to the official ideologies that preach openness and intercultural encounters, symptoms of a world tormented by the private temptations of withdrawal: self-discovery, the return to one's own, the forgetting of others, the quest for identity. As one naturist put it: "I don't do this to respect nature. I do it to be nude"[30]—to be himself, nothing but himself, as it were.

Where is Tourism, then? Where is Nature? And where is the Other, divine or human, in all this? The Other is outside, elsewhere: wiped out, erased, excluded, reported missing, "zapped." And Robinson, deprived to be sure of the company of men, but safe, can then very well declare that he has nothing more to fear here, "no furious Wolves or Tygers, . . . no Savages to murther and devour me."[31] In all respects his days can indeed be spent in safety in this place.

Here then, in response to the turbulence and threats of the Great Outside World, is the paradise of residential summer vacationing.[32]

APPENDIX

Beach and Seaside Literature

The list of works that follows is not intended to be exhaustive. In this field, as in that of travel narratives,[1] such an ambition would be madness.

The goal of this chronological bibliography is above all to provide some historical reference points that will allow the reader to discern schools of thought, to note the increasing importance of certain subjects (solitude, family, hydrotherapy, nudity, sexuality, or ecologism) within an extremely varied literary production, and to appreciate as a result some contrasts and combinations of ideas: the competition and interference among "modes"—hence the recurrence of some references cited earlier in *L'idiot du voyage*.

The works listed here are not all cited in the text, but all have contributed to its development. This bouquet of heterogeneous productions (novels, guidebooks, narratives, essays, children's literature, romantic fiction, cartoons, songs, pamphlets, tales, poems, collections of photographs, and so on) does not derive from a qualitative selection of works, which would have led some to be judged of minor literary importance. What is at issue here is a theme, not a literary genre. It is thus the former and not the latter that the chronological list is designed to reflect, as a representative sample.[2]

The dates given are those of the first edition or even those of the first draft, where there is a significant gap between the two. Given the pronounced heterogeneity of the works listed, their genre is indicated parenthetically when the title does not make this clear.

Finally, it seemed helpful to to emphasize some productions that I have found particularly important or historically significant (see asterisks).

EIGHTEENTH CENTURY

Woodes Rogers, *A Cruising Voyage Round the World* (1712)

Edward Cooke, *A Voyage to the South Sea* (1712)

Daniel Defoe, *The Life and Adventures of Robinson Crusoe** (1719)

Jonathan Swift, *Gulliver's Travels* (1726)

Dr. Richard Russell, *A Dissertation on the Use of Sea Water in the Diseases of the Glands** (1752)

Carlo Goldoni, *Trilogie de la villégiature* (1761)

H. Maret, *Mémoire sur la manière d'agir des bains d'eau douce et des bains de mer* (1769)

Dr. Ebenezer Gilchrist, *The Uses of Sea Voyages in Medicine* (1770)

Denis Diderot, *Supplément au voyage de Bougainville* (1772; published in 1796)

Joachim Heinrich Campe, *Robinson le jeune* (1779)

Jean-Jacques Rousseau, *Rêveries du promeneur solitaire* (1782)

Jacques-Henri Bernardin de Saint-Pierre, *Paul et Virginie** (1787)

NINETEENTH CENTURY

Johan David Wyss, *Swiss Family Robinson** (1812)

Honoré de Balzac, "Un drame au bord de la mer" (1823)

Louis Garneray, *Voyage pittoresque et maritime sur les côtes de la France* (1828)

Philarète Chasles, "Scènes d'un village maritime en Angleterre," *Revue de Paris* (1829)

Charles Dickens, "The Tuggses at Ramsgate" (1836)

Dr. V. Raymond, *Manuel des baigneurs, précédé de l'histoire des bains, suivi d'un traité de natation* (1840)

Fleury, *Hydrothérapie* (1841)

Dr. J. Le Coeur, *Des bains de mer. Guide medical et hygiénique du baigneur** (1846)

Karl Marx and Friedrich Engels, *Manifesto of the Communist Party** (1848)

Herman Melville, *Moby-Dick* (1851)

Emile Souvestre, *Scènes et moeurs des rives et des côtes* (1852)

Joseph Morlent, *Guide du touriste au Havre et dans ses environs* (1860)

Jules Michelet, *La Mer** (1861)

Macario, *Manuel d'hydrothérapie* (1861)

Dr. Constantin James, "Études sur les bains de mer et l'hydrothérapie," in
  Guide pratique aux eaux minérales (1861)
Victor Hugo, *The Toilers of the Sea* (1866)
Jules Verne, *Around the World in Eighty Days** (1873)
Jules Verne, *The Mysterious Island* (1874)
Gustave Flaubert, "A Simple Heart" (1877)
Bertail, *Les plages de France* (1880)
Guy de Maupassant, "Épaves" (1881)
Ernest Ameline, *Une plage normande: Villers-sur-Mer* (1882)
Jules Verne, *The Robinson Crusoe School* (1882)
Paul Lafargue, *Le droit à la paresse* (1883)
Gustave Flaubert and Maxime Du Camp (trip through Brittany in 1848), *Par
  les champs et par les grèves** (1885)
Pierre Loti, *Pêcheur d'Islande* (1886)
Jean Richepin, *La mer* (1886)
Campardon, *Guide thérapeutique aux eaux minérales et aux bains de mer*
  (1887)
Guy de Maupassant, *Pierre and Jean* (1888)
Jules Verne, *Two Years' Holiday** (1888)
Mme de Lalaing, *Les côtes de la France de Saint-Nazaire à Biarritz par la
  plage** (1889)
Robert Louis Stevenson, *The Ebb-Tide: A Trio and a Quartette* (1894)
Laura Laforgue, *Manifeste du parti communiste* (1894–95) (translation; first
  edition in French)
Jules Verne, *The Floating Island* (1895)
J. Laumonier, *Les bains de mer* (1896); *Guide des familles aux bains de mer*
  (1897)
John Meade Falkner, *Moonfleet* (1897)

FIRST HALF OF THE TWENTIETH CENTURY

René Quinton, *L'eau de mer, milieu organique** (1904)
Henri Bolland, *Excursions en France* (1909)
Thomas Mann, *Death in Venice* (1913)
Jack London, "My Hawaiian Aloha" (1919)
Robert J. Fletcher, *Isles of Illusion: Letters from the South Seas* (1923) (col-
  lected letters)
Claude Farrère, *Une jeune fille voyagea . . .* (1925)
Dr. Viaud-Grand-Marais, *Guide du voyageur à Noirmoutier* (1927)
Dr. Pierre Vachet, *La nudité et la physiologie sexuelle* (1928)
Roger Salardenne, *Le culte de la nudité. Sensationnel reportage en Allemagne*
  (1929)
Dr. Galtier-Boissière, ed. *Larousse médical illustré* (1929)

Louis-Charles Royer, *Let's Go Naked** (1929)

Paul Léautaud, *Villégiature* (1929)

Roer Salardenne, *Un mois chez les nudistes. Nouveau reportage en Allemagne* (1930)

Liselotte, *Le guide des convenances. Savoir-vivre, obligations sociales, usages mondains* (1931)

Roger Salardenne, *Le nu intégral chez les nudistes français* (1931)

Général Matton, *Par la Provence à la Côte d'Azur. Poésies* (1933)

F. Scott Fitzgerald, *Tender Is the Night** (1933)

Dr. Georges Gaubert, *Un canoë passé . . .* (1934)

Alain Gerbault, *Iles de beauté* (1941)

Etienne Jauffret, *Au pays bleu. Roman d'une vie d'enfant* (1941)

M. Boigey, *Hydrothérapie et massage* (1941)

Charles Trenet, "La mer" (1946)

SECOND HALF OF THE TWENTIETH CENTURY

Roger Vailland, *Saint-Tropez* (1950)

Ernest Hemingway, *The Old Man and the Sea** (1952)

Enid Blyton, *Noddy at the Seaside* (1953)

Pierre Probst, *Youpi en vacances* (1953)

Théodore Monod, *Bathyfolages, plongées profondes** (1954)

Claude Lévi-Strauss, *Tristes tropiques* (1955)

Enid Blyton, *Five Go Down to the Sea* (1955)

Albert Camus, *The Stranger* (1957)

Les Guides rouges, *Côte d'Azur; Provence; Corse; Riviera italienne* (1957)

Pierre Daninos, *Vacances à tous prix** (1958)

Agnès Varda, *Du côté de la côte* (1958)

Jean-René Huguenin, *The Other Side of the Summer* (1960)

Gwenn-Abel Bolloré, *Guide du pêcheur à pied et sa cuisine* (1960)

Paul Morand, *Bains de mer, bains de rêve** (1960)

Margret Wittmer, *Les Robinsons des Galapagos* (1960)

André Pieyre de Mandiargues, "La marée" (1962)

Sempé et Goscinny, *Les vacances du petit Nicolas* (1962)

Kobo Abé, *Woman in the Dunes* (1964)

Les Guides verts Michelin, *Côte de l'Atlantique, de la Loire aux Pyrénées* (1965)

J. Fauli, *Costa Brava* (1965)

Georges Brassens, "Supplique pour être enterré à la plage de Sète"* (1966)

Georges Monmarché, *La Côte d'Azur de Marseille à Menton*, Les Guides bleus (1966)

Michel Tournier, *Friday** (1967)

P. D. James, *No Hands* (1967)

Edgar Morin, *Journal de Californie* (1970)

René Richard and Camille Bartoli, *La Côte d'Azur assassinée?** (1971)
Gault and Millau, and Raymond Cartier, *Guide des nouvelles stations Languedoc-Roussillon* (1973)
Peter Benchley, *Jaws** (1974)
Pierre Daninos, *Les Touristocrates* (1974)
Sempé, *Saint-Tropez* (1968–75)
François Lourbet, *Le chef de village* (1975)
Michel Jonasz, "Les vacances au bord de la mer" (1975)
Max Gallo, *La Baie des Anges; La Promenade des Anglais; Le Palais des fêtes* (1975–76)
Jean Hureau, *La Corse aujourd'hui* (1976)
Jean-Luc Michaud, *Manifeste pour le littoral** (1976)
Michel Gall, *La vie sexuelle de Robinson Crusoé** (1977)
Anne Philippe, *Un été près de la mer* (1977)
Bonnes vacances (Collective work, 1978)
Cabu, *Le journal de Catherine* (1978)
Georges Perec, *Deux cent quarante-trois cartes postales en couleurs véritables* (1978)
Kay Thorpe, *Une île à l'abri des tempêtes* (1979)
Margerin, *Vacances de rêve* (1980)
Philippe Jacquin, *Le goémonier* (1980)
Reiser, *Ils sont moches* (1980)
Paul Theroux, *The Mosquito Coast* (1981)
Margery Hilton, *Une semaine aux Caraïbes* (1981)
Régis Franc, *Le café de la plage** (1982)
Nicole de Buron, *Dix jours de rêve* (1982)
Italo Calvino, *Palomar** (1983)
Claude Nori, *Rimini, août 82* (1983)
Mary Terence, *Sous les palmes bruissantes* (1983)
Binet, *Les Bidochon en vacances* (1984)
Annabel Murray, *Seuls sur l'île sauvage* (1984)
Christopher Frank, *L'année des méduses* (1984)
Bernadette Doka, *Bronzer sans danger* (1984)
Serres, *Les vacances* (1984)
Italo Calvino, *Collection de sable* (1984)
Hovov, *Les mâles en vacances* (1984)
Peggy Nicholson, *Privé de vacances!* (1984)
Bernard Descamps, *Balnéaires* (1985)
Christian Guidicelli, *Station balnéaire* (1986)
Max-André Rayjean, *La guerre des loisirs* (1986)
Cailleteau and Vatine, *Galères balnéaires* (1986)
Frédéric Vitoux, *Riviera** (1987)
Jannick Ser, *Le livre de l'amateur d'huîtres et de coquillages* (1987)

Marie Cardinal, *Les Pieds-Noirs* (1988)
Alain Souchon and Laurent Voulzy, "Le soleil donne" (1988)
William Boyd, *Brazzaville Beach* (1990)
Philippe Giraud, *Tropical Ladies* (1990)
Robert Doisneau and Daniel Pennac, *Les grandes vacances* (1991)
Elliott Erwitt, *Elliott Erwitt—On the Beach** (1991)
David Lodge, *Paradise News* (1991)

Notes

PREAMBLE

1. Daniel Defoe, *Robinson Crusoe*, ed. Michael Shinagel (New York: W. W. Norton, 1975), 37.

2. Ibid., 38.

3. Ibid., 160.

INTRODUCTION

1. Jean-Didier Urbain, *L'idiot du voyage. Histoires de touristes* (Paris: Payot, 1993). I should like to reassure the reader at once that, while the present book complements its predecessor, it is not merely a sequel; it is in fact an autonomous work that can stand entirely on its own. Thus subsequent references in *At the Beach* to *L'idiot du voyage* can be read in two ways: either as reminders of information or reflections already included in the first work (and made explicit once again here), or else simply as references inviting the reader to dip into the book on tourism if the present work has succeeded in arousing interest in the topic.

2. The historical and linguistic information supplied here is from Alain Rey, ed., *Dictionnaire historique de la langue française* (Paris: Le Robert, 1992).

3. See Georges Cazes, *Fondements pour une géographie du tourisme et des loisirs* (Paris: Bréal, 1992).

4. See Dennison Nash, "Tourism as Anthropological Subject," *Current Anthropology* 22, no. 5 (Oct. 1981): 461–81.

5. This terminological debate and its implications have already been discussed at length in Urbain, "Le touriste et les mots," chapter 1 of *L'idiot du voyage*.

6. See ibid., chapter 6, "L'autre du touriste."

7. Ibid., 108 n. 1.

8. Edward T. Hall, *The Silent Language* (Garden City, N.Y.: Anchor Press/ Doubleday, 1973), 53.

9. Hans Magnus Enzenberger, "Eine Theorie des Tourismus," in *Einzel- heiten I: Bewußtseins-Industrie* (Frankfurt am Main: Suhrkamp, 1964), 179–205.

10. Georges Cazes, *Le tourisme en France* (Paris: Presses Universitaires de France, 1993), 68–69. The figures given in the previous two paragraphs come from *Premiers résultats* (Paris: INSEE, 1992) and *Mémento du tourisme* (Paris: Observatoire national du tourisme, August 1992).

11. See Michel Maffesoli, *The Time of the Tribes: The Decline of Individu- alism in Mass Society,* trans. Don Smith (London: Sage Publications, 1996), 80–81.

12. See Urbain, "Le voyageur et son double oule complexe du 'faux,'" chapter 13 of *L'idiot du voyage.*

13. David Lodge, *Paradise News* (London: Secker and Warburg, 1991), 61.

14. Robert Louis Stevenson, "The Marquesas," part 1 of *In the South Seas* (Leipzig: Bernhard Tauchnitz, 1901), 14.

15. F. Scott Fitzgerald, *Tender Is the Night* (New York: Scribner's, 1934), 12.

16. Rackam, "Le cul-cul club," in *Bonnes vacances,* ed. René Durand (Paris: Le Dernier Terrain Vague, 1978), 129.

17. See Danielle Rozenberg, *Tourisme et utopie aux Baléares. Ibiza, une île pour une autre vie* (Paris: L'Harmattan, 1990), 15.

18. Michel Picard, *Bali: Cultural Tourism and Touristic Culture,* trans. Diana Darling (Singapore: Archipelago, 1996), 78.

19. See Georges Cazes, "L'île tropicale, figure emblématique du tourisme international," *Cahiers du tourisme* 112 (June 1987).

20. Paul Morand, *Bains de mer* (Paris: Arléa, 1990), 112.

21. Jack London, "My Hawaiian Aloha," in Charmian London, *The New Hawaii* (London: Mills and Boon, 1923), 48.

22. Céline, *Le Pont de Londres: Guignol's Band II* (Paris: Gallimard, 1964), 128. Cf. the English translation, *London Bridge: Guignol's Band II,* 144: "Let's hit the road, my little Virginia! You'll grow up big and beautiful out there! In the Tragacanth Seas!"

23. See Guy de Maupassant, "Histoire corse" (1881), in *Contes et nouvelles,* 2 vols. (Paris: Gallimard, La Pléiade, 1974), 1:321; Stevenson, "The Marquesas," 14.

24. Gustave Flaubert, *Voyage en Bretagne. Par les champs et par les grèves* (Brussels: Complexe, 1989); Morand, *Bains de mer,* 151.

25. J. L. Perrier, "Majorque, résidence secondaire de l'Europe," *Le Monde* (Nov. 25, 1989): 29.

26. Pascal Bruckner and Alain Finkielkraut, *Au coin de la rue, l'aventure* (Paris: Seuil, 1979), 44.

27. Bronislaw Malinowski, "Spirit Hunting in the South Seas," *The Real- ist* (1929): 398.

28. Morand, *Bains de mer*, 66.

29. One example: the Wakaya Club, in the Fiji Islands, opened in 1971. The 1993 rate was approximately $880 per day for two people, including "the bungalow, meals, wine, and even champagne"; special issue, *Paris-Match-Voyages* (1993), 114.

30. Claude Lévi-Strauss, *Tristes Tropiques*, trans. John and Doreen Weightman (New York: Athaneum, 1974), 338–39.

31. Morand, *Bains de mer*, 159–60.

32. This is Jacques Meunier's definition of the routard, in Alain Borel et al., *Pour une littérature voyageuse* (Brussels: Complexe, 1992), 146.

33. Nicole de Buron, *Dix jours de rêve* (Paris: J'ai lu, 1986), 122.

34. Let us recall that after years on the island Robinson saves the life of an Indian who is being pursued by cannibalistic savages and names him Friday.

35. For all this information, see "robinsonnade," in Rey, ed., *Dictionnaire historique.* See also Karl Marx and Friedrich Engels, "Critical-Utopian Socialism and Communism," in *Manifesto of the Communist Party* (1848), in *Collected Works* (New York: International Publishers, 1976), 6:514–17; at issue in particular are utopian robinsonnades such as Owen's home colonies, Fourier's phalanstery, or Cabet's Icarie.

36. Dominique Rouillard, *Le site balnéaire* (Brussels: Pierre Mardaga, 1984), 52.

37. Ibid., 56.

38. The opposition between "initiatory" and "experimental" is a distinction proposed in Urbain, *L'idiot du voyage*, 231ff., to differentiate between ritualized vacation practices and inaugural practices (or practices that seek to be inaugural) that mean to escape this pre-established ritualization.

39. See "robinsonnade," in Rey, ed., *Dictionnaire historique.*

40. Cf. Margret Wittmer, *Les Robinsons des Galapagos* (Paris: A. Michel, 1960), 362. Concluding Defoe's narrative, Wittmer writes: "For years, we have not been alone; the island currently boasts 45 residents. We were the first, and we showed them the way."

41. See Alain Corbin, *The Lure of the Sea: The Discovery of the Seaside in the Western World, 1750–1840,* trans. Jocelyn Phelps (Berkeley: University of California Press, 1994). We shall return to the story of this pacification, in order to account for it in the framework of contemporary seaside vacationing.

42. William Dampier was the author of two accounts of circumnavigating the globe, published in 1691 and 1706; see *Dampier's Voyages* (London: E. Grant Richards, 1906). Cf. Urbain, *L'idiot du voyage*, 262. Selkirk's adventure seems to have been published as early as 1712 by Woodes Rogers *(A Cruising Voyage Round the World)* and by Captain Edward Cooke *(A Voyage to the South Sea and round the World in the Years 1708 to 1711).* See "Selkirk," in *Grand Larousse encyclopédique,* vol. 18 (Paris: Larousse, 1970). Defoe's novel was published seven years later.

43. See Michel Gall, *La vie sexuelle de Robinson Crusoé* (Paris: J.-C. Simoen,

1977); Tournier's *Friday* and Theroux's *Mosquito Coast*; in literature, J. H. Bernardin de Saint-Pierre's *Paul and Virginia* (London: George Routledge and Sons, 1888), or, more recently, the American film *The Blue Lagoon*, directed by Randal Kleiser; Johan Wyss, *The Swiss Family Robinson*, ed. John Seelye (Oxford: Oxford University Press, 1991); Jules Verne, *The Mysterious Island*, trans. W. H. G. Kingston (New York: Heritage Press, 1959); Verne, *Two Years' Holiday* (London: Arco, 1964); and Wittmer, *Les Robinsons des Galapagos.*

44. Let us note that in his preface to *Two Years' Holiday,* Verne himself cites variants: Cooper's *The Crater, Le Robinson de douze ans, Le Robinson des glaces, Le Robinson des jeunes filles,* and so on.

45. Claude Lévi-Strauss, "The Structural Study of Myth," in *Structural Anthropology,* trans. Claire Jacobson and Brooke Grundfest Schoepf (New York: Basic Books, 1963), 210.

46. Here I am borrowing from the title of a book by David Riesmann, Nathan Glazer, and Reuel Denney, *The Lonely Crowd: A Study of the Changing American Character* (New Haven: Yale University Press, 1961).

47. See Sylvain Jouty, "Connaissance et symbolique de la montagne chez les érudits médiévaux," *Revue de Géographie Alpine* 79, no. 4 (1991): 21–34.

48. Jules Verne, *Le désert de glace,* in *Voyages et aventures du Capitaine Hatteras* (Paris: Hachette, 1966), 418.

49. Jonathan Swift, *Gulliver's Travels* (Oxford: Oxford University Press, 1999). Concerning this inversion, in which horses (the Houyhnhnms) lord it over men (the Yahoos), we can see here a prefiguration of the theme of Pierre Boulle's *Planet of the Apes,* trans. Xan Fielding (New York: Vanguard Press, 1963), a novel within which a new type of Robinson emerges: the victim of a shipwreck in space. This situation allows us to glimpse a variant of the robinsonnade in the field of science fiction. And anyone who has seen the film version of this novel (directed by Franklin Schaffner) knows that the story ends—by coincidence?—on a beach!

50. Joffre Dumazedier, *Toward a Society of Leisure,* trans. Stewart E. McClure (New York: Free Press, 1967), 31.

51. Morand, *Bains de mer,* 165.

52. Concerning this goddess, her saints, and her disciples, among the presumed heirs; there are, of course, polemics that find echoes in the discourses and practices of distinction. This "theological" debate is evoked in the epilogue to Urbain, *L'idiot du voyage,* 253–54.

53. From the Greek *kinéma,* "movement," from *kinein,* "to set in motion, move," and *philein,* "to love."

54. From the Greek *topos,* "place," and *philein.* I have borrowed this neologism from Gaston Bachelard, *The Poetics of Space,* trans. Maria Jolas (Boston: Beacon Press, 1969), 149.

55. Robert J. Fletcher, *Isles of Illusion: Letters from the South Seas,* ed.

Bohun Lynch (Boston: Small, Maynard and Co., 1923), 284; Alain Gerbault, *In Quest of the Sun* (London: Rupert Hart-Davis, 1955); Alain Gerbault, *Îles de beauté* (Paris: Gallimard, 1941), 216–17.

56. See Fitzgerald, *Tender Is the Night,* 3.

57. Morand, *Bains de mer,* 166.

58. See Urbain, *L'idiot du voyage,* chapter 4.

59. Morand, *Bains de mer,* 113.

60. Verne, *Two Years' Holiday,* 102.

PART I. THE ORIGIN OF BEACH MANNERS

1. Jean-Bernard Pouy, "Des symboles à la dérive," *Les vacances. Autrement* 111 (Jan. 1990): 106; Edward Sapir, "Speech as a Personality Trait," in *Selected Writings of Edward Sapir in Language, Culture, and Personality,* ed. David G. Mandelbaum (Berkeley: University of California Press, 1968), 533.

2. Georges Perec, "Approches de quoi?" in *L'Infra-Ordinaire* (Paris: Seuil, 1989), 11.

3. See, for example, Lévi-Strauss, *Tristes Tropiques,* 249.

4. Corbin, *Lure of the Sea,* 282.

5. Michel Marié and Jean Viard, *La campagne inventée* (Arles: Actes Sud, 1988); Philippe Joutard, *L'invention du mont Blanc* (Paris: Gallimard, 1986), 24.

6. Jules Michelet, *The Sea* (New York: Rudd and Carleton, 1861), 360.

7. Corbin, *Lure of the Sea,* 11.

8. Michelet, *The Sea,* 335.

9. Jean Delumeau, "Omniprésence de la peur," in *La peur en Occident (XIVe–XVIIe siècles): Une cité assiégée* (Paris: Fayard, 1978), 31–74. See Yvonne Bellenger, "Quelques relations de voyage vers l'Italie et vers l'Orient au XVIe siècle," in *Voyager à la Renaissance,* ed. Jean Céard and Jean-Claude Margolin (Paris: Maisonneuve et Larose, 1987), 456.

10. Delumeau, "Omniprésence de la peur," 31. "The Latins used to say: 'Praise the sea, but stay on shore.' A Russian saying advises: 'Praise the sea from your seat by the stove.'" Delumeau characterizes such sayings as "defensive reflex[es] of an essentially earthbound civilization" (ibid.).

11. Fernand Braudel, *The Identity of France,* vol. 1, *History and Environment,* trans. Siân Reynolds (London: Collins, 1988), 323.

12. Bernardin de Saint-Pierre, *Paul and Virginia;* Honoré de Balzac, "Un drame au bord de la mer," in *Oeuvres complètes,* vol. 2 (Paris: Club français du livre, 1962); Flaubert, *Voyage en Bretagne,* 135–37. On the theme of the coast as a space of clandestine trafficking, see John Meade Falkner's novel *Moonfleet* (London: Edward Arnold, 1898), and also Alain Cabantous, *Les côtes barbares* (Paris: Fayard, 1993).

13. See Rouillard, *Le site balnéaire,* 57; Jacques Lacarrière, *En cheminant avec Hérodote* (Paris: Seghers, 1981), 16–17; Flaubert, *Voyage en Bretagne,* 199–200.

14. See Urbain, "Les visiteurs des confins," chapter 10 of *L'idiot du voyage*.

15. Mme de Lalaing, *Les côtes de France de Saint-Nazaire à Biarritz par la plage* (Paris-Lille: J. Lefort, 1889), 18.

16. Corbin, *Lure of the Sea*, 52.

17. Ibid., 251.

18. Georges Cazes, Robert Lanquar, and Yves Raynouard, *L'aménagement touristique et le développement durable* (Paris: Presses Universitaires de France, 1990), 51.

19. Flaubert, *Voyage en Bretagne*, 138–39.

20. See Geneviève Heller, "Le tourisme sanitaire à l'origine de la propreté suisse?" *Urbi* 5 (1982): 80–86. See also Urbain, *L'idiot du voyage*, 29.

21. Perec, "Approches de quoi?" 11.

22. Gabriel Désert, *La vie quotidienne sur les plages normandes du Second Empire aux années folles* (Paris: Hachette, 1983), 10; Perec, "Approches de quoi?" 9.

23. Sylvia Ostrowetsky, "Dédale n'est pas Cronos et la rue ne marche pas," in *Espace & représentation* (Paris: Éditions de la Villette, 1982), 310.

24. Literally, "people who have little," i.e., the poor. See Pierre Sansot, *Les gens de peu* (Paris: Presses Universitaires de France, 1991).

1. The Death of the Fisherman

1. See Corbin, *Lure of the Sea*.

2. Bertail writes in *Les plages de France* that this "growing swell of travelers" will inevitably force the pioneer, "for fear of the crowd, to set up his tent on another beach." Cited by Rouillard, *Le site balnéaire*, 57.

3. Cited in Désert, *La vie quotidienne*, 17. According to Rémy Knafou, "the word 'discovery' is used here in a different context: it is not a matter of discovering the place itself but a different use for the place, and by people from the outside. That is why the term 'invention' is preferable to that of 'discovery' for a place that by definition was already known, if only to its own inhabitants; for the 'inventors' of a given spot succeeded both in proposing another reading . . . and in spreading that reading among their contemporaries" ("L'invention du lieu touristique: la passation d'un contrat et le surgissement simultané d'un nouveau territoire," *Revue de Géographie Alpine* 79, no. 4 [1991]: 15).

4. Rouillard, *Le site balnéaire*, 51.

5. Flaubert, *Voyage en Bretagne*, 238.

6. Cazes, Lanquar, and Raynouard, *L'aménagement touristique*, 52; emphasis added.

7. Flaubert, *Voyage en Bretagne*, 349: "There we chatted with an old sailor leaning on the parapet, who like us was smoking his pipe and digesting his meal."

8. Corbin, *Lure of the Sea*, 39.

9. Ibid., 353 n. 33; Corbin cites Philarète Chasles, "Scènes d'un village maritime en Angleterre" (1829), 82. Flaubert, *Voyage en Bretagne,* 40.

10. Lalaing, *Les côtes de France,* 185, 292; *Côte-d'Azur, Provence, Corse, Riviera italienne, Les Guides rouges* (Paris: Baneton-Thiolier, 1957), 14, 140.

11. Rouillard, *Le site balnéaire,* 57, 58. On this topic, Rouillard specifies that "the American analogy was so compelling that people went so far as to depict Indian tepees on maps of seaside cities as bathing cabins, lined up along the beach, with an Indian-style arrow pointing to the north; Celinski did this for Trouville, for example, and Leroux for Cabourg" (59).

12. The term *reduction* is to be understood here metaphorically as a reference to "physical reduction," or, if I may expand in turn on the Indian metaphor, as synonymous with "imprisonment," this time referring to the Spanish colonial *reducciones* in South America—centers where the indigenous population was rounded up under the direction of the Jesuits in Paraguay in the seventeenth and eighteenth centuries. For what happened to fishermen and other toilers of the sea is not unrelated to these other events (see below).

13. Joseph Morlent, *Guide du touriste au Havre et dans ses environs. Promenades,* cited in Rouillard, *Le site balnéaire,* 59.

14. Corbin, *Lure of the Sea,* 231.

15. Michelet, *The Sea,* 372.

16. See Corbin, *Lure of the Sea,* 367, n. 30. In *Le tourisme* (Paris: Seuil, 1982), Marc Boyer stresses that until 1890, between 85 percent and 95 percent of the winter residents in Nice, Menton, Cannes, or Hyères, were people with independent incomes; the remainder were a minority related by their social status to this aristocratic society (134).

17. See *Munch et la France* (Paris: Réunion des Musées nationaux, Munch et Spadem, Adagp, 1991), a collective work published for the exhibit by the same name at the Musée d'Orsay, 115. Max Gallo, *Le palais des fêtes,* the second volume of Gallo's *Nice trilogy* (the others being *La Baie des Anges* and *La Promenade des Anglais*), 527.

18. In this connection, see the reproductions in Philippe Jacquin, *Le goémonier* (Paris: Berger-Levrault, 1980).

19. I shall end this evocation of the theme in painting here, although I could have brought it up to date with, for example, Francis Tailleux, *Jeune fille sur la plage* (1946), Nicolas de Stael, *Le Fort d'Antibes* (1955), Salvador Dali, *La pêche au thon* (1966), Bernard Buffet, *Les plages* (1968), and so on.

20. Guy de Maupassant, *Pierre and Jean* (Westport, Conn.: Hyperion Press, 1978); Thomas Mann, *Death in Venice,* trans. H. T. Lowe-Porter (New York: Knopf, 1930); Fitzgerald, *Tender Is the Night.*

21. Gustave Flaubert, "A Simple Heart," in *Trois Contes* (Oxford: Oxford University Press, 1991); Maupassant, *Pierre and Jean,* 117; Fitzgerald, *Tender Is the Night,* 362.

22. Raymond Williams, "Pleasing Prospects," in *The Country and the City*

(New York: Oxford University Press, 1973), 125; Thorstein Veblen, *Theory of the Leisure Class* (New York: Penguin, 1979).

23. Ernest Hemingway, *The Old Man and the Sea* (New York: Scribner's, 1952), 139–40.

24. Michelet, *The Sea*, 385.

25. Corbin, *Lure of the Sea*, 264. But Île-Rousse, in Corsica, did not build its promenade until the 1980s—and even then it was merely a promenade, that is, a corridor for strolling parallel to the sea.

26. Lalaing, *Les côtes de France*, 71.

27. Cazes, Lanquar, and Raynouard, *L'aménagement touristique*, 53. If it were up to me, I would of course be inclined to speak of a "vacation" or "summering" zone.

28. The wall, as Abraham A. Moles and Elisabeth Rohmer rightly remind us, is "a condensation of distance to the extent that distance weakens, reduces, eliminates, prohibits, separates" (*Psychologie de l'espace* [Tournai: Casterman, 1972], 35).

29. Georg Hartwig, *Guide médical et topographique du baigneur à Ostende*, cited in Corbin, *Lure of the Sea*, 369 n. 111.

30. See Désert, *La vie quotidienne*, 169.

31. See "Règlement sur la récolte du goémon, art. 7," in Jacquin, *Le goémonier*, 40.

32. I shall return at greater length in part 3 to this point, which has to do with the legal definition of "beach society."

33. Let me make it clear that—after Alain Corbin (*Lure of the Sea*, 362 n. 18, and elsewhere)—I am not unaware that specialists in historical geography have analyzed the growth processes of seaside destinations, and in particular their topographical consequences in relation to the former fishing villages. But what interests me most especially here is not so much the process itself (or its stages) as its cultural significance: that toward which it seems to tend symbolically, when all is said and done. The outline of a phenomenology of the contemporary beach universe, and thus the identification of the anthropological function of today's seaside vacations, depend on the interpretation of this process.

34. Marjorie Alessandrini, "Terre de soleil. Sur les routes du Sud, jusqu'à l'extrême pointe de l'Europe," supplement, *Le Nouvel Observateur* 1435 (May 7–13, 1992): xviii.

35. See Dean MacCannell, *The Tourist: A New Theory of the Leisure Class* (New York: Schocken Books, 1989), 42–46. MacCannell distinguishes the following five stages of sight sacralization: naming (initial recognition), framing and elevation (boundary-setting and display), enshrinement (protection), mechanical reproduction (postcards, trinkets), and social reproduction (fame, notoriety).

36. Cazes, Lanquar, and Raynouard, *L'aménagement touristique*, 55. In this connection, it is important to note that 50 percent of the clientele at the

seaside consists in return visitors, as opposed to 30 percent in the country and only 15 percent in the mountains, according to Bernard Préel, based on a survey of 3,000 individuals conducted by the Bureau d'information et de prévisions économiques (BIPE), Commissariat au plan, Paris, 1990.

37. Sylvie Laloux, "67 Français 'moyens' à l'épreuve de leurs photographies de vacances: pratiques et représentations," master's thesis, Université François-Rabelais, Tours, 1987.

38. I shall address the issue of pleasure boating later on. Still, let us note here that during recent demonstrations by Breton fishermen, one way in which they chose to manifest their anger was precisely by blocking yachting ports—an eminently symbolic clash between the worlds of work and leisure, production and consumption.

39. I would of course prefer to use the term *vacationers* or *summer residents* here.

40. Yvette Barbaza, *Le paysage humain de la Costa Brava* (Paris: Armand Colin, 1966), 486.

41. Maupassant, "Épaves" (1881), in *Contes et nouvelles*, 1:324; Lalaing, *Les côtes de France*, 296ff.

42. Barbaza, *Le paysage humain*, 485.

43. Ibid., 486, 491.

44. In this connection, Michel Marié writes: "Tourism enters the local vocabulary on a massive scale in the toponymy of places: Artignosc-sur-Verdon, Fréjus-sur-Mer even before 1936" (Michel Marié and Christian Tamisier, *Un territoire sans nom* [Paris: Méridiens-Klincksieck, 1982], 107). More recently, and for the same reasons, we may recall the transformation of the Côtes-du-Nord region into the Côtes-d'Armor. Toponymic adjustments are a form of "pacification," in this instance of the shore, which thus collaborates symbolically in its own way, as painting does, with the "desavaging" process.

45. Barbaza, *Le paysage humain*, 565.

46. Ibid., 486.

47. Roger Vailland, "Saint-Tropez," *Europe* 712–13 (Aug.–Sept. 1988): 86–87.

48. Ibid., 87.

49. Morand, *Bains de mer*, 112.

50. In this connection, see Jean-Luc Hennig, *Les garçons de passe. Enquête sur la prostitution masculine* (Paris: Éditions libres-Hallier, 1978).

51. This is what the poor fisherman-guide does, for example, in Balzac's "Un drame au bord de la mer." See also Émile Souvestre's short story, "Le traîneur de grèves," mentioned in Corbin, *Lure of the Sea*, 232.

52. Related by André Thouin, *Voyage dans la Belgique, la Hollande et l'Italie*, cited in Corbin, *Lure of the Sea*, 39.

53. Louis Bertrand, *Le mirage oriental* (1910), cited by Jean-Claude Berchet, *Le voyage en Orient. Anthologie des voyageurs français dans le Levant au XIXe siècle* (Paris: Robert Laffont, 1985), 78.

54. Désert, *La vie quotidienne,* 16.

55. Barbaza, *Le paysage humain,* 565. Nevertheless, we should recall here that in Diane Kurys's autobiographical film *La Baule-les-Pins,* which depicts vacations in the 1950s, the proprietor and his wife lived in the basement while the tenants were in residence.

56. Désert, *La vie quotidienne,* 171. The same point of view had been expressed earlier in Biarritz. See Claude Bailhé and Paul Charpentier, *La côte atlantique de Biarritz à La Rochelle au temps des guides baigneurs* (Toulouse: Éditions Milan, 1983), 35.

57. Cazes, *Le tourisme en France,* 70. The outsized port of Saint-Quay-Portrieux in Brittany is one example. See "L'état des côtes en France," *Ça m'intéresse* 136 (June 1992): 32. On the theme of the shoreline's "disfigurement," of which the pleasure port is only one aspect, see below, part 2.

58. In 1989 the number of jobs directly related to pleasure boating was estimated at 13,000, and the number of indirectly related jobs at 20,000. These figures, announced by the French Fédération des industries nautiques, are found in *Tourisme, Marketing et Communication* 18 (April 1991): 17.

59. See Roland Barthes, "Myth Today," in *Mythologies,* selected and translated by Annette Lavers (New York: Hill and Wang, 1972), 123.

60. The lover of heights, the Robinson of the peaks, is excluded from this category of vacationer. See above, introduction.

61. A dream that the "real" or "deep" rural universe has precisely the reputation of realizing. See Urbain, "Les visiteurs des confins," 158ff.

62. This is the case with Deauville, as noted above. But many other seaside situations in Europe are similar in origin and concept: Cabourg in France, Knokke-le-Zoute in Belgium, Zandvoort in Holland, Scarborough and Bournemouth in England, Viareggio and Rimini in Italy. See Cazes, Lanquar, and Raynouard, *L'aménagement touristique,* 54.

63. In this connection, see Bernard Lerivray, *Guides bleus, guides verts et lunettes roses* (Paris: Éditions du Cerf, 1975).

64. Vailland, "Saint-Tropez," 87.

65. Lalaing, *Les côtes de France,* 249. In France, 400 museums are under construction, or have been completed, since the early 1980s. See the report by M. Guerrin and E. de Roux, "La fièvre des musées," *Le Monde* (March 1993).

66. Arlette Farge, *Le goût de l'archive* (Paris: Seuil, 1989), 145.

67. Lodge, *Paradise News,* 110.

68. Henri Bolland, *Excursions en France* (Paris: Hachette, 1909), 286, 328.

69. See E. André, Pierre Tardivon, and Christophe Kervran, *Étude qualitative de la demande française et européenne pour le littoral français* (Paris: HTL-Conseil, 1989), 108–10.

70. Désert, *La vie quotidienne,* 184 (note): "If one maintains good relations with the local fishing experts, it is still possible [in the 1860s] to go off on an ocean fishing expedition in their company." For the eighteenth century, see also Corbin, *Lure of the Sea,* 39.

71. From a report broadcast by Antenne 2 on the evening news, July 12, 1992.

72. In connection with this quote and the two preceding ones, see Michel de Certeau, "Les revenants de la ville," *Traverses* 40 (April 1987): 74–85.

73. *Parcours* (the magazine of the French airline Air Inter) 59 (July–Aug. 1992): 98–99.

74. This corresponds to the fourth of the five stages of sacralization included in MacCannell's typology in *The Tourist*.

75. See Richard Matheson, *I Am Legend* (New York: Walker, 1970), and *The Shrinking Man* (Cutchogue, N.Y.: Buccaneer Books, 1962).

2. THE BIRTH OF THE BATHER

1. Antoine Blondin, "Les sports d'hiver: une page blanche que l'on peut remplir à sa fantaisie," in *Voyages,* ed. J.-P. Caracalla (Paris: Olivier Orban, 1981), 53.

2. Yves Lacoste, "A quoi sert le paysage?" *Hérodote* 7 (1977): 26.

3. See Corbin, *Lure of the Sea,* 262.

4. Lacoste, "A quoi sert le paysage?" 27.

5. After Pierre Daninos, who invented "touristocrats" in 1974, I am allowing myself this neologism, soon to be followed by another, both derived along the same lines from the Greek *kratos,* "power."

6. See Urbain, "Les explorateurs du réticulaire," chapter 9 of *L'idiot du voyage,* 138–39, 146.

7. Corbin, *Lure of the Sea,* 37.

8. Ibid., 263.

9. Mme de Sévigné, letter to Mme de Grignan, May 28, 1676, in *Letters of Madame de Sévigné to Her Daughter and Her Friends,* ed. Richard Aldington (New York: E. P. Dutton, 1937), 1:219–20.

10. Cited by Philippe Perrot, *Le corps féminin. Le travail des apparences (XVIIIe–XIXe siècles)* (Paris: Seuil, 1984), 20. Concerning this complex relation to water and baths, see Georges Vigarello, *Concepts of Cleanliness: Changing Attitudes in France since the Middle Ages,* trans. Jean Birrell (Cambridge: Cambridge University Press, 1988), 173–76.

11. Michelet, *The Sea,* 334–35, 369.

12. Louis Garneray, *Voyage pittoresque et maritime sur les côtes de la France,* cited in Corbin, *Lure of the Sea,* viii, and illustrations 5–7. In some places, such as Arcachon, horse-drawn bathing cabins were also available.

13. See Rouillard, *Le site balnéaire,* 83.

14. Dr. Constantin James, *Guide pratique des eaux minérales françaises et étrangères* (Paris: Victor Masson, 1861), 413–28.

15. In reference to hot springs, see Armand Wallon, *La vie quotidienne dans les villes d'eaux (1850–1914)* (Paris: Hachette, 1981).

16. Corbin, *Lure of the Sea,* 273.

17. Bernardin de Saint-Pierre, *Paul and Virginia*, 62. (The word *quelque-fois*, "sometimes," appears in the original French text.—Trans.)

18. Morand, *Bains de mer*, 37, 30–31.

19. See Defoe, *Robinson Crusoe*, 108–11; Corbin, *Lure of the Sea*, 53.

20. Ernest Ameline, *Une plage normande, Villers-sur-Mer: Poème humor-istique* (1882), cited in Rouillard, *Le site balnéaire*, 138.

21. Désert, *La vie quotidienne*, 16.

22. Flaubert, *Voyage en Bretagne*, 328.

23. Cited in Barbaza, *Le paysage humain*, 566 (emphasis added).

24. See Lalaing, *Les côtes de France*, 186.

25. We must remember that for more than three-quarters of a century doctors advised patients to go to the sea. Thus it is not astonishing that, with rare exceptions, the establishments later called hydrotherapeutic should be the first buildings on beaches as soon as these began to be visited regularly (Désert, *La vie quotidienne*, 165).

26. Corbin, *Lure of the Sea*, 282.

27. Morand, *Bains de mer*, 32.

28. Euripides, *Iphigenia in Tauris*, ed. and trans. M. J. Cropp (Warmin-ster, England: Aris and Phillips, 2000), 149, line 1193.

29. Jacques-Bernard Renaudie, *La thalassothérapie* (Paris: Presses Uni-versitaires de France, 1984), 8.

30. Dr. Richard Russell, *A Dissertation on the Use of Sea Water in the Dis-eases of the Glands* (London, 1752).

31. James, *Guide pratique*, 6.

32. "Among the individuals who take a bath with no other need but caprice, it relaxes the parts that should not be relaxed and causes them to lose their tonus": Joseph Morin, *Manuel théorique et pratique d'hygiène;* "Too many baths are overstimulating, especially when the baths are somewhat hot": François Foy, *Manuel d'hygiène;* "Bathing is an immoral practice. Un-happy experience has taught us of the moral dangers of spending an hour naked in a bathtub": meeting of the Central Council of Health of Nantes in 1852, cited in Vigarello, *Concepts of Cleanliness*, 174.

33. James, *Guide pratique*, 428.

34. Corbin, *Lure of the Sea*, 57; James, *Guide pratique*; Michelet, *The Sea*, 369–70, 341; Désert, *La vie quotidienne*, 181.

35. See Jean Chevalier and Alain Gheerbrant, "Bath," in *A Dictionary of Symbols*, trans. John Buchanan-Brown (London: Penguin, 1996), 72–74.

36. James, *Guide pratique*, 421.

37. Cited in Lalaing, *Les côtes de France*, 186.

38. V. Raymond, *Manuel des baigneurs* (Paris: Desloges, 1840), 88.

39. James, *Guide pratique*, 425.

40. The list of diseases treated is too long to be reproduced in full here, as is the list of the various uses to which sea water could be put—not only in

baths, half-baths, foot baths, cold, warm, or hot baths and seaweed baths, but also as a lotion, a drink, an enema, or a vaginal-uterine douche.

41. Cited in Désert, *La vie quotidienne,* 20, 19.

42. A venerable euphemistic definition of ejaculation.

43. The first "true" center of thalassotherapy, according to Renaudie, was established in Roscoff in 1899 (*La thalassothérapie,* 10).

44. This was an entirely new edition with a supplement by Dr. Burnier.

45. Fitzgerald, *Tender Is the Night,* 3–4.

46. *Larousse médical illustré,* ed. Dr. Galtier-Boissière (Paris: Librairie Larousse, 1929), 739; James, *Guide pratique,* 413; Michelet, *The Sea,* 330.

47. Corbin, *Lure of the Sea,* 36.

48. Dr. James, whose reticence concerning the abuse of bathing we have already noted, writes the following: "Take a few steps in the water with [children], then get out at once and go back in again; soon what seemed terrifying to them will become on the contrary a distraction and a game" (*Guide pratique,* 425).

49. Lalaing, *Les côtes de France,* 298.

50. Michelet, *The Sea,* 369.

51. Francis Ponge, "Seashores," in *The Voice of Things,* ed. and trans. Beth Archer (New York: McGraw-Hill, 1972), 47.

52. Blondin, "Sports d'hiver," 54.

53. Désert, *La vie quotidienne,* 169.

54. Dr. Viaud-Grand-Marais, *Guide du voyageur à Noirmoutier,* 9th ed. (Fontenay-le-Comte: Lussaud, 1927), 107. "It is appropriate to bathe only the day after arriving," *Manuel du baigneur 1897,* cited in Bailhé and Charpentier, *La côte atlantique,* 39.

55. V. Raymond, *Traité de natation* (Paris: Desloges, 1840), 104; cited in Bailhé and Charpentier, *La côte atlantique,* 35; Morand, *Bains de mer,* 56; Liselotte, *Le guide des convenances. Savoir-vivre, obligations sociales, usages* (Paris: Société du petit écho de la mode, 1931), 352.

56. Daniel Pennac, in Robert Doisneau and Daniel Pennac, *Les grandes vacances* (Paris: Hoêbeke, 1991), 60.

57. In other words, drowning, which was evoked in these terms in the 1929 *Larousse médical illustré,* 814. The 36 percent who do not know how to swim are distributed as follows: 25 percent of the men surveyed and 46 percent of the women, 22 percent of the Parisians and 40 percent of the provincials, 56 percent of the farmers, 55 percent of people aged 45 or older. See Guy Mermet, *Francoscopie 1993* (Paris: Larousse, 1992), 406.

58. Claude Fischler, *L'homnivore: Le goût, la cuisine, le corps* (Paris: Jacob, 1990), 301.

59. On the subject of this ambivalence toward the sea, see Gaston Bachelard, *Water and Dreams: An Essay on the Imagination of Matter,* trans. Edith R. Farrell (Dallas: Pegasus Foundation, 1983), 159–85.

60. See Renaudie, *La thalassothérapie*, 9–11.

61. See Michel Foucault, *The Use of Pleasure*, vol. 2 of *The History of Sexuality*, trans. Robert Hurley (New York: Pantheon Books, 1985), and Foucault, *Discipline and Punish: The Birth of the Prison*, trans. Alan Sheridan (New York: Pantheon, 1977), esp. chapter 3, part 1, "Docile Bodies" 134–69. The principles of control at issue are the following: the use of time, the temporal development of the act, the establishment of a correlation between body and gesture, the articulation between body and object, and exhaustive use. These disciplinary principles are easily identified in the medical theory of sea bathing in the nineteenth century.

62. Fischler, *L'homnivore*, 305.

63. We shall return to these encodings and the ritual dimensions of beach conviviality: their deciphering and interpretation are at the heart of this study.

64. Michelet, *The Sea*, 371.

65. Jacques Lacan, "Dieu et la jouissance de la femme," in *Livre XX: Encore* (Paris: Seuil, 1975), 70.

66. According to the 1878 *Guide Joanne*, the two Zephyrs, father and son, of Étretat are "the most cooperative and the most courageous of the entire Normandy coast." Cited in Désert, *La vie quotidienne*, 170.

67. Cited in Barbaza, *Le paysage humain*, 566–67.

68. Defoe, *Robinson Crusoe*, 40.

69. Cited in Désert, *La vie quotidienne*, 175.

70. André, Tardivon, and Kervran, *Étude qualitative*, 135; Morand, *Bains de mer*, 34.

71. Corbin, *Lure of the Sea*, 272.

72. Here I am borrowing a concept of which historians of mentalities such as Philippe Ariès are quite fond.

73. As Bachelard wrote in *Water and Dreams:* "A leap into the unknown is a leap into water. It is the first leap of the novice swimmer. When an expression as abstract as 'leap into the unknown' is found to be motivated only by one real experience, it is obvious evidence of its psychological importance" (165).

3. The Era of Scandals

1. Flaubert, *Voyage en Bretagne*, 329.

2. Light verse of unknown origin from 1878, cited by Désert, *La vie quotidienne*, 177.

3. I am alluding here to Erving Goffman, *The Presentation of Self in Everyday Life* (Garden City, N.Y.: Doubleday Anchor Books, 1959).

4. See Désert, *La vie quotidienne*, 172; Corbin, *Lure of the Sea*, 279.

5. In Dieppe, for instance, in the 1920s, an Englishwoman who went from the casino to the Hotel Royal in her bathing suit was arrested and had

to pay a fine of 1000 francs! The anecdote is related by Désert, *La vie quotidienne*, 173.

6. See Corbin, *Lure of the Sea*, 369 n. 109.

7. Michelet, *The Sea*, 370.

8. Désert, *La vie quotidienne*, 173; Morand, *Bains de mer*, 56–57.

9. Morand, *Bains de mer*, 55.

10. See Jean Chevalier and Alain Gheerbrant, "Nakedness," in *A Dictionary of Symbols*, 691–93.

11. Désert, *La vie quotidienne*, 176.

12. Général Matton, "Juan-les-Pins," in *Par la Provence à la Côte d'Azur* (Nice: L'Éclaireur de Nice, 1933), 43–44.

13. Cited in Désert, *La vie quotidienne*, 20, 176.

14. Raymond, *Traité de natation*, 120–21.

15. Mentioned in Désert, *La vie quotidienne*, 177.

16. In *Histoire de la pudeur* (Paris: Olivier Orban, 1986), Jean-Claude Bologne writes: "When the Christian religion made modesty the duty of fallen man, nudity became heretical" (339).

17. See Morand, *Bains de mer*, 56; Dr. Jules Le Coeur, *Des bains de mer. Guide médical et hygiénique du baigneur* (Paris: Labé, 1846); Désert, *La vie quotidienne*, 177; and Michel Pastoureau, *The Devil's Cloth: A History of Stripes and Striped Fabric*, trans. Jody Golding (New York: Columbia University Press, 2001), 71–74.

18. In fact, according to Désert, under the July monarchy, hatmakers in Caen had already begun to manufacture "bathing shorts/vests," one-piece body suits that men began to use but that were not recommended for women, whose shape they "revealed a bit too much" (*La vie quotidienne*, 56).

19. Morand, *Bains de mer*, 56; Désert, *La vie quotidienne*, 179.

20. Liselotte, *Le guide des convenances*, 132.

21. See "Soleil et sable fin," *Modes de Paris* 712, no. 3 (1962): 50–51.

22. Morand, *Bains de mer*, 55, 56; Désert, *La vie quotidienne*, 177.

23. Désert, *La vie quotidienne*, 177; Morand, *Bains de mer*, 56.

24. Barthes, *Fashion System*, 20.

25. Pastoureau, *Devil's Cloth*, 72. This is an essential aspect of the dramaturgy of the beach; we shall return to it throughout the remainder of this study.

26. Désert, *La vie quotidienne*, 177.

27. Flaubert, letter to Louise Colet, Aug. 14, 1854; Désert, *La vie quotidienne*, 179.

28. In 1906, on the initiative of Richard Ungewitter, the first real nudist camp was created in Germany, after which the movement underwent continuous development in France as well as elsewhere in Europe. See Bologne, *Histoire de la pudeur*, 341.

29. Roger Salardenne, *Un mois chez les nudistes* (Paris: Éditions Prima, 1930), 165.

30. See Bologne, *Histoire de la pudeur,* 341. In fact, only after 1968 have certain local municipal decrees allowed nudists to occupy specified beaches without having to protect themselves with palisade fencing. See ibid. Nevertheless, in addition to stripes on bathing suits, other "palisades" of an ideological sort are still in place. I shall return to them, for, in its alternation between hatred and scorn, nudist "hunting" has not run its course even today.

31. These Wandervögel were also pioneers in forest hiking; the vast majority belonged to the Hitler Youth movement and later subscribed to Nazism. See Urbain, *L'idiot du voyage,* 190.

32. Cited by Salardenne, *Un mois chez les nudistes,* 183.

33. Jacques Laurent, *Le nu vêtu et dévêtu* (Paris: Gallimard, 1979), 180. This fanatical nudism, in the manifest forms of physical culture and other bodybuilding movements, but also in the more diffuse forms of a certain ordinary "fascism" (dietetics, sporting, or "aesthetic"), has not run its course either. I shall return to this topic as well.

34. I ask indulgence for a personal memory in the form of a quasi-confession: I remember from my own investigations that the only media windows that permitted glimpses of nude bodies in the late 1950s and early 1960s were nudist books and magazines placed on upper shelves in bookstores and newsstands.

35. Cited by Salardenne, *Un mois chez les nudistes,* 176–77.

36. Dr. Pierre Vachet, *La nudité et la physiologie sexuelle* (Paris: M. K. de Mongeot, 1928), cited in Louis-Charles Royer, *Let's Go Naked,* trans. Paul Quiltana (New York: Brentano's, 1932), 16–17; Salardenne, *Un mois chez les nudistes,* 159. Roger Salardenne is also the author of *Le culte de la nudité* (1929) and *Le nu intégral chez les nudistes français* (1931).

37. Royer, *Let's Go Naked,* 14; Salardenne, *Un mois chez les nudistes,* 7.

38. Salardenne, *Un mois chez les nudistes,* 8.

39. From an article entitled "Héliotherapie" in the 1900 *Nouveau Larousse illustré,* vol. 5: "The disinfectant power of the sun's rays has been known since the remotest times. This property is due to the action of the rays on microbes. Thus anthrax bacteria are destroyed by thirty hours of exposure to the sun; Koch's bacillae (tuberculosis) and Loeffler's (diphtheria) are considerably weakened."

40. Jean Viard, *Penser les vacances* (Arles: Actes Sud, 1984), 177.

41. Salardenne thus warmly evokes the memory of this pioneer of tanning, in *Un mois chez les nudistes,* 183.

42. See Bologne, *Histoire de la pudeur,* 341; Morand, *Bains de mer,* 110.

43. Désert, *La vie quotidienne,* 182.

44. Philippe Perrot, *Le corps féminin,* 145, 49. In the nineteenth century, remedies for tanned skin included washing one's face with chicken blood or applying thin slices of raw beef.

45. Michelet, *The Sea,* 345.

46. See Désert, *La vie quotidienne,* 174.

47. See Alain Ehrenberg, "Le Club Méditerranée, 1935–1960," *Les Vacances. Autrement* 111 (Jan. 1990): 118–19; emphasis added.

48. A great deal has already been said on this subject. See in particular Christiane Peyre and Yves Raynouard, *Histoires et légendes du Club Méditerranée* (Paris: Seuil, 1971); a well-known article by Henri Raymond, "Une utopie concrète: recherche sur un village de vacances," *Revue française de sociologie* 3 (1960): 325; the recent article cited above by Ehrenberg; and Alain Laurent, *Libérer les vacances?* (Paris: Seuil, 1973) (part 3 of Laurent's book is a monograph devoted to the Club Med in Cefalù, Sicily). I shall thus not linger further over the details of the club's chronology or its international expansion.

49. With more than 110 villages at the end of the 1980s, established in three major vacation basins: the Mediterranean, the Meso-American, and the Asian-Pacific. These villages include roughly 70,000 beds, four subsidiaries (Club Med, Valtur, Club Aquarius, and Maeva), and more than two million clients. In this connection, see Cazes, *Fondements pour une géographie du tourisme;* and by the same author, *Le tourisme international. Mirage ou stratégie d'avenir?* (Paris: Hachette, 1989).

50. Peyre and Raynouard, *Histoires et légendes,* 85.

51. Rouillard showed this clearly in *Le site balnéaire,* 157ff.

52. Morand, *Bains de mer,* 59.

53. "In use, the huts turn out to be ideal: they are better ventilated than tents, and the odiferous, living rustle of the air through the woven straw puts you in harmony with nature much better than tents do"; Peyre and Raynouard, *Histoires et légendes,* 85.

54. Ehrenberg, "Le Club Méditerranée," 126.

55. Morand, *Bains de mers,* 125, 136.

56. Paul Bénichou, cited by Charles Forrester, "Histoires de Saint-Tropez," *Vogue Hommes* (July–Aug. 1992): 58.

57. F. Giraud, cited in ibid., 64.

58. S. Bromberger, "Antibes et ses huttes polynésiennes pour milliardaires blasés," *Le Figaro* (Aug. 1, 1951): 1, 8.

59. Philippe Ariès, *Le temps de l'histoire,* preface by Roger Chartier (Paris: Seuil, 1986), 106.

60. The latter presupposes a reference to the land and to rusticity—a reference that is broadly nourished by the symbolics of "rural tourism" and by "green" vacations in the country or the mountains.

61. In 1989 5.3 percent of the French spent their summer vacations in a vacation village; 5 percent in 1990, and 4.6 percent in 1991, according to *Mémento du tourisme,* 118.

62. Ehrenberg, "Le Club Méditerranée," 119–20.

63. Ibid., 124.

64. Denis Diderot, *The Nun,* trans. Marianne Sinclair (London: New English Library, 1966), 136.

PART II. AT THE BEACH

1. André Gide, *The Journals of André Gide*, vol. 3, *1928–1939*, trans. Justin O'Brien (New York: Knopf, 1949), 128.

2. Defoe, *Robinson Crusoe*, 54.

3. Corbin, *Lure of the Sea*, 15.

4. See above, chapter 2, on the repression of the hedonist pioneers of sea bathing.

5. Ehrenberg, "Le Club Méditerranée," 126.

6. A recent story, the "minimalist" evolution of dress tells the tale beautifully, recapitulating the vicissitudes of the integration of the new seaside universe to the old.

7. Children, innocent vectors of fashion, were in fact extremely useful in introducing nudity and fanciful clothing on beaches. We shall return to this point (see below, chapter 8).

8. Viard, *Penser les vacances*, 177.

4. THE DREAM OF THE SHORE

1. Lodge, *Paradise News*, 192.

2. See Nelson H. H. Graburn, "Tourism: The Sacred Journey," in Valene L. Smith, *Hosts and Guests: The Anthropology of Tourism* (Philadelphia: University of Pennsylvania Press, 1977), 17–31 (a revised version is found in the 1989 edition, 21–36). The first detailed critical presentation of this typology is found in Urbain, *L'idiot du voyage*, at the beginning of chapter 7.

3. See Hubert Macé, "Les vacances passives. L'accès à la villégiature balnéaire," *Communications* 10 (1967): 20–24.

4. Viard, *Penser les vacances*, 176.

5. Viaud-Grand-Marais, *Guide du voyageur à Noirmoutier*, 105.

6. Corbin, *Lure of the Sea*, 258; Morand, *Bains de mer*, 158; Barbaza, *Le paysage humain*, 572.

7. Barbaza, *Le paysage humain*, 572.

8. See Corbin, *Lure of the Sea*, 263; Morand, *Bains de mer*, 143.

9. Michel Tournier, "The Taciturn Lovers," in *The Midnight Love Feast*, trans. Barbara Wright (London: Collins, 1991), 14.

10. Elliott Erwitt, *Elliott Erwitt—On the Beach* (New York: Norton, 1991), 29; James, *Guide pratique*, 421.

11. See Sansot, *Les gens de peu*, 8.

12. Lalaing, *Les côtes de France*, 245.

13. *Côte de l'Atlantique de la Loire aux Pyrénées*, Guide vert Michelin, 2nd ed. (1965), 245.

14. *Larousse médical illustré*, 740; Viard, *Penser les vacances*, 177.

15. A study by Studienkreis für Tourismus (Starnberg, 1990) reveals that, for German vacationers, among factors leading to a negative evaluation of a

site, seaweed appears in fourth position, after garbage, dirty beaches, and poor water quality, and ahead of tar-polluted sand, dead birds, and noisy boats.

16. Pierre Jakez Hélias, "Le pain de la mer," introduction to Jacquin, *Le goémonier,* 9.

17. Not to mention the "return" of seaweed in nutritional, therapeutic, and cosmetic forms, as a vegetable, medicine, or beauty product.

18. René Richard and Camille Bartoli, *La Côte d'Azur assassinée* (Paris: Roudil, 1971), 37.

19. Let us note that even those who seek to reconcile wildness with comfort anticipate, among other improvements, the removal of "dangerous" stones—a project for "cleaning" beaches that can of course be compared to the removal of seaweed. See ibid., 36.

20. "The hotel and its bright tan prayer rug of a beach were one," Fitzgerald wrote on the first page of *Tender Is the Night,* 3.

21. Jean-Luc Michaud, editor of *Tourismes, chance pour l'économie, risque pour les sociétés* (Paris: Presses Universitaires de France, 1993), interviewed by *Le Nouvel Observateur,* "Le vacancier est devenu zappeur," 51.

22. Lalaing, *Les côtes de France,* 138.

23. Désert, *La vie quotidienne,* 7.

24. *Contrée de rêve:* let us note that *contrée* is the first meaning given in the Littré dictionary for the word *plage* (beach). Its common meaning today appears only in third and last place.

25. Pierre Daninos, *Major W. Marmaduke Thompson Lives in France* (London: Jonathan Cape, 1955), 173.

26. Christian Giudicelli, *Station balnéaire* (Paris: Gallimard, 1986).

27. Ibid., 80.

28. Ibid., 127.

29. Robert Louis Stevenson, *The Ebb-Tide: A Trio and a Quartette,* ed. Peter Hinchcliffe and Catherine Kerrigan (Edinburgh: Edinburgh University Press, 1995), 68.

30. "Sand not only flows, but this very flow *is* the sand"; Kobo Abe, *The Woman in the Dunes,* trans. E. Dale Saunders (New York: Knopf, 1964), 99.

31. Bachelard, *Water and Dreams,* 47; Jack London, "The Water Baby," in *Short Stories of Jack London,* ed. Earle Labor, Robert C. Leitz III, and I. Milo Shepard (New York: Macmillan, 1990), 714.

32. Poem by Cowper, cited in Morand, *Bains de mer,* 39.

33. Jean Chevalier and Alain Gheerbrant, "Bath," in Chevalier and Gheerbrant, *Dictionary of Symbols,* 72–73. See below, chapter 9.

34. Monique Lange, *The Bathing Huts,* trans. Barbara Beaumont (London: Marion Boyars, 1986), 31.

35. Morand, *Bains de mer,* 13.

36. Albert Camus, *The Stranger,* trans. Matthew Ward (New York: Vintage International, 1989), 58.

37. William Boyd, *Brazzaville Beach* (London: Sinclair-Stevenson, 1990), xi.

38. Lodge, *Paradise News*, 85.

39. Georges Brassens, "Supplique pour être enterré à la plage de Sète" (Phillips, 1966).

40. Bachelard, *Water and Dreams*, 83.

41. See Arnold Van Gennep, *The Rites of Passage*, trans. Monika B. Vizedom and Gabrielle L. Caffee (Chicago: University of Chicago Press, 1960).

42. Chevalier and Gheerbrant, "Baptism," in Chevalier and Gheerbrant, *Dictionary of Symbols*, 68.

43. In this connection, see Dr. James's discourse on "reaction" in *Guide pratique*, 423.

44. Michelet, *The Sea*, 345; René Quinton, *L'eau de mer, milieu organique* (1904). Cf. Renaudie, *La thalassothérapie*, 10.

45. Désert, *La vie quotidienne*, 19.

46. On this subject, see Alain Laurent, "Le thème du soleil dans la publicité des organismes de vacances," *Vacances et tourisme. Communications* 10 (1967): 35–50.

47. Cited by Salardenne, *Un mois chez les nudistes*, 180.

48. Lange, *Bathing Huts*, 31.

49. Général Matton, "Bronzage," in *Par la Provence à la Côte d'Azur*, 116.

50. "Cet été en vacances," *Santé Magazine* 201 (Sept. 1992): 28ff.

51. This time a couple is featured, also laughing, "surprised" upon emerging from the water (*Top Santé* 22 [July 1992]: 12ff.).

52. Morand, *Bains de mer*, 13, 14.

53. Michelet, *The Sea*, 370.

54. Etienne Jauffret, *Au pays bleu. Roman d'une vie d'enfant*, an elementary school textbook (Paris: Belin, 1941), 77.

55. According to the legend of Endymion, a handsome young shepherd, Zeus promised to grant him a wish. "[Endymion] chose the gift of eternal sleep, and fell asleep, remaining young forever." See Pierre Grimal, *Dictionary of Classical Mythology*, trans. A. R. Maxwell-Hyslop (Oxford: Blackwell, 1986), 145–46.

56. "Madrid," in *Diario de Ibiza* (Sept. 6, 1969). See also *La voix du Nord* (Aug. 5, 1972), cited by Rozenberg, *Tourisme et utopie*, 15–16.

57. Lodge, *Paradise News*, 142.

58. The magazine *Elle* applied this label to the hippies of Ibiza (July 10, 1972). Cf. Rozenberg, *Tourisme et utopie*, 15.

59. From Peslages, the population that preceded the Hellenic settlements on both shores of the Aegean sea.

60. Pennac, in Doisneau and Pennac, *Les grandes vacances*, 60.

61. In this connection, see Michel Maffesoli's "Le rhythme social," in *La transfiguration du politique* (Paris: Grasset, 1992), 181ff.

62. Peyre and Raynouard, *Histoire et légendes*, 22.

63. Gall, *La vie sexuelle de Robinson Crusoé*, 19.

64. See Urbain, *L'idiot du voyage*, 170.

65. Boyd, *Brazzaville Beach,* 260–61.

66. Pouy, "Des symboles à la dérive," 106.

67. Peyre and Raynouard, *Histoire et légendes,* 36.

68. It is the opening sentence in Urbain, *L'idiot du voyage.*

69. Peyre and Raynouard, *Histoire et légendes,* 60.

70. Wittmer, *Les Robinsons de Galapagos,* 362.

71. Peyre and Raynouard, *Histoire et légendes,* 39.

72. Erwitt, *Elliott Erwitt,* 13.

73. Laurent, "Thème du soleil," 48.

74. See Urbain, *L'idiot du voyage,* 107ff.

75. Louis Marin, "L'effet Sharawadgi ou le jardin de Julie," in *Jardins contre nature. Traverses* 5–6 (Oct. 1976): 127.

76. Italo Calvino, *Mr. Palomar,* trans. William Weaver (San Diego: Harcourt Brace Jovanovich, 1985), 29.

77. See Yves Luginbuhl, in "Désir de rivage," *Atelier du Conservatoire du littoral* 3 (Oct. 1993): 7.

78. Patrick Süskind, *Perfume: The Story of a Murderer,* trans. John E. Woods (New York: Knopf, 1986), 121.

79. Ehrenberg, "Le Club Méditerranée," 123.

80. André, Tardivon, and Kervran, *Étude qualitative,* 81.

81. Verne, *Le désert de glace,* 419.

82. Linda Chase, *Hyperrealism* (New York: Rizzoli, 1975), 71.

83. Balzac, "Un drame au bord de la mer," 694.

84. "I took refuge under a glass bell, I could see everything, hear everything around me, but nothing had gotten through to me"; Michael Pollack, *L'expérience concentrationnaire* (Paris: Métailié, 1990).

85. Elias Canetti, *Crowds and Power,* trans. Carol Stewart (New York: Viking Press, 1963), 345–46.

86. Stevenson, *The Ebb-Tide,* 100.

5. The Overcrowded Desert

1. Bernard Pouy, "Des symboles à la dérive," 106.

2. Cf. Macé, "Les vacances passives."

3. Fitzgerald, *Tender Is the Night,* 12. "They just stick around with each other in little cliques," she says of the summer beach people.

4. See Urbain, "Portraits du touriste en chien triste," part 1 of *L'idiot du voyage.*

5. Maupassant, *Pierre and Jean,* 115–16.

6. Jean-René Huguenin, *The Other Side of the Summer,* trans. Richard Howard (New York: G. Braziller, 1961), 44.

7. See Urbain, *L'idiot du voyage,* 37ff.

8. Dr. Georges Gaubert, *Un canoë passe . . .* (Paris: Stock, 1934), 155.

9. Morand, *Bains de mer,* 105–6.

10. Cited in Enzenberger, "Eine Theorie des Tourismus," 182–83. See also Urbain, *L'idiot du voyage*, 40.

11. Corbin, *Lure of the Sea*, 279. "Several works of fiction and fragments of diary writing illustrate the growing diatribe against the changes in this form of leisure." The author cites Jane Austen (1817), William Cobbett (1822), John Constable (1824), Charles Dickens ("The Tuggses at Ramsgate," 1836), and, in France, Henri Monnier and Eugène Labiche (Corbin, *Lure of the Sea*, 279–80). On the same subject, see above, part 1, for an evocation of the critical attitudes of writers such as Flaubert and Michelet.

12. Perrot, *Le corps féminin*, 263, n. 41; Jules and Edmond Goncourt, *Journal des Goncourt: Mémoires de la vie littéraire*, vol. 6. (Paris: E. Fasquelle, 1894–1908), cited in ibid.

13. Morand, *Bains de mer*, 67.

14. Claude Farrère, *Une jeune fille voyagea* . . . (Paris: Flammarion, 1925), 20–21.

15. Charles de Secondat, Baron de Montesquieu, *The Spirit of Laws*, trans. Thomas Nugent, Great Books of the Western World 38 (Chicago: Encyclopedia Britannica, 1952), 102–3.

16. Anne de Mishaegen, *Dans la forêt canadienne* (Brussels: La Renaissance du livre, 1946), 18.

17. Lévi-Strauss, *Tristes Tropiques*, 339, 338.

18. Morand, *Bains de mer*, 166, 167.

19. Philippe Simonnot, *Ne m'appelez plus France* (Paris: Olivier Orban, 1991), 213.

20. Serre, *Les vacances*.

21. Morand, *Bains de mer*, 107.

22. Lodge, *Paradise News*, 73.

23. "L'état des côtes de France"; "SOS Bretagne," *L'événement du jeudi* (Sept. 5–11, 1991): 141–45; "Opération spéciale: sauvons la pointe du Raz," *Le Point* 977 (June 10–16, 1991).

24. Opinion survey by SOFRES-Le Point, carried out May 3–6, 1991, using a representative sample of 1,000 people at least eighteen years old. The total percentage is greater than 100 percent, since the respondents could give more than one answer.

25. See "Le littoral a atteint la cote d'alerte," *Que Choisir* 296 (July–Aug. 1993): 34ff.

26. Lodge, *Paradise News*, 63.

27. Serre, *Les vacances*.

28. Calvino, *Mr. Palomar*, 17.

29. Pierre Ziegelmeyer, "Objectif vacances," in *Bonnes vacances*, ed. René Durand (Paris: Le Dernier Terrain Vague, 1978), 30.

30. Théodore Monod, *Plongées profondes: Bathyfolages* (Arles: Terres d'Aventure-Actes Sud, 1991), 182.

31. Caroline Brizard, "Méditerranée, le cancer vert," interview with Charles-François Boudouresque, *Le Nouvel Observateur* (Dec. 1991–Jan. 1992): 60.

32. Morand, *Bains de mer*, 28.

33. Paul Léautaud, *Villégiature* (Paris: Mercure de France, 1986), 27.

34. Lodge, *Paradise News*, 4–5.

35. Michelet, *The Sea*, 372–73.

36. Morand, *Bains de mer*, 66.

37. Frédéric Vitoux, "Deux femmes," in *Riviera* (Paris: Seuil, 1987), 155–56.

38. Laurence Sterne, *A Sentimental Journey through France and Italy* (New York: Knopf, 1925), 16. See also Urbain, *L'idiot du voyage*, 28.

39. Reiser, *Ils sont moches* (Paris: Éditions du Square, 1980), 4–5.

40. Olivier Burgelin, "Le touriste jugé," *Vacances et tourisme. Communications* 10 (1967): 78; Urbain, *L'idiot du voyage*, 202.

41. Léautaud, *Villégiature*, 26; Tournier, "The Taciturn Lovers," 14.

42. Cited by M. Tricot, "Les 'salopards' en vacances (II)," in *L'Humanité* (July 3, 1979): 9.

43. *Dictionnaire Hachette de la langue française* (Paris: Hachette, 1980), 332.

44. Pierre-Marie Doutrelant, "Le Touquet des quatre saisons," *Le Nouvel Observateur* 816 (June 28–July 4, 1980): 38–39; Pennac, in Doisneau and Pennac, *Les grandes vacances*, 60; Morand, *Bains de mer*, 140.

45. *Modes de Paris* 1285 (August 1973): 38.

46. Christopher Frank, *L'année des méduses* (Paris: Seuil, 1884).

47. Boyd, *Brazzaville Beach*, 260.

48. In this connection, see Françoise Cribier, *La grande migration d'été des citadins en France* (Paris: Centre national de la recherche scientifique, 1969).

49. Paul Theroux, *The Old Patagonian Express: By Train Through the Americas* (Boston: Houghton Mifflin, 1979), 69.

50. Hemingway, *The Old Man and the Sea*, 139.

51. B. Giansetto, "Le sable des plages passé au crible," *Top-santé* 23 (Aug. 1992): 79; "Où se baigner en Europe?" *Que choisir* 237 (March 1988): 36–46; Lodge, *Paradise News*, 143.

52. A. Herbeth, "La machine à laver les plages," *Tourisme, Marketing and Communication* 6 (Sept. 1990): 31–32.

53. "Opération plage propre. Une initiative d'estivants," in *Corse-Matin* (Aug. 22, 1992).

6. BORDERLAND

1. Braudel, *Identity of France*, 1:15: "For I am determined to talk about France as if it were another country, another fatherland, another nation: 'to observe France' as Charles Péguy said, 'as if one were no part of it.'"

2. Anne Philippe, *Un été près de la mer* (Paris: Gallimard, 1977), 64–65.

3. Léon-Paul Fargues, cited in Morand, *Bains de mer*, 138.

4. Benigno Cacérès, *Loisirs et travail du Moyen Age à nos jours* (Paris: Seuil 1973), 189–90; Borie, preface to Michelet, *La mer,* 23; Michelet, *The Sea,* 337.

5. Barthes, "Myth Today," in *Mythologies,* 143.

6. Advertisements: "L'Espagne, une passion: la vie!" Spanish Tourist Bureau, May 1992; "Jersey. L'oasis du charme," Island of Jersey Tourist Bureau, March 1991; "Ile de la Réunion, Ile intense," Réunion Tourist Board, May 1992.

7. Michelet, *The Sea,* 340.

8. *La perception du littoral par les touristes français (été 1992), Les Cahiers de l'observatoire* 25 (Ministry of Development, Transportation and Tourism, 1993), 3; Cazes, *Le tourisme en France,* 68.

9. For these statistics see Cazes, Lanquar, and Raynouard, *L'aménagement touristique,* 48–50.

10. "L'état des côtes de France," 32; "Plages mode d'emploi," *Que choisir?* 34; Cazes, Lanquar, and Raynouard, *L'aménagement touristique,* 69.

11. Report broadcast on Antenne 2 during the 1:00 p.m. television news, Aug. 20, 1992; Cazes, *Le tourisme en France,* 73.

12. According to a comment made by D. Charpentier, director of the CRT Riviera-Côte d'Azur, during a conference titled "Le tourisme international entre tradition et modernité," Nice, November 1992.

13. *La perception du littoral:* results and analyses established on the basis of a survey undertaken by SOFRES on 898 questionnaires from a representative sample of 1,000 individuals. 4–5 nights, 94.2 percent satisfaction; 1–2 weeks, 94.5 percent; 2–3 weeks, 96.3 percent; 34 weeks, 98 percent; 1 month or more, 98.8 percent (p. 55).

14. Boyd, *Brazzaville Beach,* 287.

15. André, Tardivon, and Kervran, *Étude qualitative,* 94.

16. On the distinction between experimental and initiatory, see above, introduction, and Urbain, *L'idiot du voyage,* 231ff.

17. *La perception du littoral,* 30; Morand, *Bains de mer,* 105.

18. André, Tardivon, and Kervran, *Étude qualitative,* 81.

19. See *La perception du littoral,* 68. Only nine elements were retained in this study: from most to least important, they are cleanliness, beauty, tranquility, the price/quality relation, lodging, services, transportation, sports and cultural activities, and entertainment.

20. Ibid., 56; Morand, *Bains de mer,* 131; Vitoux, "Avanti!" in *Riviera,* 23.

21. See *La perception du littoral,* 24.

22. Defoe, *Robinson Crusoe,* 54; Maffesoli, *Time of the Tribes,* 79. See also Edgar Allen Poe, "The Man of the Crowd," in *Collected Works of Edgar Allan Poe,* ed. Thomas Ollive Mabbott (Cambridge: Belknap Press of Harvard University Press, 1978), 2:505–18.

23. Edward T. Hall, *The Hidden Dimension* (Garden City, N.Y.: Anchor Books/Doubleday, 1969), 171–73.

24. Phyllis Passariello, "Never on Sunday? Mexican Tourists at the Beach," *Annals of Tourism Research* 10 (1983): 109–22.

25. Perrot, *Le corps féminin*, 206. This paradox was formulated by Arthur Schopenhauer and cited by Guy Benamozig in "Enfermement et psychose," Ph.D. diss., Paris V-Sorbonne, 1992, 186.

26. Roland Barthes, "L'usager de la grève," in *Mythologies* (Paris: Seuil, 1957), 153. (This essay is not included in the Lavers translation cited above.—Trans.) Let us note an amusing coincidence: while Barthes is not speaking of the same thing at all, since in his article he uses the word *grève* in the sense of "strike" ("a work stoppage organized by salaried workers in defense of common interests" [*Dictionnaire Hachette*, 1980]), his reflection nevertheless applies to our object, *grève* in its second meaning, "shore." But the French terms for "strike" and "beach" in fact have a common origin: the Place de Grève beside the Seine in Paris was both a shore and a gathering place for workers waiting to be hired ("Grève," in Rey, ed., *Dictionnaire historique*, 918).

27. Gilles Bonnot, "Savons-nous partir?" *Le Nouvel Observateur* (Aug. 2, 1980): 40–41; Defoe, *Robinson Crusoe*, 108–11.

28. André, Tardivon, and Kervran, *Étude qualitative*, 101.

29. See *La perception du littoral*, 39.

30. Advertisement, "Spain, a passion: life," Spanish National Tourist Office, April 1993.

31. Ibid.

32. Vitoux, "L'incendiaire," in *Riviera*, 85.

33. Vacation literature and reading practices would warrant an in-depth study of their own.

34. As Rachid Amirou has emphasized, in *Imaginaire touristique et sociabilités du voyage* (Paris: Presses Universitaires de France, 2000). According to a survey conducted by Ipsos-Télérama-France Culture in July 1992, of 1,000 respondents, 63 percent asserted that they took advantage of summer vacations to watch television less (*Télérama*, July 1992, 8).

35. Patrick Francès, "Faut-il tuer les touristes?" *Les Vacances. Autrement* 111 (Jan. 1990): 72.

36. See in this regard Michel Tournier's Robinson in *Friday*. This Robinson takes his island the way a man takes a woman. Moreover, he finds that his island has a female form, and he names it Speranza.

37. Benamozig, "Enfermement et psychose," 171: "In order to break this terrifying silence, as we have been told by all these imprisoned or encapsulated beings, traces of the world one has known, the world in which people talk to one another, have to be preserved."

38. Michel Maffesoli, *The Contemplation of the World: Figures of Community Style*, trans. Susan Emanuel (Minneapolis: University of Minneapolis Press, 1996), 43; Macé, "Les vacances passives."

39. Enzensberger, "Eine Theorie des Tourismus"; cf. above, introduction.

40. Raymond Radiguet, *Le diable au corps* (Paris: B. Grasset, 1923).

41. Lévi-Strauss, *Tristes Tropiques*, 317.

42. To borrow the interpretation proposed by Amirou in *Imaginaire*

touristique to characterize vacation strategies of isolation. As for the notion of "full fortress," it is of course an allusion to Bruno Bettelheim's "empty fortress"; *The Empty Fortress: Infantile Autism and the Birth of the Self* (New York: Free Press, 1967).

43. Vitoux, "Les deux Paris-Match," in *Riviera*, 59.

44. Alessandrini, "Terre de soleil," xviii.

45. Alain Ehrenberg, "C'est au Club et c'est nulle part ailleurs: Essai dur la société décontractée," *Le Débat* 34 (March 1985): 130–45.

46. See in this connection Danielle Léger and Bernard Hervieu, *Le retour à la nature* (Paris: Seuil, 1979).

47. See Urbain, *L'idiot du voyage*, 94–95; Ehrenberg, "C'est au Club," 142.

48. In *La nudité humaine* (Paris: Fayard, 1973), Jean Brun writes: "At various moments in Western history revolutionary movements appeared that were characterized by the following program: a desire to rediscover original nudity, a rejection of the environment . . ." (125).

49. Lacoste, "A quoi sert le paysage?" 27.

50. See Corbin, *Lure of the Sea*, 265.

51. Liselotte, *Le guide des convenances*, 341.

52. Lalaing, *Les côtes de France*, 9.

53. Désert, *La vie quotidienne*, 174: "Thus no beaches without cabins. No cabins without peepholes, one might add. Those of Yport, in any case, are renowned for their peepholes 'clustered at the height of the bust and the pelvis.' Curiosity was not limited to Yport. In 1926, part of the 'advice to swimmers' was the following: 'In the cabin, watch out for indiscreet onlookers. When you have taken off your shirt, use it to block the keyhole.' All times and all places have had their voyeurs"—some more audacious than others.

54. Matton, "Juan-les-Pins," 43.

55. Barbaza, *Le paysage humain*, 567.

56. In this connection, see Régis Franc, *Le café de la plage*, 2 vols. (Bondy: Les BD du matin, 1982), a remarkable Proustian seaside saga.

57. Cited in Bailhé and Charpentier, *La côte atlantique*, 34.

58. Claude Nori, "Rimini, août 92," in Gilles Mora and Claude Nori, *L'été dernier. Manifeste photobiographique* (Paris: Éditions de l'Étoile, 1983); Bernard Descamps, *Balnéaires* (Amiens: Trois Cailloux, 1985); Erwitt, *Elliott Erwitt*.

59. Jean-Pierre Dupuy, "Le signe et l'envie," in Paul Dumouchel and Jean-Pierre Dupuy, *L'enfer des choses: René Girard et la logique de l'économie* (Paris: Seuil, 1979), 43.

PART III. IN THE LAND OF NAKED MEN

1. Claude Lévi-Strauss, "Introduction: History and Anthropology," in *Structural Anthropology*, trans. Jacobson and Schoepf, 18.

2. Ibid., 18–19.

3. Morand, *Bains de mer,* 100; Edgar Morin, *Journal de Californie* (Paris: Seuil, 1983), 115.

4. Krzystof Pomian, interview in *Libération* (July 13, 1990): 26.

5. Cf. Marc Laplante, "La révolution du voyage d'agrément," *Loisir et sociétés* 11, no. 1 (1988).

6. Lévi-Strauss, "Introduction," 18. From an institutional viewpoint, the beach, a public domain, has become considerably more complicated in France over the years. Its formal complexity is now managed jointly by local mayors, commissioners of the Republic, and prefects of the maritime departments. Mayors, responsible for safety on beaches and swimming sites developed for public use, are charged with designating access channels for sailboards and unlicensed craft (pedalboats, canoes, etc.). They must also delimit zones reserved for swimming and those closed to all nautical sports, and they are responsible for the overall supervision of beaches and marinas. Commissioners named by the central government are in charge of supervising land use and water quality. Finally, prefects define access channels for waterskiing, motor boats, and yachts, as well as zones of navigation closed to motor boats and sea-going boats, zones generally beginning 300 meters from shore.

7. Louis-Jean Calvet, *Les jeux de la société* (Paris: Payot, 1978), 220.

8. Émile Durkheim, *The Elementary Forms of Religious Life,* trans. Daren E. Fields (New York: Free Press, 1995), 38.

9. Viard, *Penser les vacances,* 175.

10. Peyre and Raynouard, *Histoire et légendes,* 125.

11. We may recall that in *To Catch a Thief,* a 1955 film by Alfred Hitchcock shot on the Riviera, Cary Grant gets away from the police by taking off his street clothes and mingling with the crowd of swimmers.

12. Verne, *Two Years' Holiday,* 1:146.

13. See Peyre and Raynouard, *Histoire et légendes,* 60, 103, and elsewhere.

14. Margaret Mead, *From the South Seas: Studies of Adolescence and Sex in Primitive Societies* (New York: Morrow, 1939), 14.

15. In this connection, see Désert, *La vie quotidienne,* 174.

7. Tribes and Territories

1. Alain Souchon and Laurent Voulzy, *Le soleil donne* (Paris: Éditions Laurent Voulzy, 1988).

2. Royer, *Let's Go Naked,* 33.

3. Peyre and Raynouard, *Histoire et légendes,* 64.

4. Erwitt, *Elliott Erwitt,* 12; Joël Bonnemaison, "Les voyages et l'enracinement: Formes de fixation et de mobilité dans les sociétés traditionnelles des Nouvelles-Hébrides," *L'espace géographique* 8, no. 4 (1979): 306.

5. Claude Lévi-Strauss, *Structural Anthropology,* vol. 2, trans. Monique Layton (New York: Basic Books, 1976), 329. (A close parenthesis omitted in the 1976 translation has been restored.—Trans.)

6. Bruckner and Finkielkraut, *Au coin de la rue, l'aventure*, 55; Peyre and Raynouard, *Histoire et légendes*, 11. The idea of "mini-socialism" seems to be almost synonymous with that of a robinsonnade, according to Marx.

7. The French word *plagiaire*, "plagiarist," which comes from *plage*, "beach," according to the 1973 *Petit Robert Dictionary*, is thought to derive from the Greek root *plagios*, meaning "oblique, deceitful."

8. See Corbin, *Lure of the Sea*, and, more recently, *Désir de rivage. Des nouvelles représentations aux nouveaux usagers du littoral* (Ateliers du Conservatoire du littoral, 1993). See also above, chapter 1.

9. "Souvenir d'Alger," *L'événement du jeudi* (March 5–11, 1992): 59.

10. See Corbin, *Lure of the Sea*, 277.

11. The practice of commercial adjudication on beaches is not new. In *La vie quotidienne*, Désert reports that in Houlgate, a lease awarded in 1900 and renewed in 1908 "grants a Parisian proprietor the right to exploit 220 meters of beach for an annual sum of 305 francs. The limits will be marked 'perpendicular to the shore, by ropes strung at high tide and loosened at low tide . . .' In exchange for the obligations imposed on him, the adjudicator may collect an annual fee of 10 francs per square meter on the various shelters that private parties may erect in the part that has been rented to them" (p. 168).

12. In 1981, Louis Le Pensec, Minister of Maritime Affairs, ordered the destruction of fences on private beaches in order to make them public.

13. Charles Dickens, "The Tuggses at Ramsgate," cited in Corbin, *Lure of the Sea*, 278, 317.

14. Erwitt, *Elliott Erwitt*, 20; "Les états d'Étretat," a report broadcast on FR3 on Sept. 8, 1991, as part of the "Estivales" program.

15. See *La perception du littoral*, 14.

16. André, Tardivon, and Kervran, *Étude qualitative*, 83.

17. Morand, *Bains de mer*, 89.

18. Claude Soula, "'Club Med': le soleil quand même!" *Le Nouvel Observateur* (Jan. 2–8, 1992): 49.

19. "Histoires de Saint-Tropez," *Vogue-Hommes*, 65.

20. By municipal decree, for reasons of hygiene and safety, dogs are more and more often banned from developed beaches.

21. This seasonal countermigration is strongly encouraged by economic factors. See Jean-Didier Urbain, "Les vacanciers des équinoxes," *Le continent gris. Communications* 37 (1983): 137–48.

22. The national average of vacationers under age fifty-five on the coast during summer 1992 was 76.5 percent. On the Atlantic coast, those under thirty-five reached 45.3 percent, and those under fifty-five constituted nearly 80 percent. The best-represented age group is from thirty-five to forty-four, with 23 percent as opposed to 22.6 percent for ages twenty-five to thirty-four and 19.5 percent for ages fifteen to twenty-four. The "oldest" coasts are those of the English Channel and Brittany, with people fifty-five and older rep-

resenting respectively 28.2 percent and 30.3 percent of vacationers—while the national average for this age group is 31.2 percent. See *La perception du littoral*, 7–10.

23. Cf. the comment by Lévi-Strauss cited above in n. 5.

24. A division that paralleled a social discrimination, moreover. See above, chapter 3.

25. Erwitt, *Elliott Erwitt*, 12.

26. "Le tour de France des plages chaudes," special report, *VSD* 725 (July 1991): 25–35.

27. Concerning this normative appreciation of tourists, see Urbain, *L'idiot du voyage*, chapter 5.

28. "Vacances: le classement des stations françaises," *L'Express* 1614 (June 18, 1982): 74.

29. Morand, *Bains de mer*, 65.

30. Fitzgerald, *Tender Is the Night*, 6.

31. Irene Pennacchioni has already done this successfully in describing marital relations, in *De la guerre conjugale* (Paris: Mazarine, 1986).

32. Désert, *La vie quotidienne*, 168.

33. Georges Perec, *Tentative d'épuisement d'un lieu parisien* (Paris: Union Générale d'Éditions, 1975).

34. "'Critical distance' encompasses the narrow zone separating flight distance from attack distance" (Hall, *Hidden Dimension*, 12).

35. Reported in "Vacances: le classement des stations françaises," 114.

36. Hall, *Hidden Dimension*, 113–29. What is important here is not the precision of these figures, which vary from culture to culture, but rather the idea that there exists a universal overlapping of spheres of relationship.

37. I am again borrowing terms from Hall (ibid., 108).

38. *La perception du littoral*, 7–9; Macé, "Les vacances passives," 22.

39. "In fact we have every theoretical reason to suppose that from the beginning human groups have given their spatial establishments a set of meanings and attributions connected with a set of social and symbolic practices and representations"; Françoise Paul-Lévy and Marion Segaud, *Anthropologie de l'espace* (Paris: Centre Georges Pompidou/Centre de création industrielle, 1983), 28.

40. Peter Benchley, *Jaws* (New York: Doubleday, 1974), 198.

41. Fitzgerald, *Tender Is the Night*, 6, 19; Wyss, *Swiss Family Robinson*. The Robinson of this novel is a father who, after saving his family from a shipwreck, gives his children sound practical lessons in homemaking and craftsmanship.

42. An attribute André Gide ascribes to families in *The Fruits of the Earth*, trans. Dorothy Bussy (New York: Knopf, 1952), 68.

43. According to Macé, "Les vacances passives."

44. Émile Durkheim, in *The Rules of Sociological Method*, trans. Sarah A. Solovay and John H. Muelle, ed. George E. G. Catlin (Chicago: University of

334 / Notes to Chapter 7

Chicago Press, 1938), 82–83, says that the horde is "a social aggregate which does not include, and has never included within itself any other more elementary aggregate, but is directly composed of individuals . . . in atomic juxtaposition."

45. A reference to Erving Goffman, who contrasts "focused" and "unfocused interaction" in *Behavior in Public Places: Notes on the Social Organization of Gatherings* (New York: Free Press, 1963), 24.

46. "When Claude Lévi-Strauss notes that Salesian missionaries had only to bring about the spatial transfer of the Bororo from their circular villages to a village built on the European model to get the Bororo to give up their vision of the world and convert to Christianity [in *Tristes Tropiques*, 220–21], he makes it necessary to recognize that *spatial organizations are guarantors of social and cultural identity, and ensure its reproduction*" (Paul-Lévy and Segaud, *Anthropologie de l'espace*, 29; emphasis added).

47. Viard, *Penser les vacances*, 178; Corbin, *Lure of the Sea*, 253.

48. See Erving Goffman, *Relations in Public: Microstudies of the Public Order* (New York: Basic Books, 1971), 49–58; Bachelard, *Poetics of Space*, 37.

49. Bachelard, *Poetics of Space*, 32; Daniel Pennac, *Comme un roman* (Paris: Gallimard, 1992), 57.

50. Quotations are from Laloux, "67 Français," interviews 5 and 7.

51. Viard, *Penser les vacances*, 178.

52. Erwitt, *Elliott Erwitt*, 24.

53. Passariello, "Never on Sunday?"

54. See Van Gennep, *Rites of Passage*.

55. According to surveys carried out by the Centre de recherche pour l'étude et l'observation des conditions de vie (Credoc), to the statement "the family is the only place where I feel good and can relax," the proportion of positive reactions by the French went from 61 percent in 1982 to 69 percent in 1991. As for divorce, the rise was steep: France saw 30,000 divorces in 1960, 104,000 in 1990. These results are reprinted in Mermet, *Francoscopie 1993*, 126, 141. For its part, Villages Vacances Familles (VVF) noted during roughly the same period a sharp increase in single-parent families, families extended to include grandparents, and "even couples or single people searching for a familial ambiance" (in *Bonheur*, a magazine published by the Caisse d'allocations familiales [February 1992]: 22).

56. See Raymond Boudon, *Effets pervers et ordre social* (Paris: Presses Universitaires de France, 1977).

57. According to *La perception du littoral*, 51.

58. Let us recall here the meaning of the French word *endémisme:* "The fact, for a living species, of having a distribution limited to a very specific region." *Endémie* comes from the Greek *endêmon (nosema)*, "indigenous (illness)," according to the entry "épidémie," *Dictionnaire Hachette de la langue française*, 552.

59. Fitzgerald, *Tender Is the Night*, 3.

60. François Truffaut, letter to Marcel Moussy, in *Correspondance,* ed. G. Jacob and Cl. Givray (Paris: Hatier, 1988), 148.

61. These are just a few names of hotels and boardinghouses mentioned in *Le Pouliguen: sa plage, son bois, son port, sa côte,* a guidebook published by the syndicat d'initiative in Le Pouliguen in 1936.

62. Roland Barthes, "The Nautilus and the Drunken Boat," in *Mythologies,* 66.

63. Ehrenberg, "Le Club Méditerranée," 122; Peyre and Raynouard, *Histoire et légendes,* 95–96. In 1955, Gilbert Trigano explained: "We chose to make a clean break in order to appeal to couples and families. Initially, children under the age of ten were not admitted. Now, children less than one year old can come for free."

64. See Laurent, *Libérer les vacances?* 147; Peyre and Raynouard, *Histoire et légendes,* 36.

65. Raymond, "Une utopie concrète," 325.

66. See François Lourbet, *Le chef de village* (Paris: Balland, 1975). Lourbet recounts life in the village of Agadir during a two-week period.

67. Rackam, "Le cul-cul-club," 127.

68. Gall, *La vie sexuelle de Robinson Crusoé;* Umberto Eco, "Un art d'oublier est-il concevable?" *Théâtres de la mémoire. Traverses* 40 (April 1987): 124–35.

69. Lalaing, *Les côtes de France,* 246; See Marc Augé, *Domaines et châteaux* (Paris: Seuil, 1989), 126ff.

70. Rouillard, *Le site balnéaire,* 302; Roland Barthes, "'Blue-Blood' Cruise," in *Mythologies,* 33.

71. Enid Blyton, *Five Go Down to the Sea* (1955; Chicago: Reilly and Lee, 1961), 40.

72. Ponge, "Notes for a Shell," in *The Voice of Things,* 60. See also Baudry de Saunier, Charles Dollfus, and Edgar de Geoffroy, *Histoire de la locomotion terrestre* (Paris: L'Illustration, 1936), 417; here we learn that camping, considered exclusively as a form of "sporting tourism" at the time, saw purist campers deny the label "camping" to those who did not sleep on the ground; the latter were engaged in "caravaning," "a sport that only retains the outward appearance of sport." (The term *caravanage* is used in French today.)

73. See Cazes, *Le tourisme en France,* 73; *Mémento du tourisme* (Paris: Observatoire national du tourisme, August 1992), 118.

74. The term *cabanisme* was used by Guy Premel and Bernard Kalaora in the summary of the introductory report of the Atelier du conservatoire du littoral, 4.

75. Bruckner and Finkielkraut, *Au coin de la rue,* 40; cited in Boyer, *Le tourisme,* 234–35; Sansot, *Les gens de peu,* 220.

76. Sansot, *Les gens de peu,* 167. To get an idea of the atmosphere of these "trailer parks," see *Week-end ou la qualité de la vie,* a documentary film made by P. Manuel and Jean-Jacques Péché in 1972 that offers a humorous recounting

of a Belgian family's brief stay in the Fabiola camp, near Blankenberghe (film broadcast on Arte, on the "Grand Format" program, Feb. 26, 1994).

77. Augé, *Domaines et châteaux*, 141. See also Defoe, *Robinson Crusoe*: "This Fence was so strong, that neither Man nor Beast could get into it or over it: This cost me a great deal of Time and Labour, especially to cut the Piles in the Woods, bring them to the place, and drive them into the Earth . . . and so I was compleatly fenced in . . . and consequently slept secure in the Night, which otherwise I could not have done, tho, as it appear'd afterward, there was no need of all this Caution" (49).

78. "When we think we have found the meaning of a word or an idea, it is because we grasp a multiplicity of equivalences in different realms. And the justification results in the final analysis from all these equivalences" (Claude Lévi-Strauss, interview with Didier Eribon, *Le Nouvel Observateur* 1092 [Oct. 1985]: 72–73).

79. An observation made by Frédéric Vitoux about vacation villas, in "Deux Femmes," in *Riviera*, 155. He adds that these are "houses without souls, without a past, without madness or memory."

80. See Sansot, *Les gens de peu*, 173; André, Tardivon, and Kervran, *Étude qualitative*, 96.

8. BEACH SOCIETY

1. "Like language, the social *is* an automonous reality (the same one, moreover)," as Claude Lévi-Strauss says in *Introduction to Marcel Mauss*, 37.

2. Viard, *Penser les vacances*, 31.

3. I am referring here to Norbert Elias, *The Court Society*, trans. Edmund Jephcott (1969; New York: Pantheon Books, 1983).

4. Simonnot, *Ne m'appelez plus France*, 199–200.

5. Defoe, *Robinson Crusoe*, 162–63.

6. In *The System of Objects*, trans. James Benedict (London: Verso, 1996), Jean Baudrillard writes: "it . . . cannot be denied that even superficial differences are real as soon as someone invests them with value" (153). The same holds true for equalities, however epidermic they may be.

7. Bertail, *La vie hors de chez soi*, cited by Rouillard in *Le site balnéaire*, 277.

8. In *La vie quotidienne*, Désert writes: "Bathing requires that one undress, décence oblige, away from the public eye" (172). The same requirement applied in Spain in the late nineteenth century. See above, chapter 2, and Barbaza, *Le paysage humain*, 467.

9. Laurent, *Le nu vêtu et dévêtu*, 18.

10. See Roland Barthes, "Histoire et sociologie du vêtement," *Les Annales* (1957): 430–41; Peyre and Raynouard, *Histoire et légendes*, 223.

11. Goffman, *Behavior in Public Places*, 34; Morand, *Bains de mer*, 120.

12. Laurent, *Le nu vêtu et dévêtu*, 183.

13. Cacérès, *Loisirs et travail*, 189; Morand, *Bains de mer*, 149.

14. Pastoureau, *Devil's Cloth*, 74; Laurent, *Le nu vêtu et dévêtu*, 51–52.

15. Technical details are given in Françoise Vincent-Ricard, *Les objets de la mode* (Paris: Éditions Du May, 1989), 28.

16. Pennac, in Doisneau and Pennac, *Les grandes vacances*, 73.

17. Laurent, *Le nu vêtu et dévêtu*, 52.

18. Vachet, *La nudité*, 9.

19. This is the category of games of simulation ("mimicry"), as opposed to competitive play ("agôn"), games of chance ("alea"), and play based on vertigo ("ilinx"). See Roger Caillois, *Man, Play, and Games,* trans. Meyer Barash (New York: Free Press of Glencoe, 1961).

20. Vachet, *La nudité*, 5.

21. See Carl Gustav Jung, "The Psychology of the Child Archetype," in Carl Gustav Jung and Karl Kerényi, *Essays on a Science of Mythology: The Myth of the Divine Child and the Mysteries of Eleusis,* trans. R. F. C. Hull (Princeton, N.J.: Princeton University Press, 1971), 97, 96. On the subject of dolphins, see below, chapter 9.

22. This is how the father was dressed in Laurent's *Le nu vêtu et dévêtu,* 15. These signs were in fact given up only gradually, and fairly late. Pastoureau notes this in relation to navy blue stripes, which were initially a sign of the high seas, then transformed into a sign of the seaside, then of sports and leisure; in the nineteenth century, these stripes invaded all sorts of beach objects (bathing suits, towels, umbrellas, windbreakers, tents, chairs, balls, bags, and so on); "[w]e must wait until the seventies, even the eighties, for the phenomenon to begin to slow down and then to decline" (*Devil's Cloth,* 73). Similarly, some borrowings from local dress have been forgotten, like the "kabig, the dress of seaweed harvesters of Kerlouan," adopted by summer residents around 1939, according to Jacquin, *Le goémonier,* 56. But isn't the fact that the borrowing was forgotten precisely what is significant, in that it reveals the abandonment of a reference?

23. Laurent, *Le nu vêtu et dévêtu*, 176.

24. Erwitt, *Elliott Erwitt,* 20; Perrot, *Le corps féminin,* 205.

25. Ziegelmeyer, "Objectif vacances," 32; Perrot, *Le corps féminin,* 206.

26. Morand, *Bains de mer,* 168; Laurent, *Le nu vêtu et dévêtu,* 176; Perrot, *Le corps féminin,* 92.

27. "Pour hâler bien," *Vogue-Hommes* 151 (July–August 1992); the "Practical Beauty" column in *Vogue-Beauté* 656 (April 1992): 42 (emphasis added).

28. "Practical Beauty" column.

29. *Elle* 2481 (July 19, 1993), 46; *Nous Deux* 516 (April 1957): 46.

30. Marie de Saint-Ursin, cited in Perrot, *Le corps féminin,* 151; V. Leca, in *L'almanach du viveur,* cited in Perrot, *Le corps féminin,* 151–53.

31. Catherine Carlson, *L'amour, ça fait pas grossir: Lettre aux femmes ou à ce qu'il en reste* (Paris: Régine Deforges, 1991), 66; from the Christian Dior advertising campaign of 1992–93.

32. Eugène Chapus, *Manuel de l'homme et de la femme comme il faut* (Paris: M. Lévy, 1862), 63; Laurent, *Le nu vêtu et dévêtu,* 143.

33. See in this connection Alain Rey and Sophie Chantreau, *Dictionnaire des expressions et locutions* (Paris: Le Robert, 1987), under the heading "Nature": "Parties sexuelles" and "Instinct sexuel."

34. Perrot, *Le corps féminin,* 151.

35. Jean Baudrillard, *Symbolic Exchange and Death,* trans. Ian Hamilton Grant (London: Sage Publications, 1993), 105.

36. In this connection see Johan Huizinga, *Homo Ludens: A Study of the Play-Element in Culture* (1939; Boston: Beacon Press, 1950), chapter 1. As for the distinction between simulacrum and simulation, Jean Baudrillard cites an entry from the Littré dictionary: "Whoever fakes an illness can simply stay in bed and make everyone believe he is ill. Whoever simulates an illness produces in himself some of the symptoms" (*Simulacra and Simulations,* trans. Sheila Faria Glaser [Ann Arbor: University of Michigan Press, 1994], 3).

37. Chevalier and Gheerbrant, "Hair," in *A Dictionary of Symbols,* 463. Here viewers may recall the character of Jérôme, played by Christian Clavier in *Les Bronzés,* a film by Patrice Leconte, a veritable caricature of this sort of hairy ostentation.

38. Huizinga, *Homo Ludens,* 11.

39. William Sansom, *A Contest of Ladies,* 230–32, cited in Goffman, *Presentation of Self in Everyday Life,* 4–5.

40. Fitzgerald, *Tender Is the Night,* 5.

41. Sansom, in Goffman, *Presentation of Self,* 5.

42. Baudrillard, *System of Objects,* 83.

43. Frank, *L'année des méduses,* 15–16.

44. Cited by Désert, *La vie quotidienne,* 180.

45. See Barthes, "The World of Wrestling," in *Mythologies,* 18.

46. Jacques Sauvestre, "Premier bain," in *Mon ami Bob,* an elementary-level reader, 76.

47. I am alluding to Étienne Souriau, *Les deux cent mille situations dramatiques* (Paris: Flammarion, 1950).

48. Here I am borrowing the opposition between "a world of roles" and "the new world of jobs" as presented and analyzed by Marshall McLuhan, in *The Gutenberg Galaxy: The Making of Typographic Man* (1962; Toronto: University of Toronto Press, 1966), 14–15.

49. Sauvestre, *Mon ami Bob,* chapter 24.

50. Morand, *Bains de mer,* 167, 108.

51. Laloux, "67 Français 'moyens,'" interview 12.

52. For in order to exist, "Utopia, in fact, never admits anything external to itself; Utopia is for itself its own reality," as Louis Marin writes in *Utopics: Spatial Play,* trans. Robert A. Vollrath (Atlantic Highlands, N.J.: Humanities Press, 1984), 102.

53. Bernadette Doka, *Bronzer sans danger* (Montreal: Éditions de l'Homme, 1984), 37 (emphasis added).

54. See André, Tardivon, and Kervran, *Étude qualitative*, 146.

55. Barbaza, *Le paysage humain*, 677. This "defensive laughter" has already been studied in other contexts, for example among the Pueblo Indians confronted with tourists. See Jill D. Sweet, "Burlesquing 'the Other' in Pueblo Performance," in *Semiotics of Tourism*, ed. Dean MacCannell, special issue of *Annals of Tourism Research* 16, no. 1 (1989): 62–75.

56. Reported by Premel and Kalaora, introductory report, 5.

57. According to Premel, on the basis of a study involving coastal populations whose results were presented at the third Atelier du conservatoire du littoral. Numerous incidents attest to this intensification of the conflict between locals and summer resident campers, for example the following: "Bastia: coups de feu contre des campings-cars à l'Arinella" (Bastia: shots fired on camping vans at Arinella), *Corse-Matin* (Aug. 24, 1992). Arinella is the main beach in Bastia.

58. See Premel and Kalaora, introductory report.

59. An interview published in *Kyrn, le magazine de la Corse* 56 (Aug.–Sept. 1975): 66–67.

60. See Premel and Kalaora, introductory report, 2.

61. In this connection, see Marié and Tamisier, *Un territoire sans nom*, 121ff.

62. Reported by Premel and Kalaora, introductory report, 4.

63. See Urbain, *L'idiot du voyage*, 70.

64. Let us recall that those who practice sailing, surfing, or motorboating represent only 6.5 percent of seaside vacationers. See *La perception du littoral*, 39.

65. This is a return to a critique I have already undertaken in the framework of the anthropology of tourism (Urbain, *L'idiot du voyage*, chapter 5).

66. Premel and Kalaora, introductory report, 5.

9. THE NAKED AND THE RAW

1. "Spécial maigrir," *Vital* 139 (April 1992); 218,000 copies printed.

2. "Spécial maigrir," *Prévention santé* 127 (April 1992); "Maigrir. Bas les masques!" *50 millions de consommateurs* 261 (April–May 1993); "Spécial mode été," *Elle* 242 (June 1992): 36.

3. "Spécial mode été," 37.

4. Licht-Land, "light-land," is what Dr. Franzel called the nudist space in his naturist center near Luneburg in Germany, between the two world wars. See Salardenne, *Un mois chez les nudistes*, 18.

5. "Maigrir. Bas les masques!"

6. Perrot, *Le corps féminin*, 69.

7. The "wrecks" that wash up on the beach at Étretat, in Maupassant's short story "Épaves" (in *Contes et nouvelles*, vol. 1), were social pariahs; today,

they are rejected on aesthetic grounds. Discrimination has thus not disappeared; it has simply been displaced.

8. Perrot, *Le corps féminin,* 204.

9. Fischler, *L'homnivore,* 14, 31.

10. Advertisement for "Côte d'Azur, Star du Siècle," Comité régional du tourisme (CRT), Nice, spring 1991.

11. See Chevalier and Gheerbrant, "Salt," in *A Dictionary of Symbols,* 822–24.

12. See Véronique Nahoum, "La belle femme ou le stade du miroir en histoire," *Communications* 31 (1979): 25; Laurent, *Le nu vêtu et dévêtu,* 182; reported by Royer in *Let's Go Naked,* 40.

13. Morand, *Bains de mer,* 15.

14. See in this connection Gwenn-Abel Bolloré, *Guide du pêcheur à pied et sa cuisine* (Paris: Gallimard, 1986). See also Jannick Ser, *Le livre de l'amateur d'huîtres et de coquillages* (Toulouse: Éditions D. Briand-R. Laffon, 1987).

15. "Pour hâler bien," *Vogue-Hommes* 151 (July–Aug. 1992).

16. As Roland Barthes says in "Ornamental Cookery," in *Mythologies* (1972), 78. But gastronomy based on raw food does not hesitate either before a certain dream staging, an aestheticization of uncooked dishes.

17. Claude Lévi-Strauss, *The Raw and the Cooked,* trans. John and Doreen Weightman (Chicago: University of Chicago Press, 1990).

18. Seaweed washed up on the beach, perceived as garbage, the residue of a natural process of degradation, is also on the side of the rotten, hence the disgust it inspires.

19. We may recall in this connection that Grenouille, the hero of Süskind's novel *Perfume,* retreats into the mountains to seal (provisionally) his total break with the world; there he lives exclusively on raw foods: salamanders, ring snakes, lichen, and grass.

20. This simplicity on the part of the camper, as Sansot rightly notes with respect to "families of modest means" in *Les gens de peu,* here stops being the sign of "economic precariousness. It leads them toward the beginning of the human adventure, when one had to be ingenious to survive and invent little by little the conquests of elementary culture" (170).

21. Viard, *Penser les vacances,* 178. See above, chapter 6.

22. Commercial broadcast on French television in 1991–92.

23. Erwitt, *Elliott Erwitt,* 16, 18.

24. Frank, *L'année des méduses,* 125.

25. Morand, *Bains de mer,* 15; Laurent, *Le nu vêtu et dévêtu,* 179.

26. Corbin, *Lure of the Sea,* 251.

27. Reported in Alain Corbin, *Le territoire du vide: l'Occident et le désir du rivage, 1750–1840* (Paris: Aubier, 1988), 390–91 n. 54. [This passage was omitted in the English translation, *Lure of the Sea.*—Trans.]

28. Cf. the section titled "Ophelia Devoured," in chapter 9 below.

29. Abe, *Woman in the Dunes,* 42.

30. See on "ungraspable" the lovely text by Italo Calvino, *Collection de sable,* trans. J.-P. Manganaro (Paris: Seuil, 1986).

31. Jacques Brel, "Le plat pays," in *Chansons* (Paris: Tchou, 1967), 74.

32. Enid Blyton, *Noddy at the Seaside* (1953; London: Macdonald, 1990), 20; Fitzgerald, *Tender Is the Night,* 7; Franc, *Le café de la plage.*

33. Camus, *The Stranger,* 57: "The sea gasped for air with each shallow, stifled little wave that broke on the sand."

34. Morand, *Bains de mer,* 147, 57; Philippe, *Un été près de la mer,* 68; Nori, "Rimini, août 82," 80.

35. For example, in Brian Coe, *The Birth of Photography* (New York: Taplinger Publishing, 1977), an anonymous photograph from 1908 represents two female bathers exposing themselves (for pleasure) to the "assaults" of the waves (134). One cannot help thinking here of the famous picture of Burt Lancaster and Deborah Kerr clinging together in the surf, in Fred Zimmerman's film *From Here to Eternity,* 1953.

36. "La marée" (1962), an erotic tale by André Pieyre de Mandiargues that was used in a film by Walerian Borowczyk (*Contes immoraux* [Immoral tales]), develops precisely this theme.

37. Margery Hilton, *Une semaine aux Caraïbes,* no. 383 (Paris: Harlequin, 1983), 122.

38. *Lui* 42 (May 1977): 100–103; *New Look* 105 (April 1992): 66ff. (the source of the statistic is not indicated); *Jeune et jolie* 61 (July 1992): 40ff. The article offers a typology of "guys" that goes from the "breakneck adventurer" by way of the "ecological true-believer" and the "sweep-them-off-their-feet-fast" type to the "behind-the-times party-goer."

39. "Votre été 92: amour, sexe et séduction," *Biba* 150 (August 1992); "L'été érotique: six nouvelles inédites de femmes écrivains," *Marie-Claire* 480 (August 1992); "L'amour à la plage" and "Comment transformer un coup en Love Story?" *20 ans* 73 (August 1992); "Vos amours d'été. Qui séduire? Qui fuir?" *Marie-France* 449 (July–August 1993); "Sexualité: les Français et l'amour," *Top Santé* 23 (August 1992); "Le tour de France des plages chaudes"; "Le tour de France des nuits chaudes. Du Touquet à Biarritz, de Perpignan à Saint-Tropez," *VSD* 778 (July 1991); "Le hit-parade des plages SEXY," *L'écho des savanes* 118 (July–August 1993).

40. *Ça m'intéresse* 150 (August 1993); "Les Français, l'été et l'amour." This survey, conducted Aug. 9–10, 1991, by *Paris-Match BVA,* was based on a representative sample of 801 French people aged eighteen to forty-nine.

41. This is confirmed, with some minor differences, by the survey conducted by Panorama and Conseils Sondages Analyses (CSA) in January 1993: 80 percent of the French people interviewed asserted that they had always been faithful on the level of sexual relations (men 72%; women 86%).

42. "Couple. Sex. Take advantage of the summer to try everything": this was the invitation on the cover of the journal *Interview* in June 1993.

43. Reported by Bruno Péquignot, in *La relation amoureuse: analyse sociologique du roman sentimental moderne* (Paris: L'Harmattan, 1991), 65.

44. See Patrick Tacussel, "L'attraction amoureuse dans l'observation sociale," *Cahiers de l'imaginaire* 5 (1989): 80.

45. In an interview published in *Le Monde* (Jan. 7, 1992, 2), Gérard Demuth, the director of Cofremca, emphasized that today's social climate no longer seems to favor strong and permanent bonds with a limited number of social groups (in terms of social class, religion, occupation). The contemporary individual establishes many more and weaker ties with a large number of groups, "connecting" and "disconnecting" more quickly in relation to certain modes of exchange and conviviality. This is "social zapping."

46. This remains true even after Corbin's in-depth study, *Lure of the Sea*.

47. Michelet, *The Sea*, 330.

48. See Bronislaw Malinowski, "A Savage Myth of Incest," in *The Sexual Life of Savages in North-Western Melanesia* (1929; New York: Harcourt, Brace and World, 1962), 539–72.

49. Let me refer once again here to Roger Vadim's well-known film starring Brigitte Bardot, *And God Created Woman* (1976), in which the action takes place at Saint-Tropez.

50. In this connection, see Bachelard, *Water and Dreams*, 115–32.

51. Jean Richepin, *La mer* (1886; Paris: Gallimard, 1980), 111.

52. Michelet, *The Sea*, analyzed by Bachelard, *Water and Dreams*, 118–19.

53. In *Bains de mer*, 52, Morand reminds us that a novel by Willy, situated in Biarritz, is called *Une plage d'amour*.

54. Mann, *Death in Venice*; Theroux, *Old Patagonian Express*, 72.

55. The French term for "floating on one's back" is *faire la planche*, "act like a board."—Trans.

56. Lodge, *Paradise News*, 162.

57. Monod, *Plongées profondes*, 50–52.

58. Flaubert, *Voyage en Bretagne*, 335; Marie Cardinal, *Les pieds-noirs* (Paris: Belfond, 1988), 289.

59. The expression is from Gaston Bachelard, *La terre et les rêveries du repos* (Paris: José Corti, 1948), 14.

60. Jean Duvignaud, Françoise Duvignaud, and Jean-Pierre Corbeau, *La banque des rêves. Essai d'anthropologie du rêveur contemporain* (Paris: Payot, 1979), 97–98.

61. Morand, *Bains de mer*: "My mother, frightened to see that my head was now just a barely discernible spot on the surface, had gotten used to these disappearances of her son the Cartesian diver" (16).

62. Philippe, *Un été près de la mer*, 18–19. The notion of proprioceptism refers to "the perception man has of his own body." See A. J. Greimas and Joseph Courtès, *Sémiotique* (Paris: Hachette, 1979), 299.

63. Monod, *Plongées profondes*, 46.

64. See Véronique Nahoum-Grappe, "Les conduites de vertige," in *Possessions. Galaxie anthropologique* 2, nos. 4–5 (1993): 66–71.

65. See Gaston Bachelard, *Air and Dreams: An Essay on the Imagination of Movement,* trans. Edith R. Farrell and C. Frederick Farrell (Dallas: Dallas Institute Publications, 1988).

66. Regarding the myth of surfing, see Hugo Verlomme's novel, *L'homme des vagues* (Paris: Gallimard, 1992).

67. Morin, *Journal de Californie,* 191; Philippe, *Un été près de la mer,* 68.

68. As Nahoum-Grappe emphasizes in "Les conduites de vertige." The pleasure of falling may be experienced vicariously, through some intermediate substance: "The anticipatory pleasure of falling produces its effect of vertigo even if it is not experienced [physically], but only imagined" (67).

69. In *La terre et les rêveries du repos,* Bachelard recalls that one "of the most normal and regular imaginary functions [is] that of miniaturizing" (13). From the little shell to the kites on northern beaches, a great deal could be said on this topic.

70. Corbin, *Lure of the Sea,* 30. *The Big Blue,* released in 1989, is a remake of *Le grand bleu,* a 1988 film directed by Luc Besson.

71. See Chevalier and Gheerbrant, "Dolphin," in *A Dictionary of Symbols,* 303–4.

72. Let us recall that for Plato, in *Timaeus,* trans. Donald J. Zeyl (Indianapolis: Hackett Publishing, 2000), death is inseparable from the color blue.

73. In the film, Jacques has a loving companion who is expecting his child, but this is not enough to hold him back.

74. Excerpt from commentary in a report devoted to Jacques Mayol, "L'homme dauphin" (P. Amory and Ph. Montoisy), broadcast on France 2, during a program titled "Envoyé spécial," Jan. 3, 1994.

75. Even when it is termed "internal" or "national."

76. Heading, *Hara-Kiri* 131 (Aug. 1972).

77. Hypocapnia is the name given to the decrease in the level of carbonic gas contained in the blood. It is produced by pulmonary hyperventilation and leads to apnea.

78. Hilton, *Une semaine aux Caraïbes,* 120.

79. Flaubert, *Voyage en Bretagne,* 160–61; S. James, *Pour que tu m'appartiennes* (Paris: Duo, 1983), 154, emphasis added.

80. Monod, *Plongées profondes,* 145.

81. *Édredonde,* from *édredon,* "comforter," and *onde,* "wave," is a portmanteau word coined by Alain Finkielkraut and defined as *mer chaude et confortable,* a "warm and comfortable sea," in *Petit Fictionnaire illustré* (Paris: Seuil, 1981), 32.

82. Benchley, *Jaws,* 57.

83. *New Look* 108 (July 1992): 64–79. In this connection, see Patrick Baudry, *Le corps extrême. Approche sociologique des conduites à risque* (Paris: L'Harmattan, 1991), chapter 3, especially 123ff.

84. "L'Espagne. Tout sous le soleil," *Télérama* (March 1991).

85. Events along the Atlantic coast in late 1993 and early 1994 made the latter dangers clear.

86. In "Omniprésence de la peur," Jean Delumeau gives numerous mythical and historical examples of this phobic archetype linked with water and its depths, from Polyphemus to Lorelei via the Strigones and the Leviathan.

87. In Dr. Eric Caumes, *Les maladies en voyage* (Paris: Seuil, 1988), we find the following advice: "Refrain if possible from swimming alone in distant lands, and respect local customs and practices (no swimming beyond the bar at Dakar, for example). In fact, a brief verbal (or gestural!) exchange with the local population is better than an unwelcome surprise from which there may be no return: dangerous waters, sharks, stone-fish (damaging to feet, sometimes deadly), scorpion-fish, poisonous shellfish, jellyfish, and so on" (45).

88. "The Greeks appreciated oysters highly, and knew how to prepare them in various ways. . . . Furthermore, we know that they used oyster shells for voting. On the pearly surface of a shell, the voter inscribed his sentence with a stylus, and this is why banishment took the name of ostracism"; Prosper Montagné and Dr. Alfred Gottschalk, *Larousse gastronomique* (Paris: Larousse, 1938), 610.

89. Benchley, *Jaws*, 82.

90. Daniel Pennac is recalling a stay on the Atlantic coast near Bilbao, in Doisneau and Pennac, *Les grandes vacances*, 51.

91. For sunscreen, above and beyond the medical arguments that justify it, also undoubtedly shares in this fantasmatic schema of safety. Advertising slogans such as "Mastering the sun" (Roc, 1992) or "The sun tamed" (Lancaster, 1992) can also be read in terms of a fantasmatic construct that can even turn into collective psychosis, as in Australia where an obsession with the hole in the ozone layer has led swimmers to go back to bathing fully dressed.

92. Thus in "Ludic and Liminoid Aspects of Charter Yacht Tourism in [the] Caribbean," *Annals of Tourism Research* 10 (1983): 35–56, J. W. Lett notes that vacationing young (white) Americans do not hesitate to have sexual adventures with people of color to whom they would tend to pay little attention at other times. Presumably, since 1983, another monster, AIDS, has considerably modified behaviors by reinforcing strategies of protection.

Epilogue

1. See *La perception du littoral*, 139.

2. See Robert Lanquar and Robert Hollier, *Le marketing touristique: la mercatique touristique* (Paris: Presses Universitaires de France, 1981), 38–40; see also Robert Lanquar, *Sociologie du tourisme et des voyages* (Paris: Presses Universitaires de France, 1985), 68–69.

3. In this connection, see Jules Verne once again (he seems indeed to have imagined all the possibilities): *The Floating Island* (1895; London: Kegan Paul International, 1990).

4. Cited by Peyre and Raynouard, *Histoire et légendes*, 5; Laloux, "67 Français 'moyens,'" 70; Pennac, *Comme un roman*, 57.

5. Sylvie Rimbert, *Paysages urbains*, cited by Georges Cazes, "Le tourisme international dans le tiers monde," Ph.D. diss., University of Bordeaux III, 1983, 489; Pennac, *Comme un roman*, 33.

6. Augé, *Domaines et châteaux*, 133. In *La voix et le regard* (Paris: Seuil, 1978), Alain Touraine writes: "If love is acknowledged as being so important in our culture, this is because it is experienced as the opposite of a social relationship, as a choice, as an encounter between individuals, as desire and as passion" (51).

7. I am referring here to J. E. Adler, "Mobility and the Creation of the Subject: Theorizing Movement and the Self in Early Christian Monasticism," in *Le tourisme international entre tradition et modernité. International tourism between tradition and modernity*, 407–15 (Nice: Laboratoire d'ethnologie-Université de Nice, 1994).

8. See Jean Baudrillard, *The Illusion of the End*, trans. Chris Turner (Stanford: Stanford University Press, 1994), esp. 21–27.

9. Bernardin de Saint-Pierre, *Paul and Virginia*, 18–19.

10. See Didier Masurier, *Hôtes et touristes au Sénégal: Imaginaires et idéologies touristiques de l'exotisme* (Paris: L'Harmattan, 1998).

11. According to Pierre Tsartas, "Identité et mobilité de deux groupes des acteurs sociaux du tourisme en Grèce: les touristes et les autochtones," in *Le tourisme international entre tradition et modernité*, Proceedings of international colloquium, Nice, Nov. 1992 (Nice: Laboratoire d'ethnologie-Université de Nice, 1994), 381.

12. In this connection, see Léger and Hervieu, *Le retour à la nature*; and, by the same authors, "La nature des néoruraux," in *Protection de la nature* (Paris: L'Harmattan, 1982), 152ff.

13. I shall not attempt to do so here, as the present book has a different aim.

14. Also by the statistics. See *La perception du littoral*, 39.

15. Premel and Kalaora, introductory report, 3–4.

16. I owe the expression "shell hotels" to Georges Cazes.

17. Macé, "Les vacances passives," 23.

18. André, Tardivon, and Kervran, *Étude qualitative*, 155. Let us recall that in 1992, only 3.7 percent of seaside vacationers went sailing or sailboarding, and only 2.8 percent used motorboats (*La perception du littoral*, 39).

19. Ibid., 163–64.

20. G. Bremond, president of Pierre & Vacances, in *Désir du rivage*, 6–7.

21. J.-C. Lévy, "Les aquaboulevards ou la nature artificialisée," *Les vacances. Autrement* 111 (Jan. 1990): 155.

22. Advertisement for Aquaboulevard in Paris, June 1992; Royer, *Let's Go Naked*, 34.

23. Philippe Couderc, "Israël: Eilat, drôle de bout du monde en maillot de bain," *Le Nouvel Observateur* (Jan. 9–15, 1992): 102.

24. Gérard Blitz, "Il y a aussi une prospective des vacances," *Planète* 22 (May–June 1965): 39.

25. D. Desré, referring to "Thalasso Business," a report on the program "Thalassa," broadcast on FR3 on May 10, 1991 (*Télérama* 2155, 131).

26. See André, Tardivon, and Kervran, *Étude qualitative*, 101, 159.

27. Center Parcs is a Dutch group with headquarters in Rotterdam. It has facilities in Belgium, Great Britain, and France as well as in Holland. There are several centers in France, including one opened in Verneuil-sur-Avre (Normandy) in 1988, and another opened in Chaumont-sur-Tharonne (Sologne) in 1993.

28. Information communicated by M. Loeffen, director general of Center Parcs, during a seminar held by the Commissariat au plan, Paris, October 1990.

29. *Hydroponic* is the term used to describe crops grown in water, without soil. The analogy should be clear enough, since these vacation bubbles are the site of a balnearity that is "cultivated" away from the beach and the sea.

30. "Vivre nu, à la recherche du paradis perdu," a report included in the program "Grands Reportages," broadcast on TF1, Dec. 7, 1993.

31. Defoe, *Robinson Crusoe*, 104.

32. For its 1994 advertising campaign, Center Parcs kept "like nowhere else" as its motto, and "OVNI" (UFO) as its slogan. But this well-known acronym is translated here into new terms: "Oasis de Verdure Nouvelle et Inimaginable" (Oasis of Unimaginable New Greenery). As a figure of paradise, we thus find the image of Swift's floating island (see Introduction, above), via the contemporary reference to "Objets Volants Non Identifiés" (Unidentified Flying Objects), that is, the concept of a place of sojourn fantasized as extraterrestrial . . .

APPENDIX

1. See Urbain, *L'idiot du voyage*, annex, 261ff.

2. For brevity's sake, films, reviews, magazines, and other newspaper articles mentioned in the text are not included here. Moreover, a filmography of the shore and the beach remains to be undertaken; it would include in particular the American "beach movie" as a genre.

Works Cited

Abe, Kobo. *The Woman in the Dunes.* Translated by E. Dale Saunders. New York: Knopf, 1964.

Adler, Judith E. "Mobility and the Creation of the Subject: Theorizing Movement and the Self in Early Christian Monasticism." In *Le tourisme international entre tradition et modernité. International tourism between tradition and modernity,* 407–15. Nice: Laboratoire d'ethnologie–Université de Nice, 1994.

Alessandrini, Marjorie. "Terre de soleil. Sur les routes du Sud, jusqu'à l'extrême pointe de l'Europe." Supplement, *Le Nouvel Observateur* 1435 (May 7–13, 1992): xviii.

Amirou, Rachid. *Imaginaire touristique et sociabilités du voyage.* Paris: Presses Universitaires de France, 2000.

André, Éric, Pierre Tardivon, and Christophe Kervran. *Étude qualitative de la demande française et européenne pour le littoral français.* Paris: HTL-Conseil, 1989.

Ariès, Philippe. *Le temps de l'histoire.* Preface by Roger Chartier. Paris: Seuil, 1986.

Augé, Marc. *Domaines et châteaux.* Paris: Seuil, 1989.

Bachelard, Gaston. *Air and Dreams: An Essay on the Imagination of Movement.* 1943. Translated by Edith R. Farrell and C. Frederick Farrell. Dallas: Dallas Institute Publications, 1988.

———. *La terre et les rêveries du repos.* Paris: José Corti, 1948.

———. *The Poetics of Space.* 1957. Translated by Maria Jolas. Boston: Beacon Press, 1969.

———. *Water and Dreams: An Essay on the Imagination of Matter.* 1942. Translated by Edith R. Farrell. Dallas: Pegasus Foundation, 1983.

Bailhé, Claude, and Paul Charpentier. *La côte atlantique de Biarritz à La Rochelle au temps des guides baigneurs.* Toulouse: Éditions Milan, 1983.

Balzac, Honoré de. "Un drame au bord de la mer." 1823. In *Oeuvres complètes,* vol. 2. Paris: Club français du livre, 1962.

Barbaza, Yvette. *Le paysage humain de la Costa Brava.* Paris: Armand Colin, 1966.

Barthes, Roland. *The Fashion System.* 1967. Translated by Matthew Ward and Richard Howard. New York: Hill and Wang, 1983.

———. "Histoire et sociologie du vêtement." *Les Annales* (1957): 430–41.

———. *Mythologies.* Selected and translated by Annette Lavers. New York: Hill and Wang, 1972. Originally published as *Mythologies* (Paris: Seuil, 1957).

"Bastia: Shots fired on camping vans in Arinella." *Corse-Matin* (Aug. 24, 1992).

Baudrillard, Jean. *The Illusion of the End.* 1992. Translated by Chris Turner. Stanford: Stanford University Press, 1994.

———. *Simulacra and Simulations.* 1981. Translated by Sheila Faria Glaser. Ann Arbor: University of Michigan Press, 1994.

———. *Symbolic Exchange and Death.* 1976. Translated by Ian Hamilton Grant. London: Sage Publications, 1993.

———. *The System of Objects.* 1968. Translated by James Benedict. London: Verso, 1996.

Baudry, Patrick. *Le corps extrême. Approche sociologique des conduites à risque.* Paris: L'Harmattan, 1991.

Bellenger, Yvonne. "Quelques relations de voyage vers l'Italie et vers l'Orient au XVIe siècle." In *Voyager à la Renaissance,* ed. Jean Céard and Jean-Claude Margolin, 453–65. Paris: Maisonneuve et Larose, 1987.

Benamozig, Guy. "Enfermement et psychose." Ph.D. diss., Paris V-Sorbonne, 1992.

Benchley, Peter. *Jaws.* New York: Doubleday, 1974.

Berchet, Jean-Claude. *Le voyage en Orient. Anthologie des voyageurs français dans le Levant au XIXe* siècle. Paris: Robert Laffont, 1985.

Bernardin de Saint-Pierre, J. H. *Paul and Virginia.* 1787. London: George Routledge and Sons, 1888.

Berto, Emmanuel, Carol Illouz, Antoine Casubolo, and Sylvie Lotiron. "Le tour de France des nuits chaudes. Du Touquet à Biarritz, de Perpignan à Saint-Tropez." *VSD* 778 (July 30–Aug. 5, 1992): 28–40.

Bettelheim, Bruno. *The Empty Fortress: Infantile Autism and the Birth of the Self.* New York: Free Press, 1967.

Blitz, Gérard. "Il y a aussi une prospective des vacances." *Planète* 22 (May–June 1965): 39–41.

Blondin, Antoine. "Les sports d'hiver: une page blanche que l'on peut remplir à sa fantaisie." 1959. In *Voyages,* preface by P.-J. Rémy, ed. J.-P. Caracalla, 53–56. Paris: Olivier Orban, 1981.

Blyton, Enid. *Five Go Down to the Sea.* 1955. Chicago: Reilly and Lee, 1961.

———. *Noddy at the Seaside*. 1953. London: Macdonald, 1990.

Bolland, Henri. *Excursions en France*. Paris: Hachette, 1909.

Bolloré, Gwenn-Abel. *Guide du pêcheur à pied et sa cuisine*. Paris: Gallimard, 1986.

Bologne, Jean-Claude. *Histoire de la pudeur*. Paris: Olivier Orban, 1986.

Bonnemaison, Joël. "Les voyages et l'enracinement. Formes de fixation et de mobilité dans les sociétés traditionnelles des Nouvelles-Hébrides." *L'espace géographique* 8, no. 4 (1979): 303–18.

Bonnot, Gilles. "Savons-nous partir?" *Le Nouvel Observateur* (Aug. 2, 1980): 40–41.

Borel, Alain, et al. *Pour une littérature voyageuse*. Brussels: Complexe, 1992.

Borie, Jean. Preface to Jules Michelet, *La Mer*. Reprint ed. Paris: Gallimard, 1983.

Boudon, Raymond. *Effets pervers et ordre social*. Paris: Presses Universitaires de France, 1977.

Boulle, Pierre. *Planet of the Apes*. Translated by Xan Fielding. New York: Vanguard Press, 1963.

Boyd, William. *Brazzaville Beach*. London: Sinclair-Stevenson, 1990.

Boyer, Marc. *Le tourisme*. Paris: Seuil, 1982.

Brassens, Georges. "Supplique pour être enterré à la plage de Sète." In *Poèmes et chansons*, 185–87. Paris: Éditions musicales 57, 1973.

Braudel, Fernand. *The Identity of France*. 1986. Vol. 1, *History and Environment*. Translated by Siân Reynolds. London: Collins, 1988.

Brel, Jacques. *Chansons*. Paris: Tchou, 1967.

Brizard, Caroline. "Méditerranée, le cancer vert." Interview with Charles-François Boudouresque. *Le Nouvel Observateur* (Dec. 1991–Jan. 1992): 60.

Bromberger, S. "Antibes et ses huttes polynésiennes pour milliardaires blasés." *Le Figaro* (Aug. 1, 1951): 1, 8.

Bruckner, Pascal, and Alain Finkielkraut. *Au coin de la rue, l'aventure*. Paris: Seuil, 1979.

Brun, Jean. *La nudité humaine*. Paris: Fayard, 1973.

Burgelin, Olivier. "Le tourisme jugé." *Vacances et tourisme. Communications* 10 (1967): 65–96.

Buron, Nicole de. *Dix jours de rêve*. Paris: J'ai lu, 1986.

Cabantous, Alain. *Les côtes barbares*. Paris: Fayard, 1993.

Cacérès, Benigno. *Loisirs et travail du Moyen Âge à nos jours*. Paris: Seuil, 1973.

Caillois, Roger. *Man, Play, and Games*. 1958. Translated by Meyer Barash. New York: Free Press of Glencoe, 1961.

Calvet, Louis-Jean. *Les jeux de la société*. Paris: Payot, 1978.

Calvino, Italo. *Collection de sable*. 1984. Translated by J.-P. Manganaro. Paris: Seuil, 1986.

———. *Mr. Palomar*. 1983. Translated by William Weaver. San Diego: Harcourt Brace Jovanovich, 1985.

Camus, Albert. *The Stranger.* 1957. Translated by Matthew Ward. New York: Vintage International, 1989.

Canetti, Elias. *Crowds and Power.* 1960. Translated by Carol Stewart. New York: Viking Press, 1963.

Cardinal, Marie. *Les pieds-noirs.* Paris: Belfond, 1988.

Carlson, Catherine. *L'amour, ça fait pas grossir: Lettre aux femmes ou à ce qu'il en reste.* Paris: Régine Deforges, 1991.

Caumes, Dr. Eric. *Les maladies en voyage.* Paris: Seuil, 1988.

Cazes, Georges. *Fondements pour une géographie du tourisme et des loisirs.* Paris: Bréal, 1992.

———. *Le tourisme en France.* Paris: Presses Universitaires de France, 1993.

———. *Le tourisme international. Mirage ou stratégie d'avenir?* Paris: Hachette, 1989.

———. "Le tourisme international dans le tiers monde." Ph.D. diss., University of Bordeaux III, 1983. Published as *Le tourisme international à la conquête du Tiers-Monde* (Paris: L'Harmattan, 1989).

———. "L'île tropicale, figure emblématique du tourisme international." *Cahiers du tourisme* 112 (June 1987).

Cazes, Georges, Robert Lanquar, and Yves Raynouard. *L'aménagement touristique et le développement durable.* Paris: Presses Universitaires de France, 1990.

Céline [Louis-Ferdinand Destouches]. *Le Pont de Londres: Guignol's Band II.* Paris: Gallimard, 1964. English translation: *London Bridge: Guignol's Band II,* trans. Dominic Di Bernardy (Normal, Ill.: Dalkey Archive Press, 1995).

Certeau, Michel de. "Les revenants de la ville." In *Théâtre de la mémoire. Traverses* 40 (April 1987): 74–85.

"Cet été en vacances." *Santé Magazine* 201 (Sept. 1992): 28ff.

Chapus, Eugène. *Manuel de l'homme et de la femme comme il faut.* Paris: M. Lévy, 1862.

Chase, Linda. *Hyperrealism.* Introduction by Salvador Dali. New York: Rizzoli, 1975.

Chevalier, Jean, and Alain Gheerbrant. *A Dictionary of Symbols.* 1969. Translated by John Buchanan-Brown. London: Penguin, 1996.

Coe, Brian. *The Birth of Photography.* New York: Taplinger Publishing, 1977.

"Comment transformer un coup en Love Story?" *20 ans* 73 (August 1992).

Cooke, Captain Edward. *A Voyage to the South Sea and round the World in the Years 1708 to 1711.* 1712. New York: Da Capo Press, 1969.

Corbin, Alain. *The Lure of the Sea: The Discovery of the Seaside in the Western World, 1750–1840.* 1988. Translated by Jocelyn Phelps. Berkeley: University of California Press, 1994.

Côte de l'Atlantique de la Loire aux Pyrénées. Guide vert Michelin, 2nd ed. Paris: Éditions Michelin, 1965.

Côte-d'Azur, Provence, Corse, Riviera italienne. Les Guides rouges. Paris: Baneton-Thiolier, 1957.

Couderc, Philippe. "Israël: Eilat, drôle de bout du monde en maillot de bain." *Le Nouvel Observateur* (Jan. 9–15, 1992): 102.

Cribier, Françoise. *La grande migration d'été des citadins en France.* Paris: Centre national de la recherche scientifique, 1969.

Dampier, William. *Dampier's Voyages.* London: E. Grant Richards, 1906.

Daninos, Pierre. *Major W. Marmaduke Thompson Lives in France.* 1954. London: Jonathan Cape, 1955.

Defoe, Daniel. *Robinson Crusoe.* 1726. Edited by Michael Shinagel. New York: W. W. Norton, 1975.

Delumeau, Jean. "Omniprésence de la peur." In *La peur en Occident (XIVe–XVIIe siècles): Une cité assiégée,* 31–74. Paris: Fayard, 1978.

Demuth, Gérard. Interview. In *Le Monde* (Jan. 7, 1992): 2.

Descamps, Bernard. *Balnéaires.* Amiens: Trois Cailloux, 1985.

Désert, Gabriel. *La vie quotidienne sur les plages normandes du Second Empire aux années folles.* Paris: Hachette, 1983.

Désir de rivage. Des nouvelles représentations aux nouveaux usagers du littoral. Ateliers du Conservatoire du littoral. 1993.

Diderot, Denis. *The Nun.* 1796. Translated by Marianne Sinclair. London: New English Library, 1966.

Doisneau, Robert, and Daniel Pennac. *Les grandes vacances.* Paris: Hoëbeke, 1991.

Doka, Bernadette. *Bronzer sans danger.* Montreal: Éditions de l'Homme, 1984.

Doutrelant, Pierre-Marie. "Le Touquet des quatre saisons." *Le Nouvel Observateur* 816 (June 28–July 4, 1980): 38–39.

Dubois, Véronique, Silvie Lotiron, and Marc Daum. "Le tour de France des plages chaudes." Special report, *VSD* 725 (July 25–31, 1991): 25–35.

Dumazedier, Joffre. *Toward a Society of Leisure.* 1962. Translated by Stewart E. McClure. New York: Free Press, 1967.

Dupuy, Jean-Pierre. "Le signe et l'envie." In Paul Dumouchel and Jean-Pierre Dupuy, *L'enfer des choses: René Girard et la logique de l'économie,* 17–134. Paris: Seuil, 1979.

Durkheim, Émile. *The Elementary Forms of Religious Life.* 1912. Translated by Daren E. Fields. New York: Free Press, 1995.

———. *The Rules of Sociological Method.* 1895. Translated by Sarah A. Solovay and John H. Muelle. Edited by George E. G. Catlin. Chicago: University of Chicago Press, 1938.

Duvignaud, Jean, Françoise Duvignaud, and Jean-Pierre Corbeau. *La banque des rêves. Essai d'anthropologie du rêveur contemporain.* Paris: Payot, 1979.

Eco, Umberto. "Un art d'oublier est-il concevable?" *Théâtres de la mémoire. Traverses* 40 (April 1987): 124–35.

Ehrenberg, Alain. "C'est au Club et nulle part ailleurs . . . Essai sur la société décontractée." *Le Débat* 34 (March 1985): 130–45.

———. "Le Club Méditerranée, 1935–1960." *Les Vacances. Autrement* 111 (Jan. 1990): 117–29.

Elias, Norbert. *The Court Society.* 1969. Translated by Edmund Jephcott. New York: Pantheon Books, 1983.

Enzenberger, Hans Magnus. "Eine Theorie des Tourismus." In *Einzelheiten I: Bewußtseins-Industrie,* 179–205. Frankfurt am Main: Suhrkamp, 1964.

Erwitt, Elliott. *Elliott Erwitt—On the Beach.* New York: Norton, 1991.

Euripides. *Iphigenia in Tauris.* Edited and translated by M. J. Cropp. Warminster, England: Aris and Phillips, 2000.

Falkner, John Meade. *Moonfleet.* London: Edward Arnold, 1898.

Farge, Arlette. *Le goût de l'archive.* Paris: Seuil, coll. "La librairie du XXe siècle," 1989.

Farrère, Claude. *Une jeune fille voyagea . . .* Paris: Flammarion, 1925.

Ferrand, J.-B. *A Dissertation on the Use of Sea Water in the Diseases of the Glands.* London, 1752. In French as *Le traitement de la rage par les bains d'eau de mer,* 1753.

Finkielkraut, Alain. *Petit Fictionnaire illustré.* Paris: Seuil, 1981.

Fischler, Claude. *L'homnivore: Le goût, la cuisine, le corps.* Paris: Jacob, 1990.

Fitzgerald, F. Scott. *Tender Is the Night.* New York: Scribner's, 1934.

Flaubert, Gustave. "A Simple Heart." In *Trois contes.* 1877. Oxford: Oxford University Press, 1991.

———. *Voyage en Bretagne. Par les champs et par les grèves.* 1848. Brussels: Complexe, 1989.

Fletcher, Robert J. *Isles of Illusion: Letters from the South Seas.* Edited by Bohun Lynch. Boston: Small, Maynard and Co., 1923.

Forrester, Charles. "Histoires de Saint-Tropez." *Vogue Hommes* (July–Aug. 1992): 53–65, 142.

Foucault, Michel. *Discipline and Punish: The Birth of the Prison.* 1975. Translated by Alan Sheridan. New York: Pantheon, 1977.

———. *The Use of Pleasure.* 1984. Vol. 2 of *The History of Sexuality.* Translated by Robert Hurley. New York: Pantheon Books, 1985.

Franc, Régis. *Le café de la plage.* 2 vols. Bondy: Les BD du matin, 1982.

Francès, Patrick. "Faut-il tuer les touristes?" *Les Vacances. Autrement* 111 (Jan. 1990): 71–75.

Frank, Christopher. *L'année des méduses.* Paris: Seuil, 1884.

Gall, Michel. *La vie sexuelle de Robinson Crusoé.* Paris: J.-C. Simoen, 1977.

Gallo, Max. *La Baie des Anges* (1975); *Le palais des fêtes* (1975); *La Promenade des Anglais* (1976). Paris: Robert Laffont, 1982.

Gaubert, Dr. Georges. *Un canoë passe . . .* Paris: Stock, 1934.

Gerbault, Alain. *Îles de beauté.* Paris: Gallimard, 1941.

———. *In Quest of the Sun.* 1929. London: Rupert Hart-Davis, 1955.

Giansetto, B. "Le sable des plages passé au crible." *Top Santé* 23 (Aug. 1992): 79.

Gide, André. *The Fruits of the Earth.* 1897. Translated by Dorothy Bussy. New York: Knopf, 1952.

———. *The Journals of André Gide.* Vol. 3, *1928–1939.* Translated by Justin O'Brien. New York: Knopf, 1949.

Gilchrist, Ebenezer. *The Uses of Sea Voyages in Medicine.* 1770.

Giudicelli, Christian. *Station balnéaire.* Paris: Gallimard, 1986.

Goffman, Erving. *Behavior in Public Places: Notes on the Social Organization of Gatherings.* New York: Free Press, 1963.

———. *The Presentation of Self in Everyday Life.* Garden City, N.Y.: Doubleday Anchor Books, 1959.

———. *Relations in Public: Microstudies of the Public Order.* New York: Basic Books, 1971.

Gozlan, Martine. "Souvenir d'Alger." *L'événement du jeudi* (March 5–11, 1992): 59.

Graburn, Nelson H. H. "Tourism: The Sacred Journey." In Valene L. Smith, *Hosts and Guests: The Anthropology of Tourism.* Philadelphia: University of Pennsylvania Press, 1977.

Greimas, A. J., and Joseph Courtès. *Sémiotique.* Paris: Hachette, coll. "Université," 1979.

Grimal, Pierre. *Dictionary of Classical Mythology.* 1951. Translated by A. R. Maxwell-Hyslop. Oxford: Blackwell, 1986.

Guerrin, M., and E. de Roux. "La fièvre des musées." *Le Monde* (March 1993).

Hall, Edward T. *The Hidden Dimension.* Garden City, N.Y.: Anchor Books/ Doubleday, 1969.

———. *The Silent Language.* Garden City, N.Y.: Anchor Press/Doubleday, 1973.

Heller, Geneviève. "Le tourisme sanitaire à l'origine de la propreté suisse?" *Urbi* 5 (1982): 80–86.

Hemingway, Ernest. *The Old Man and the Sea.* New York: Scribner's, 1952.

Hennig, Jean-Luc. *Les garçons de passe. Enquête sur la prostitution masculine.* Paris: Éditions libres-Hallier, 1978.

Herbeth, A. "La machine à laver les plages." *Tourisme, Marketing and Communication* 6 (Sept. 1990).

Hilton, Margery. *Une semaine aux Caraïbes.* 1981. Paris: Harlequin, 1983.

Hugo, Victor. *The Toilers of the Sea.* 1866. New York: Hurst, 1907.

Huguenin, Jean-René. *The Other Side of the Summer.* 1960. Translated by Richard Howard. New York: G. Braziller, 1961.

Huizinga, Johan. *Homo Ludens: A Study of the Play-Element in Culture.* 1939. Boston: Beacon Press, 1950.

Jacquin, Philippe. *Le goémonier.* Paris: Berger-Levrault, 1980.

Jakez Hélias, Pierre. "Le pain de la mer." Introduction to Philippe Jacquin, *Le goémonier.* Paris: Berger-Levrault, 1980.

James, Constantin. *Guide pratique des eaux minérales françaises et étrangères,* 413–28. Paris: Victor Masson, 1861.

James, S. *Pour que tu m'appartiennes.* Paris: Duo, 1983.

Jauffret, Etienne. *Au pays bleu. Roman d'une vie d'enfant.* Paris: Belin, 1941.

Joutard, Philippe. *L'invention du mont Blanc.* Paris: Gallimard, 1986.

Jouty, Sylvain. "Connaissance et symbolique de la montagne chez les érudits médiévaux." In Bernard Debarbieux and Jean-Olivier Majastre, *Homo turisticus: Du tourisme ordinaire en montagne. Revue de Géographie Alpine* 79, no. 4 (1991): 21–34.

Jung, Carl Gustav. "The Psychology of the Child Archetype." In Carl Gustav Jung and Karl Kerényi, *Essays on a Science of Mythology: The Myth of the Divine Child and the Mysteries of Eleusis.* 1941. Translated by R. F. C. Hull. Princeton, N.J.: Princeton University Press, 1971.

Knafou, Rémy. "L'invention du lieu touristique: la passation d'un contrat et le surgissement simultané d'un nouveau territoire." In Bernard Debarbieux and Jean-Olivier Majastre, *Homo Turisticus: Du tourisme ordinaire en montagne. Revue de Géographie Alpine* 79, no. 4 (1991): 11–19.

"L'Espagne. Tout sous le soleil." *Télérama* (March 1991).

"L'état des côtes en France." *Ça m'intéresse* 136 (June 1992).

"L'été érotique: six nouvelles inédites de femmes écrivains." *Marie-Claire* 480 (August 1992).

La perception du littoral par les touristes français (été 1992). Les Cahiers de l'observatoire 25. Ministry of Development, Transportation and Tourism, 1993.

Lacan, Jacques. "Dieu et la jouissance de la femme." In *Livre XX: Encore.* Paris: Seuil, 1975.

Lacarrière, Jacques. *En cheminant avec Hérodote.* Paris: Seghers, 1981.

Lacoste, Yves. "A quoi sert le paysage?" *Hérodote* 7 (1977).

Lalaing, Mme de. *Les côtes de France de Saint-Nazaire à Biarritz par la plage.* Paris-Lille: J. Lefort, 1889.

Laloux, Sylvie. "67 Français 'moyens' à l'épreuve de leurs photographies de vacances: pratiques et représentations." Master's thesis, Université François-Rabelais, Tours, 1987.

Lange, Monique. *The Bathing Huts.* 1982. Translated by Barbara Beaumont. London: Marion Boyars, 1986.

Lanquar, Robert. *Sociologie du tourisme et des voyages.* Paris: Presses Universitaires de France (coll. "Que sais-je?"), 1985.

Lanquar, Robert, and Robert Hollier. *Le marketing touristique: la mercatique touristique.* Paris: Presses Universitaires de France (coll. "Que sais-je?"), 1981.

Laplante, Marc. "La révolution du voyage d'agrément." *Loisir et sociétés* 11, no. 1 (1988).

Larousse médical illustré. Supplement by Dr. Burnier. Edited by Dr. Galtier-Boissière. Paris: Librairie Larousse, 1929.

Laurent, Alain. "Le thème du soleil dans la publicité des organismes de vacances." *Vacances et tourisme. Communications* 10 (1967): 35–50.

———. *Libérer les vacances?* Paris: Seuil, 1973.

Laurent, Jacques. *Le nu vêtu et dévêtu.* Paris: Gallimard, coll. Idées, 1979.

"Le classement des stations françaises." *L'Express* 1614 (June 18, 1982): 70–74.

Le Coeur, Jules. *Des bains de mer. Guide médical et hygiénique du baigneur.* Paris: Labé, 1846.

"Le hit-parade des plages SEXY." *L'écho des savanes* 118 (July–August 1993).

"Le littoral a atteint la cote d'alerte." *Que Choisir* 296 (July–Aug. 1993): 34ff.

Le Pouliguen: sa plage, son bois, son port, sa côte. Le Pouliguen: Syndicat d'initiative, 1936.

"Le vacancier est devenu zappeur." Interview with Jean-Luc Michaud. *Le Nouvel Observateur* (Aug. 12–18, 1993): 50–51.

Léautaud, Paul. *Villégiature.* 1929. Paris: Mercure de France, 1986.

Léger, Danièle, and Bertrand Hervieu. "La nature des néoruraux." In *Protection de la nature,* ed. A. Cadoret, 152–60. Paris: L'Harmattan, 1982.

———. *Le retour à la nature.* Paris: Seuil, 1979.

Lerivray, Bernard. *Guides bleus, guides verts et lunettes roses.* Paris: Éditions du Cerf, 1975.

Lett, James William. "Ludic and Liminoid Aspects of Charter Yacht Tourism in [the] Caribbean." *Annals of Tourism Research* 10 (1983): 35–56.

Lévi-Strauss, Claude. Interview with Didier Eribon. *Le Nouvel Observateur* 1092 (Oct. 1985): 72–73.

———. *Introduction to the Work of Marcel Mauss.* Translated by Felicity Baker. London: Routledge and Kegan Paul, 1987.

———. *Race et histoire.* Paris: Unesco, 1968.

———. *The Raw and the Cooked.* 1975. Translated by John and Doreen Weightman. Chicago: University of Chicago Press, 1990.

———. *Structural Anthropology.* 1958. Translated by Claire Jacobson and Brooke Grundfest Schoepf. New York: Basic Books, 1963.

———. *Structural Anthropology.* Vol. 2. 1973. Translated by Monique Layton. New York: Basic Books, 1976.

———. "The Structural Study of Myth." In *Structural Anthropology.* 1958. Translated by Claire Jacobson and Brooke Grundfest Schoepf. New York: Basic Books, 1963.

———. *Tristes Tropiques.* 1955. Translated by John and Doreen Weightman. New York: Atheneum, 1974.

Lévy, Jean-Claude. "Les aquaboulevards ou la nature artificialisée." *Les vacances. Autrement* 111 (Jan. 1990): 155–60.

Lionnet, Dominique. "Votre été 92: amour, sexe et séduction." *Biba* 150 (August 1992).

Liselotte. *Le guide des convenances. Savoir-vivre, obligations sociales, usages mondains.* Paris: Société du petit écho de la mode, 1931.

Lodge, David. *Paradise News.* London: Secker and Warburg, 1991.

London, Jack. "My Hawaiian Aloha." 1919. In *The New Hawaii,* ed. Charmian London, 9–59. London: Mills and Boon, 1923.

———. "The Water Baby." 1918. In *Short Stories of Jack London,* ed. Earle Labor, Robert C. Leitz III, and I. Milo Shepard, 712–21. New York: Macmillan, 1990.

Loti, Pierre. *Iceland Fisherman.* 1886. Translated by W. P. Baines. London: J. M. Dent, 1961.

Lourbet, François. *Le chef de village.* Paris: Balland, 1975.

Luginbuhl, Yves. *Désir de rivage. Atelier du Conservatoire du littoral* 3 (Oct. 1993).

MacCannell, Dean. *The Tourist: A New Theory of the Leisure Class.* 1976. New York: Schocken Books, 1989.

Macé, Hubert. "Les vacances passives. L'accès à la villégiature balnéaire." In *Vacances et tourisme. Communications* 10 (1967): 20–24.

"Madrid." In *Diario de Ibiza,* Sept. 6, 1969.

Maffesoli, Michel. *The Contemplation of the World: Figures of Community Style.* 1993. Translated by Susan Emanuel. Minneapolis: University of Minneapolis Press, 1996.

———. "Le rythme social." In *La transfiguration du politique: la tribalisation du monde.* Paris: Grasset, 1992.

———. *The Time of the Tribes: The Decline of Individualism in Mass Society.* 1988. Translated by Don Smith. London: Sage Publications, 1996.

"Maigrir. Bas les masques!" Special report. *50 millions de consommateurs* 261 (April–May 1993).

Malinowski, Bronislaw. *The Sexual Life of Savages in North-Western Melanesia.* 1929. New York: Harcourt, Brace and World, 1962.

———. "Spirit Hunting in the South Seas." *The Realist* (1929): 398–417.

Mandiargues, André Pieyre de. "La marée." 1962. In *Mascarets.* Paris: Gallimard, 1971.

Mann, Thomas. *Death in Venice.* 1913. Translated by H. T. Lowe-Porter. New York: Knopf, 1930.

Marié, Michel, and Christian Tamisier. *Un territoire sans nom.* Paris: Méridiens-Klincksieck, 1982.

Marié, Michel, and Jean Viard. *La campagne inventée.* Arles: Actes Sud, 1988.

Marin, Louis. "L'effet Sharawadgi ou le jardin de Julie." In *Jardins contre nature. Traverses* 5–6 (Oct. 1976): 114–31.

———. *Utopics: Spatial Play.* 1973. Translated by Robert A. Vollrath. Atlantic Highlands, N.J.: Humanities Press, 1984.

Marx, Karl, and Friedrich Engels. "Critical-Utopian Socialism and Communism." In *Manifesto of the Communist Party* (1848), in *Collected Works,* 6: 477–519. New York: International Publishers, 1976.

Masurier, Didier. *Hôtes et touristes au Sénégal: Imaginaires et idéologies touristiques de l'exotisme.* Paris: L'Harmattan, 1998.

Matheson, Richard. *I Am Legend.* New York: Walker, 1970.

———. *The Shrinking Man.* Cutchogue, N.Y.: Buccaneer Books, 1962.

Matton, Général. *Par la Provence à la Côte d'Azur. Poésies.* Nice: L'Éclaireur de Nice, 1933.

Maupassant, Guy de. *Contes et nouvelles.* Preface by A. Lanoux. Introduction by Louis Forestier. 2 vols. Paris: Gallimard, La Pléiade, 1974.

———. *Pierre and Jean.* 1888. Westport, Conn.: Hyperion Press, 1978.

Mauss, Marcel. *Seasonal Variations of the Eskimo: A Study in Social Morphology.* 1908. Translated by James J. Fox. London: Routledge and Kegan Paul, 1979.

McLuhan, Marshall. *The Gutenberg Galaxy: The Making of Typographic Man.* 1962. Toronto: University of Toronto Press, 1966.

Mead, Margaret. *From the South Seas: Studies of Adolescence and Sex in Primitive Societies.* New York: Morrow, 1939.

Melville, Herman. *Moby-Dick, or the Whale.* New York: Harper, 1851.

Mémento du tourisme. Paris: Observatoire national du tourisme, August 1992.

Mermet, Guy. *Francoscopie 1993.* Paris: Larousse, 1992.

Michaud, Jean-Luc, ed. *Tourismes, chance pour l'économie, risque pour les sociétés.* Paris: Presses Universitaires de France, 1993.

Michelet, Jules. *The Sea.* New York: Rudd and Carleton, 1861.

Mishaegen, Anne de. *Dans la forêt canadienne.* Brussels: La Renaissance du livre, 1946.

Moles, Abraham A., and Elisabeth Rohmer. *Psychologie de l'espace.* Tournai: Casterman, 1972.

Monod, Théodore. *Plongées profondes: Bathyfolages.* 1954. Arles: Terres d'Aventure-Actes Sud, 1991.

Montagné, Prosper, and Dr. Alfred Gottschalk. *Larousse gastronomique.* Paris: Larousse, 1938.

Montesquieu, Charles de Secondat, Baron de. *The Spirit of Laws.* 1748. Translated by Thomas Nugent. Great Books of the Western World 38. Chicago: Encyclopedia Britannica, 1952.

Morand, Paul. *Bains de mer, bains de rêves.* Lausanne: Guide du livre and Clairefontaine, 1960. Reprinted as *Bains de mer* (Paris: Arléa, 1990).

Morin, Edgar. *Journal de Californie.* 1970. Paris: Seuil, 1983.

Munch et la France. Paris: Réunion des Musées nationaux, Munch et Spadem, Adagp, 1991.

Nahoum, Véronique. "La belle femme ou le stade du miroir en histoire." *La nourriture. Communications* 31 (1979): 22–32.

Nahoum-Grappe, Véronique. "Les conduites de vertige." In *Possessions. Galaxie anthropologique* 2, nos. 4–5 (1993): 66–71.

Nash, Dennison. "Tourism as Anthropological Subject." *Current Anthropology* 22, no. 5 (Oct. 1981): 461–81.

Nori, Claude. "Rimini, août 82." In Gilles Mora and Claude Nori, *L'été dernier. Manifeste photobiographique.* Paris: Éditions de l'Étoile, 1983.

"Opération plage propre. Une initiative d'estivants." In *Corse-Matin,* "Ghisonaccia," Aug. 22, 1992.

"Opération spéciale: sauvons la pointe du Raz." *Le Point* 977 (June 10–16, 1991).

Ostrowetsky, Sylvia. "Dédale n'est pas Cronos et la rue ne marche pas." In *Espace et représentation,* 302–21. Paris: Éditions de la Villette, 1982.

"Où se baigner en Europe?" *Que choisir* 237 (March 1988): 36–46.

Passariello, Phyllis. "Never on Sunday? Mexican Tourists at the Beach." *Annals of Tourism Research* 10 (1983): 109–22.

Pastoureau, Michel. *The Devil's Cloth: A History of Stripes and Striped Fabric.* 1991. Translated by Jody Golding. New York: Columbia University Press, 2001.

Paul-Lévy, Françoise, and Marion Segaud. *Anthropologie de l'espace.* Paris: Centre Georges Pompidou/Centre de création industrielle, 1983.

Pennac, Daniel. *Comme un roman.* Paris: Gallimard, 1992.

Pennacchioni, Irene. *De la guerre conjugale.* Paris: Mazarine, 1986.

Péquignot, Bruno. *La relation amoureuse: analyse sociologique du roman sentimentale moderne.* Paris: L'Harmattan, 1991.

Perec, Georges. "Approches de quoi?" In *L'infra-Ordinaire,* 9–13. Paris: Seuil, 1989.

──────. *Tentative d'épuisement d'un lieu parisien.* Paris: Union Générale d'Éditions, 1975.

Perrier, J. L. "Majorque, résidence secondaire de l'Europe." In *Le Monde* (Nov. 25, 1989): 29.

Perrot, Philippe. *Le corps féminin. Le travail des apparences (XVIIIe–XIXe siècles).* Paris: Seuil, 1984. Repr. coll. "Points," 1991.

Peyre, Christiane, and Yves Raynouard. *Histoire et légendes du Club Méditerranée.* Paris: Seuil, 1971.

Philippe, Anne. *Un été près de la mer.* Paris: Gallimard, 1977.

Picard, Michel. *Bali: Cultural Tourism and Touristic Culture.* 1992. Translated by Diana Darling. Singapore: Archipelago, 1996.

Picard, Muriel. "L'amour à la plage." *20 ans* 72 (August 1992): 46–51.

Pinchon, Joseph-Porphyre [Annaïk Labournez], and Caumery [Maurice Languereau]. *Les cent métiers de Bécassine.* Paris: Éditions Gautier-Languereau, 1929.

Plato. *Timaeus.* Translated by Donald J. Zeyl. Indianapolis: Hackett Publishing, 2000.

Poe, Edgar Allan. "The Man of the Crowd." 1840. In *Collected Works of Edgar Allan Poe,* ed. Thomas Ollive Mabbott, 2:505–18. Cambridge: Belknap Press of Harvard University Press, 1978.

Pollack, Michael. *L'expérience concentrationnaire.* Paris: Métailié, 1990.

Pomian, Krysztof. Interview in *Libération* (July 13, 1990): 26.

Ponge, Francis. *The Voice of Things.* 1942. Edited and translated by Beth Archer. New York: McGraw-Hill, 1972.

"Pour hâler bien." *Vogue-Hommes* 151 (July–Aug. 1992).

Pouy, Jean-Bernard. "Des symboles à la dérive." *Les vacances. Autrement* 111 (Jan. 1990): 106–10.

Premel, Guy, and Bernard Kalaora. Summary, introduction to the Report of the Atelier du Conservatoire du littoral. Oct. 13, 1993.

Quinton, René. *L'eau de mer, milieu organique.* Paris: Masson, 1904.

Rackam. "Le cul-cul club." In *Bonnes vacances,* ed. René Durand. Paris: Le Dernier Terrain Vague, 1978.

Radiguet, Raymond. *Le diable au corps.* Paris: B. Grasset, 1923.

Rayjean, Max-André. *La guerre des loisirs.* Paris: Fleuve noir, 1986.

Raymond, Henri. "Une utopie concrète: recherche sur un village de vacances." *Revue française de sociologie* 3 (1960): 325.

Raymond, Dr. V. *Manuel des baigneurs,* preceded by *L'histoire des bains* and followed by *Traité de natation.* Paris: Desloges, 1840.

Reiser. *Ils sont moches.* Paris: Éditions du Square, 1980.

Renaudie, Jacques-Bernard. *La thalassothérapie.* Paris: Presses Universitaires de France, 1984.

Rey, Alain, ed. *Dictionnaire historique de la langue française.* Paris: Le Robert, 1992.

Rey, Alain, and Sophie Chantreau. *Dictionnaire des expressions et locutions.* Paris: Le Robert, 1987.

Richard, René, and Camille Bartoli. *La Côte d'Azur assassinée.* Paris: Roudil, 1971.

Richepin, Jean. *La mer.* 1886. Paris: Gallimard, 1980.

Riesmann, David, Nathan Glazer, and Reuel Denney. *The Lonely Crowd: A Study of the Changing American Character.* New Haven: Yale University Press, 1961.

Rogers, Woodes. *A Cruising Voyage Round the World.* 1712. New York: Da Capo Press, 1969.

Rouillard, Dominique. *Le site balnéaire.* Brussels: Pierre Mardaga, 1984.

Royer, Louis-Charles. *Let's Go Naked.* 1929. Translated by Paul Quiltana. New York: Brentano's, 1932.

Rozenberg, Danielle. *Tourisme et utopie aux Baléares. Ibiza, une île pour une autre vie.* Paris: L'Harmattan, 1990.

Russell, Dr. Richard. *A Dissertation on the Use of Sea Water in the Diseases of the Glands.* London, 1752.

Salardenne, Roger. *Le culte de la nudité.* Paris: Éditions Prima, 1929.

———. *Le nu intégral chez les nudistes français.* Paris: Éditions Prima, 1931.

———. *Un mois chez les nudistes.* Paris: Éditions Prima, 1930.

Sansot, Pierre. *Les gens de peu.* Paris: Presses Universitaires de France, 1991.

Sapir, Edward. "Speech as a Personality Trait." 1927. In *Selected Writings of Edward Sapir in Language, Culture, and Personality,* ed. David G. Mandelbaum, 533–43. Berkeley: University of California Press, 1968.

Saunier, Baudry de, Charles Dollfus, and Edgar de Geoffroy. *Histoire de la locomotion terrestre.* Paris: L'Illustration, 1936.

Ser, Jannick. *Le livre de l'amateur d'huîtres et de coquillages.* Toulouse: Éditions D. Briand-R. Laffon, 1987.

Serre. *Les vacances.* Grenoble: Serre and Glénat, 1984.

Sévigné, Marie de Rabutin-Chantal. *Letters of Madame de Sévigné to her Daughter and her Friends.* Vol. 1. Edited by Richard Aldington. New York: E. P. Dutton, 1937.

"Sexualité: les Français et l'amour." *Top Santé* 23 (August 1992).

Simonnot, Philippe. *Ne m'appelez plus France.* Paris: Olivier Orban, 1991.

Smith, Valene L., ed. *Hosts and Guests: The Anthropology of Tourism.* Philadelphia: University of Pennsylvania Press, 1977. Rev. ed., 1989.

"Soleil et sable fin." *Modes de Paris* 712, no. 3 (1962): 50–51.

"SOS Bretagne." *L'événement du jeudi* (Sept. 5–11, 1991): 141–45.

Soula, Claude. "'Club Med': le soleil quand même!" *Le Nouvel Observateur* (Jan. 2–8, 1992): 47–49.

Souriau, Étienne. *Les deux cent mille situations dramatiques.* Paris: Flammarion, 1950.

Sterne, Laurence. *A Sentimental Journey through France and Italy.* 1768. New York: Knopf, 1925.

Stevenson, Robert Louis. *The Ebb-Tide: A Trio and a Quartette.* 1894. Edited by Peter Hinchcliffe and Catherine Kerrigan. Edinburgh: Edinburgh University Press, 1995.

———. "The Marquesas." Part 1 of *In the South Seas* (1896). Vol. 1. Leipzig: Bernhard Tauchnitz, 1901.

Süskind, Patrick. *Perfume: The Story of a Murderer.* 1985. Translated by John E. Woods. New York: Knopf, 1986.

Sweet, Jill D. "Burlesquing 'the Other' in Pueblo Performance." In *Semiotics of Tourism,* ed. Dean MacCannell, special issue of *Annals of Tourism Research* 16, no. 1 (1989): 62–75.

Swift, Jonathan. *Gulliver's Travels.* 1726. Oxford: Oxford University Press, 1999.

Tacussel, Patrick. "L'attraction amoureuse dans l'observation sociale." *Cahiers de l'imaginaire* 5 (1989).

Theroux, Paul. *The Mosquito Coast.* Boston: Houghton Mifflin, 1981.

———. *The Old Patagonian Express: By Train Through the Americas.* Boston: Houghton Mifflin, 1979.

Touraine, Alain. *La voix et le regard.* Paris: Seuil, 1978.

Tournier, Michel. *Friday.* 1967. Translated by Norman Denny. New York: Pantheon Books, 1985.

———. "The Taciturn Lovers." In *The Midnight Love Feast.* 1989. Translated by Barbara Wright. London: Collins, 1991.

Tricot, Michel. "Les 'salopards' en vacances (II)." In *L'Humanité* (July 3, 1979): 9.

Truffaut, François. *Correspondance.* Edited by G. Jacob and Cl. Givray. Paris: Hatier, 1988.

Tsartas, Pierre. "Identité et mobilité de deux groupes des acteurs sociaux du tourisme en Grèce: les touristes et les autochtones." In *Le tourisme international entre tradition et modernité,* 381. Proceedings of international colloquium, Nice, Nov. 1992. Nice: Laboratoire d'ethnologie-Université de Nice, 1994.

Urbain, Jean-Didier. *L'idiot du voyage. Histoires de touristes.* Paris: Plon, 1991. Reprint, Paris: Payot, 1993.

———. "Les vacanciers des équinoxes." *Le continent gris. Communications* 37 (1983): 137–48.

"Vacances sans fin: noyez vous." *Hara-Kiri* 131 (Aug. 1972).

Vachet, Pierre. *La nudité et la physiologie sexuelle.* Paris: M. K. de Mongeot (coll. "Vivre intégralement"), 1928.

Vailland, Roger. "Saint-Tropez." 1950? reprinted in *Roger Vailland*, special issue, *Europe* 712–13 (Aug.–Sept. 1988): 84–87.

Van Gennep, Arnold. *The Rites of Passage.* 1909. Translated by Monika B. Vizedom and Gabrielle L. Caffee. Chicago: University of Chicago Press, 1960.

Veblen, Thorstein. *Theory of the Leisure Class.* 1899. New York: Penguin, 1979.

Verlomme, Hugo. *L'homme des vagues.* Paris: Gallimard, coll. "Jeunesse", 1992.

Verne, Jules. *Around the World in Eighty Days.* 1873. Translated by William Butcher. Oxford: Oxford University Press, 1995.

———. *The Floating Island.* 1895. London: Kegan Paul International, 1990.

———. *Le désert de glace.* 1866. In *Voyages et aventures du Capitaine Hatteras.* Paris: Hachette, 1966.

———. *The Mysterious Island.* 1874. Translated by W. H. G. Kingston. New York: Heritage Press, 1959.

———. *Two Years' Holiday.* 1888. 2 vols. London: Arco, 1964.

Viard, Jean. *Penser les vacances.* Arles: Actes Sud, 1984.

Viaud-Grand-Marais, Dr. *Guide du voyageur à Noirmoutier.* 9th ed. Fontenay-le-Comte: Lussaud, 1927.

Vigarello, Georges. *Concepts of Cleanliness: Changing Attitudes in France since the Middle Ages.* 1985. Translated by Jean Birrell. Cambridge: Cambridge University Press, 1988.

Vincent-Ricard, Françoise. *Les objets de la mode.* Paris: Éditions Du May, 1989.

Vitoux, Frédéric. *Riviera.* Paris: Seuil, 1987.

"Vos amours d'été. Qui séduire? Qui fuir?" *Marie-France* 449 (July–August 1993).

Wallon, Armand. *La vie quotidienne dans les villes d'eaux (1850–1914).* Paris: Hachette, 1981.

Williams, Raymond. "Pleasing Prospects." In *The Country and the City*, 120–26. New York: Oxford University Press, 1973.

Wittmer, Margret. *Les Robinsons des Galapagos.* Paris: A. Michel, 1960.

Wyss, Johan. *The Swiss Family Robinson.* 1812. Edited by John Seelye. Oxford: Oxford University Press, 1991.

Ziegelmeyer, Pierre. "Objectif vacances." In *Bonnes vacances,* ed. René Durand. Paris: Le Dernier Terrain Vague, 1978.

FILMOGRAPHY

And God Created Woman. Directed by Roger Vadim. 1976.

The Blue Lagoon. Directed by Randal Kleiser. 1980.

Contes immoraux. Directed by Walerian Borowczyk. 1974.

Dupont Lajoie. Directed by Yves Boisset. 1974.

From Here to Eternity. Directed by Fred Zimmerman. 1953.

Hell in the Pacific. Directed by John Boorman. 1968.

La Baule-les-Pins. Directed by Diane Kurys. 1989.

Le grand bleu. Directed by Luc Besson. 1988. English version, *The Big Blue* (1989).

Les Bronzés. Directed by Patrice Leconte. 1978.

Les quatre cents coups. Directed by François Truffaut. 1959.

M. Hulot's Holiday. Directed by Jacques Tati. 1952.

Never on Sunday. Directed by Jules Dassin. 1960.

Pierrot le fou. Directed by Jean-Luc Godard. 1965.

Planet of the Apes. Directed by Franklin Schaffner. 1968.

Roma. Directed by Federico Fellini. 1972.

To Catch a Thief. Directed by Alfred Hitchcock. 1955.

Week-end ou la qualité de la vie. Directed by P. Manuel and Jean-Jacques Péché. 1972.

Jean-Didier Urbain, professor of sociology at the University of Versailles, has also taught at the University of Paris V. His earlier works include *La société de conservation, L'archipel des morts,* and a companion volume to *At the Beach, L'idiot du voyage.* In his most recent book, *Secrets de voyage,* he examines the role of secrecy in relation to travel.

Catherine Porter is professor emerita of French at the State University of New York, College at Cortland. She has translated more than twenty works of contemporary French nonfiction in the areas of literary theory and criticism, philosophy, psychoanalysis, history, and sociology.